Real Estate Law

Real Estate Law

Benjamin N. Henszey
Associate Professor of Business Law,
The Pennsylvania State University;
Member of the Pennsylvania Bar

Ronald M. Friedman
Member of the Pennsylvania
and New Mexico Bars

WARREN, GORHAM & LAMONT
Boston and New York

ISBN 0-88262-310-9
Library of Congress Catalog Card Number 78-24808

First Printing—March 1979
Second Printing—September 1979

PRINTED IN THE UNITED STATES OF AMERICA

Preface

REAL estate law consists of a vast body of rules and regulations that determine what one's rights and duties are with respect to real property. Many of these rights and duties can be traced back directly to ancient common law principles and practices developed in England to meet the political and economic needs of the times.

Early English common law has been substantially incorporated into modern real estate law in the United States. It has been modified and supplemented by federal and state constitutional, statutory, and case law. For example, under the federal constitution private property cannot be taken for a public purpose except upon payment of just compensation; under state statutory law, contracts for the sale of real estate are generally required to be in writing; and by court decision, the case law in most states provides that landowners, with certain exceptions, owe no duty to trespassers. Statutory and case law may vary from state to state. In Colorado, for example, statutory and case water law is far different from water law in Pennsylvania. Each state develops its own law according to its unique economic and topographical conditions. The problem for the student of basic real estate law is to understand the numerous legal principles that affect real property.

Many textbooks on real estate law present the complex array of laws affecting real estate by stating the basic principle or rule and supporting it with citations of statutes or cases. It has been our experience that such citations are of little value to beginning students. In addition, many traditional textbooks tend to emphasize principles that have little if any significance or value to these students. In this volume we have opted for simplicity and practicality and have thus omitted what we believe to be superfluous material. By avoiding a purely academic approach to the presentation of real estate law and by including material that is professionally relevant, we have attempted to convey useful information without sacrificing content. Legal citations from law reviews, cases, periodicals, and so forth have not been included, because we believe that in an introductory course such reference material is unnecessary and is often a cause of confusion. Where a legal principle is particularly difficult to explain, and in other appropriate situations, a simple example is called upon to illustrate the principle.

Ample use is also made of sample documents to illustrate legal practices. Diagrams and charts throughout the book clarify and summarize the text. Each chapter begins with a preview of the material to be presented and places it in the overall framework of the book. Chapters end with questions for discussion; all but two also have sets of sample cases, which have been extracted from cases reported in the national appellate reporter system from jurisdictions throughout the United States.

Terms with which the reader may not be familiar are defined briefly in the Glossary at the end of the book. (For more extensive definitions, the reader is referred to *The Arnold Encyclopedia of Real Estate,* Warren, Gorham & Lamont, 1978). There is also a subject index.

Real Estate Law has been structured to meet a variety of educational needs. It is suitable for use as a basic textbook in both undergraduate real estate courses and programs designed for the real estate professional. All the topics traditionally covered in real estate law books are to be found here, including real estate interests, deeds, property descriptions, transfer of interests, titles and title protection, easements, and financing. Two more unusual entries are the chapters on real estate settlements and on the tax consequences of real estate transfers. The latter (Chapter 13) incorporates changes in the law brought about by the Tax Reform Act of 1976 and the Revenue Act of 1978.

With a basic understanding of real estate law, the reader should be able to answer many professionally relevant questions and problems pertaining to real estate. More important, perhaps, he or she will be better equipped to recognize those areas in which the complexity and changing nature of real estate law make it appropriate to consult legal counsel or other experts.

In writing this textbook we have received help, directly and indirectly, from a number of individuals. We especially wish to thank the following: Dean Eugene J. Kelley and Professor John J. Coyle of the College of Business Administration, The Pennsylvania State University, for their continuing support; J. Alvin Hawbaker, former president of the Pennsylvania Association of Realtors, for his help in reviewing the outline and for other assistance in the preparation of the manuscript; and Sol Polan of the Real Estate Institute of New York University and Alvin L. Arnold, Editor of *Real Estate Review*, for their critical evaluations of the final draft. We also thank Jean L. Januszkiewicz, senior honors student at The Pennsylvania State University, for her research assistance in the writing of Chapter 12, and Deborah Strouse for her typing and editorial contributions.

BENJAMIN N. HENSZEY
RONALD M. FRIEDMAN

Contents

Chapter 1
Introduction to Real Estate and Real Estate Interests

REAL ESTATE DEFINED

PHYSICAL CHARACTERISTICS OF REAL PROPERTY

Immobility and Indestructibility

Nonhomogeneity

PERSONAL PROPERTY DEFINED

PERSONAL PROPERTY AND REAL PROPERTY DISTINGUISHED

Law of Fixtures

Trade Fixture Exception

CLASSIFICATION OF INTERESTS IN REAL PROPERTY

Ownership Interests

Possessory Interests

Nonpossessory Interests

WHO MAY HOLD INTERESTS IN REAL PROPERTY

Individuals

Corporations and Partnerships

Other Private Entities

Governmental Units

REAL estate can be distinguished from other forms of property by its physical and legal characteristics. The interests, rights, and duties associated with real estate make it a unique form of property. This chapter describes the characteristics of real estate that make it unique and discusses the types of individual and governmental interests that exist in real estate.

REAL ESTATE DEFINED

Real estate, often referred to as real property, realty, or land, is, in its broadest definition a portion of the earth extending above and below the surface and including all fixed and immovable objects both on and within the earth.

Land refers to real property with no improvements. *Improvement* as used in this text means any addition to the land. Improvements may be constructed items such as houses, water systems, or fences, or they may be an alteration of the land's surface such as a channel dug as a means of distributing water for irrigation purposes. The term "improvement" is not qualitative, and an addition to land that depreciates the value of property or is not appealing esthetically is still an improvement in the context of real estate law.

PHYSICAL CHARACTERISTICS OF REAL PROPERTY

Immobility and Indestructibility

Real property has two important characteristics. First, it is immobile and indestructible. This characteristic is important to taxing authorities

3

because, unlike other forms of property, real property cannot be hidden or moved to avoid the assessment and collection of taxes. This characteristic also makes it important to judgment creditors, who may attach a debtor's real property, force its sale, and apply the proceeds toward satisfaction of the judgment debt. The debtor cannot abscond with his/her real property to prevent a forced sale.

Nonhomogeneity

The second characteristic of real property is its physical nonhomogeneity. No two tracts of real estate are identical. A difference will always exist because they are located upon different geographical points of the earth's surface. This characteristic also has important legal consequences. Because no two parcels are the same, as a matter of law one parcel may not be substituted for another. Thus, when a buyer of land bargains for a particular tract of real estate, the seller may not make the buyer accept another. The law allows the buyer to sue the seller to force the sale in an equitable action called *specific performance*.

PERSONAL PROPERTY DEFINED

Personal property is all property subject to ownership that is not real property. Personal property is sometimes referred to as *chattels* or *personalty*. Its physical characteristics differ from those of real property in that personal property is by definition movable. Even though certain items of personal property are large and present logistical problems for anyone wishing to move them, unless they are permanently affixed and incorporated into real property they are considered to be personalty. Chattels have the physical characteristic of destructibility in that they may be physically changed into another form.

Most items of personal property are not unique, and as a matter of law another such item may be substituted without legal consequences. For example, one new late model refrigerator may be substituted for another similar appliance, even though in a technical sense each would be different. However, some items of personal property are considered unique, and in these cases the equitable remedy of specific performance would be available to force a sale of a unique item of personalty. An example of such an item would be an original work of art or a rare postage stamp.

Personal property may be classified into two groups: tangible personal property and intangible personal property. *Tangible personal property* is personal property that has a physical existence—for example, a diamond ring or an automobile. *Intangible personal property* does not have a physical existence; copyrights and patents, for example, are intangible. Intangible property is usually a contract right that does not have physical presence but is nevertheless capable of being owned. Often an item of intangible personal property may be represented by a certificate or other written document, but in such cases the writing is only evidence of the intangible property and not the personal property itself.

The law that governs basic transactions in personal property of modern business is the *Uniform Commercial Code,* which has been adopted in all jurisdictions in the United States except Louisiana. The Uniform Commercial Code, or UCC, is designed to modernize and standardize commercial transactions in personal property throughout the United States. Basic ownership, possessory, and nonpossessory interests in personal property between merchants and nonmerchants are set forth in the Uniform Commercial Code.

PERSONAL PROPERTY AND REAL PROPERTY DISTINGUISHED

Both personal property and real property are distinct forms of property at law. Both have certain rights and duties attached to their ownership, transfer, and use. However, real property has always enjoyed a higher standing before the law because of the historical importance and uniqueness of real estate itself.

The transfer of an ownership interest in real property requires certain legal formalities that are not required in a transfer of ownership of personal property. Generally, with certain exceptions, an agreement for the transfer of any interest in real estate must be in writing in order to comply with the Statute of Frauds. The transfer of personal property generally does not require a written agreement at common law. In addition, ownership rights in real estate are transferred with an instrument called a *deed,* and the law imposes certain requirements as to proper execution of this deed. Ownership rights in most personal property can be transferred without instruments of conveyance. An example of such transfers would be grocery items purchased at a food store, where only a receipt for payment is given without an executed itemization of the personal property sold and accompanying words of conveyance. Where an instrument of transfer is required, such as in the sale of an automobile, a bill of sale is generally used to evidence the transfer.

When personal property is permanently affixed to real property, it becomes part of the real estate. Such a transmutation of personal property to real property occurs when building material is used to construct a house, for example. Before construction, the bricks, mortar,

TABLE 1   Summary of Major Differences Between Real and Personal Property

	Personal Property	*Real Property*
Physical characteristics		
destructibility	Yes	No
mobility	Yes	No
nonhomogeneity	No, with exceptions	Yes
tangibility	Tangible or intangible	Tangible only
Instrument of transfer	Bill of sale	Deed
Contract for sale required to be in writing	No, unless value exceeds $500	Yes
Form changeable	Yes, to real property under law of fixtures	Yes, to personalty, as when minerals are extracted from land
Laws governing ownership transfer and rights	Uniform Commercial Code	Jurisdiction's law of real property

wood, and other materials are movable items of personal property, but as they are permanently incorporated into the building, they become real property.

Just as personal property may become real property, it is possible to change real property to personal property. Minerals upon or within the land or products of the land may be severed from the land and moved to another place for use or sale. Coal, gravel, oil, gas, and timber are chief examples of this.

Table 1 summarizes the major differences between real and personal property.

Law of Fixtures

It is a general rule of law that, unless the parties agree otherwise, the transfer of ownership or possessory rights to real property includes all the real estate. This includes all items that were once personal property but have been incorporated into the real estate. Thus, when an individual's home is sold, in the absence of an agreement to the contrary the seller may not remove items of personal property that have been affixed permanently to the real estate.

In a landlord–tenant agreement, unless otherwise agreed, the lessor leases all the real estate to the lessee. In addition, a lessee who installs personal property in the leased premises and affixes it permanently to the real estate must leave these leasehold improvements at the termination of his/her tenancy.

The general rule is easily applied to certain items of personal property that clearly become part of the real estate. Examples of such clear cases are landscaping, fences, and paneling. However, in many instances, it is difficult to classify property as real or personal. Frequently, the buyer, seller, or former lessee is dissatisfied with an adverse party's classification of property. As a result, the issue of distinguishing personal and real property has been much litigated in the courts.

The test or standard most often applied by courts is threefold:

First, the courts will determine whether the item of personal property was affixed to the real estate. The item may be attached to improvements upon the property and need not be affixed to the land itself.

Second, if the court determines that the item is affixed to the real estate, it will examine the character of the item to ascertain whether the article is adapted to the use or purpose of that part of the real estate. If the item is affixed to the real estate and augments the use to which the real estate is being put, it is an indication that it is part of that real estate.

Third, and perhaps most important, the court will inquire into the intention of the party who affixed the personalty to the real estate. Here the court looks at objective manifestations of intent such as the method by which the item was attached and the removability of the article without injury to the real estate. Loosely attached items are less likely to indicate an intention to permanently affix personalty to the real estate. The more substantial the attachment, the more likely the intention was to incorporate the item into the real estate.

For example, it has been held that a gas range attached by pipe to the apartment gas supply was personalty because it could be removed simply by unscrewing connecting pipes. This indicated an intention that the range not become part of the real estate. In contrast, a pull-down bed that was bolted to the wall was declared to be part of the real estate even though the character of the article was not one that would usually be considered real estate.

Items of personal property whose removal from the real estate would cause considerable damage to the real estate are more likely to be considered to have become incorporated into the real property. The person making such an affixation is usually considered to have manifested an intention to make the item permanently part of the real estate because of the difficulty or expense in restoring the real estate after removal. An example of such a situation would be the installation of an underground on-site sewage system, which could not easily be removed without damage to both the system and the land. This would indicate an intention of permanent annexation by the person who installed the system.

The law of fixtures applies only when the parties have not agreed otherwise. Many potential problems can be avoided in real estate transactions if the parties clearly set out in writing an inventory of all items of personal property that are not to be included in the transfer.

Trade Fixture Exception

As a general rule, upon termination of a lease, the lessee may not remove any real property. One important exception to the law of fixtures is the law that has been developed regarding a merchant lessee's right to remove items of personal property used to store, handle, or display the lessee's goods or services even though these items of personalty may be affixed to the real estate and otherwise might be considered part of the real estate. Examples of such trade fixtures are beauticians' equipment, refrigerators, gas tanks, and air-conditioning units.

The apparent theory behind the trade fixture exception is that it is desirable to encourage trade and that the lessor should not be unjustly enriched at the expense of the merchant lessee. The exception may be statutory, as it is in some states, or it may be developed by custom and usage given effect by court decisions. In order for the exception to apply, the merchant tenant must remove the trade fixture before termination of the lease without causing damage to the leasehold premises. The lessee is obligated to restore the premises to their original condition, except for reasonable wear and tear.

The trade fixture exception applies only to trade fixtures themselves. If the lessee makes improvements to the leasehold premises in the absence of an agreement with the lessor to the contrary, the leasehold improvements remain at the termination of the lease and become part of the real estate. There is no duty on the part of the lessor to compensate the lessee for such improvements.

As with the law of fixtures, many problems may be avoided if the parties clearly set forth in the lease document a schedule of trade fixtures that the merchant lessee intends to install in the leasehold premises and has the right to take upon the termination of the lease. In the absence of an agreement to the contrary, the trade fixture exception applies.

CLASSIFICATION OF INTERESTS IN REAL PROPERTY

Among other things, real estate law deals with the creation, transfer, and division of a variety of rights that make up real property. "Bundle of rights" has been frequently used to describe real property, to convey the idea that many distinct interests may be involved in any one tract of real estate, each such interest being identifiable and protected at law.

To provide a framework for an understanding of this variety of rights and duties coexisting in a parcel of real estate, it is possible to classify interests into three broad categories: (1) ownership interests; (2) possessory interests; and (3) nonpossessory interests.

Ownership Interests

Among the three categories of interests in real estate, the one most likely to come to mind is ownership. *Ownership* is the right to exclusive dominion and control over real property, including the right to create or transfer ownership to another. Ownership is fully discussed in Chapter 2.

Possessory Interests

In addition to ownership rights, possessory interests may also exist in real estate. A *possessory interest* in real estate is the right to physical possession of the property, but does not include the right to create ownership rights in another. The chief example of a possessory interest is a lease. Possessory interests in real estate are discussed in Chapter 2.

Nonpossessory Interests

Nonpossessory interests in real property are legally protected rights that an individual may have in the real property of another, not including the right to physical possession. Some nonpossessory interests involve limited rights to the nonexclusive use of another's land. Another nonpossessory right that an individual may have is interest in the real estate held as security for the repayment of a debt, such as a mortgage. There are many nonpossessory rights in real estate, the most common of which are discussed within this text.

The coexistence of a variety of rights or interests in one parcel of real estate is the rule rather than the exception for most urban and suburban real property in the United States. In any tract of real property, there are usually outstanding interests other than ownership. This fact has many important legal consequences that will be discussed throughout this book.

WHO MAY HOLD INTERESTS IN REAL PROPERTY

Individuals

It is a general principle of law that any individual person may have an ownership, possessory, or nonpossessory interest in real property. Even if a person does not have contractual capacity because he or she is a minor, is insane, or has some other disability, that person still has the legal right to hold an interest in real property. However, a person with such a contractual disability usually does not have the absolute right to transfer that interest without compliance with the local laws of estate guardianship. This rule is important for persons dealing in real estate, because a transfer from a person without contractual capacity may be either voidable or absolutely void and without legal effect.

Corporations and Partnerships

The law recognizes the rights of certain groups of individuals to hold interests in real property. An example is a group comprising a business corporation. A *corporation* is generally defined as one or more individuals doing business as an entity separate and apart from themselves as individuals. It is created under authority of and recognized by the state or national government. The corporation may hold an ownership, possessory, or nonpossessory right or interest in real property and has all the rights of an individual provided that it has complied with the laws applicable to corporations.

The interest held by the corporation is held separate from the individuals or stockholders who make up the corporation. The law looks to the corporation for the performance of duties incident to the interest held. For example, the corporation would be liable for taxes assessed against the interest. On the other hand, the corporation receives the benefits of the interest held, such as rents and profits.

A joint interest in real property may also be held by a partnership. A *general partnership* is two or more persons engaged in business for profit with joint management and control of the partnership business and its assets. A general partnership can hold an interest in real property in its own name, but unlike a corporation, the interest enjoyed by a partnership is not separate and apart from the partners. Each partner is separately liable for the performance of the duties associated with the interest held by the partnership, and each partner has rights individually in the benefits derived from the interest held by the partnership.

Other Private Entities

In addition to business corporations and partnerships, there are other recognized entities that can hold interests in real property. Nonprofit corporations and certain special unincorporated associations are two examples. A *nonprofit corporation* is a corporation created to carry out certain legally recognized charitable or nonprofit operations. The law looks to the corporate entity as the holder of the interest. An *unincorporated association* is a specialized form of association, and the rules for liability vary among the many jurisdictions. An example of an unincorporated association would be a fraternal order whose existence is recognized apart from the individual members.

Governmental Units

Federal, state, and local governmental units may also hold ownership, possessory, and nonpossessory interests in real property in their performance of governmental functions.

IDENTIFICATION OF INTERESTS IN REAL PROPERTY

It is a general rule of law that a purchaser of real estate takes ownership of that real estate subject to any and all ownership, possessory, or nonpossessory interests that may already exist in the property. Thus, it becomes very important for the prospective purchaser to be able to identify all interests in the real estate that affect his/her potential ownership rights.

The identification of the holder of a particular interest is important because the rules governing the transfer of interests will vary according to the form of the holder. For example, with corporations it may be necessary to obtain an appropriate certified copy of a corporate resolution authorizing the transfer in order for the transferee to be certain that the corporate officer executing the instrument of transfer has authority to do so. Local law may require each individual partner within a partnership to join in instruments of conveyance when the partnership transfers an interest in real property. Transfer from a governmental unit may require an authorizing resolution of the local legislative unit. Unless the law prescribing the form of execution is complied with, a transfer of an interest in real estate from such an entity may be null and void.

Coexisting rights in real estate may be identified or discovered by (1) a physical inspection of the real estate and (2) a search of the public record for any matters that a reasonable inspection would reveal.

By Physical Inspection

A physical inspection of Sunny Acre (see Figure 1) by a potential buyer would reveal that there are several interests in the real property other than the ownership interest enjoyed by the owner.

A portion of Sunny Acre is leased for farming purposes to the adjacent landowner to the west. While the owner has an ownership right in the leased portion of Sunny Acre, the lessee has the right to exclusive

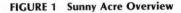
FIGURE 1 Sunny Acre Overview

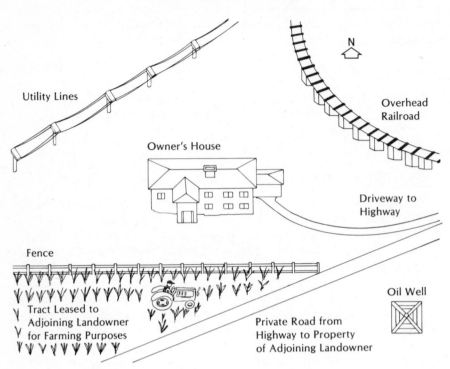

possession of that portion during the term of the lease. Thus, if Sunny Acre were sold, the new owner would not be entitled to possession of the leased portion of the premises until the expiration or prior termination of the possessory interest held by the lessee. Leases are discussed more fully in Chapter 11.

A further inspection of the premises would reveal that there is a private road across the southern portion of Sunny Acre from the highway to the property of the adjacent owner to the south. This limited right to the use of a portion of Sunny Acre for a particular purpose is known as an *easement* or *right-of-way*. The right or interest enjoyed by the adjacent landowner to the south is a nonpossessory one, and the owner of that tract does not have the right to physical possession of the portion of Sunny Acre he uses. However, the nonpossessory right is legally protected, and the owner of Sunny Acre may not interfere with the adjacent owner's free passage across Sunny Acre along the private road. The buyer who purchases the real property would be legally obligated to continue to recognize the nonpossessory interest of the adjacent landowner.

The physical inspection of Sunny Acre would also reveal that there is an overhead utility line running across Sunny Acre. It would be apparent that one or more utility companies has a utility easement across the property. The utility company does not have any right to physical possession of Sunny Acre because its interest is nonpossessory. The owner of Sunny Acre can make free use of the area under the lines but cannot interfere with the utility's right to use the property for the maintenance of its distribution line across Sunny Acre. As with all other such interests, a new owner of Sunny Acre would legally be required to honor the utility company's easement.

Easements are more fully discussed in Chapter 2.

The inspection of Sunny Acre would also disclose an oil well and an overhead railroad track. These indicate that both the oil company and the railroad company have interests in Sunny Acre, and their physical presence is notice to a potential buyer that further inquiry should be made as to the nature of these interests. The inspection itself does not disclose whether the interests enjoyed by the oil company and the railroad company might be possessory interests held under lease, nonpossessory interests in the form of easements, or ownership rights.

As previously noted, real estate is that portion of the earth extending above and below the surface of the land in which a person has certain rights. Under the law of most jurisdictions, it is possible to have separate rights or interests in the area above the surface of the real estate and below the surface of the real estate. The rights to or interests in the area below the surface of the land are *subterranean rights* and are most commonly referred to as *mineral rights*. Rights to and interests in the space directly above the surface of the real estate are commonly referred to as *air rights*. (See Figure 2.) In most cases, the owner of the surface is also owner of both the subterranean and air rights. However, as with Sunny Acre, when there is evidence that the subsurface is owned separately from the surface, the buyer is required to make an inquiry into the rights or interests of the parties involved. In any case, the new owner would take Sunny Acre subject to the nonpossessory, possessory, or ownership rights and interests held by the oil company and the railroad company. Both mineral rights and air rights are discussed more fully in Chapter 3.

By Inspection of the Public Record

A physical inspection of the premises will not disclose all interests in the real property. Ownership, possessory, and nonpossessory interests may exist in a tract of real estate even though there is no physical evidence of them on the real estate itself. In order to discover such interests, it would be necessary to inspect the public records.

FIGURE 2   Sunny Acre Elevation

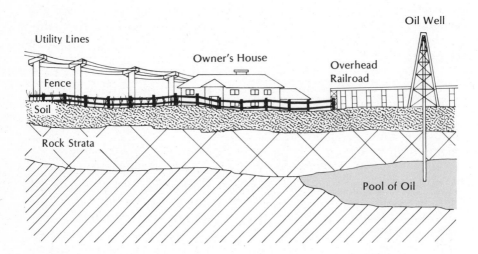

In the United States, most local governmental units, usually at the county level, have a central registry of documents relating to real property. If the holder of the interest in real estate does not give physical evidence of that interest, he/she usually must make it known by placing the document creating the interest in the public record. The record of the document gives notice to all parties interested in the property that there is an outstanding ownership, possessory, or nonpossessory interest. With a few exceptions, it is a general principle of law that if the interest is properly recorded, any subsequent interest is subordinate to the prior interest. Thus, it becomes just as important to review the public record as it does to physically inspect the real property. The process of searching the public record is discussed in Chapter 6.

GOVERNMENTAL POWERS OVER REAL PROPERTY INTERESTS

As previously noted, a governmental unit may be the holder of an ownership, possessory, or nonpossessory interest in real property. In addition, it has certain rights and powers over the interest of others.

Eminent Domain

The first of these governmental rights over interests in real property is eminent domain. *Eminent domain* is the governmental power to claim private property for public purposes. The taking must be for a purpose that is public in nature, and just compensation must be paid the holder of the interest. The power of eminent domain is exercised in a legal proceeding known as a *condemnation suit*. Eminent domain is more fully discussed in Chapter 2.

Police Powers

Police power is a governmental power over interests in real estate that is incident to the function of government to provide for the health, welfare, morals, and safety of the members of the community. Police powers are generally powers that are exercised over the uses to which real property can be put by those holding interests in it. An example of police power is zoning, which is more fully discussed in Chapter 2.

Escheat

Escheat is the power or right of the government to take ownership of property if its owner dies without having disposed of the property by will and has no heirs-at-law surviving. The right of escheat was part of the feudal law system whereby the sovereign had the right to reenter vacated property when there were no legal heirs to take possession of it. The right has been carried forward to the present day and has been assumed by the states. However, as a practical matter, the escheat of real estate rarely occurs because there is usually some surviving heir to press a claim to the property of a person who died without having made a valid will.

SUMMARY

Both real and personal property are distinct forms of property. Different rules of law control their ownership and transfer. Under the law of fixtures, certain personal property may become real property by its permanent attachment to other real property, and certain parts of real property may become personal property upon severance from the land.

Any one tract of real property may include ownership interests, possessory interests, and nonpossessory interests. The identification of the various interests may be accomplished by a physical inspection of the property and a search of the public record. Individuals, business associations, and governmental units may hold interests in real property subject to certain rights and powers of others.

QUESTIONS FOR DISCUSSION

1. What is the historical basis for the proposition that real property has a "higher standing" than personal property?

2. Is there any basis for the distinction in treatment under the law of fixtures between improvements made by a merchant lessee and those made by a residential lessee?

3. What are the practical purposes behind the requirements that the buyer inspect the property and the public record?

4. What are some economic characteristics of real estate?

CASES

Case 1. Seller and Buyer entered into a written agreement for the purchase and sale of a single-family residence. After paying the purchase price and taking possession of the house, Buyer discovered that Seller had removed the following items from the house: electric hot-water heater, venetian blinds, a crystal chandelier of good quality, and a fireplace screen. The chandelier was replaced by Seller with one of inferior quality. All the venetian blinds that had been removed had conformed to the sizes of the various windows in the house. The fireplace screen was not attached to the fireplace structure, but it had been constructed to fit the odd shape of the fireplace opening. Nothing in the written agreement between Buyer and Seller mentioned the items that were removed.

Applying the tests usually employed by courts, may the buyer recover damages for any or all of the items removed by Seller? If so, which ones and why?

Case 2. Defendants were lessees of a one-acre tract of real property along a major highway. There was a five-year written lease between Plaintiffs and Defendants. After taking possession of the property, the defendants constructed five small cabins on the property and began operating a tourist cabin rental business. Each cabin had running water and was equipped with a wood-burning stove for heating purposes. Upon expiration of the lease, Defendants removed the five cabins and relocated them directly across the highway on land they had purchased. Nothing in the written lease agreement dealt with the right to remove the cabins. Plaintiffs brought suit against Defendants, seeking damages for Defendants' wrongful removal of the cabins at the expiration of the lease terms.

What arguments may be made on behalf of Plaintiffs in their action to collect damages from the lessees? What defenses might be used to support Defendants' removal of the cabins? What is the likely result at trial?

Case 3. Seller agreed to sell a farm property to Buyers. Several feeding pens used to fatten cattle before shipment to market were located on the property. The food used to fatten the cattle was grain that was grown on the farm premises. Prior to the closing of the transaction, Seller removed 660 tons of manure from the feeding pens. The agreement between Seller and Buyers was silent as to the ownership of the manure removed by Seller. Buyers brought suit against Seller for damages, claiming that the manure removed by Seller was part of the real estate and was included in the sale of the farm. Seller defended on the grounds that the manure was personal property and was rightfully removed prior to settlement.

Applying the tests usually used by courts for the law of fixtures, what disposition might be made of Buyers' claim? Are there any other considerations that might play a part in the decision of the court?

Case 4. Coal Company entered into a long-term lease with Land Company for the letting of a large tract of remote mountain land. Coal Company took possession of the land and erected buildings on the premises for the purpose of equipment storage and temporary housing for the miners at the job site. The buildings were necessary for Coal Company to carry on its exploration and mining operations. The buildings stood on piles and were constructed of wood frame, complete with doors, windows, and interior partitioning.

The state highway department found it necessary to purchase the property for construction of a turnpike. Both Coal Company and Land Company agreed on the value of their respective interests in the land, and the state has paid each, but both parties claim compensation for the buildings. Land Company claims ownership, stating that the buildings were part of the real estate, and Coal Company claims the buildings were trade fixtures.

To whom should the state highway department make payment for the value of the buildings? Why?

Chapter 2
Ownership and Possession of Real Property

OWNERSHIP OF REAL PROPERTY

Classification of Ownership Interests
Fee Simple Absolute   Fee Simple Determinable   Fee Simple
Subject to a Condition Subsequent   Life Estate

How Ownership May Be Held
Severalty   Concurrent Ownership   Community Property
Tenants in Partnership   Ownership in Trust   Other Forms
of Ownership

Rules of Construction

POSSESSION AND ADVERSE POSSESSION

Classification of Possessory Interests
Estate for Years   Estate from Year to Year   Tenancy at Will
Tenancy at Sufferance

Adverse Possession

FUTURE INTERESTS

Classification of Future Interests
Reversionary Interests   Remainder Interests

NONPOSSESSORY INTERESTS RELATED TO USE

Easements
Easements Appurtenant   Easements in Gross   Termination of
Easements   Rights of the Parties

Profits a Prendre

Licenses
Ordinary License   License Coupled with an Interest

NONPOSSESSORY INTERESTS RELATED TO CONTROL

Private Control

Public Control
Eminent Domain   Zoning

QUESTIONS FOR DISCUSSION

CASES

THE purpose of this chapter is to specifically identify and describe the more common forms of ownership, possessory, and nonpossessory interests in real property. Persons dealing in real property such as real estate salespersons, brokers, mortgage lenders, investors, and lawyers may never encounter some of the interests discussed, but in gaining a basic understanding of these interests, they gain a foundation for understanding other real estate law concepts that may lead to important practical applications in the future.

OWNERSHIP OF REAL PROPERTY

Ownership interests in real property are sometimes referred to as *freehold estates.* The basic rights associated with an ownership interest or estate in real property include the right to use, abuse, enjoy, possess, and dispose of specific real property. The degree to which these rights can be exercised depends in part on the nature or classification of the ownership interest.

Classification of Ownership Interests

All estates in real property are either freehold or nonfreehold. The term *freehold* dates back to feudal England, where it meant that land was possessed by a "freeman" for an uncertain duration. Hence, the primary characteristic of a freehold estate is its uncertain duration. It can endure forever—that is, it can be passed on from one generation to another—in which case it is called a *freehold estate of inheritance.* Or it can endure for the life of either the tenant or a third person; under this circumstance, it

21

is called a *life estate*. In either case, the exact duration of the estate cannot be determined.

By contrast, a *nonfreehold estate* can be measured in exact intervals of time; its duration is said to be for *a term that is less than a life*. In addition, because it is only a possessory interest, it is commonly referred to as a *leasehold*. A ninety-nine-year lease, for example, may be longer than a life estate. However, it is a leasehold; it is not a freehold estate since its duration is definite.

Freehold estates can be subclassified into various estates, the most important of which, based on an owner's rights in descending order of quality, are (1) fee simple absolute, (2) fee simple subject to a condition subsequent, (3) fee simple determinable, and (4) life estate. It is important to recognize the language used to create the estate for identification purposes and the characteristics applicable to the estate after it has been identified. Obviously, the greater an owner's interest is in an estate, the greater its value.

The diagram in Figure 3 will help to illustrate the concept of freehold quality. The quality of an estate is determined by the ownership rights that are incident to it. Thus, if the entire area of a circle represents maximum ownership rights in real property, then as rights are removed, the area becomes smaller and the quality of the estate decreases.

Fee Simple Absolute

This estate is created by the conveyancing language "to B" or "to B and his/her heirs." Modern law has eliminated the necessity of strict formal conveyancing language and in its place has substituted the concept of *total intent*. Therefore, if it appears that a grantor meant to convey in fee simple absolute, no matter how informal the conveyancing language the grantor's intent will prevail.

A fee simple absolute is characterized as being the estate to which the greatest number of ownership rights attach. Consequently, subject to

FIGURE 3   Freehold Estates

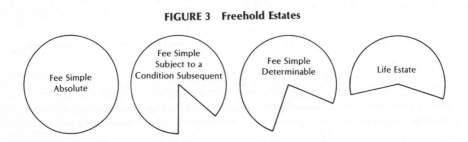

certain private and public restraints, its owner can use, abuse, exclusively possess, take the fruits of, or dispose of it by deed or will.

Fee Simple Determinable

This estate can also be easily identified by language of condition. Typically, the conveyancing language includes the words "as long as" or "until" a certain condition occurs. For example, "to B as long as alcohol is not sold on the premises," or "to B until he marries." Since a condition has been attached to the use of the property, the grantee in fee simple determinable does not possess the same quality of estate as an owner in fee simple absolute. The grantee has clearly been deprived of unrestricted use of the land; hence, it is safe to say that in most cases the intrinsic value of the fee simple determinable is less than that of a fee simple absolute. Since it is not a pure estate, it is often called a *qualified* or *base* estate.

A fee simple determinable is characterized by the fact that the instant the property is no longer used for the intended purpose, it reverts back to the grantor, or to his or her heirs if the grantor is dead. A grantee who continues in possession after the condition of the grant is violated could be considered a trespasser and might be liable to the grantor or the grantor's heirs for damages.

Fee Simple Subject to a Condition Subsequent

This estate can be easily identified by language of condition plus a provision for reentry and repossession. For example, "to B, but if the property is not used for educational purposes, then Grantor has the right to reenter and repossess the property," or "to B, until it is incorporated within the city limits, then Grantor has the right to reenter and repossess the property." The language used to create this estate, similar to a fee simple determinable, creates a conditional use. However, unlike the determinable estate, the primary characteristic of the fee simple subject to a condition subsequent estate is that it will continue in the grantee unless and until the power to reenter and repossess is exercised. The grantor can exercise the power by physical reentry or by a legal action in equity.

In summary, the determinable estate comes to an end when the condition occurs, whereas the condition subsequent estate comes to an end when the condition occurs *if* followed by actual reentry or repossession. Therefore, it can be argued that the quality of the grantee's fee simple subject to a condition subsequent is slightly better than a fee simple determinable. The grantor would probably prefer to convey a fee simple determinable estate, and the grantee would probably prefer to receive a fee simple subject to a condition subsequent.

Life Estate

Life estates can be created by grant or by operation of law under principles of dower and curtesy.

By Grant   A life estate created by grant arises from an express agreement between a grantor and grantee. The duration of a life estate is measured by the life of either the grantee or some third party. Therefore, the conveyancing language "to B for life" creates a life estate in B as measured by B's life. The conveyancing language "to B for the life of C" creates a life estate in B for the life of C, a third party. The life estate in this example is measured not by the life of the life tenant B, but by the life of C, a third party.

Characteristically, the grantee of a life estate can use the land just as if he/she were an owner in fee simple absolute. The grantee has the right to take and enjoy any rents and profits from the land but cannot commit waste on the premises.

By Operation of Law (Dower and Curtesy)   At common law and by statute in certain states, a life estate may arise by operation of law. Examples of legal life estates are dower and curtesy. *Dower* is a legal life estate that the widow has in real property owned by her deceased husband. *Curtesy* is the legal life estate that the surviving husband has in the real property owned by his deceased wife. At common law, the surviving husband was entitled to curtesy only if a child was born of his marriage to the decedent.

Sometimes a dower or curtesy interest is referred to as an *inchoate* or incomplete right. Upon the death of the spouse, the inchoate right becomes consummate and the legal life estate arises. At common law, the life estate of the surviving spouse attached not only to the real property owned by the decedent at time of death but to all property owned at any time during marriage.

When a married individual sold his/her ownership interest in real property, the spouse would have to join in the conveyance in order to release his/her inchoate right in the property conveyed. If the surviving spouse did not join in the conveyance, the dower or curtesy right would attach to the property regardless of who the owner might be when the right became consummate. Dower and curtesy become effective whether or not the deceased spouse died with a will.

At common law, dower and curtesy were designed to ensure the surviving spouse a means of support by granting a life estate in the

TABLE 2   Freehold Estates

Type of Freehold Estate	Language Used to Create	Characteristics and Duration	Type of Future Interest
Fee simple absolute	"To B" or "To B and his heirs"	B's estate is inheritable; thus it can endure forever	None
Fee simple determinable	"To B as long as the land is used for a specific purpose"	The instant B's estate is not used for the stated purpose, it reverts back to Grantor	Possibility of reverter in G
Fee simple subject to a condition subsequent	"To B, but if the land is not used for a specific purpose, G has the right to reenter and repossess the land"	If B's estate is not used for the stated purpose, it continues in B until G reenters and repossesses it	Possibility of reverter in G
Life estate	"To B for life, remainder to C"	B's estate will revert back to G on B's death	Remainder interest in C

Note: B = Grantee
        C = Third party
        G = Grantor

property of the decedent. However, in modern practice, only about half the states continue to recognize some form of dower rights, and less than one-fourth continue to recognize curtesy. In most states these legal life estates have been supplanted by laws permitting the surviving spouse to set aside the provisions of a deceased spouse's will and take a share of the estate.

It should be readily apparent that the life estate, owing to its uncertain and limited existence, is economically the least desirable, and the fee simple absolute the most desirable, of the freehold estates discussed. Table 2 summarizes the different freehold estates, the language used to create them, their characteristics, and related future interest, if any (see subsequent discussion in this chapter on future interests).

How Ownership May Be Held

Freehold and nonfreehold estates can be held by one or more persons or entities, such as corporations, partnerships, or trusts. Where interests are held by two or more persons or entities, certain problems may arise as to the respective rights and duties between or among the concurrent owners; therefore, how ownership is held will in part determine an owner's rights in the real property.

Severalty

An *estate in severalty* occurs when one person or an entity such as a corporation owns the real property. The owner's interest is severed from any other person. When an individual owner dies, the real property is probated and passes to his/her heirs or devisees. Since a corporation is an artificial person, the real property remains in the corporation until sold, traded, or distributed in some other manner. Most corporations own real property in severalty.

Concurrent Ownership

Concurrent ownership exists when two or more persons or other entities simultaneously hold title to real property. Concurrent ownership may take the form of (1) joint tenancy, (2) tenancy by the entirety, or (3) tenancy in common. It is important that a person dealing in real property recognize the language used to create the concurrent interest and know the characteristics that typify it so that sound advice can be offered as to how two or more persons or entities should title real property they plan to purchase or have retitled.

Joint Tenancy   This form of concurrent ownership may be created by use of the language "to A and B as joint tenants." Preferably, words of survivorship such as "to A and B as joint tenants with the right of survivorship" should be included, because some jurisdictions require it to avoid having it construed as a tenancy in common. Other jurisdictions infer survivorship, and the language is omitted.

The right of survivorship is one of the primary characteristics of joint tenancy. It means that on the death of one of the co-owners, his/her joint interest in the real property will pass automatically, by operation of law, to the surviving co-owner. Thus, a joint tenant cannot dispose of his/her interest by will. A joint interest can be disposed of, however, during the joint tenant's lifetime. If this happens, the characteristic of unity of title has been destroyed and the person or entity acquiring the interest becomes a *tenant in common* with the remaining joint owners, who remain joint tenants with respect to each other.

Unity of title simply means that the joint tenants acquired their interest at the same time and from the same source, by deed or will; that each joint tenant has the same identical interest as every other joint tenant;

and that the possession of each is the possession of all. Clearly, where one of the joint tenants disposes of his/her interest during life, the unity does not exist between the new owner and the remaining owner(s).

Another characteristic of joint tenancy is that creditors of any of the individual joint tenants can proceed against the debtor's joint interest and use the proceeds from a forced sale to satisfy the debt. If the creditor acquires title, he/she will obviously become a tenant in common with the remaining joint owners.

Tenancy by the Entirety   This form of concurrent ownership may be held only by a husband and wife. Therefore, the preferable conveyancing language will state "to H and W, husband and wife, as tenants by the entirety with the right of survivorship." A number of jurisdictions have concluded that a conveyance "to H and W, his wife," without survivorship language, is sufficient to create a tenancy by the entirety. If the parties are not married, a joint tenancy is created. If the parties are married and subsequently obtain a divorce, the tenancy by the entirety becomes a tenancy in common.

The characteristics of tenancy by the entirety ownership are basically identical with those of joint tenancy. Survivorship and unity of title are identical. The difference lies in the fact that creditors of the individual spouses cannot satisfy their debts by proceeding against the entirety interest; hence, tenancy by the entirety ownership shields real property from the individual obligations of each spouse. In some jurisdictions it has the added advantage of being a tax-free transfer in the estate of the deceased spouse for estate tax purposes.

Tenancy in Common   This form of concurrent ownership may be created by use of the conveyancing language "to A and B as tenants in common." Each tenant in common is treated as if he/she owned an equal undivided fractional interest in the whole, unless the conveyancing instrument clearly indicates that the fractional interest will not be equal. A tenancy in common can be created automatically, by operation of law, when a joint tenant disposes of his/her interest during his/her lifetime or when a tenant by the entirety obtains a divorce. In addition, where the conveyancing language is vague as to the nature of the concurrent ownership interest, tenancy in common under modern law is generally the preferred construction.

Thus, when a grantor conveys real property to "A and B" and A and B are not husband and wife, the law presumes that it was the intention of the grantor to create a tenancy in common between A and B.

The survivorship characteristic of joint tenancy and tenancy by the entirety is not applicable to tenancy in common. Consequently, a tenant in common is free to dispose of his/her interest by will. Judgment creditors of individual tenants in common can have a debt satisfied by a forced sale of a tenant-in-common's interest in the real property. This characteristic also applies to joint tenants but not to tenants by the entirety.

Choosing the Form of Ownership   The form of concurrent ownership to be selected may be an important personal or business decision. Typically, for example, the first major real estate purchase by a husband and wife is a residential house. If they take title as tenants by the entirety, they will shield their house from their individual debts and provide for automatic transfer of ownership to the survivor on the death of either spouse. This would be particularly appropriate when one spouse is just starting into a high-risk business. On the other hand, two unrelated individuals investing in real property may want to be able to freely dispose of their interest in the real property at their death. Their only alternative would be to co-own the property as tenants in common. Other objectives will, of course, enter into a titling decision, but they will invariably focus on the characteristics surrounding each form of concurrent ownership.

Termination of Concurrent Ownership   Termination of concurrent ownership can occur by operation of law, when, for example, a tenant by the entirety dies and is survived by a spouse or all but one joint tenants die. Due to the survivorship characteristic, interests not disposed of during the deceased's lifetime pass to the sole survivor. Termination can also result from either a voluntary division of the concurrently owned estate or, where agreements between or among concurrent owners cannot be obtained, by a court-ordered partition or separation of the real property into several parts. When the court cannot equitably divide the real property, a sale can be ordered and the proceeds divided between or among the concurrent owners. Such partition sales are generally applicable only to joint tenancy and tenancy in common.

Community Property

A minority of jurisdictions (California, Louisiana, Arizona, New Mexico, Nevada, Washington, Texas, and Idaho) are community property states. In a community property state, all property acquired by a husband or wife after marriage is considered by law to belong to the community, that is, to belong to both. Only property acquired before marriage or by gift or devise after marriage is considered separate property. Furthermore, in the majority of community property states, both husband and wife have the power of testamentary disposition as to one-half the property. Only a few community property states provide for passage of title to the surviving spouse by operation of law.

Tenants in Partnership

Under the Uniform Partnership Act, which has been adopted in whole or in part by many states, a partnership is simply an association of two or more persons who voluntarily agree to carry on a business for profit. It is not difficult to recognize that the managerial and economic needs of a partnership would not be practically met by joint tenancy or tenancy in common forms of ownership where the concurrent owners can sell their individual interests during their lifetime. Therefore, under the Uniform Partnership Act, Section 25, the concept of tenancy in partnership was created whereby the partners are treated much like tenants by the entirety. Partnership property must remain in the partnership; individual partners cannot dispose of the property during their lifetime or at death nor can it be encumbered by a partner's personal debts.

Ownership in Trust

The laws of most states provide for ownership of real property in trust. By definition, a *trust* arises when legal title to property is conveyed by a settlor or trustor to a *trustee,* who holds it for the benefit of one or more persons or entities known as *beneficiaries.* The beneficiaries retain an ownership interest known as *equitable title.*

Mechanically, the trust is created by an agreement called a *declaration of trust.* In the declaration of trust, the settlor usually sets forth in full the duties of the trustee with respect to the property conveyed. Hence, the trustee is immediately put in a position of responsibility. The trustee is said to have a *fiduciary duty* to the settlor and beneficiary, and performance of this duty will in part be based upon the express duties. For example, he/she might be given the specific instruction to sell certain properties if their actual or anticipated yield falls below 6 percent. A more general instruction would be to buy or sell at his/her discretion. In the above example, the trustee may be breaching his/her fiduciary duty if he/she allows the trust assets to yield less than 6 percent over a period of time.

Trusts can be broadly classified into two groups depending upon when the settlor intends the trust to become operative. With an *inter vivos trust,* it must appear that the settlor intended the trust to become operative during his or her lifetime. With a *testamentary trust,* the settlor intends the trust to become operative upon his or her death. Like a will, a testamentary trust can be revoked by the settlor at any time before death.

TABLE 3   Characteristics of Concurrent Ownership

Type of Concurrent Ownership	Survivorship	Disposal Allowed During Life	At Death	Subject to Individual Debts
Joint tenancy (with the right of survivorship)	Yes	Yes	No	Yes
Tenancy by the entirety	Yes	No	No	No
Tenancy in common	No	Yes	Yes	Yes
Tenancy in partnership	Yes	No	No	No

Other Forms of Ownership

The forms of ownership discussed in the preceding sections are the most common vehicles by which the average individual or other entity can own real property. Other forms of ownership that will be covered later, but in a different context, are corporate ownership, real estate investment trusts (REITs), cooperative ownership, and condominium ownership. It is important for the person dealing in real property to recognize the characteristics that distinguish one form of ownership from another so that the intended results will be achieved. Recognition of the alternatives is the first major step. After that, an in-depth analysis can be made by legal, accounting, or other specialists in the field to determine the most appropriate form of ownership.

Table 3 summarizes the more important characteristics applicable to joint tenancy, tenancy by the entirety, tenancy in common, and tenancy in partnership.

Rules of Construction

On occasion, particularly with documents drafted by laypersons, it may be difficult to classify the estate being conveyed or reviewed. If, for example, G, an owner in fee simple absolute, conveyed Sunny Acre

"to B, and her heirs, for her life, then at B's death to be divided equally among the living grandchildren of G,"

the question is whether B has acquired a fee simple absolute in Sunny Acre or a life estate. Several general rules of construction have been developed in the law for the purpose of determining the probable intent of the parties. These rules are not exhaustive nor are they stated in any order of priority. They are merely indicative of how probable intent can be established.

1. All parts of the conveyancing instrument should, if possible, be given some consideration in its construction. This concept is known as the *four corners doctrine*. This means that certain words and phrases in the conveyancing language cannot be ignored. In the example above, if all the words after "to B, and her heirs" were discarded, B's estate would clearly be a fee simple absolute. But if consideration were given to all the conveyancing language, it could justifiably be argued that the probable intent of the grantor was to convey a life estate to B.

2. An agreement is construed most strongly against its draftor because he/she is in a better position to eliminate ambiguities in the first place. If the conveyancing language were "to B, and her heirs, remainder to G, the grantor," the question is whether G, the draftor of the language, intended to convey a life estate to B with the estate to revert to herself at B's death, or a fee simple absolute to B. If the conveyancing language is construed most strongly against the grantor-draftor, the grantor may not retain any interest and B will receive a fee simple absolute.

3. Where the instrument contains two contradictory clauses, the first clause prevails. In the Sunny Acre example, under this rule, B will receive a fee simple absolute since the first clause is "to B, and her heirs."

4. A fee simple absolute is the favored estate.

In the example discussed above, it would appear that the third and fourth rules favor an interpretation that would give B a fee simple absolute. On the other hand, by applying the first rule it could be argued that the grantor intended to convey a life estate to B. The question is arguable and may have to be resolved in court, since no single rule or combination of rules necessarily prevails.

It is important to draft documents that clearly convey the intended meaning by use of precise legal terminology. It is equally important, from a buyer's point of view, to recognize when an uncertainty exists in the conveyancing language that may adversely affect the buyer's ownership interest.

POSSESSION AND ADVERSE POSSESSION

The concepts of possession and ownership of real property are not interchangeable. *Ownership* has been defined as a collection of rights that can endure for at least a life, as in a life estate, and possibly forever, as in a fee simple absolute. Without ownership, possession of real property will continue for only a definite period of time. In short, ownership denotes some form of freehold estate, whereas possession denotes a nonfreehold estate.

Classification of Possessory Interests

Possessory interests can be classified into various nonfreehold estates based primarily on the duration of the possessor's interest as follows: (1) estate for years, (2) estate from year to year, and (3) tenancy at will.

Estate for Years

An estate for years arises when a landlord leases real property to a tenant "from 1/1/X0 to 12/31/X1, a period of two years." As the conveyancing language characteristically indicates, the lease is for a definite period of time. If the tenant continues to occupy the premises after the expiration of the stated period, a tenancy at sufferance might exist. A tenancy existing at the sufferance of the landlord could be terminated by the landlord at any time without notice. In the alternative, the tenant could be considered a trespasser and liable for resulting damages. If the tenant dies during the stated period, his/her personal representative will assume the deceased tenant's responsibility under the lease.

Estate from Year to Year

An estate from year to year arises when a landlord leases real property to a tenant "from 1/1/X0 to 12/31/X0, rent payable in advance on or before the first day of each month." When the landlord accepts payment for the month following 12/31/X0, the lease continues for another year under the same terms and conditions specified in the original lease.

The primary characteristic of an estate from year to year, as distinguished from the estate for years, is the indefiniteness of its duration. It is conceivable, but not realistic, that the lease will continue forever under the same terms and conditions that existed in the original lease. The tenancy will not terminate until proper notice is given by either party, whereas termination is automatic under an estate for years.

Tenancy at Will

A *tenancy at will* arises when a landlord leases real property to a tenant "for as long as landlord wishes." As the conveyancing language indicates, the tenancy can be terminated by either party at any time; hence, the estate is of indeterminate duration at the will of either party. Generally, notice of termination is not required by either party.

Tenancy at Sufferance

Tenancy at sufferance is the lowest form of nonfreehold estate. It arises when a tenant, without the owner's consent, continues to exercise

TABLE 4 Nonfreehold Estates

Type of Estate	Language Used To Create	Characteristics and Duration
Estate for years	"To T from 1/1/X0 to 12/31/X1, a period of two years"	T's tenancy is for a definite period of time
Estate from year to year	"To T from 1/1/X0 to 12/31/X0, rent payable in advance on or before the first day of each month"	T's tenancy can renew itself each year and therefore is indefinite
Tenancy at will	"To T as long as L wishes"	T's tenancy can be terminated by either T or L at any time and therefore is indeterminate
Tenancy at sufferance	None	Since T's possessory interest is without contractual foundation, the interest can be terminated at any time at the will of L

Note: L = Landlord
       T = Tenant

possessory interest in the real property after the possessory or leasehold interest has terminated. Such a tenancy can be terminated at the will of the owner without the necessity of giving notice.

If you were the farmer-lessee in the Sunny Acre example (see Figure 1), which form of nonfreehold estate would you select?

Table 4 summarizes the type of language used to create the various nonfreehold estates discussed and their duration.

Adverse Possession

A possessory interest or estate has been characterized as being synonymous with a leasehold interest. A lease, of course, denotes an agreement between two parties, a lessor-owner and a lessee-possessor. However, a possessor who occupies an owner's land without a pre-arranged agreement such as a lease or without permission may be an *adverse possessor* and, under the doctrine of adverse possession, may eventually be entitled to an ownership interest. For a possessor to hold title adversely to the owner, his/her possession must meet three basic requirements:

1. The possessor's occupancy must be *open, visible,* and *notorious.* This means that the possession is not secretive and that the possessor is treating the real property as if he/she were its true owner.   This requirement depends in large part on the nature and character of the real property. If the real property were remote, unimproved mountain land, a person who occasionally camped on the land would probably not be considered an adverse possessor.   But if a person moved into a vacated house in an urban residential neighborhood, his/her possession would probably be adverse. Generally, only a true owner moves into a house, whereas campers who are not owners frequently camp on privately owned remote land. Also, a house occupant's use in an urban setting is more visible than a camper's use in a remote mountain setting.

2. The possessor's occupancy must be *hostile* and *adverse.* This means that possession is taken under a claim of right that is inconsistent with the rights of the owner and without the consent or permission of such owner.   In short, the possessor is laying a claim to the real property against the whole world, including its owner.

3. The possessor must maintain occupancy for the required statutory period, which may be from five to twenty-one years depending on the state.   The running of the statutory period can be discontinued or interrupted either by physical eviction or by court action. However, it is possible to tack the period of one possessor's use onto another possessor's use if there is privity of contract between the two possessors. If, for example, F openly, notoriously, continuously, and adversely farmed the southwest portion of Sunny Acre for 25 years, and did not have permission to do so, he could lay claim to an ownership interest in the southwest corner of Sunny Acre by adverse possession.   This is one reason why it is suggested in Chapter 1 that a buyer carefully inspect real property before purchasing it.

A few western states have two additional requirements for adverse possession: color of title and payment of taxes. An adverse possessor is said to hold *color of title* to real property when there exists a written document such as a deed, will, or agreement that purports to convey an ownership interest to the adverse possessor. Thus, in these states a mere "squatter" can never obtain an ownership interest by adverse possession. Under the *payment of taxes* requirement, the adverse possessor must provide evidence that he/she paid applicable real estate taxes on the property during the statutory period. That is, those who receive the benefits of ownership are required to pay for them.

FUTURE INTERESTS

Where a future interest in real property has been conveyed to a grantee, the grantee technically has neither ownership nor possessory rights in that property. The grantee has only an expectancy. His/her rights will materialize on the occurrence of a specified event at some later date. Because the person dealing with real property is not likely to encounter a future interest, only the more common forms will be briefly considered.

Classification of Future Interests

Future interests can generally be classified as *reversionary* in nature, when the real property reverts back to the grantor at some future date, or *remainder* in nature, when the real property is transferred at some future date to a third party, not the grantor.

Reversionary Interests

There are two types of reversionary interests. An *absolute reversionary interest,* usually called simply a *reversionary interest,* provides the grantor absolute assurance of getting the real property back at some future date. Such a reversionary interest is created by the language "to B for life, remainder to G, the grantor." The effect of the conveyancing language is to create a life estate in B, thus leaving G with something less than a fee simple absolute. The grantor technically retains a future or reversionary interest, which will absolutely materialize into a fee simple absolute on the death of B.

In contrast, the grantor with the *possibility of a reverter* is not assured of getting the real property back at some future date, although the possibility exists. The possibility of a reverter is created by the use of conditional language. For example, "to B as long as the property is used for recreational purposes," or "to C until his gross income exceeds $100,000 per year." Any condition that does not violate law or public policy will suffice. The effect here is to create a fee simple determinable in B, with the grantor retaining the possibility that the estate might, at some future time, revert back to him/her or his/her heirs. Whether or not the property reverts depends, of course, on the occurrence of the stated condition. Thus, in the examples just given, the condition would be violated if B made a use of the property that was not associated with recreation or if C grossed over $100,000 per year.

In summary, the interest retained by the grantor is called either a reversionary or possibility of a reversionary interest, and the grantee acquires a life estate, a fee simple determinable, or a fee simple subject to a condition subsequent, depending upon the conveyancing language used.

Remainder Interests

There are two types of remainder interests. A *vested remainder* is identical to a reversionary interest except that someone other than the grantor has an absolute right to enjoy the property in the future. Therefore, the conveyancing language "to B for life, remainder to T (a third party)" illustrates T's vested remainder interest in the property. A *contingent remainder* is identical to a possibility of a reversionary interest except that the right to future enjoyment rests in someone other than the grantor. For example, the conveyancing language "to B so long as the property is used for recreational purposes, then to T (a third party)" or "to B until he marries, then to T (a third party)" shows that for T's interest to become absolute, the contingency must occur. Although the average person dealing in real property may never encounter a future interest, it is nevertheless helpful to understand how and when it relates to other interests in real property.

NONPOSSESSORY INTERESTS RELATED TO USE

As previously noted, ownership of real property includes the rights of use, enjoyment, possession, and disposition. Possession of real property includes the right of occupancy and control for a limited period of time, but not disposition of the real property. By contrast, a nonpossessory or incorporeal interest in real property gives its owner only a limited right to use for a limited purpose real property that is owned or possessed by another. The more common types of nonpossessory interests related to use are (1) easements, (2) profits a prendre, and (3) licenses.

Easements

Easements can be broadly classified into two groups: (1) *easements appurtenant,* which involve some relationship between or among two or more tracts of land, and (2) *easements in gross,* which are personal in nature and do not require a relationship between or among two or more tracts of land.

Easements Appurtenant

By definition, an *easement appurtenant* is an interest that one owner of real property may enjoy in the real property of another. The property burdened by the use is called the *servient tenement,* since it serves the other tract. The property benefited by the use is called the *dominant tenement,* since it is in a dominant position with respect to the use being made of the servient tenement (tract). For example, if two tracts of property owned by A and B, respectively, were contiguous one to the other and A acquired an easement through B's property, A's property would benefit and therefore is the dominant tenement, whereas B's property is burdened by the use and therefore is the servient tenement.

If an easement appurtenant is not personal, it continues to affect the property through changes in ownership. Under those circumstances, the easement is said to *run with the land.* Each new owner of the dominant tract acquires the predecessor's rights in the tract including the benefit of the previously established easement. Each new owner of a servient tract, even though continuing to own the property under the easement, is subject to the dominant owner's reasonable use.

Creation of Easements Appurtenant By express agreement. An easement appurtenant is most commonly created by express grant or reservation. If A and B own contiguous tracts of real property and A agrees to sell to B an easement appurtenant through A's property for use as a single-lane road, B would acquire an *easement by express grant.* However, if B owned two contiguous tracts of real property and sold one of them to A, B could, in a deed to A, reserve to herself and her heirs an easement for use as a single-lane road through A's newly acquired property. In this case, B has acquired an *easement by reservation.* Both methods of creating an easement appurtenant must be in writing to be valid.

By implication upon severance. A written agreement is not required to create an easement by implication upon severance. As the term indicates, the implication is that when an owner of real property subdivides it into two or more tracts, each grantee will be provided with access to his/her particular property. The implication arises under two circumstances:

1. When the grantee is landlocked. The implication here is based on "ways of necessity." The grantor and grantee will have to resolve their access problem by express agreement or, in the absence of such agreement, the grantee will be forced to seek a court order to gain access.

2. When a grantor, prior to conveying to the grantee, subjects one part of the property to an obvious, visible use for the benefit of another part, then conveys away his/her interest in the land benefited. The use made by the grantor must be not only clearly visible, but also permanent and continuous, thereby allowing a prospective grantee to easily ascertain its existence by physical inspection before purchasing the property.

If, for example, A owned a large tract of real property and many years ago constructed a gravel road from the front (servient tract) to the back (dominant tract) of the property to provide access to a sawmill business he had operated for ten years and continues to operate, it should appear obvious to prospective grantees by visual inspection that if they purchased the front part of the property the grantor could continue to use the gravel road in the absence of an agreement to the contrary.

Even if the easement is not mentioned in the deed from grantor to grantee, or in any other agreement, it can arise by implication, as in the above example, because of prior use. This is another very good reason why a buyer should carefully inspect real property before purchase. Otherwise, he/she may discover that the newly acquired interest in the property is subject to an easement interest of another party.

By prescription. An easement by prescription is generally created by an adverse, hostile, open and notorious, and continuous use of the servient tenement by the dominant owner for the statutory period of prescription. Each descriptive word defining the nature of the use must be established.

A use is *adverse* when it occurs without license or permission from the servient owner. A use is *hostile* when the use made by the dominant owner invades a proprietary interest of a servient owner. A neighbor, for example, who trespasses onto a servient tract of property and cuts down a fruit tree has invaded a proprietary interest of the servient owner; but a neighbor who constructs his/her house so that it will interfere with a servient owner's light and air has not made hostile use of the servient tract, since generally a legal right to light and air does not exist.

A use is *open and notorious* when it gives the servient owner an opportunity to appraise the situation and take appropriate action to protect his/her right. A secretive use is not hostile.

A *continuous* use throughout the statutory period does not mean that the use must be constant or at regular intervals, but it must be something more than an occasional trespass. It must clearly appear that the user has attempted to establish a definite property right in the servient tract. A well-worn footpath across a neighbor's lawn used as a shortcut to work would probably be sufficient.

The statutory period for which the use must be made varies from state to state, but is usually between ten and twenty-one years. Generally, the servient owner cannot legally interrupt the statutory period by mere protest. He/she must either physically prevent the use, perhaps by installing a gate or fence across the used portion of the property, or sue in equity to obtain injunctive relief. Nor will the same use made by a new owner of a dominant tract serve to interrupt the statutory period. The general rule here is that there is a sufficient contractual relationship (privy) between successors' interests in the dominant tract to permit them to tack one period of use onto another. Most of these requirements are similar to those for establishing adverse possession.

Therefore, it is again emphasized that a buyer of real property should inspect it carefully to ascertain the existence of easements that may arise by operation of law.

Easements in Gross

Whereas an easement appurtenant requires dominant and servient tracts of real property, an easement in gross is personal to its user and consequently does not require the user to have an ownership interest in another tract. An *easement in gross* is a mere personal interest in the real property of another; a utility easement is a common example.

Since an easement in gross is considered to be personal to its user, it generally cannot be assigned to another user unless the parties intend its assignability or the right in question was intended for commercial exploitation rather than personal enjoyment.

Creation of Easements in Gross   An easement in gross is most commonly created by an express written grant. A less common method is by prescription coupled with estoppel. States differ as to whether or not easements in gross can be acquired by the same prescriptive requirements necessary for obtaining an easement appurtenant by prescription. However, it seems that if prescription is coupled with the element of estoppel, an easement in gross can be established.

Estoppel arises when the owner of a servient tenement stands idly by and watches another substantially change position in reliance on the expectation that the use he/she has begun will be allowed to continue. If, for example, A owned a large tract of land that was contiguous to a government range of mountains designated as a wilderness area, and B, without protest from A, substantially improved a jeep route through A's property so that he would be able to better carry on his back-packing business in the mountains, and then after thirty years A suddenly sought to enjoin B from using the jeep road, A would probably be estopped from denying B's use. Since the jeep road had been substantially improved, it would be unjust to B to deny the existence of an easement in gross.

Termination of Easements

An easement can generally be terminated either (1) by the expiration of a period of time stated in a written easement agreement or deed or (2) by extinguishment, the occurrence of some event subsequent to its creation.

By Expiration   Whether an easement is appurtenant or in gross, the parties can specifically agree that it will terminate at the end of a stated period of time. For example, if A conveyed an easement appurtenant or in gross to B until 1/1/XX, the easement will terminate on that date.

By Extinguishment   An easement can be terminated by extinguishment on the occurrence of an event. The most common events that can cause extinguishment of an easement are (1) express release, (2) merger, (3) abandonment, and (4) prescription.

An *express release* occurs when the dominant owner, by written agreement, expressly gives up the right to use the easement. A *merger* occurs when an easement appurtenant exists and the dominant and servient properties come under the ownership of the same person. In a related situation, when the owner of an easement in gross becomes the owner of the servient property that was burdened by the easement, the reason for the easement in gross no longer exists, so it is considered to be extinguished.

An *abandonment* occurs when the dominant owner, through his/her conduct, demonstrates an intent to discontinue use of the easement. Generally, mere statements of nonuse or an actual nonuse of the easement will not be sufficient to prove abandonment. Abandonment is a question of fact that must be shown from all the surrounding circumstances. Anything short of denial of the existence of the easement by the dominant owner by acts that are contrary to its existence will not be sufficient to show abandonment.

For example, if A, owner of a dominant tract, built a fence on her property where it enters a right-of-way on B's servient tract, and A tells B that she no longer intends to use the right-of-way, this statement alone would not be enough to prove abandonment, but the statement coupled with the act of blocking entrance to the right-of-way easement might be sufficient.

Finally, an easement can be *terminated by prescription* when the servient owner makes an adverse, hostile, open, notorious, and continuous use of the easement for the statutory period of prescription. For example, if A, owner of the servient property across which B has constructed a road in accordance with an express easement agreement, plowed up the road and planted a vegetable garden every year for the statutory period, the easement would be terminated by prescription.

Rights of the Parties

Whether the easement was created expressly or by implication, the burden of the servitude should not be expanded to include a use that was not authorized or contemplated by the parties. In general, the use made by the dominant owner must be reasonable and within the scope of the express grant or implied purpose.

For example, B, whose house and land were situated in a rural area, by express written agreement used a private lane over A's property to gain access to his house. The agreement specifically stated that B and his heirs could use the land "for domestic purposes only." Coal was discovered on B's land and large coal trucks began to haul it over the private lane. Since this is a commercial use that expands the intended purpose of the easement, A could enjoin the coal trucks from using the lane. B's expanded use was not reasonable.

On the other hand, since the servient owner continues to own the property subject to the easement, he/she can exercise full ownership rights over his/her property but cannot interfere with the dominant owner's reasonable use of the easement. Generally, unless stated in an agreement, the obligation to maintain and repair an easement rests with the user.

Profits a Prendre

An easement gives its owner the right to use another's property without removing anything from it, but a *profit a prendre* gives its owner the right to remove natural resources such as timber, minerals, and fish from the property. It is similar to an easement in that it must be in writing since it represents an interest in real property.

The owner of the profit has the right to use the property in such a way as to be able to enjoy the profit. Thus, if the owner of a profit has the right to remove timber, by necessity he/she has the right to do whatever is reasonably necessary to cut it down and haul it away.

A profit a prendre should not be confused with a natural resource lease. In the latter, an owner of real property leases the property to a developer and retains the right to receive a royalty payment, which is usually based on a certain percentage of the amount of natural resource extracted. For example, an oil or gas royalty might be one-fifth the net sales price of the amounts extracted, or ten cents per ton of sand removed.

Licenses

A *license,* like an easement or profit, allows its owner to make personal use of property that is in the possession of another, but it does not confer an interest or estate in the property. The fundamental difference lies in the legal relationship established between the parties. A license, unless coupled with an interest, is revocable. An easement or profit is not revocable. Further, a license does not have to be in writing, and no particular formality is necessary for its creation. Therefore, the right of a licensee to use another's property is less substantial than that which arises out of an easement or profit. It is more in the nature of a personal privilege and not an interest in real property. However, if a license is coupled with an interest, that is, if it is in some way relied on to the detriment of the licensee, it takes on all the attributes of an easement.

Licenses, then, can be classified into two groups: (1) ordinary licenses and (2) licenses coupled with an interest.

Ordinary License

An ordinary license is a mere revocable privilege or a right to do something on real property owned or possessed by another. For example, an ordinary license can be obtained from an owner of real property to sell farm products on the owner's property. In this case, the license can be revoked by the licensor at will, and since it is technically not an interest in the property itself, but a mere personal privilege, it cannot be transferred or assigned by the licensee to another.

License Coupled with an Interest

The general rule that a license is a mere revocable personal privilege and consequently cannot be transferred or assigned is subject to an important exception. Where a licensee substantially changes his/her economic position while exercising his/her license and reasonably relies on misrepresentations made by the licensor as to the duration of the license, the licensor may thereafter be equitably estopped from revoking the license.

For example, A obtained permission from B to connect into B's spring, which was the only known source of water in the area. Relying on the promise, A built a house and ran an underground pipe to carry the water from B's spring to her new house. Since A has spent a considerable amount of money in reliance on B's promise, a *license coupled with an interest* has arisen and B cannot revoke the license.

In this example, the duration of the license will probably be as long as the life of the house that it serves. However, unlike an easement, a license coupled with an interest generally is not irrevocable forever. It lasts until such time as the licensee realizes a reasonable return on his or her investment. Otherwise, it would create an interest in the property and be equivalent to an easement.

Table 5 summarizes the need for the various nonpossessory interests to be in writing.

TABLE 5 Nonpossessory Interests Related to Use

Type of Interest	Written Agreement Required
Easement appurtenant by:	
Express grant	Yes
Implication upon severance based on:	
ways of necessity	No
prior use	No
Prescription	No
Easement in gross	
Express grant	Yes
Prescription coupled with estoppel	No
Profit a prendre	Yes
License	No

NONPOSSESSORY INTERESTS RELATED TO CONTROL

Nonpossessory interests in real property exist not only with respect to a use that is made by one who is not an owner or possessor on or over a servient property, but also in the various methods by which both the private and public sectors of society can control, from a distance, the use that the owners or possessors can make of their own real property. Those rights that an owner has in a fee simple absolute estate or any other form of estate are never absolute where subject to public or private regulation. Outside control is one of the most important factors that must be taken into consideration before a developer or investor buys real property. In most cases, the more restricted the use, the less desirable the tract for development purposes.

Private Control

Historically, land use was controlled almost exclusively by private contractual agreement. Contained in the agreements were restrictive covenants that permitted some uses and denied others. For a restrictive covenant to run with the land in the sense that it would bind subsequent purchasers of the same property to the same restrictions, the following must exist:

1. There must be an element of *privity of estate*. Although there is not universal agreement as to its definition, privity generally means that one who is not a party to the original covenant or agreement can sue or be sued based on the restrictions expressed in the covenant if he/she is a successor to the interest in the estate of one of the parties to the

covenant. If, for example, A conveys the northeast portion of Sunny Acre (see Figure 1) to B and in the conveyance both parties agree to restrict further development of their land to single-family residential houses, and B subsequently conveys his interest in Sunny Acre to C, C is clearly a successor in interest to B and consequently will be bound by the original covenant between A and B. There is little doubt in this case that the A-B covenants run with the land and will bind each subsequent grantee.

2. The covenant must *touch and concern* the land in the sense that the obligation relates to an ownership interest in the property. In the example above, use of property, a fundamental ownership interest, has been restricted by a covenant, so the covenant clearly touches and concerns the land.

3. The parties to the covenant must *intend* the restrictions not only to be binding as between themselves, but also to be equally binding on their transferees. Intent will be established from the language of the document creating the covenant and the surrounding circumstances. In the example given in (1), it is not absolutely clear from the brief information given that the covenantor and covenantee intended the use restriction to affect subsequent transferees. However, a strong argument can be made, based on the use presently being made of Sunny Acre, that both parties desire to preserve the low-density residential character of the property. However, since commercial activity is also taking place on Sunny Acre, the opposite point of view could probably be argued too.

Covenants running with the land are created for the most part by express agreement. They are extinguished either by the passage of an expressly stated period of time or, where the covenant no longer makes practical sense, by implication. For example, a century-old covenant restricting the use of a tract of land that is located in the middle of an intensely used commercial district to single-family residential housing would not make practical sense, and hence probably would not be enforced in court.

Covenants running with the land are the most direct form of private control of real property use, but there are many other kinds of controls. For example, a mortgagee has the right to prevent a mortgagor-owner-possessor from committing waste on the mortgaged property (see Chapter 7); a landlord has the same right with respect to a tenant (see Chapter 11); a judgment creditor has certain claims in a debtor's real property (see Chapter 6). The point is that the rights surrounding ownership and possession are deceptively simple, especially when ownership and possession are subject not only to covenants running with the land but also to a multitude of other private nonpossessory interests relating to control.

Public Control

In recent years, due to increased recognition of the need to control and regulate the environment for the good of all, property use has been publicly regulated either through the legislative power of eminent domain exercised primarily on the state level or through state zoning statutes implemented at the local level of government.

Eminent Domain

The concepts of eminent domain and condemnation are often confused. *Eminent domain* refers to a state's power to take private land for public use, and *condemnation* is the name of the legal process by which the power is exercised. Under eminent domain, property can be condemned or taken if it is required for either a public purpose, such as public housing, redevelopments, or a highway, or for a private purpose necessary to the development of a natural resource of the state. It is possible that a private way to gas-bearing property could be condemned to allow a private company to develop the publicly needed natural resource.

The owner of a condemned property must be paid *just compensation* for the property, which is often difficult to measure. Generally, however, a condemnee is entitled to the difference between fair market value of the property owned before and after the taking. Obviously, if the entire property were condemned, just compensation would be the difference between the fair market value before the taking and zero. Fair market value is generally determined by taking into account all relevant and material evidence such as location, comparable selling prices, income production, and improvement. In addition, a property owner may be entitled to consequential damages when the property is not actually condemned but is detrimentally affected as the result of a nearby taking. A restaurant cut off from highway access is an example of such an entitlement.

Zoning

Zoning has been defined as the legislative division of a community into various areas, such as commercial, residential, and industrial, in which only certain designated uses of real property are permitted. The purpose of zoning is to benefit the community as a whole through planned development. However, those who oppose zoning argue from a practical point of view that each individual property owner is best able to determine the use to which his/her property will be put, that property values are artificially inflated because each zone contains a limited amount of space and, as a consequence, development is impeded, and that the law of supply and demand would tend to set a natural pattern of development if there were no zoning. In some parts of the country, these arguments have had an impact.

The power to zone and the validity of zoning statutes or ordinances are based on a state's police power. *Police power* is the constitutional authority of a state to adopt and enforce laws and regulations that promote the health, safety, morals, and general welfare of the public. To conform to police power standards, any zoning statute or ordinance must first be *reasonable*, not arbitrary, and *nondiscriminatory*. That is, there must be a rational basis for the classification. Second, the zoning statute or ordinance must be *nonconfiscatory*. That is, the property should be used for the purpose for which it is best suited.

Thus, if Sunny Acre (see Figure 1) were within the city limits, and a city ordinance divided Sunny Acre into low-density residential, medium-density residential (both requiring off-street parking), and light industrial zones, without knowledge of further facts, the ordinance would appear to be valid because it bears some relationship to public health and safety and is reasonable in its application.

Within the context of zoning law, several concepts and terms that should be understood are (1) nonconforming use, (2) spot zoning, (3) variance, and (4) exception.

Nonconforming Use   A *nonconforming use* is a use that was in effect at the time a zoning ordinance was passed. The general rule is that such a use may be continued but not expanded upon or changed without appropriate permission of the governing authority. If a person was using his property as a gas station before the zoning ordinance became effective, he could continue that use after enactment of an ordinance that placed his property in a single-family residential zone. Depending on the language of a particular zoning ordinance, a nonconforming use can be terminated (1) by abandoning the use, (2) by making another use of the property, (3) by passage of an expressly stated period of time, or (4) by rezoning to include the nonconforming use as a permitted use.

Spot Zoning   Spot zoning, sometimes called *contract zoning*, arises when a single tract or a limited number of tracts of real property are placed in a zone that does not conform to surrounding tracts. Such an arrangement is usually not valid because it results in unreasonable discrimination and as a consequence violates constitutional dictates.

Variance   If a zoning ordinance causes disproportionate hardship to one tract of real property as compared to others in the same zoning classification, the owner of the property against whom the hardship was worked can seek administrative relief by application to the appropriate body for a *variance* from the existing zoning.

For example, in an area zoned for single-family houses, A owned a corner lot that was originally 100 feet by 100 feet but was now 95 feet by 95 feet because 5 feet on both sides was condemned for road construction purposes. After the condemnation, A could not build a single-family house on the property because the zoning ordinance required that each lot have at least 100 front feet. A's only recourse would be to apply for a variance. Clearly, noncompliance with the zoning ordinance was caused by a circumstance that was beyond A's control and was probably not anticipated. It resulted in a practical difficulty and unnecessary hardship.

Generally, one or a combination of the following conditions should exist for a variance to be granted: (1) Under the circumstances, the land in question could not yield a reasonable return if used solely as zoned; (2) the plight of the owner is unique compared to other owners in the general area; and (3) the use permitted by the variance will not materially alter the general character of the locality. In the example above, it can be clearly shown that conditions (2) and (3) have been met. A more difficult and not uncommon fact situation arises when a building is constructed and is found to encroach a matter of inches on another's property, or to be over a setback line established by a particular zoning classification.

Exception An *exception* is written into the zoning ordinance to permit certain uses that are not in general compliance with other uses in the locality. For example, an office may be permitted in a home in a neighborhood that is zoned exclusively for residential use.

Summary A basic understanding of modern zoning law is absolutely necessary for the person dealing in real property because zoning establishes use that may have a direct bearing on price. For the public in general, zoning is even more important because it sets the pattern of growth in the community and consequently may have a direct effect on the environment.

QUESTIONS FOR DISCUSSION

1. Describe the similarities and differences among the following ownership interests: (a) fee simple absolute, (b) fee simple determinable, and (c) fee simple subject to a condition subsequent.

2. H and W were just married. W was an orphan and had no significant accumulated wealth. H, on the other hand, had a savings account in his name alone in the amount of $100,000. H was advised by F, a friend, that he could get a better return on his money by investing it in a large apartment complex. F proposed that he and H each contribute $100,000 toward the purchase price. Assuming it is a good investment, what advice would you give to H as to how they should concurrently own the apartment building? Make whatever assumptions you feel are necessary to arrive at a logical conclusion.

3. If both adverse possession and creation of an easement by prescription require hostile, open, notorious, and continuous use of the subject property for a statutory period, what is the difference between them? Which would you prefer?

4. Describe the ways by which land can be privately and publicly controlled. What is the legal basis for private and public control? Do you think public control alone would be sufficient?

5. Arnold, an avid fisherman, entered into a valid written agreement with Brenda, wherein Brenda agreed to give to Arnold, for a stated consideration, a right-of-way through her property so that Arnold would have easy access to a famous fishing stream. The conveyancing language read in part "to Arnold as long as he enjoys fishing." Arnold then recorded his right-of-way agreement with Brenda and purchased the land next to Brenda's property. Arnold used the right-of-way for several years, lost interest in fishing, and sold his land next to Brenda's to Casey. Does Casey, an avid fisherman, have the right to use the right-of-way? (What is the difference between an easement in gross and an easement appurtenant, and how does that difference relate to the problem?)

CASES

Case 1. In 1962, A signed a contract to purchase a house. The contract contained the following provision: "Use of apartment swimming pool to be available to purchaser and his family." S, the seller, orally told A that use of the pool went with ownership of the house being purchased and that subsequent purchasers would have the same right to use the pool.

The pool was located in an adjoining apartment complex that was being developed by S at the time. When S delivered the deed to the house to A, there was no mention of the pool in the deed.

A sold the house to B in 1969. Although B was informed by A that use of the pool went with the property, no mention of this appeared either in the sales contract between A and B or in the deed from A to B. When B attempted to obtain a free pass from S to use the pool, S refused to comply with the request.

What argument would you make for B? What would be S's defense?

Case 2. In 1949, O became the owner of a parcel of land upon which a gristmill had been located until 1949, when it was torn down. The deed to O contained an express easement provision that allowed O the right to run a millrace through the property of S. This express easement had been contained in all the deeds to the property since 1873.

In the 1930s, the gristmill was converted to gasoline power, thereby eliminating the necessity for the millrace. Further, a road had been built over part of the millrace, and no water had actually run through the millrace since the late 1930s.

In 1972, O attempted to reopen the millrace through S's property pursuant to the express easement contained in his deed.

What legal argument could S make to prevent O from opening the millrace?

Case 3. Grantor owned a certain tract of land that she wanted to share with her beloved cousin. The grantor and grantee cousins entered into an agreement whereby the grantor agreed to convey "the said hereinafter described land equally, jointly, as tenants in common, with equal rights and interest in said land, and to the survivor thereof, in fee simple . . . ." The agreement further recited the fact that both parties had grown up together, had been closely associated and devoted to each other, and that the grantor desired to share ownership and possession with her cousin.

If the grantor died a short time after the conveyance, what interest, if any, would her surviving cousin have in the said tract of land?

Case 4. Two tracts of land were conveyed to Grantee City in 1965 and 1966, respectively. Both conveyances contained the following provision: "Subject to the restriction that the . . . real property shall be operated and maintained solely for park, recreational, and public accommodation, and convenience purposes." There was no language in the conveyancing document to indicate that the grantor had the right to reenter and repossess the land if the restrictions were violated.

In 1973, P made application to Grantee City for a sales tax permit to conduct various commercial activities on the two tracts of land. Grantee

City rejected the application in part on the ground that the deed restriction on the land prohibited its commercial exploitation and that if the sales tax permit were granted, the land would revert back to the grantor who conveyed it to Grantee City.

What argument would you make on behalf of P to undermine Grantee City's contentions?

Case 5. M and T owned adjoining lots on the shore of a navigable lake. The only access that M had to his lot by land was over T's lot.

Previously, the lots owned by M and T had been under common ownership. The common owner had simultaneously conveyed both lots to predecessors in title of M and T, who in turn conveyed to the present owners. At the time the common owner simultaneously conveyed the lots now owned by M and T, no one portion of the land was physically used for the benefit of another portion.

If M wanted to continue his use of the access path running over T's lot and T at the same time wanted to stop M's use, what legal argument would you make on behalf of both M and T?

Case 6. In 1968 Defendant purchased a farm through a portion of which ran a road that was used by Plaintiff and other individuals to gain access to their respective properties. The realtor who handled the sale to Defendant, pursuant to instructions from Defendant's predecessor in title, informed her that the sale was subject to Plaintiff's use of the road and testified that the road was clearly visible for everyone to see and that Defendant was very much aware of Plaintiff's use of the road to reach his farm. Plaintiff continued to use the road until 1971, at which time Defendant notified Plaintiff that he would not be permitted to cross her lands. She posted "No trespassing" signs and locked a gate across the road. Plaintiff then brought an injunction action against Defendant for the purpose of forcing her to remove the gate.

What legal argument would Plaintiff raise, and would he be successful?

Case 7. Plaintiff desires to expand its present clubhouse facilities. It has just purchased an adjoining tract of property and proposes to build a new building on it. Between the present clubhouse and the proposed new structure is an 8-foot alley, over which Plaintiff intends to connect its present clubhouse with the proposed new building by placing a walkway 16 feet above ground level over the alley. Defendants own a tract of land that adjoins the tract on which Plaintiff's clubhouse is located. Defendants' predecessor in title had been granted "a right-of-way over and the privilege of the free use of a public alley," specifically the 8-foot alley that separated Plaintiff's present clubhouse and the proposed new construction.

What legal arguments could the defendants raise to prevent Plaintiff from constructing the 16-foot high walkway over the 8-foot wide alley to connect the two buildings? Do you think the argument would be successful?

Case 8. Certain real property was willed to B "in fee simple with the proviso that he shall never deny access or occupation to the several heirs hereinafter named during their lifetime." Based upon this provision in testator's will, how would you classify the ownership interest obtained by B?

Case 9. In 1971, the town of New Castle adopted a zoning ordinance that provided for twelve types of districts. However, in none of the twelve districts would the development of multiple-family dwellings be permitted. The rationale was that the town of New Castle was a quiet and relatively undeveloped suburban community, and the town fathers, through the zoning ordinance, were trying to preserve as much of the rustic character of the town as they could.

Plaintiffs owned a 50-acre tract of land within the town of New Castle that they had planned to develop as a complex, part of which would include multifamily dwellings. The town refused to grant Plaintiff's petition to develop the 50-acre tract of land as planned, based on the 1971 zoning ordinance.

If you were the plaintiff, what legal arguments would you make against the decision of the town of New Castle?

Case 10. T, who is a commercial waste hauling operator, owns two tracts of land in an area zoned for single-family residential and agricultural purposes. T maintains his residence on one of the tracts, and he sought permission from the governing authorities to park his commercial refuse truck on the other. D, who owns property adjacent to the lot where T sought to park his commercial refuse truck, objected.

A local zoning ordinance provided that "all off-street parking areas shall be reserved and used for automobile parking only . . . . The parking of one (1) commercial vehicle up to one (1) ton is permitted if needed by an individual for his livelihood for a business not conducted on the premises; . . ." T sought to park his commercial refuse truck on one of his vacant lots because he could not comply with the parking ordinance in that his truck weighed more than one ton.

If you were T, what procedure would you have to follow to obtain the desired permission? If you were D, on what basis would you seek to have the permission denied?

Case 11. Plaintiff and her husband farmed three tracts of land called Parcels 2, 3, and 4 from 1919 until 1948, since when their son, Joe, has farmed Parcel 4 continuously. From sometime prior to 1918 to the present date, a fence has existed along the west side of Parcel 4 clearly separating it from Parcel 5. The fence was repaired in 1939 by Plaintiff's husband. Also, Plaintiff's brother farmed the property west of the fence, Parcel 5, until 1939 when he sold it.

Unknown to Plaintiff, record title to Parcel 4 is owned by Defendant and is now claimed by him.

If you were Plaintiff, how would you attempt to establish your ownership interest in Parcel 4?

Chapter 3
Rights Incident to Ownership of Real Property

ABOVE AND BELOW THE SURFACE

Airspace

Subsurface

TREES, SHRUBS, AND OTHER VEGETATION

Permanent Growth

Temporary Growth

LATERAL AND SUBJACENT SUPPORT

Lateral Support

Subjacent Support

WATER RIGHTS

Navigable Water

Nonnavigable Surface Lakes and Streams
Riparian Rights   Prior Appropriation Doctrine

Subterranean Water
Percolating Water   Subterranean Lakes and Streams

Surface Water

NUISANCE

TRESPASS

Rights

Duties

WASTE

  Depreciating Waste

  Ameliorating Waste

SUMMARY

QUESTIONS FOR DISCUSSION

CASES

THE various rights associated with an ownership interest in real property were defined in Chapters 1 and 2 to include the general right to use, abuse, enjoy, possess, and dispose of real property. This chapter focuses on the specific nature of an owner's right to use and enjoy real property.

Some important rights that are incident to an owner's use and enjoyment of real property are (1) the right to possession above and below the surface; (2) the right to trees, shrubs, and other vegetation growing on or near the boundary line; (3) the right to lateral and subjacent support; (4) water rights; (5) the right to be free from nuisance; (6) the right to prevent and recover for trespass; and (7) the right to prevent and recover for waste. Although this listing is certainly not exhaustive, it includes the more common rights that are incident to ownership of real property. Owners and possessors should have knowledge of these rights to protect their interests in the real property. Buyers and investors should also be aware of them, because the price they are willing to pay or the amount they are willing to invest may depend on the extent to which these rights can be enforced or utilized.

In summary, Chapter 2 identified the ownership interest in real property. This chapter describes some of the rights that are incident to an ownership interest.

ABOVE AND BELOW THE SURFACE

Airspace

The general rule is that owners or possessors of real property have the right to exclusively possess that airspace above their land, limited by its perimeter boundaries extended vertically upward, which is reasonably necessary to the use and enjoyment of the surface. Before the existence of airplanes, the rule was that ownership rights went from the surface to infinity. Now, the statutes and cases say either that airspace rights are subject to overhead flights or that owners own only that airspace which they can effectively possess. Under either theory, there is no definite lineal footage limitation to airspace ownership. It depends ultimately on the nature of the non-owner's act and how it affects the surface owners' use of their land.

At the very least, the owner of Sunny Acre (see Figure 2, page 14) has a right in the airspace to the top of her house and the owners of the utility and railroad easements have rights in the airspace to the top of the utility lines and overhead railroad, respectively, since each effectively occupies and uses such airspace. The question is, how far above the point of effective occupancy and possession does the right to airspace go? It depends on the facts. A low-flying jet plane traveling over Sunny Acre might violate the owner's right to the quiet use and enjoyment of her house, but it probably would not interfere with the utility or railroad easements short of physically striking them. The answer depends on the facts of each case.

Subsurface

A surface owner's right to the soil beneath the surface is identical to the right to the airspace above the property. The general rule is that owners of real property have the right to exclusively possess the soil underneath their surface property, limited by its perimeter boundaries extended vertically downward, that is reasonably necessary to the use and enjoyment of the surface. Thus, if the owner of the tract of land adjoining Sunny Acre dug a mine shaft on his property and in the process accidentally mined under the surface of Sunny Acre, he would be liable in trespass.

The same rule does not apply to the removal of fluid substances. A landowner can remove water, oil, or similar fluid substances from the subsurface of an adjoining tract of property as long as the well, shaft, or other vehicle used for the removal does not itself trespass onto or beneath the surface. For example, the shaft drilled into the substrata of Sunny Acre (Figure 2) will lawfully result in the removal of oil from Sunny Acre's subsurface and that of the adjoining property, since the pool of oil appears to be situated under both properties.

TREES, SHRUBS, AND OTHER VEGETATION

Trees, perennial plants, and grasses are more or less permanent in nature and as a consequence are considered to be part of the real property. However, crops produced by permanent growth, such as apples by an apple tree, and growing crops, such as wheat, are considered to be temporarily affixed to the land and thus are personal property. Different rules of law are applicable to each.

Permanent Growth

Problems often arise between adjoining landowners with respect to ownership rights of trees or shrubs growing on or close to a boundary line. The prevailing rule is that adjoining landowners are tenants in common of trees whose trunks are partially located on two adjoining tracts of land. As a consequence of common ownership, each adjoining owner has the right to prevent the other from destroying the tree. However, an adjoining owner has the right to remove any part of a tree, including branches and roots, that extends over or under his/her property as long as such removal is not done in a negligent or malicious manner. Similarly, where a tree trunk is located entirely on one owner's land, an adjoining owner can remove encroaching roots and overhanging branches to the common boundary line. This is called the *right of self help*. The fruit produced by the tree is personal property. Hence, the tree's owner has a special right to retrieve the fruit from the tree if it falls on the land of an adjoining property owner.

Tree and shrub ownership also imposes certain duties. No longer can property owners ignore the condition of trees growing on their property. In many jurisdictions, they have a duty to inspect the trees from time to time to determine if they pose a threat to an adjoining property owner. The duty to inspect is greater in urban areas than rural areas, due in part to the fact that trees appear less frequently in urban areas and the potential for personal and property damage is greater in the urban environment.

Temporary Growth

Growing crops that are harvested annually—for example, corn, wheat, and cotton—are generally classified as personal property. The rule is that when a lease is of uncertain duration and has been terminated through no fault of the tenant, or when a life estate expires, the tenant is entitled to harvest the crops planted during the period of the lease. In the Sunny Acre example (see Figure 1, page 12), the farmer-lessee would be entitled to harvest his crops if the landlady-owner terminated a lease of uncertain duration and the farmer gave her no legal cause for such termination. But if the lessee were in wrongful possession of the land, he would be entitled only to those crops harvested during the time of his possession and may be required by the rightful owner to pay reasonable rent for the period of occupancy.

LATERAL AND SUBJACENT SUPPORT

The right of owners to support of their property from surrounding property (*lateral support*) and underneath their property (*subjacent support*) is not a right in the land of an adjoining owner; it is a right incident to the property entitled to the support. Hence, the general rights of lateral and subjacent support do not involve easements in the land of another.

Lateral Support

Subject to modification by state statute or local ordinance, the right to lateral support applies to land in its natural condition. It does not, therefore, include the right to support for the additional weight of artificial structures such as buildings or other improvements. Where lateral support has been removed and the land would have fallen in its natural condition, the determination of damages depends on the jurisdiction in which the land is located. Some states have adopted the rule that the injured party can recover only for the land in its natural condition, whereas other states also permit recovery for damage done to artificial structures on the land.

As previously indicated, a property owner does not have a right to lateral support provided by liquid substances such as water and oil because adjoining owners have the right to remove such substances that naturally flow under their land. However, if the substance is semiliquid, such as asphalt or quicksand, liability will result if its removal directly affects lateral support.

Subjacent Support

Problems involving subjacent support arise when an ownership interest in real property has been divided. For example, the owner of Sunny Acre may convey a profit a prendre to B so that B can mine and remove coal deposits under Sunny Acre. In the absence of an express or implied agreement to the contrary, B's nonpossessory interest is subject to the burden of surface support. The rule is the same as that applicable to lateral support. Basically, the surface owner has a right to the subjacent support of his/her land in its natural condition. If a subsidence occurred, the surface owner could recover damages to a building or other improvement if the excavation were negligent or if the land, in its natural condition, would have subsided.

WATER RIGHTS

Water may be classified into four general categories: (1) navigable bodies of water, (2) nonnavigable surface lakes and streams, (3) subterranean water, and (4) surface water. In addition to having its own individual physical characteristics, each category creates distinctly different rights, which are based on ownership interests in property underneath or beside the water.

Navigable Water

Navigable water is generally defined as a watercourse or lake that can be used for commerce. This does not mean that the watercourse or lake must accommodate large commercial vessels. But it does mean that it can be used for more than mere recreational purposes. No clear definition can be given, since it depends on the facts of each case.

Navigable waters are distinguished from other categories of water primarily with respect to ownership interests in the land beneath the water. The state usually owns the land over which a navigable stream flows or a lake is located. Where the stream or lake is subject to high and low water marks, some states permit private ownership to the high water mark, others to the low water mark. Similarly, where land borders an ocean, private ownership goes to the high tide mark. The area between the high tide and low tide marks, the *shore,* is usually held by the state in trust for use by the public. The waters beyond the low water mark, the *ocean,* are controlled by the federal government for a certain number of miles, and beyond that are subject to international regulation.

When land is privately owned and is submerged by a navigable body of water, a public right to use the water over the private land exists subject to the landowners' right to reclaim their property. Thus, if a navigable stream flooded, washing away the banks of a large tract of private land, the water that now flowed over the private land would be used by the public until such time as the owner rebuilt the bank.

Nonnavigable Surface Lakes and Streams

Nonnavigable surface lakes and streams are water that is contained in a natural watercourse or lake or an artificial body of water where the water is supplied by natural means that cannot be used in commerce. Generally, land that is benefited by nonnavigable surface lakes and streams is called *riparian land* if it touches on the water, is under one ownership, and is within the natural watershed.

For example, B owns a rectangular tract of land that has 50 feet of frontage on a nonnavigable stream and is 400 feet deep, all of which is in the natural watershed. Thus the entire tract is riparian. But if B sold the back half of his land to C, the land would then be under two ownerships and C's land would not be riparian, because it would not touch the water.

There are two systems of water rights in the United States that relate to riparian land ownership: (1) riparian rights, which is the predominant system in the eastern part of the United States; and (2) the prior appropriation doctrine, which is the predominant system in the western United States.

Riparian Rights

A riparian landowner's right to use the water depends on the law of the state in which the land is located. Some states apply the *natural flow rule* of riparian rights. This rule states that riparian owners may use all the water they need for natural or artificial purposes as long as the natural condition of the stream or lake is generally maintained and the water is used only on the riparian land. Under this rule, the rights of all riparian owners are equal; therefore, if an upper riparian owner unreasonably diminished the quantity or quality of the water, his/her action could be enjoined by any lower riparian owner.

Other states apply the *reasonable use rule*. This rule states that riparian owners may use all the water they need for natural or artificial purposes as long as their use does not unreasonably interfere with a use being made by another riparian owner. The water can be used on or off the riparian land. The emphasis under the reasonable use rule is placed not on the effect the use has on the stream or lake, but on the effect it has on other riparian owners. As a consequence, a lower riparian owner cannot complain about an upper riparian owner's use, even if it interferes with the quantity or quality of the stream or lake, unless the owner of the lower tract can prove such use damaged him/her personally.

If, for example, A and B were upper and lower riparian owners, respectively, along the same stream, and A made a use of the stream that decreased its level by one foot, B, who was not using any water from the stream, could enjoin A's use under the natural flow rule because A's use caused the quantity of the water to be well below the natural level. However, B could not enjoin A's use under the reasonable use rule because it would not interfere with B's nonexistent use.

Under both rules, the use to which water is put plays an important role in determining rights. Water used for domestic purposes such as drinking, washing, and irrigating takes precedence over water used for artificial purposes such as mining and manufacturing. In some states, for example, an upper riparian owner is permitted to use all of the water for domestic purposes.

Prior Appropriation Doctrine

This doctrine states that the first person to beneficially use a water supply has priority to it over all others to the extent of that use. In other words, first in time, first in right. Riparian land ownership is not required. It is sufficient to demonstrate (1) the intent to appropriate, (2) the actual diversion from the source, and (3) a beneficial use. The theory behind the prior appropriation doctrine is that if the available water were equally divided among all potential users, it would not be adequate for anyone and would produce nothing, but if its use were concentrated in a few, it could produce something.

In some of the more arid regions of the United States, all surface waters are owned by the state subject only to the rights of landowners whose prior appropriation predates the state's ownership rights.

Subterranean Water

Subterranean water is water beneath the surface of the earth. When subterranean water is not confined to a known and well-defined channel or bed, it is called *percolating water;* when it is so confined, it is classified as a *subterranean lake or stream.*

Percolating Water

Some states apply the *absolute ownership rule* to percolating water. Under this rule, in the absence of negligence, a landowner may use all the water that comes from beneath the surface of the land no matter how severe the effect on other landowners. A number of states do, however, provide by statute that the use cannot be wasteful or malicious.

Most states apply the *reasonable use rule,* which means that land owners are entitled to make reasonable use of percolating water under the surface of their land.

But there is a diversity of opinion among those states as to what constitutes reasonable use. Some hold that a landowner can withdraw as much water as he/she needs, even to the detriment of other landowners, if it is used beneficially on the land from under which it is withdrawn or used in the development of such land. Use of water off the land from under which it was withdrawn is unreasonable if it interferes with a beneficial use being made by an adjoining landowner. Other states hold that percolating water must be shared by all landowners. A few states apply the prior appropriation rule, under which the first user takes priority over subsequent users.

Obstruction or diversion of percolating water, in the absence of negligence, is permissible in most states no matter what rule is followed. Thus, a mining or quarrying operation would not be legally responsible to A for diverting percolating water away from A's land if such diversion were reasonably necessary to operate the mine or quarry.

Subterranean Lakes or Streams

In most states, the rules applicable to percolating waters are equally applicable to subterranean lakes or streams, with one important exception: Landowners have no right to obstruct or divert a subterranean lake or stream when its existence is clearly known to them. A public policy exception exists for mining and similar operations in many states that apply this general rule.

Surface Water

Surface water is water that does not flow in a well-defined channel and has not reached a natural watercourse or basin. Water from rain, melting snow and ice, and springs are examples. Two rules govern surface water rights: the common enemy rule and the natural or free flow rule.

In the majority of states, under the *common enemy rule*, surface water can be warded off by a lower tract owner if not done negligently or maliciously, since it is the "common enemy" of both the upper and lower tract owners. But under the *natural flow rule*, the owner of the lower tract does not have a right to ward off water from an upper tract, since water should be allowed to flow in its natural path.

If A carefully constructed a concrete wall around her property that caused surface water to back up on B's land, under the common enemy rule A would not be responsible for damages to B, but under the natural flow rule she would be responsible.

Some states apply the natural flow rule to rural areas and the common enemy rule to urban areas. In any event, under either rule, landowners can impound surface water and use all of it, but they cannot discharge it in such a way as to damage another's land.

For example, since X did not have any access to groundwater for domestic use, he collected all the rainwater from his roof in a large cistern. The cistern overflow was discharged through a four-inch drain pipe directly onto Y's property, causing her property to wash away and her basement to flood during heavy rains. X has a right to contain and use all the surface water he can collect, but he does not have a right to discharge it at one point causing damage to Y's property.

NUISANCE

The rights of landowners or possessors to the reasonable use and enjoyment of their real property may be interfered with by activities of their neighbors without the neighbors physically entering or technically trespassing on the property. Examples of such activities are loud noises, noxious odors, and offensive sights. An interference of this sort, which tends to offend one of the senses, is called a nuisance. A *nuisance* is specifically defined as a nontrespassory invasion of the use and enjoyment of the land of another.

Generally, three elements must be established before a nuisance becomes actionable:

1. The nontrespassory invasion must be both substantial and unreasonable. The occasional loud playing, perhaps three weekends throughout the year, of rock music on the neighbor's stereo system may not be substantial or unreasonable enough to establish a nuisance; but a continuous playing, perhaps every weekend, may be. In determining what is substantial and unreasonable, the conduct must be such that it would offend an average, normal person with ordinary sensitivities. An opera buff, for example, may be offended by loud rock music played by his neighbor three times a year, but the average person may not be offended.

2. The act producing the injury must be either intentional and unreasonable or unintentional and negligent, reckless, or ultrahazardous. If a city ordinance prohibits the burning of leaves within the city limits, and A, knowing this fact, intentionally sets fire to a large leaf pile on her land, causing smoke damage to B's house, A's act is both intentional and unreasonable per se because it violates the city ordinance. But if A stores her leaves in a compost pile next to B's land, causing a continuous noxious odor to permeate B's house, A's act is unintentional and may be negligent. If A were warned that the compost pile could ignite due to spontaneous combustion and did nothing to correct the situation, any smoke damage caused thereby might be attributed to A's recklessness.

3. The injury must result from a legally protected interest. There is, for example, no legal right to light and air. Thus, B could not rely on a nuisance theory if A built a large barn next to B's house that deprived B of the air flow and light he had previously received. Nor would the unsightliness of the barn create an actionable nuisance, since appearance is generally not a legally protected interest.

TRESPASS

Rights

A landowner or possessor has the right to be free from trespass. Generally, trespass to real property occurs when one intentionally intrudes upon land that is in the possession of another. Land in this context includes improved real property such as houses, apartment buildings, and stores, as well as unimproved real property such as lawns, fields, or vacant lots.

Trespassers are liable for all harm done while on the real property. For example, if A intentionally drove her car through B's rose garden and into B's front porch, B could recover for the damage done to both the rose garden and porch as a result of the trespass. However, certain trespasses are privileged and hence cannot serve as the basis for a cause of action. *Privileged trespasses* include reasonable overflights by aircraft, reasonable reclamation of personal property, service of legal process, and prevention of waste.

Duties

Landowners or possessors not only have a right to be free from trespass, but they also owe a duty to certain trespassers. The nature of the duty depends primarily on the purpose or age of the trespasser. The general rule is that, in the absence of intentionally willful, wanton, or reckless conduct, landowners owe no duty to ordinary trespassers, so if an ordinary trespasser falls and injures her/himself while trespassing, the owner or possessor is not responsible. But if the trespasser is an invitee, guest, or licensee such as garbage disposal personnel, meter readers, or mail carriers, then the owner or possessor is more responsible for negligent conditions of the land.

For example, if A knew that a step was loose on an interior staircase, and B, a guest, fell and injured himself on the loose step, A probably would be liable to B for the damage incurred. A had a duty to repair the step. But if B were a thief and were injured on the same loose step while in the process of robbing A's house, A probably would not be liable. She owes no duty to repair a step for a person whose purpose is to commit robbery.

If the trespasser is a child, it imposes a special duty on the owner or possessor under the *attractive nuisance doctrine.* This doctrine states that an owner or possessor will be liable for injuries to trespassing children if all of the following conditions are met:

1. The possessor knew or should have known that children are likely to trespass.

2. The possessor maintained a patently harmful condition on the property.

3. The children were unaware of the danger.

4. The cost of removing or remedying the danger was slight compared to the potential harm that could result.

If P, a possessor, stored a used refrigerator in his back yard in plain view of all the children in the neighborhood, who, with P's knowledge, used the yard as a playground, P may be liable for injuries caused to a five-year-old child who accidentally locked himself in the refrigerator while playing hide-and-seek. Applying the attractive nuisance doctrine, P knew that children trespassed on his property; P should have realized that a refrigerator is a potentially dangerous device to children; the average five-year-old child is not aware of the danger of being trapped inside a refrigerator; and the cost of removing the refrigerator is slight compared with the risk involved.

WASTE

Depreciating Waste

Depreciating waste, usually called *waste,* occurs when someone in possession, other than a fee simple owner, uses or abuses the real property so that the value of the reversionary or remainder interest is impaired. For example, if T, a tenant for years who was farming Sunny Acre, removed all the topsoil from the acreage under lease, he committed waste because he injured L's remainder interest. Or if R, a life tenant of Sunny Acre, cut down a valued row of protective trees, he committed waste because L's remainder interest was impaired.

However, if the possessor's act was consistent with good husbandry or was something the owner of the reversionary or remainder interest would have done anyway, then waste may not have occurred. For example, T, a life tenant and farmer, cleared and plowed part of the acreage under lease. The other part had been cleared, plowed, and used to raise crops for many years by L, owner of the remainder interest. If L had planned to clear and plow the other part of the leased real property, then T was only doing what L had planned to do anyway, and if it were consistent with good husbandry, no waste occurred.

Ameliorating Waste

Ameliorating waste occurs when someone in possession, other than a fee simple owner, performs an unauthorized act that augments the value of the reversionary or remainder interest. For example, T, a life tenant, shores up the foundation of the leasehold premises by digging below the foundation and installing a larger, more substantial concrete footing. As a result of T's labor, L's remainder interest increases 20 percent in value. Usually, the tenant is not liable for ameliorating waste, since it increases the worth of the future interest. On the other hand, the owner of the future interest does not have to pay for the improvement.

SUMMARY

In summary, all the rights and duties discussed in this chapter are incident to an ownership interest in real property. An understanding of these rights helps to further clarify the real property concept of ownership. In essence, this chapter has provided substance to the area of the circle represented in Figure 3 (Chapter 2, page 22) as merely consisting of a bundle of rights. Therefore, the circle can now be further clarified, for example, as in Figure 4.

FIGURE 4   Rights Under Fee Simple Absolute

QUESTIONS FOR DISCUSSION

1. The common law rule that ownership of land extended to the periphery of the universe has been substantially modified to accommodate the needs of modern society. Describe how this common law rule has been changed, and discuss the justification for the change.

2. Discuss how the law has limited the various rights that are incident to an ownership interest in real property. Do you think ownership rights in real property will be further limited in the future?

3. Discuss how the many different legal principles applicable to water rights reflect the needs of landowners in different geographic locations.

4. It has been suggested that the general concepts of ownership and possession are not always interchangeable. Which of the rights discussed in this chapter are applicable to both ownership and possession?

CASES

Case 1. Plaintiffs owned certain farm land that was next to acreage owned by defendants. Defendants divided their property into three separate subdivisions containing a total of 114 houses. The subdivisions were approved by the appropriate governmental units, and various streets and driveways were constructed accordingly. Plaintiffs claimed that during the construction of the subdivision, Defendants changed the course of natural drainage by bringing water from a different watershed into the natural drainage system that drained both Plaintiffs' and Defendants' lands. Because of this change or diversion, Plaintiffs claimed, Plaintiffs' land received greater quantities of water than it had naturally received previously.

What legal arguments could be made in Plaintiffs' behalf for an injunction and damages for the alleged alteration of natural drainage? Defendants would counter with what legal arguments?

Case 2. Defendants purchased 160 acres of grapefruit orchards and 20 acres of vineyards from Plaintiffs. As part of the purchase price, Defendants signed and delivered to Plaintiffs a promissory note and a deed of trust. After Defendants took possession, they failed to cultivate, irrigate, fertilize, fumigate, or prune the citrus trees and vines, which led to decreased production and a general decrease in the value of the land. Defendants defaulted on the promissory note, and Plaintiffs bought in the property at a foreclosure sale. Assuming that Plaintiffs retained an ownership interest in the property until the promissory note was completely paid off, on what legal basis could Plaintiffs sue Defendants for the decrease in value of the property? Would they be successful?

Case 3. A and B were adjoining landowners. In 1942, A planted an elm tree on her property approximately 15 inches on her side of the common boundary line. In 1954, B constructed a chain-link fence on his property approximately 4 inches south of the common boundary line. When the fence was completed, A's elm tree was 6 inches away from the fence and 2 inches from the common boundary line. By 1968, the elm tree had grown to such proportions that it now protruded 8 inches onto B's property. The roots pushed B's fence out of alignment and caused other damage to B's property. It was shown at trial that if B cut off the roots of the elm tree that encroached on his land, the tree might fall in a severe windstorm and damage A's house as well as his own.

Could B force A to remove the elm tree at her own expense? What would be A's defense?

Case 4. Lisa and Amy were both six years old. Lisa came to play in Amy's backyard at Amy's invitation. During the course of play, they entered a treehouse that had been built by Amy's father. After playing in the treehouse for some time, Lisa attempted to come down the ladder from the treehouse to the ground. She slipped and fell, sustaining injuries to her back.

Lisa sued Amy's father for the injuries she sustained. Amy's father relied upon the defense that the only duty he owed Lisa was not to be willful or wanton in his conduct toward her. How would Lisa respond to this argument, and with what success?

Case 5. Plaintiff and Defendant owned adjoining parcels of land. Defendant had owned both parcels before they were subdivided. During the period when Defendant owned both parcels, he filled the land with a substantial amount of soil. After the subdivision, a second layer of groundfill was placed on the land. Presently, Defendant excavated close to the common boundary line, causing both layers of fill on Plaintiff's land to slough. Plaintiff contended that (1) the fill on his land constitutes an "improvement" that is entitled to lateral support; and (2) the fill has existed for such a long period of time that it has now become the natural level of the land for which lateral support is required.

Do you agree with Plaintiff's contentions?

Case 6. L purchased a lot from D, a real estate developer. L's lot adjoins D's property in the rear and is at a much lower elevation than D's property. Rocks, soil, water, and debris constantly wash down the steep slope from D's property to L's in spite of L's effort to prevent it. In addition, the constant washing away of the soil has caused roots from a tree located on D's property to be precariously exposed. The tree is located close enough to L's property that it presents a clear danger to L.

If L sued D to compel D to erect a retaining wall to prevent D's land from eroding onto L's land, and to compel D to remove the tree, what legal arguments would he make on his own behalf and with what success?

Case 7. Lewis' residence-farm property adjoined property used by Miller as a service station. Miller had gasoline storage tanks installed that leaked large quantities of gasoline into the ground and eventually contaminated Lewis's water wells, which were approximately 250 feet away. Lewis sued Miller for the damages sustained as a result of the well contamination. What legal arguments might Miller make to avoid liability? Would he be successful?

Case 8. Defendant owns and operates an airport that is located immediately adjacent to and abuts land owned by Plaintiff, an Indian tribe. Plaintiff sought injunctive relief and damages, claiming that its airspace had been trespassed by airplane approaches and departures from Defendant's airport. Most of the airplanes crossed the common boundary line at heights of 150 feet or less. The facts also showed that Plaintiff's land was uninhabited, unimproved, and vacant for a distance of 3.4 miles from the boundary line.

Plaintiff argued that it was entitled to a judgment because the low-flying aircraft interfered with its possessory rights in the land. Do you agree with this argument? State your legal reasons.

Chapter 4
Transfer of Interests in Real Property

REAL PROPERTY INTERESTS SUBJECT TO TRANSFER

CLASSIFICATION OF METHODS OF TRANSFER

Voluntary Transfers
Bargain and Sale   Gift

Testamentary Transfers
Real Estate Interest Subject to Testamentary Disposition
Who May Make a Will   Formal Requirements for Execution of a Will
Procedure for Testamentary Transfers   Tax Consequences of a
Testamentary Transfer

Real Property Interest Passing by Descent
Real Property Interests Subject to Descent and Distribution
Heirs-at-Law under Statutes of Descent and Distribution
Administration of the Estate of an Intestate   Tax Consequences of
Transfer by Descent

Involuntary Transfers
Transfers to Enforce a Judgment for Money   Mechanic's and
Materialman's Liens   Tax Liens   Municipal Liens
Adverse Possession

TRANSFER OF LAND BY FORCES OF NATURE

Accretion and Erosion

QUESTIONS FOR DISCUSSION

CASES

IN the United States, most interests in real property are transferable from one party to another. The most common method of transfer is by bargain and sale, whereby one party sells his/her interest to another in exchange for money, property, or other valuable consideration. The sale of ownership, possessory, or nonpossessory real property interests has been discussed in the preceding chapters. However, there are several other ways in which such interests may be transferred.

In discussing the transfer of real property interests, it is important to distinguish between the method of transfer and the document or instrument by which the transfers are accomplished. For example, in real property, the document used to transfer an ownership interest is a *deed*. The deed is not the *method* of transfer; it merely provides written evidence of the transfer.

REAL PROPERTY INTERESTS SUBJECT TO TRANSFER

It is a general legal principle that real property interests are subject to transfer. The law favors the transferability of real property, and when the language of an instrument creating an interest is vague as to its transferability, there is a strong presumption that the interest is transferable. Any restraint on alienation (transfer) of real property interests must be clearly stated in the instrument by which the interest is created, and any such restraint must be reasonable and cannot violate either law or public policy. For example, a limitation in a deed that states that the owner may not transfer the property to a person of a certain race or religion is unenforceable in court because it is contrary to both law and public policy.

Certain types of interests in real property are not transferable because of the nature of the interests themselves. For example, a nonpossessory interest that a landowner in a subdivision has to enjoin the violation of a restrictive covenant may not be assigned to another outside the subdivision who has no actual interest in the enforcement of the covenant. Another example is an easement in gross, which is not assignable or transferable by the holder unless the right to assign or transfer has been reserved in the original grant or reservation of the easement.

CLASSIFICATION OF METHODS OF TRANSFER

The methods by which interests in real property are transferred may be generally classified into four groups: (1) voluntary transfers, (2) transfer by will (transfer by devise), (3) transfer by a person dying intestate (transfer by descent), and (4) involuntary transfers.

These four groups are not legal classifications; rather, they are set forth to provide a framework for organization of the topic materials. It may properly be argued that any method could be appropriately included in one or more of these classifications.

Voluntary Transfers

With the voluntary transfer of a real property interest, the holder of the interest exercises his/her free will in accomplishing the transfer. A voluntary transfer is sometimes referred to as an *inter vivos* transfer, because the actual transfer occurs during the lifetime of the transferor. This distinguishes voluntary transfers from transfers by will, which can occur only after the death of the transferor.

Bargain and Sale

The most common example of a voluntary transfer of real property is a bargain and sale. The chief characteristic of transfer by bargain and sale is the existence of a bargained-for exchange between buyer and seller. The owner transfers an interest in real property for money, property, services, or other valuable consideration. Transfers of ownership interests by bargain and sale are usually initiated through a *real estate contract* that sets forth the rights and performance obligations of the buyer and seller. Upon completion of the performance obligations of the buyer, the seller delivers a properly executed deed to the buyer. Upon acceptance of the deed by the buyer, the original contract is terminated or "merged" into the deed, and the transfer of the ownership interest is completed.

It is also common to transfer possessory and nonpossessory interests by bargain and sale. Possessory interests are transferable unless restricted in the lease document, and the sale of leases is quite common. Certain nonpossessory interests such as mortgages can also be bought and sold. The document used to accomplish the transfer of possessory or nonpossessory rights is an *assignment*. The seller of the possessory or nonpossessory interest transfers and "assigns" his/her interest to the buyer. The assignment usually

1. Names the seller-assignor and the buyer-assignee.
2. Identifies the interest being assigned.
3. Contains words manifesting an intention on the part of the seller-assignor to transfer the interest to the buyer-assignee.

The assignment of most possessory and nonpossessory interests must be in writing to be enforceable under the Statute of Frauds. When the properly executed instrument of assignment is delivered to and accepted by the buyer-assignee, the assignment is complete and the interest transferred to the new party.

Gift

Another method of voluntary transfer of interests in real estate is by gift. A *gift* is a transfer of an interest in real property from a *donor* to a *donee* made gratuitously and without consideration. The primary characteristics of a gift are that the transfer is made during the lifetime of the donor without a bargained-for exchange. A gift is distinguishable from a sale by the lack of consideration; it is distinguishable from a transfer by will because a transfer by gift is initiated during the lifetime of the donor.

Requirements of a Valid Gift The general legal requirements of a completed gift are (1) capacity of the donor to make a gift; (2) intention of the donor to make a gift; (3) delivery of the property to the donee; and (4) acceptance of the property by the donee.

Capacity of donor. To qualify to make a gift, the donor must have legal capacity; that is, he/she must not be acting under some disability at the time of the gift. For example, a gift from a person who had been judicially declared to be insane would not be effective to transfer the interest even if the property were delivered to and accepted by the donee.

Intention of donor. The intention of the donor to make a gift must be a present intention. Such intention often is manifested through acts or words. The donor has manifested an intention to make a gift during his/her lifetime if a reasonable person with knowledge of the surrounding circumstances would believe that the donor intended to permanently relinquish dominion and control over the real property interest without any exchange from the donee. If the donor acts under duress, the vital element of intention is absent.

Delivery. The requirement of delivery of the property to the donee presents a special problem when real property interests are involved. There may be no physical delivery of the real property interest from donor to donee as there may be with an item of personal property such as a watch. The delivery must be symbolic. To deliver the gift of an ownership interest, a deed is used; with a possessory or nonpossessory interest, an assignment may be used to symbolize the actual delivery.

The key element of delivery is the donor's relinquishment of dominion and control over the property. That is, the donor may no longer exercise the incidents of ownership. If the gift takes place during the donor's lifetime, both the donor and donee are available to testify about the facts surrounding the delivery.

The delivery requirement has been the subject of much litigation when the donor started the gift during his or her lifetime and actual delivery was not accomplished until after death. The issue in such cases is whether the donee or the estate is entitled to the real property interest. The following is a typical example: Donor ordered his attorney to draft a deed to his mountain cabin, naming his nephew as donee-grantee. The lawyer complied, and Donor executed the deed and gave the deed to a trusted friend with instructions to deliver the deed if he did not return from a safari in Africa. Donor died while on safari, and upon hearing the news the trusted friend delivered the deed to the nephew.

Some courts have held that the intermediary such as the trusted friend in the example is acting as agent for the donor. During his lifetime, the donor set into motion the chain of events that led to delivery, there is a completed gift, and the property should not be included in the estate. Other courts faced with similar facts have held that if the donor retains the right, or even the possibility, of recovering the deed from the intermediary before delivery to the donee, there can be no completed gift because the donor continued to exercise dominion and control over the property. Applying that rule to the case cited, Donor could at any time have instructed his friend to withhold delivery and destroy the deed, and as a result the delivery should be set aside, the deed canceled, and the property included in the estate.

Still other courts, when faced with similar issues, have held that any such transfer is an attempt to make a gift of property after death, and there can be no completed gift in the absence of compliance with the applicable laws regarding execution of wills. The case law in this area is by no means settled.

Acceptance. The requirement of acceptance of the gift is usually presumed in the absence of an affirmative rejection by the donee. Whether or not there has been acceptance of the gift is rarely an issue in a legal proceeding.

It is a general rule that any real property interest that is capable of being owned may be the subject of a gift. Ownership, possessory, and certain nonpossessory interests may be given by one party to another. One of the key characteristics of ownership of a real property interest is the ability of the holder to transfer that interest to another. Any restriction or restraint upon the right of a holder of an interest to transfer or assign that interest must be reasonable and not violate law or public policy.

Tax Consequences Making a gift of an interest in real property may have important tax consequences. With certain exemptions and exclusions, the federal government assesses a tax on gifts from one party to another. The Tax Reform Act of 1976 has unified the estate and gift tax rates so that the same amount of tax is applied whether the property is given during life or passed after the death of the holder of the interest. Under former law the gift tax was assessed at a lower rate than the estate tax. Another innovation in the Tax Reform Act of 1976 is the required inclusion in the estate for estate tax purposes of the value of all gifts made by the decedent during a three-year period preceding death. This may have important ramifications for survivors if a decedent has depleted his or her estate with gifts made less than three years prior to death and the estate has no liquid assets with which to satisfy the estate tax due.

Many estate and gift tax problems can be anticipated and avoided if expert advice is sought prior to any sizable gift of a real property interest.

Testamentary Transfers

Another method by which interests in real property may be passed from one to another is by testamentary transfer. A *testamentary transfer* is the transfer of an interest in property by one party called a *testator* after death to an heir without a bargained-for exchange and pursuant to a valid will. A testamentary transfer is distinguished from a gift in that it occurs after the death of the holder; it is distinguished from a sale in that there is no bargained-for exchange. A transfer of a real property interest may result from the death of a party such as a life tenant; however, this could not be considered a testamentary transfer because the remainderman's

interest is vested by operation of law on the death of the life tenant and
not pursuant to the life tenant's will.

The right to make a testamentary disposition of property is taken for
granted. There has been much philosophical discussion about whether
the right to pass property upon death is a "natural right." Nevertheless,
all jurisdictions permit testamentary dispositions of property, and in each
state there are statutes that set out the specific formal requirements of a
valid will. The principles set forth in this section are general principles;
and local statutory and case law should be consulted and expert assistance obtained before drafting any testamentary instrument.

Real Estate Interest Subject to
Testamentary Disposition

As a general principle of law, all interests in real property that are held
at death and survive the life of the testator may be transferred by will.
The testator would have testamentary power over all interests
—ownership, possessory, and nonpossessory— of which he or she was
owner at the time of death. Of course, this rule would not apply to
interests that automatically terminate either by operation of law or by
prior agreement of the testator and another party. For example, interests
held by the decedent in joint tenancies or tenancies by the entirety, or as
life tenant, automatically terminate by operation of law upon death.

Certain leasehold interests such as tenancy at will may terminate by
operation of law upon death of either landlord or tenant. Certain
nonpossessory interests such as profits and easements in gross, which are
personal, may terminate upon death of the holder. Any interest held
under an agreement may, by its terms, terminate the holder's interest at
death. Some states by statute limit the testamentary transfer of more
remote interests in real estate such as possibilities of reverter.

The will speaks at the moment of the testator's death, and property
acquired after the execution of the will but before death would be
included under the terms of the will and pass by testamentary disposition. Similarly, property owned at the time of the execution of the
will and included in the dispositive provisions of the will, but transferred
before death, would be excluded from the operation of the will.

The right to testamentarily dispose of property may be limited by
statutes that give a surviving spouse or children the right to have the will
set aside as to a certain portion of the estate if their expectations are not
realized under the terms of the testator's will. In many states, a surviving
spouse may have the right to elect to take property as it passes by will or
take the share that would be received if a valid will did not exist. This is
commonly referred to as a "widow's election," although usually it also

applies to a surviving husband. Therefore, to a certain extent, the power to dispose of all property by will is limited if all or part of the testamentary transfer may be set aside after death.

Who May Make a Will

As discussed in Chapter 1, there are many entities that may hold interests in real property; however, only natural persons have the right to transfer property by will. Most states by statute set forth the age requirements for the making and execution of a valid will. Some states limit the rights of convicted felons to execute valid wills.

A testator must also have legal mental competency to make a will. The law refers to "sound mind" as being the standard of mental capacity. The testator must possess this mental competency or soundness of mind to make a will at the time the will is executed. If he/she later lacks mental capacity and dies without regaining capacity, the will may still be considered valid even though the will speaks at the time of death. The standard for mental capacity to make a will is not as stringent as for mental capacity to make a contract for the sale of real property interests, and some courts have upheld the validity of wills executed by persons who had been judicially declared to be insane.

The soundness of mind of the testator becomes an issue only when a will is presented for processing by the appropriate court and its validity is challenged by an interested party. The soundness of mind of the testator is a factual question. Since the testator is not available for examination, courts must rely on other evidence before determining whether the testator lacked competency to make a will. Certain tests have been used by courts to determine soundness of mind:

1. The testator must be able to clearly understand the nature of the testamentary act in which he is engaging. He must know that he is making a will and what effect that will will have.

2. The testator must know the nature and extent of his property. That is, he must have a clear idea of what he owns and what may be disposed of by will.

3. He must be able to recall the natural objects of his bounty. He must understand his relationship to family members and others who would naturally expect to be beneficiaries under the will.

4. The testator must be able to arrive at an orderly disposition of his property based on his understanding of the nature and extent of the property and the persons who would naturally be the objects of his bounty.

There is a basic presumption of soundness of mind. Courts have held that basic unfairness of a will, a testamentary gift that excludes helpful and loving family members, temporary intoxication, the advanced age of testator, a low grade of intelligence, or even the presence of a mental illness are not sufficient alone to show unsoundness of mind, so long as the basic tests outlined above are present. For example, the exclusion of the natural objects of testator's bounty from the dispositive provisions of the will is not enough, in itself, to destroy the validity of the will if at the time of execution of that will the testator knew who those natural objects were and made a free choice to exclude them from sharing in his or her estate.

Implicit in the "sound mind" requirement is that the testator must be exercising his/her free will and not be under duress at the time of engaging in the testamentary act. Some influence is often exerted on a testator when a will is being made, but the legal requirement is that influence must not be "undue." *Undue influence* is the exertion of pressure that would make it possible for a party to substitute his/her intention for that of the testator. The party contesting a will has the burden of proving undue influence. If it is found by the judge or jury that there was undue influence, the entire will fails, and either a former will takes effect or the property passes as if the testator had no will at death.

Formal Requirements for Execution of a Will

The historical roots of formal requirements for the proper execution of a will are found in ancient English common law and statute. The Statute of Wills of 1540 permitted the testamentary transfer of real property interests from one person to another. In the next century, the English Statute of Frauds included minimum requirements necessary to testamentarily dispose of interests in real property. Today, all states have statutes that specifically set forth the formal elements necessary to make a valid will. These statutes are designed to protect against fraud and undue influence and to provide written evidence of the testator's wishes and intended disposition of property.

The statutes setting forth the rules for formal execution of witnessed wills vary from state to state. In 1969 the National Conference of Commissioners on Uniform State Laws approved the Uniform Probate Code. The objective of the Uniform Probate Code is to modernize and standardize probate procedures including the requirements for proper execution of testamentary instruments. The Uniform Probate Code has been adopted in whole or in part by many states and is under consideration by others.

Signature   All states require that a testamentary transfer of real property be evidenced by a written will signed by the testator. In some states, the signature may appear anywhere on the document, but in others it must be signed at the end.

Witnesses Most states require that there be witnesses to the signature of the testator, although the number of required witnesses varies from state to state. Attesting witnesses must also sign or subscribe their names upon the will document in the presence of the testator after the testator has signed. Most states prohibit parties interested in the will as beneficiaries or executors from serving as witnesses.

Publication In some states, a testator must "publish" the will by making an oral declaration that the document signed and witnessed is in fact his/her last will and testament. States requiring publication do so as an additional safeguard that the testator understands the nature of the document being executed.

Change of Domicile Most states have statutes that validate a will and entitle it to probate if it conforms to the law of the state in which it was executed. Thus, a will properly executed in one state would be valid if the testator were to die domiciled in another state. However, there are exceptions to this rule, and to avoid an unintended result a person moving from one jurisdiction to another should consult local counsel concerning the validity in that state of a will executed in another.

Procedure for Testamentary Transfers

After a person dies testate, the person named in the will as executor or personal representative presents the will to the appropriate court for proving. The proving of the will and the carrying out of the provisions of the will are referred to as *probate*. Each state has its own rules of practice and procedure for probating wills. Often the procedures for probating wills differ between large and small estates.

When the will is presented and an accompanying petition is filed, the judicial process requires that all interested parties in the potential estate of the testator be given notice of the proceedings and be given a chance to contest the will. When the will is proved and the executor or personal representative is appointed by the court, general notice of the opening of the estate is usually required so that any one having a claim against the testator or the estate may come forward and make that claim known to the court.

The executor is usually charged by law with the responsibility of marshaling the assets, inventorying the estate, and assuring that all just debts of the testator or estate are paid. The executor or personal representative is also charged with the responsibility of seeing that all federal estate taxes and state inheritance taxes are paid. After all debts are paid and the appropriate tax returns and documents are completed, the executor in most states is required to file an accounting with the court. In most states, the court will enter an order or decree of distribution, and the executor, in reliance on the decree, will execute and deliver a deed to real property to the named beneficiaries of the will. After all distribution of the estate is made and all matters completed, the executor is discharged by the court and the estate is closed.

Probate and estate administration procedures vary widely from state to state. Expert assistance should be obtained before any probate is attempted.

Tax Consequences of a Testamentary Transfer

A testamentary transfer of an interest in real property may result in the assessment of federal *estate taxes* and state *inheritance* or *succession taxes*. The measure of these taxes is the value of the property passing from the testator to the beneficiaries. Estate tax rates vary. The federal estate tax is a graduated tax; the greater the value of the gross estate, the higher the rate at which the tax is assessed.

The impact of the estate and inheritance taxes may be mitigated through the use of estate planning. One key to successful estate planning is the inclusion of appropriate dispositive provision of the last will and testament to maximize advantages offered by exemptions, exclusions, and credits. Estate planning is not only for the rich. Persons with modest estates can often benefit through a will drafted with an eye toward lessening the tax burden on property passing to survivors. Estate planning is a highly specialized area of law and accountancy, and expert assistance always should be obtained before an attempt is made to draft a will to achieve an anticipated tax result.

Real Property Interest Passing by Descent

A third method by which interests in real property pass from one to another is through descent. *Transfer by descent* is the transfer of property by operation of law from a person dying intestate (without a valid will) to his/her heirs-at-law. The laws of *descent and distribution* in jurisdiction of the domicile at the time of the owner's death control the disposition of the estate. *Intestacy* results either from the failure of the decedent to make a will or the invalidity of a will that fails because of improper execution or lack of testamentary capacity. A *partial intestacy* may also result when a decedent's will does not account for the disposition of the decedent's entire property.

A large percentage of the population of the United States does not have a will at the time of death. Therefore, the laws of descent and distribution, sometimes referred to as *laws of intestate succession,* are important. Under common law, real property interests *descended* to the heirs of an intestate, who were referred to as having taken the interests by *descent.* Interests in personal property passed by *distribution,* and heirs receiving personal property interests were referred to as *distributees.*

Under modern law, if a person cannot or does not make a last will and testament that sets forth the disposition of his/her property after death, the local *statute of descent and distribution* takes effect. With each such statute, the state legislature has attempted to prescribe the disposition that most testators would make if they had died testate. It is clear that there is no unanimous agreement among legislatures as to the probable intention of testators, because the statutes of descent and distribution vary widely from state to state.

Real Property Interests Subject to Descent and Distribution

As a general rule, all real property interests that a decedent has at the time of death will pass by intestate succession to his/her heirs-at-law. Excluded from intestate succession are interests that terminate at death such as interests in joint tenancies, tenancies at will, life estates, and interests that by agreement may terminate at death, such as easements or profits. As a general rule, any restriction on the transfer of property must be reasonable and not violate law or public policy.

The laws of descent take effect at the moment of death, and all real property interests—ownership, possessory, and nonpossessory—immediately pass to the heirs-at-law. At common law, there could be no "gap" in the interest, and someone was always designated as being responsible for the interest. In theory, this is still true today; however, most states require that a decedent's estate be administered before the heirs or their respective interests are confirmed.

Heirs-at-Law under Statutes of Descent and Distribution

Many persons wrongly assume that upon death without a will all property passes to the surviving spouse. Under most statutes of descent and distribution, the spouse is not the only heir to share in the estate of an intestate.

Generally, the statutes of descent and distribution divide heirs into classes depending on their relationship to the decedent. These relationships are founded either upon *affinity* through marriage or founded upon *blood* through a child, parent, or grandparent. There are commonly four classes of heirs:

1. Surviving spouse. A decedent may have only one spouse at the time of death who is qualified to take possession of property under the laws of intestate succession. This classification of relationship is founded upon affinity.

2. Descendants: Children, children of children (grandchildren), and so forth. Descendants include legally adopted children of the decedent but in some states do not include legally adopted grandchildren.

3. Ascendants: Parents, grandparents, and greatgrandparents of the decedent.

4. Collaterals: Brothers and sisters and their children.

Classes 2 through 4 are "founded upon blood."

Each state treats the different classes of heirs somewhat differently. Figure 5 is a typical scheme of intestate succession, although it does not represent the scheme for any one jurisdiction.

In Figure 5, each group of heirs is subject to the rights of the preceding group. For example, in order for parents to inherit from a child who dies intestate, that child cannot be survived by either spouse or children.

Administration of the Estate of an Intestate

There are two major purposes of court administration of an intestate's estate: (1) to oversee the technical aspects of settling the financial affairs of the decedent and (2), since the decedent did not identify the persons intended to share the estate, to judicially determine the heirs of the decedent.

When a person dies without having made a valid will, an heir-at-law or other interested party may petition the court for the opening of an estate in the decedent's name. If the petition is granted, an administrator is appointed by the court to marshall the decedent's assets, inventory the estate, pay all just claims and taxes, render a final accounting, and comply with the jurisdiction's rules of intestate succession. After the administration is completed and a final accounting is approved by the court, a final decree or order of distribution is entered and the administrator distributes personal property and conveys the real property to the heirs entitled to receive a share of the estate.

In some jurisdictions, the administrator has a deed prepared and delivered to the heir. In others, the determination of heirship as stated in the order or decree of distribution is sufficient to provide evidence of ownership.

One common problem affecting land titles involves deeds that are executed by heirs of an intestate. The surviving heirs of an intestate

FIGURE 5 **Order of Descent and Distribution Under a Typical Intestate Statute**

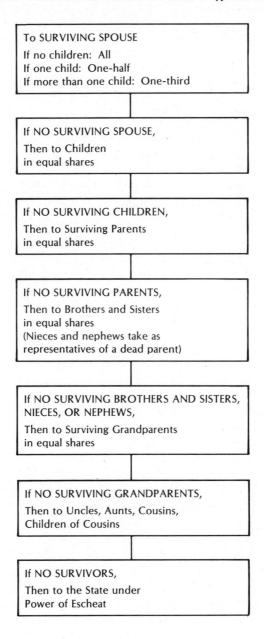

sometimes do not institute an administration of the decedent's estate because the value of the property involved does not warrant the expense and trouble of a court proceeding. Instead, at the time that the property is sold, they all join in conveying to a third party the real property interest left by the intestate. In such cases, there has been no judicial determination as to the heirship of the decedent, and without such a determination the conveyance is subject to possible attack by a person claiming to be an heir of the decedent.

In most jurisdictions, the lack of a judicial determination of the heirs to an intestate's estate may render title to real property unmerchantable. In many jurisdictions, this potential problem may be avoided through use of simplified procedures for administering a small estate. In jurisdictions where these summary procedures are not available, it may still be worthwhile to administer a small estate. Expert counsel should be consulted before the decision is made not to administer an intestate's estate.

Tax Consequences of Transfer by Descent

Both the federal and state governments assess a tax on the transfer of property after death. There is no practical difference in tax treatment between a testamentary transfer and a transfer by descent. A person who fails to make a valid will may forfeit some of the benefits of planning the disposition of his/her estate to take advantage of exemptions, exclusions, and credits in the estate and inheritance tax laws. Even young people and persons with modest estates should consult expert counsel about the disposition of their estates because of the possible tax and legal consequences of dying intestate.

Involuntary Transfers

Transfers of interests in real property may take place when the holder of the interests either does not consent or is powerless to stop the transfer. For example, in a mortgage foreclosure action, the ownership interest in real property is transferred without consent under judicial process to a third party at a public sale to satisfy a debt due the mortgagee. This type of transfer is involuntary because the owner has lost the right to transfer the property. Interests are also transferred involuntarily when an adverse possessory interest in the property ripens into an ownership interest and when property is condemned by governmental authority under the power of eminent domain. In each case, the holder of the interest subject to involuntary transfer loses the right to exercise free choice in the transfer. It is the loss of the right to control the time of transfer and identity of the transferree that gives the transfer its involuntary character.

Transfers to Enforce a Judgment for Money

One common involuntary transfer in effect in all but a few states is a transfer to enforce a money judgment. Under this type of involuntary transfer, a debtor's interest in real property may be subject to sale to satisfy an outstanding debt that has been reduced to judgment. The legal effect of the judgment is to place a lien on the real property of the judgment debtor to secure payment of the debt. The resulting judgment lien is a nonpossessory security interest that gives the judgment creditor the right to have the property sold to satisfy the debt.

The mere fact that the creditor is owed money by the debtor is not sufficient to subject the debtor's property to a nonsecurity interest in favor of the creditor. In order for a creditor to be entitled to a judgment lien on a debtor's real property, in most states the creditor must first have his/her claim litigated in a suit for money damages. After the judgment is entered and becomes final, the judgment creditor has the right to have that judgment entered against the debtor; upon such entry, a lien or nonpossessory security interest in the debtor's real property attaches.

Some states permit a debtor to agree in advance to an entry of a judgment without the creditor's having to first obtain a judgment in court. In such states, a judgment may be entered "by confession," and a judgment so entered has the same force as one obtained through a lawsuit. Confession of judgment is unpopular with debtors, and its use has been severely limited by statute or case law in states where it is still permitted.

Prerequisites of a Valid Judgment Lien   The right to have a judgment entered as a lien on the real property interests of a debtor is a statutory right that varies widely among the states. For example, in some states, the entry of a money judgment on the court records or dockets automatically places a lien on the judgment debtor's real property in the county where the court is located. In other states, the court rendering the judgment must issue an abstract or transcript of the judgment, which the judgment creditor then is required to enter in the county records affecting land titles before the lien can arise.

Despite the differences in procedures for entry of the judgment lien, each judgment must meet certain requirements in order to give rise to an enforceable nonpossessory security interest.

1. The court proceeding on which the judgment is based must have been procedurally correct. The court had to have jurisdiction over the

person against whom the court judgment is entered; the order giving rise to the judgment must have been both final and for a definite sum of money.

2. The judgment giving rise to the lien must not be stale. That is, the prescribed time limit must not have expired for entry of a court judgment on the appropriate judgment docket to create the lien.

Therefore, if the court proceeding that results in the judgment was procedurally correct and that judgment has not lapsed, the judgment is entitled to be accorded lien status. The judgment lien is a general lien and attaches to all real property of the debtor in the county where the lien is entered.

Interests in Real Property Subject to Judgment Liens   As a general rule, the judgment lien applies to all real property owned by the debtor at the moment the lien is entered. Interests that the debtor has conveyed to third parties before actual entry of the judgment are not subject to the lien. In addition, in some states, property acquired *after* the entry of the judgment is not subject to the lien unless the judgment is reentered. A transfer of an ownership interest before entry of judgment may be set aside and canceled if the transfer can be shown to have been a fraudulent attempt to avoid subjecting the property to possible sale by the creditor.

The exact interests in real property that may be subject to judgment liens vary from state to state. As a general rule, all freehold estates may be subject to judgment liens. However, in some states, if the judgment debtor holds a freehold estate as co-owner, the judgment against one co-owner may not affect the property. For example, in states recognizing tenancies by the entirety and community property, a judgment against a spouse individually will not affect the jointly held property. Interests where the judgment debtor is holding title as trustee for the benefit of others are not generally subject to judgment liens.

The judgment lien affects only property within the county where the judgment has been entered. However, the scope of the judgment may be enlarged through compliance with the state's filing requirements in any county where the judgment debtor has property. In each case, the judgment is not effective against property until the filing requirement has been met. Interstate filing of judgment is possible in all states, so that a judgment entered properly in another state is entitled to enforcement provided local filing requirements have been met.

Exemptions   By statute, certain real property is exempt from claims of creditors. This exemption may arise because the debtor enjoys a certain status or because the real property interest qualifies for special treatment. For example, most governmental units are exempt from judgment liens, so a creditor of a governmental authority may not have public property sold to satisfy the debt. This protection usually extends to quasi-governmental units such as sanitation authorities and irrigation districts. In addition, for reasons of social policy, many states have enacted *homestead exemptions* that specifically exclude the family home from property that may be sold pursuant to a judgment lien. The basic theory is that each family should be guaranteed that their home could not be taken to satisfy the debts of a family member.

Not all states recognize the homestead exemption, and in states that do, the provisions vary widely. In some jurisdictions, there is a dollar limit on the exemption that may be claimed. In others, the debtor is permitted to elect between a dollar amount and specific real and personal property. In most states recognizing the homestead exemption, the property sought to be exempted must be used for family residential purposes. Often farm properties are accorded special exemptions for acreage surrounding the farmstead.

It is a general rule that the homestead exemption does not apply when the debt arises from the purchase of a homestead itself. Thus, the homestead exemption may not be affirmatively asserted as a defense by the mortgagor in a mortgage foreclosure action against the homestead property.

Priority of Judgment Liens Often a debtor with more than one creditor will have assets whose combined value is less than the total debt. Therefore, among creditors it becomes important to establish a priority by which their debts may be satisfied using the proceeds of the debtor's available assets. For establishing a priority, creditors are classified as secured or unsecured.

Secured creditors have either a specific or general lien against the real property of the debtor that has been "perfected" through compliance with certain filing requirements. Secured creditors have the first right to the proceeds from the sale of the debtor's assets in the order in which their liens were perfected. For example, a *mortgage lien* is a specific lien on property that, upon proper recordation of the mortgage document, attaches to specific real property; any other general or specific lien filed subsequently is inferior and subordinate to the mortgage. Upon forced sale of that property by creditors, the first mortgagee would be entitled to receive the proceeds up to the amount of the debt due before any other secured creditor would be entitled to receive any funds produced through the sale. After all secured creditors have been satisfied, any surplus is returned to the debtor.

Unsecured creditors are those who have no lien on the debtor's real or personal property. As a general rule, unsecured creditors' debts are satisfied only after those of secured creditors.

In most states the priority of liens is established by the chronological order in which the liens were filed. However, there are exceptions to this general rule. In some states, for example, a purchase money mortgage has a preferred status, and the priority date of the purchase money mortgage lien can relate back to a time prior to the actual filing for record. Mechanics' and materialmen's liens, which are discussed subsequently, also enjoy this preferred status for priority purposes by relating back to a prior date even though entered for record later.

Termination of Judgment Liens   A judgment lien may terminate by lapse of time. Each state has its own time limits on the life of judgment liens; the length of time may vary from a few years to many. Often, the statutes prescribe a minimum length of time but permit judgment creditors to renew or "revive" a judgment lien for additional periods of time. A judgment lien binds real property interests only as long as it is effective, and after the statutory period has run without a revival the lien loses its priority. If the lien is reentered after it has lapsed without revival, it takes a new priority date. The expiration of the judgment lien does not discharge the debt upon which it is based. The expiration affects only the judgment creditor's right to have real property sold to satisfy the debt.

A judgment lien may be terminated through release or by the issuance of a satisfaction by the judgment creditor. In some cases, the lien may be terminated by the discharge of the underlying debt through bankruptcy of the debtor. The lien is also terminated upon forced sale of the property.

Enforcement of Judgment Liens   After the judgment lien has been perfected, the judgment creditor has a right to enforce the judgment by executing upon the real property interest of the judgment debtor. The procedures are statutory and vary from state to state. Usually, the creditor prepares a writ of execution directing the appropriate local authority such as the sheriff to take control or levy upon the property of the debtor. Since real property cannot be taken into physical possession, the sheriff posts the land or improvements with copies of the writ. After the posting requirement has been met and the debtor notified of the proceedings, the public is notified of the intended sale of the property, usually through advertisements and notices posted in public places.

The sale is held at the time and place stated by the court in the notice, with the property going to the highest bidder. Any proceeds realized at the sale are applied first to costs, with the balance going to the debtor's account. If the proceeds are sufficient to satisfy the debt, the lien is terminated. If the proceeds are not sufficient to liquidate the underlying debt, the judgment lien continues, but the amount of the lien is reduced by the proceeds realized at the sale. In some states, the judgment debtor has the right to redeem the property after it has been sold at public auction. This *statutory right of redemption* after judicial sale is similar to the mortgagor's right to redeem the property after foreclosure.

The document used to transfer title from judgment debtor to the successful bidder at the public sale is a deed issued by the sheriff or other court-appointed individual who conducts or supervises the public sale. The debtor usually does not personally execute an instrument of conveyance to the new owner. The judicial proceedings have foreclosed the debtor's interest and he/she subsequently has no right to make a conveyance of the ownership interest.

Mechanic's and Materialman's Liens

Another lien that may result in an owner subjecting a property interest to involuntary transfer is a mechanic's and materialman's lien.

Definition   *Mechanic's and materialman's liens* are nonpossessory security interests in real property to secure payment to workers and suppliers for services and supplies provided for the improvement of real property. The labor and material incorporated into the real property enhances the value of that property, and a property owner who failed to pay for the improvements would be unjustly enriched in an amount equal to the value of the improvements. Therefore, a mechanic or supplier may secure payment by claiming a special lien upon the improved property.

Mechanic's liens and materialman's liens are statutory liens and, unlike many real estate laws and principles, have no historical precedent in English law. The first mechanic's lien statute was passed in 1791 by the Maryland legislature and provided that contractors engaged in the construction of the new national capital should have a lien on the real property to secure payment by the government of charges for labor and materials supplied to the project. Today, each state has a mechanic's and materialman's statute designed to ensure payment to workers and suppliers of amounts due for improvements to real property. The specific procedures for claiming a mechanic's lien vary from state to state, but their general principles are similar.

1.   A contractual relationship must exist between the mechanic or materialman and the owner at the time the claim arises. If a contractual relationship does not exist, then a claim cannot be supported.

2.   The mechanic's efforts or materialman's supplies must have *actually* been used for the benefit of the owner. This requirement is met if the claimant shall have performed services or supplied materials to the job site that were incorporated into the improvements on real property.

3.   The mechanic must have "substantially completed" his/her work

before the right to claim a lien accrues. A mechanic or supplier cannot partially perform a contract and then claim the benefits of the mechanic's lien statute.

Enforcement Procedures   Enforcement procedures for mechanic's and materialman's liens vary widely from state to state. Usually, the contractor is required to file a claim of lien that contains the name of the owner, the name of the person who contracted for the furnishing of services or supplies, a brief summary of the contract duties, a description of the land affected by the claim of lien, and a statement of the amount due and owing the claimant. A mechanic's lien is usually filed with the appropriate governmental official to provide notice to third parties of the existence of the mechanic's claim against the property. If a third party purchases the property before the lien is discharged, the lien continues to bind the property if the claimant has met all procedural requirements.

Most statutes provide a time limit within which the mechanic or materialman must file claim. Usually the period is from two to six months after "substantial completion" of the work or supplying of materials. If the claim is not filed within the time limit, the right to a claim of lien is forfeited. After the lien is filed and perfected, the mechanic then has a certain time limit within which to move to foreclose on the lien. The time limit varies from one jurisdiction to another; however, a one-year time limit is common. A mechanic's lien is a specific lien and in most states is foreclosed in much the same way as a mortgage.

Since the value of the work performed or the materials supplied is incorporated into the improvements on the real property, the owner is enriched proportionately. The claim of lien is limited to the value of the improvements attributable to the labor or material supplied and not for additional damages.

In most states, mechanic's and materialman's liens are accorded special priority. If the time limit is met and the lien is filed properly, it is accorded a priority date that relates back to either the date of substantial completion or the date the labor or materials were last supplied to the project. For example, if a house is substantially completed on June 1 and the mechanic's lien is filed August 1 within the prescribed time limit for filing such liens, the priority date of the lien relates back to June 1 for the purpose of establishing priority among secured creditors. If another lienholder were to enter a lien on July 1, before the mechanic filed his lien, its lien would be subordinate to the mechanic's lien.

This special priority status accorded mechanic's and materialman's liens is especially troublesome to mortgage lenders because of the risk that their mortgage might be subordinate to a mechanic's lien recorded after the mortgage document. Often, the mortgage lender will require an affidavit from the mortgagor that no improvements have been made to the premises within the statutory period for filing mechanics' liens. Because each state has its own mechanic's and materialman's statute, it is always wise to consult counsel before entering a lien whose priority is essential to the transaction and that might be subordinated to a subsequently recorded mechanic's or materialman's lien.

Tax Liens

Another involuntary method by which the holder of a real property interest may lose it is through foreclosure of a tax lien for unpaid federal, state, or local taxes. Federal, state, and local governments each have the power to raise revenue through the assessment and collection of taxes.

Federal Taxes Federal taxes include assessments on income, gifts, transfers of property after death, and taxes on certain consumer goods such as alcohol. In addition, the federal government may make an individual responsible for collection and payment of employees' taxes as well as his/her own taxes. If an individual fails or refuses to pay income tax, gift tax, estate tax, or excise tax, or fails to report and forward employees' payroll taxes, under United States statutory law the Internal Revenue Service has the right to file a *tax lien* against the taxpayer. This tax lien is a general lien on all the property of the tax debtor in any county where the lien is recorded. Its priority depends on the time it was entered and the types of other liens against the debtor-taxpayer.

State Taxes Most states impose a tax on earned income and require employers to withhold such taxes from employees. In addition, most states have inheritance or succession taxes that are assessed on the transfer of property after death. Failure to pay any of the taxes or report and forward taxes withheld from employees may result in the entry of a state tax lien. A *state tax lien* is a statutory lien that permits the state government to enter a lien against a debtor-taxpayer's property for nonpayment of taxes. The state tax lien is a general lien and affects all real property of the taxpayer in any county where the lien is recorded. By statute, most states have accorded state tax liens special priority over other general liens. However, as a general rule, such liens do not take priority over federal tax liens or specific prior liens such as mortgages. State tax liens are foreclosed upon under the procedures set out in statutes that are usually similar to those used for judgment liens.

Local Taxes Local governmental units in most jurisdictions are permitted to assess and collect taxes on the real property interests within their jurisdiction. These taxes are sometimes referred to as *ad valorem* taxes, because they are based on the value of the property being taxed.

The local governmental units that may have the right to impose *ad valorem* taxes include counties, townships, cities, towns, boroughs, school districts, and special governmental subunits such as irrigation and conservancy districts. The failure of a taxpayer to pay the tax assessed against his/her property may result in the entry of a tax lien against the property.

Local tax liens differ from the federal and state liens because the local lien affects only the specific property against which the tax is assessed. Other property of the owner is not affected by the local tax lien.

The lien against the owner's property is a nonpossessory security interest to secure payment of the property taxes that have accrued but have not been paid. However, the government may enter its lien only after the taxes have been billed and the time for payment has expired. The actual foreclosure procedures for nonpayment of local taxes vary widely from state to state. Usually, the taxpayer is notified of the impending sale and given a chance to pay the taxes plus penalty and interest. If the payment is not made, then the governmental authority charged with tax collection advertises the property for public sale. At the appointed time and place, the property is sold at public auction to the highest bidder. After payment of the auction price, the new owner receives a tax deed to the property evidencing the purchase of the property from the governmental authority.

In most jurisdictions, the purchase of the property at tax sales does not cut off the rights that any other lienholder may have in the property. For example, if there were a mortgage on the property being sold for unpaid taxes, the successful bidder would be entitled to receive a deed from the taxing authority, but the mortgagee would continue to have a mortgage lien on the premises. In some states, the taxpayer whose property has been involuntarily transferred in a tax sale has a certain time period within which he/she may redeem the property by paying the purchase price plus costs to the tax deed grantee.

Municipal Liens

In some jurisdictions, a local governmental unit may make improvements that are publicly owned but specifically benefit a privately owned parcel of real estate. In such cases, the governmental authority has the right to specially assess the landowner for the cost of the improvements. For example, if the municipality were to construct a public sewer line adjacent to a tract of land, enhancing the value of the specific tract and making it possible for the landowner to use the public sewage facilities, the landowner would be assessed a certain amount to defray the cost of the public improvement.

The methods of assessment vary, but usually the assessment is based on the front footage of the property being benefited by the public improvement. If the expense of the improvement is a substantial amount, the landowner may be permitted to defer payment of the special assessment over several years. By statute, if a payment is not made when due, the local governmental authority has the right to enter a lien against the property that has been benefited by the improvement. In some jurisdictions, these liens are referred to as *municipal liens.* Municipal liens usually acquire their priority from the date of filing, although they may be accorded special priority in some states. Under most state statutes, municipal liens are foreclosed in the same manner as other specific liens.

Special assessments are distinguishable from general property taxes in both the method of assessment and the use of the proceeds realized through collection.

Adverse Possession

Another method of involuntarily transferring ownership interests in real property is through adverse possession. *Adverse possession* is the holding of possession of real property openly, hostilely, notoriously, and adversely against the true owner of the property. If the adverse possession continues for a prescribed period, and all other requirements of adverse possession are met, then the adverse possession ripens into full ownership. The requirements of adverse possession are fully discussed in Chapter 2.

Statutes that permit adverse possession to ripen into ownership reflect the public policy that favors the use of available land. If an owner fails to use his/her land and another makes use of that land, having met all the requirements set forth in the statute governing adverse possession, then the adverse possessor becomes the owner of the land and the former owner is forever barred from asserting ownership rights.

TRANSFER OF LAND BY FORCES OF NATURE

Accretion and Erosion

In some geographical areas of the United States, it is a common occurrence that quantities of real property are transferred through natural processes. The chief examples of this are the loss of area by erosion and the acquisition of area by accretion. Accretion is an increase in the quantity of land by the gradual deposit of soil or rock through the action of a river or a body of water. When there is a gradual buildup of land by the deposition of soils to an existing riparian bank, there is often a gradual decrease in the riparian bank of another parcel of real property.

Thus, what one owner gains by the process of accretion, another may lose through erosion. In each case, there is no actual transfer of ownership interest, only an increase or decrease in the quantity of land through these natural processes.

In order for accretion to be recognized as an increase in the area of land owned, the land must be bounded by water and the process of depositing soil must be both natural and gradual. A violent change in the course of a stream or river brought on by a flood that alters the course of the water will change neither the original boundaries nor the quantity of land owned.

The chief justification for the rule recognizing accretion is the maintenance of riparian rights by parties whose land was originally bounded by water. Thus, a party may not be cut off from the water if there is a deposit of soil between his/her original boundary at water's edge and the new bank. Accretion and erosion are ways by which the quantity or area of land may be changed through natural processes; they should not be confused with other natural processes such as flood or wind erosion, by which the physical characteristics of nonriparian land are changed.

QUESTIONS FOR DISCUSSION

1. Is there any difference to the grantee from a legal standpoint whether his/her title has been obtained by descent, devise, or gift? If so, what is that difference?

2. What problems may be presented in transferring ownership of real property from the estate of a person who has died intestate from the point of view of the estate? From the point of view of the grantee? If the decedent had minor children at the time of death?

3. At present, the federal estate and gift tax rates are unified so that the same rate is applied whether the gift is made before or after death. Assuming that the person's estate includes valuable real estate that is appreciating in value, discuss the advantages and disadvantages of transferring the property to heirs before death through a systematic plan of giving rather than holding the property to be included in the estate after death.

4. Not all real property interests are transferable. Name some real property interests that are generally not transferable by descent or devise.

5. There is a public policy that limits the restraints that a grantor can impose upon future transfer of possessory, nonpossessory, and ownership interests in real property. What is the basis of this policy, and what arguments may be made in favor of or against restraints upon alienation of real property interests?

CASES

Case 1. Husband and wife, who were owners of 160 acres of land, had two deeds prepared giving each of two sons 80 acres. However, the deeds were never delivered or recorded during the lifetime of the grantors. Before either owner died, the husband told one of the two sons about the deeds and gave him a key to the safe deposit box where the deeds were kept. The son who had not been told of the deeds died before his parents. Upon the death of the husband and wife, the surviving son claimed ownership of both tracts of land as closest surviving heir on grounds that there had been no delivery during the lifetime of the grantors. Who is entitled to receive the 80 acres of the deceased son, the brother or the heirs of the deceased brother? Why?

Case 2. River X was navigable and the land under the surface was owned by the state. Over a period of time, accretion formed an island in the middle of River X, which gradually grew until it reached and connected with the lands of the riparian owner, who brought suit against the state to quiet his title to the accreted land. Is the plaintiff entitled to a court decree quieting title to the accreted land? Why or why not?

Case 3. X was the owner of real property in fee simple at the time of his death. By will he devised the property to his wife for her use during her life with a remainder to his children. The wife had several judgments entered against her and then died. The judgment creditors sought to enforce their judgments against the property. The remaindermen children brought suit against the judgment creditors to have the liens declared null and void. What arguments may be made on behalf of the children to have the liens declared null and void? What is the most likely result of the case?

Case 4. A parcel of real property was conveyed to "Harry Hornby and Wilma Hornby, his wife, and Xavier Allen as tenants in common with rights of survivorship." Wilma died intestate, leaving a son by a prior marriage as sole heir-at-law. Shortly thereafter, Harry died testate, leaving his entire estate to his brother. The jurisdiction recognized tenancy by the entirety. Wilma's surviving son brought suit against Harry's brother for a declaration that one-third of the property belonged to him. What was his argument, and what argument could be made on behalf of Harry's brother? What is the most likely result at trial?

Chapter 5
Initiating the
Real Estate Transaction

A *real estate transaction* can generally be defined as any arrangement or agreement between or among two or more parties, the subject matter of which is real property. Common examples of real estate transactions are the transfer of an ownership interest, where one party sells real property to another; the creation of a possessory interest, where an owner of real property leases a portion of it to another person; or the creation of a nonpossessory right or interest in real property, where an interest is mortgaged or an easement granted. In each case, where there is either a transfer of an existing interest or the creation of a new interest, the transaction may involve many different parties each of whom has certain rights, duties, and responsibilities to others involved in the transaction.

This chapter will specifically consider the relationship between and among a seller, buyer, and real estate broker. The landlord–tenant relationship will be dealt with in Chapter 11.

PARTIES TO THE REAL ESTATE TRANSACTION

Seller and Buyer: Rights and Duties

In transactions in which an ownership right in real property is transferred in exchange for money, property, or other valuable consideration, the party making the transfer of the real property is the *seller* and the party receiving the ownership interest is the *buyer*. The basic rights and duties of each are primarily governed by the terms and conditions of the agreement or *real estate contract,* which gives the buyer the right to receive merchantable title and the duty to pay for it and gives the seller the corresponding right to receive payment and the duty to deliver merchantable title.

Merchantable Title

Unless the parties agree to the contrary, the seller is obligated to transfer his/her ownership interest in real property free and clear of liens and encumbrances. The legal term used to describe such an ownership interest is *merchantable title* or *marketable title*. Merchantable title has also been described as title to real estate that would be accepted by a prudent person well advised of the facts pertaining to the property. In short, the property is said to be free of all legal and factual claims. The term is descriptive of the quality of the ownership interest enjoyed by the seller or transferor.

It is a general rule of law that a buyer may not be compelled to complete a real estate transaction if the seller's title to the property is not merchantable. As a result, the issue of merchantability of title has been much litigated in the courts. For example, courts have held that any one of the following circumstances may render the seller's title unmerchantable:

1. An unsatisfied mortgage on the property.
2. Outstanding mineral rights.
3. Violations of local zoning ordinances.
4. Encroachments.
5. Existence of a right in the property superior to that of the seller.

On the other hand, courts have held that an unproved adverse claim, an expired defect in the ownership rights of seller, or a restrictive covenant less strict than applicable zoning ordinances do not render the title unmerchantable.

Defects in title that can be corrected before or at the time of closing the real estate transaction do not render the title unmerchantable. If the proceeds of the sale from seller to buyer are sufficient to satisfy outstanding interests in the real property, the buyer may not object to seller's title. For example, if seller's property is encumbered by a first mortgage and the proceeds of the sale are sufficient to satisfy the outstanding mortgage, the buyer must complete the transaction. In such a case, the buyer would be entitled to assurance that the proceeds of the sale will be applied to the outstanding indebtedness.

If the title cannot be made merchantable through the application of funds to be produced by the buyer, the buyer generally has the election to either take ownership of the property with the defect or rescind the contract. A buyer who elects to take ownership might be entitled to an abatement of the purchase price in recognition of the existence of the defect. Courts have ordered the completion of a sale at the election of the buyer and forced the seller to abate the purchase price in an amount necessary to account for the defect in the title. This rule helps prevent a seller from self-inducing a defect or encumbrance after the contract is made in an effort to avoid the sale to the buyer. However, where the buyer knows of the defect when entering into the contract, the presumption is that the buyer was compensated for the risk by a reduction in price, and hence the contract cannot be rescinded or the price abated.

Many problems may be avoided between seller and buyer if the agreement between them clearly sets forth all restrictive covenants, easements, or other encumbrances and the seller ascertains in advance that the proceeds of the sale would be sufficient to satisfy any liens on the property. If the encumbrances are set forth in the agreement and the buyer agrees to accept the property subject to the encumbrances, the buyer may not avoid the contract on the grounds that seller's title is unmerchantable.

Payment

The primary duty of the buyer to the seller is to pay the exchange bargained for at the time specified in the contractual agreement. If the contract does not indicate that "time is of the essence," the buyer may have a few days following the date set for payment to perform or pay. Where "time is of the essence," the buyer is in default if payment is not made within the specified time period. This language emphasizes that prompt performance is an essential part of the contract.

Disclosure of Defects

A seller's duty to disclose defects is generally not included in the contractual agreement between seller and buyer. In the past, buyers were responsible for satisfying themselves as to the physical condition of the property under the doctrine of *caveat emptor*—"Let the buyer beware." Recently, however, there has been a growing trend toward imposing on the seller the duty to disclose all known defects that could not be readily discoverable by the buyer during the course of an ordinary and reasonable inspection of the property. For example, the seller may be required to disclose to the buyer a defect in the plumbing or sewage system or the presence of termites on the property. Where this rule is in effect, an affirmative duty to disclose arises, and a seller who remains mute may not compel the buyer to complete the purchase if the defect is discovered after the contract is made. In addition, if the sale is consummated and the defect subsequently becomes known to the buyer, the buyer may have the right to rescind the contract and also have a potential claim for damages from the seller.

In addition to the affirmative duty to disclose known latent defects, the seller should permit the buyer reasonable access to the property so that the buyer can discharge the duty imposed at law to inspect the premises for the purpose of ascertaining the rights and interests of third parties that would be disclosed by such an inspection. The seller is generally not required to disclose discoverable defects or interests in the property, but if the seller should make an incorrect representation to the buyer concerning the presence or absence of interests or defects, the seller may be liable for misrepresentation and subject him/herself to damage claims by the buyer.

The Real Estate Broker: Rights and Duties

Often, a seller or buyer will retain the professional services of a real estate broker to assist in the sale or purchase of an ownership interest in real estate. Usually, it is the seller who employs a broker to assist in finding a buyer for the real estate. However, in some cases a broker may be employed to find property for a buyer.

A broker is in the business of performing the service of bringing together seller and buyer or lessor and lessee. In all states, a person engaged in the real estate brokerage business must be licensed to engage in his/her profession or business. The license laws usually define a *real estate broker* as one who buys, sells, or leases, or assists in the buying, selling, or leasing, of real property of another. The license laws provide rules and regulations concerning the powers and responsibilities of brokers and the persons working for them in their dealings with the general public. These rules vary among the states, but all states impose by statute certain standards of conduct for licensed brokers. In addition, the laws provide that real estate salespersons must be licensed and work directly under a licensed broker.

The educational, experiential background, and character requirements for both brokers and salespersons vary widely among the states. However, there is a general trend toward stricter requirements for persons seeking to enter the real estate brokerage business.

Listing Agreements

For services rendered by the broker, the seller or buyer usually pays compensation. When the broker represents the seller, the compensation is usually a percentage commission based on the ultimate sales price of the real property being sold. The seller does not usually compensate the broker unless a sale is consummated.

The mutual rights and duties of broker and seller are a matter of contractual agreement between the parties. Such employment contracts, called *listing agreements,* are just as enforceable as any other contract unless public policy, law, or regulation is violated by the terms of the contract. Many states require that listing agreements be in writing to be enforceable.

The broker and the client may bargain for the terms and conditions of the listing agreement; however, a few types of listing agreements are generally recognized throughout the country. These are (1) open listing, (2) exclusive agency, and (3) exclusive right.

Open Listing   Under an *open listing* agreement, the client reserves the right to employ other real estate brokers to assist in the sale of the listed property. The client may have concurrent agreements with a number of different brokers but is obligated to pay a commission only to the broker who actually accomplishes the sale. The client also retains the right to buy or sell the real property her/himself without being obligated to pay a commission to any broker. Although open listings are in general use, they are not favored by brokers, who are forced to compete against other brokers and the client him/herself in seeking a buyer or seller for the property.

Exclusive Agency   Under an *exclusive agency* agreement, the client agrees to list his/her property with one particular real estate broker only. During the term of the agreement the client may not list the property with another broker without being obligated to pay a commission to the broker under the exclusive agency. The client reserves the right to buy or sell the property him/herself without being obligated to pay a commission to the broker. The exclusive agency listing agreement provides protection to the broker from other agencies but not from the client's own sale.

Exclusive Right   Under an *exclusive right* agreement, the client appoints one broker to represent him/her in the sale and agrees that compensation wll be forthcoming no matter who accomplishes the desired result. With an exclusive right to sell or buy, the broker is protected from competition both from other agents and from the client. This type of listing agreement is most favored by real estate brokers.

Other Listing Agreements   Another type of listing agreement is the *net listing* agreement, in which the seller wishes to realize a specific amount and agrees to pay the broker all or a portion of the excess above the expected sales price. Because this type of listing has a potential for fraud, it is not lawful in some states.

A type of listing arrangement growing in use is multiple listing. Under a *multiple listing* arrangement, brokers in a geographic or market area agree to pool their listed properties. Upon sale of a property, the broker who listed the property and the one who sold it share the compensation. Multiple listing arrangements vary widely throughout the United States. Generally, brokers who are members of a local multiple listing organization are required within a specified time to share their listings. The agreement between the client and his/her broker may be an open listing or an exclusive right to sell; the obligation of the listing broker to share the listing with other brokers is the distinguishing characteristic of the multiple listing agreement.

Agency Relationship

The broker and the seller or buyer client may agree on their respective rights and duties. However, even though the parties have the right to vary their mutual undertakings, certain rights and duties result no matter what type of listing agreement is in force between them. The legal relationship created by the employment or listing agreement is a type of agency relationship. However, it is not usually a pure agency relationship.

An *agency relationship* results in giving one person the power to affect the contractual liability of another. Under an agency arrangement, one party, the *agent*, acts on behalf of another party, the *principal*, in dealing with a third party. The agent can act under the express authority created in the agreement between him/herself and the principal or pursuant to the express direction of the principal in dealing with the third party. The agent can also act in certain cases where implied authority exists, that is, where it reasonably appears to the third party that the agent has the authority to so act.

For example, Agent A contacts Third Party T about the possible purchase of T's ownership interest in T's farm by A's principal, P. T contacts P to verify that A is P's agent. P informs T that A is his agent and has authority to negotiate the purchase of the farm from T. Unknown to T, P has given A authority to pay up to $50,000 for the farm. After lengthy negotiations between A and T, T offers to sell the farm to P for $60,000 and A accepts on behalf of P. A has exceeded the scope of her authority by binding P to pay $60,000 for the farm. P may not avoid the contract on the grounds that A was not authorized to accept T's offer of $60,000. P must complete the contract with T. P's remedy for the $10,000 damages he has suffered is against A for breach of A's duty to P under the agency agreement.

If express or implied authority exists, the agent has the power to bind the principal to a contract with the third party even though the principal has not personally negotiated the contract.

In a *pure agency relationship,* the agent owes certain duties to his/her principal. These duties may be included in the agreement between principal and agent and they may be imposed by statutory law. They include the duties of accounting, loyalty, notice, care, and obedience. The principal, in turn, owes the agent certain duties, the most important being the duty of compensation for services.

An example of a pure agency relationship is a relationship created by a power of attorney where the person granting the power, the principal, authorizes his/her *attorney-in-fact,* the agent, to act on his/her behalf. The holder of the power has the right to carry out specific functions and duties, usually including the right to execute legal documents on behalf of the principal. A pure agency relationship is often established between an attorney at law and his/her client whereby the attorney has the power to bind the client in legal matters and proceedings.

The legal relationship between a broker and his/her client is usually not a pure agency relationship. The listing agreement that sets forth the respective rights and duties of broker and client usually does not give the broker the authority to bind the client to a contract with a buyer or seller. Under the typical relationship, the broker agrees only to assist the client in the procurement of a buyer or seller. Once a potential buyer or seller third party is found by the real estate broker, the broker solicits an offer from the third party and reports that offer to the client. The client is free to accept or reject the offer made by the prospective buyer or seller. The pure agency relationship and the agency relationship that exists between a broker and a seller or buyer are illustrated in Figure 6.

The main difference between the pure agency relationship and the broker-client relationship is that the broker brings buyer and seller together but does not customarily have the power to negotiate or to bind the client to a contract with a third-party buyer or seller.

Even though the relationship between broker and client is not one of pure agency, many of the duties an agent owes a principal under the law of agency are imposed on the real estate broker. All states have laws and regulations regulating the conduct of real estate brokers and their sales staff. In addition, courts have given recognition to the special relationship that exists between broker and client and have imposed higher standards of conduct on real estate brokers than the standards that ordinarily exist in a business contractual relationship between two parties. Trade organizations within the real estate brokerage industry also set standards of ethical conduct to be met by their members in dealing with clients and with others in the real estate brokerage business. Real estate brokers who violate their duty to their clients may be subject to criminal and civil litigation and to discipline by local real estate commissions.

FIGURE 6   Agency Relationships

Pure Agency Relationship

Real Estate Broker–Client Relationship

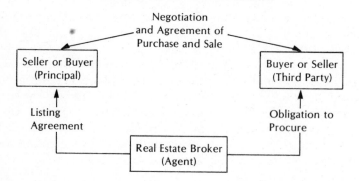

Commissions and Finder's Fees

The primary duty that the client owes the real estate broker is the duty to pay compensation for services rendered. The terms of payment are set forth in the listing agreement. If the broker is employed by a client seller, the compensation payable is a percentage of the ultimate gross sales price and is generally referred to as a *commission.* If employed by the buyer to find property, the compensation is usually a flat rate that is sometimes referred to as a *finder's fee.*

The real estate broker is entitled to a commission or finder's fee if the following requirements are met:

1. The broker is a licensed broker legally competent to represent the seller or buyer

2. An employment contract exists between the broker and the client buyer or seller

3. The broker is the "procuring cause" of the sale or purchase of the property.

Because real estate brokers are licensed by the state, any listing or employment contract with an unlicensed broker is not enforceable in court, under the general rule that an illegal contract will not be enforced by the courts. The broker must be licensed at the time of the agreement and at the time of the sale or purchase.

There must be an employment contract in existence between the broker and the client at the time of the purchase or sale. If there is no contract, the broker is deemed to be a volunteer and cannot force the buyer or seller to pay a commission or fee. However, if the broker is led to believe through the words or actions of the client buyer or seller that he/she will receive compensation for performing certain services, and the broker performs those services in reasonable reliance on those representations, the client may not defend against a claim for compensation on grounds that there existed no agreement between them.

For example, Broker A knows of a seller who might be interested in selling real property and a buyer who is interested in purchasing real property. The broker suggests to the potential seller that she contact the potential buyer. A sale is effectuated between the parties. Broker A would not normally be entitled to receive a commission or fee upon the successful completion of the transaction, because even though he might be the "procuring cause" of the sale he had no employment or listing agreement with either the seller or the buyer.

The final requirement for entitlement to a commission or fee is that the broker be the "procuring cause" of the sale or purchase. This requirement is met if the broker set into motion the chain of events that led to the consummation of the transaction. The issue of whether the broker was, in fact, the procuring cause of a sale will not arise in cases where an exclusive right to sell listing agreement existed between broker and seller, because the broker is entitled to a commission no matter who was the procuring cause of the sale. The issue most often arises when the employment relationship between broker and client was under an open or exclusive agency listing agreement where the seller retained the right to sell the property him/herself. For example, there is in force an exclusive agency agreement between B, a licensed real estate broker, and S, seller. An agreement of purchase and sale is made between S and purchasers PH and PW, who are husband and wife. Prior to the sale, on the same day and unknown to each other, S contacted PW about selling the property and B contacted PH. PH and PW visited the property together, with both S and B present, and later the two purchasers made an offer to buy that was accepted by S. Here there may be a question of whether the broker was the procuring cause of the sale and entitled to a commission.

Courts have found it difficult to apply a specific standard to the question of whether a real estate broker was the procuring cause of a purchase or sale. The issue is factual. The test generally applied is whether a reasonable person with full knowledge of the surrounding facts and circumstances would believe that the efforts of the real estate broker substantially contributed to the ultimate consummation of a purchase or sale. Applying this rule to the facts in our example, it appears that both S and B made contacts that resulted in a sale of the property to PH and PW. A judge or jury deciding the facts might find that B's contribution to the sale was substantial and he was entitled to a commission from S.

Another area of potential difficulty with a broker's right to compensation arises when a broker procures a buyer or seller who is ready, willing, and able to purchase or sell real property under the terms stated in the listing agreement and the client refuses to consummate the transaction. In such cases it has been held that if there are no reasonable grounds for the client's refusal to complete the transaction, the real estate broker has performed his/her obligations under the listing agreement and would be entitled to receive the bargained-for compensation.

Many areas of potential conflict between real estate broker and client may be avoided by each party's having a clear understanding of their mutual obligations. Often the real estate broker is in the best position to ensure the complete understanding because the listing agreement is contained in a form used and provided by the broker. Potential clients who have questions should be referred to independent legal counsel.

Liability to Seller or Buyer

As previously stated, the real estate broker's chief obligation under the listing agreement is to bring together the client and a buyer or seller; the duty to negotiate rests with the client and the buyer or seller. Since the broker's fee or commission depends on the successful consummation of the negotiations between the client and the buyer or seller, there is the potential of fraud or misrepresentation. In recognition of this possibility, some courts have begun to impose a duty on the broker not only to the client but to all parties in the transaction. A broker who misrepresents or does not deal fairly with all parties to the transaction may be liable for damages suffered by one of the parties even though the injured party had no agency relationship with the broker. If there is reliance on a misrepresentation made by the broker, or the broker perpetrates a fraud on any party to the transaction, the broker may be subject to a lawsuit for such misrepresentation or fraud and also subject to certain sanctions under the state's real estate licensing laws and regulations.

TRANSFER OF OWNERSHIP INTERESTS

For an ownership interest in real property to be transferred, the parties must mutually agree to the terms of the transfer. Their mutual agreement is ultimately expressed in the form of a contract that may be called an *article of agreement,* a *purchase agreement,* a *real estate contract,* an *agreement for the purchase of real estate,* or some other name. No matter what its label, if valid it means that a seller has agreed to sell and a buyer has agreed to buy certain real property. However, before the point of agreement has been reached, there are usually preliminary negotiations followed by an offer, usually made by the buyer and accompanied with an earnest money deposit, which is formalized into a written contract or agreement to sell and buy specific real property.

Preliminary Negotiations

The transfer of an ownership interest in real property typically follows the same general pattern whether or not the seller is acting on his or her own behalf or through a broker. Initially, preliminary negotiations take place between the seller and the buyer, each of whom may negotiate directly or through an agent. Terms such as price, method of payment, date of delivery of possession and ownership, items of personal property to be included, payment of applicable fees, and proration of taxes are discussed, and if the terms are agreed upon, the buyer will submit a formal written offer of purchase to the seller that incorporates the agreed-upon terms. Where the seller is represented by a broker, the broker will not only actually solicit offers, but will often prepare them for the buyer as part of his/her service to the seller. Because of the agency relationship between the seller and broker, the broker has a duty to communicate all written and oral offers to the seller even though they may be less than the amount stated in the listing agreement. If the offer is in accordance with the agreement reached during preliminary negotiations, it will usually be accepted.

Deposit

As evidence of his or her good-faith intention to complete the transaction, the prospective buyer usually makes a cash deposit immediately following the seller's signed acceptance of the offer. This deposit is called *earnest money, hand money,* or a *binder,* depending upon the local custom. The amount of the deposit depends on what the parties agreed to during their preliminary negotiations. Usually, however, it does not exceed 10 percent of the purchase price. Since the deposit can act as a source of funds to pay damages in the event the buyer decides to back out of the contract, the seller is interested in receiving as large a deposit as possible. Applying the same rationale, the buyer is interested in paying as small a deposit as possible. In any event, the deposit is not necessary to the formation of a valid contract for the sale and purchase of real property.

Where a broker has been retained, the deposit is usually turned over to the broker. Under the licensing laws of the various states, the broker cannot commingle this money with his/her own funds; therefore, it is placed in a client trust account where, after the transaction has been consummated, it will be credited toward the purchase price. In the event the seller defaults, the broker will consult with the buyer, because the buyer may decide to sue the seller for specific performance of the contract. In the event the buyer defaults, as indicated above, the deposit may have to be turned over to the seller as damages. A broker who improperly dispenses such funds from a client trust account—for example, where buyer defaults and the deposit is returned—could be held personally responsible for repayment of the improperly dispensed funds.

THE REAL ESTATE CONTRACT

The real estate contract is perhaps the most important document in the process of transferring an ownership interest in real property from seller to buyer. Ideally, it incorporates the full understanding of the parties as derived from their preliminary negotiations. It creates legally enforceable rights and duties for both parties. It specifies the basic duty of the seller to convey marketable title and the corresponding right to receive payment, and the basic duty of the buyer to make payment and the corresponding right to receive the ownership interest. In addition, the parties may agree on other performance obligations. For example, the contract may state that repairs and improvements will be made by the seller prior to transfer of full ownership rights; the seller then has the duty and the buyer the right to have such repairs and improvements made.

These are several of many rights and duties created by the real estate contract. If the transaction does not involve a real estate broker, a lawyer for either seller or buyer usually prepares the contract, which is reviewed by the other party or his or her counsel to ensure that all pertinent items have been included and are understood. If the transaction involves a broker, usually the broker will prepare the contract on a standard preprinted form. A typical form for a purchase agreement is illustrated in Figure 7.

FIGURE 7   A Typical Purchase Agreement

PURCHASE AGREEMENT

Property Description

Received   of _____, Address
_____ Phone _____, the   sum   of
$_____ in the form of cash ___, check ___ dated _____ as
deposit to be escrowed with broker as part payment for the
purchase   of _____, located   at
(Type of Property)
_____, lot ___ block ___ in _____ addition, and to
include the following improvements:_____
_____
together with all planting and improvements except _____
_____

Terms and Conditions of sale

THE FULL PURCHASE PRICE is $_____ to be paid as follows:
total down payment including above deposit to be approximately
$_____ cash, plus or minus prorations, upon execution of
formal instruments; Purchaser assumes and agrees to pay the existing mortgage or lien of record, current as of date of transfer in the
approximate amount of $_____ with monthly payments of
approximately $_____ on said mortgage and balance, if any, to
be paid as follows:
_____
_____

Seller shall make payments due on above incumbrance(s) before
closing date, Purchaser thereafter.   Survey, if required, to be
furnished at expense of _____. Warranty deed and abstract
continued to date or a policy of title insurance in Purchaser's name,
at option of Seller, showing merchantable title clear of liens and
assessments except as set out herein, to be furnished at Seller's
expense as soon as practicable.   Lien of Conservancy Districts,
easements, restrictions, zoning and patent reservations, if any, to be
assumed by Purchaser.

Paving _____ to be paid by _____.   Existing trust
funds in the approximate amount of $_____ to be assigned to
Purchaser at _____ expense.   Rent, taxes, interest, hazard
and FHA mortgage insurance, if any; water, sewer and garbage
charges, if any, are to be prorated to _____.   Seller
agrees to keep property adequately insured and to give possession
of the premises to Purchaser on _____ and certifies that property
will be in the same condition, reasonable wear and tear excepted, as
of the date of this agreement.   Venetian blinds, screens, screen
doors, awnings, traverse rods, electric fixtures complete and
clothesline poles must remain with the house, if same are in
property at this date. Closing date _____.   All parties
undersigned agree to complete closing within 72 hours after notification that papers are ready.   Purchaser agrees to buy and Seller

agrees to sell according to the terms and conditions set out hereinabove. Time is of the essence. This instrument comprises the entire understanding and agreement of the parties hereto on the subject matter herein contained and shall be binding upon and inure to the benefit of the parties, their heirs, executors, adminis- trators, successors, and assigns. Seller agrees to pay customary costs of closing the transaction. Purchaser pays his own attorney fees. In event Seller accepts this offer and Purchaser refuses or fails to consummate the purchase, Seller shall have the option of retaining the earnest money as liquidated damages and terminating this contract or of enforcing the same. Purchaser(s) hereby give(s) broker hereinafter named a specific period of _____ days to com- plete the purchase agreement, and agrees to keep this offer open for that time. If broker is unable to complete this agreement, earnest money is to be refunded in full to Purchaser and this agreement canceled.

Dated this __ day of _____, 19___, at _____ (A.M.) (P.M.)

_____

Realtor(s) Broker

By:_____

_____   _____

Identity Purchaser   Purchaser
of
parties   I/we hereby accept above offer to purchase and agree to pay agent a commission of __% on the full purchase price plus __% sales tax on the commission. In the event purchase is not consummated and earnest money forfeited, said earnest money is to be divided between Seller and Agent according to the bylaws of the _____ Board of Realtors.

_____   _____

Seller   Seller

Contents of the Real Estate Contract

Basic Requirements

The contents of a real estate contract do not have to rigorously follow any prescribed form. However, in order to be valid and enforceable, it must at least (1) identify the parties, (2) state the terms and conditions of the sale including the consideration or price to be paid, and (3) sufficiently describe the property so that it can be easily identified. Any agreement containing these essential items that is in writing and signed by at least one of the parties can be enforced in a court of law against the signator(s). The typical real estate contract will contain more information.

Other Conditions

In addition to the basic requirements, other important conditions are usually included in a standard contract for the sale of real property:

1. It will be dated so that a reference point in time can be firmly established for performance of its various provisions.

2. The place where the contract was entered into will be indicated. This is important because under conflict of law rules, the laws of the state where the contract was entered into may ultimately be used in consideration and enforcement of the contract.

3. The consideration will be stated, including the method of payment and the amount of the deposit.

4. Financing requirements will usually be included primarily for the buyer's benefit so that the buyer's obligation is contingent upon his/her ability to qualify for adequate and reasonable financing.

5. The type of deed—quit claim, special warranty, or general warranty—the seller will deliver to the buyer at closing will be specified so that the buyer will know what kind of guarantee the seller will give as to the merchantability of the title being transferred.

6. The dates of possession and closing or settlement will be stated. Usually, possession and closing occur at the same time. However, where possession is transferred before closing, the seller may require that compensation be paid for the period of occupancy between possession and closing. The closing or settlement date generally fixes a time beyond which a breach of contract occurs if payment is not made, merchantable title not delivered, or other provisions not fulfilled.

7. Since certain expenses arise as a result of real property being transferred from one party to another, the parties usually agree who will pay for them or how they will be prorated. Examples of such expenses are real estate school taxes, real estate transfer taxes, and utility costs.

8. The parties usually insert a risk of loss statement, which names the party who will be responsible for the loss incurred if the property is damaged or destroyed during the period of time the contract is operative. If such a statement is not included, the risk normally falls upon the buyer.

9. The contract will generally include a default provision giving the seller the right to either retain buyer's deposit as liquidated damages or

sue for any other permissible legal remedy including damages at law and rescission in equity.

10. Other provisions may include statements relative to the condition of the property (whether seller warrants its condition or sells it "as is"), a statement including certain personal property in the sale, a provision for assignment of the contract rights and duties, a statement that the contract will be binding upon the heirs of either party, and a statement pertaining to time and whether or not it is of the essence.

11. Finally, the real property contract should be signed by all parties in interest so that they will be bound by its terms, and acknowledged by an authorized person such as a notary public. In many jurisdictions, a contract for the sale of real property will not be accepted for recordation unless it has been acknowledged.

This listing is certainly not exhaustive of all the provisions that could be contained in a real estate contract. It does, however, identify the conditions that are common to most contracts.

The Statute of Frauds

Every state has a Statute of Frauds that requires contracts for the sale of real property to be in writing and signed by the party against whom enforcement is sought. The purpose of the statute is not to prevent the enforcement of oral contracts, but to prevent the perpetration of fraud by one who may seek to enforce an agreement that never existed. The statute does not require a formal, legalistic written document. It can be satisfied by an informal, signed written memorandum, or a series of memoranda, which generally must identify the parties, describe the property in such a way that it can be easily identified, state the purchase price, and contain the promise of the seller to sell and the buyer to buy.

For example, in a written correspondence to B, A wrote: "Dear B, I understand you are interested in a house. I plan to give my house located at 145 Smith Street to a broker to sell for $50,000; however, I can offer it to you for $48,000 if you accept within ten days of the date of this letter. (Signed) A." B replied two days after he received A's letter: "Dear A, I accept your offer to sell for $48,000. (Signed) B." Although the two letters are not formal legal documents, they contain all the requirements necessary to a written memorandum or series of memoranda.

An oral contract for the sale of real property can, under certain circumstances, be enforced where part performance has occurred. The states generally are not uniform as to the nature or degree of part performance. However, the acts most commonly relied upon are (1) total or part payment of the purchase price, (2) delivery of possession to the buyer, and (3) improvements made on the premises by the buyer. The presumption is that these acts would never occur in the absence of a contractual agreement. In some states, a single act is sufficient to circumvent the Statute of Frauds. In other states, a combination of acts is required.

If, for example, S and B entered into an oral contract wherein S agreed to sell and B agreed to buy a certain described house and tract of land for a stated dollar amount, and B paid S half the purchase price in cash, moved in, and built an addition, the oral contract would be clearly enforceable. The same result might not be reached if B's only act in reliance on the oral agreement was to take possession, because the transfer of possession is not in itself unequivocally referable to a contract of sale. The transfer of possession may have been pursuant to a lease.

The Parol Evidence Rule

Under the *parol evidence rule,* after the parties reduce their negotiations to a written real estate contract, all previous or contemporaneous oral agreements merge into the writing and cannot be offered into evidence to change the key terms of the written contract. Thus, if S, during preliminary negotiations, orally agreed to pay all applicable transfer taxes, and the written contract said that such taxes were to be paid one-half by S and one-half by B, the written contract would prevail, since evidence of the prior oral agreement is not admissible. This rule, similar to the Statute of Frauds, is designed to prevent fraudulent claims and to achieve some degree of certainty in the contracting situation.

The parol evidence rule is subject to many exceptions. For example, oral evidence of subsequent agreements or of illegality, fraud, mistake, duress, and misrepresentation is admissible. Most of these exceptions do not attack the key terms of the contract but concern the very existence of the contract.

If S signed a contract to sell certain real property to B at a reduced price because B threatened S's life, S could offer this fact into evidence, not to change the terms of the contract, but to disaffirm it entirely. In essence, the contract never existed in the first place, because there was never a voluntary mutual agreement between seller and buyer.

Legal and Equitable Title

After a contract for the sale of real property has been properly executed, that is, signed by the parties, the seller continues to hold legal title for the benefit of the buyer until actual delivery of a deed and payment of the purchase price. The seller, therefore, holds *legal title* as security for payment of the purchase price. The buyer obtains *equitable title,* or the right to receive legal title. In essence, the seller is the owner of the purchase money and the buyer is the owner of the real property.

This fictitious division of an ownership interest into legal and equitable title is called the *doctrine of equitable conversion.* It generally governs the rights and duties of seller and buyer between the time the contract is executed and the settlement or closing date, when the deed is delivered to the buyer and the buyer pays the remainder of the purchase price. For example, in most states, in the absence of a contract provision to the contrary or a showing of fault on the part of the seller, the buyer bears the risk of loss from casualty, accident, or destruction of the purchased real property.   The rationale is that risk of loss ordinarily follows ownership and the buyer is regarded as the real owner in equity.

The law in some states imposes the risk of loss on the seller, and others impose it upon the person in possession. Where the risk of loss is borne by the buyer and the real property subject to the contract has been destroyed, any insurance benefits received by the seller would be held for the benefit of the buyer, to be delivered to the buyer at the time of closing. Thus, if S contracted to sell B his residential property on January 1 with a closing date of January 30, and the house was accidentally destroyed by fire on January 15, the law in most states would enforce the contract. However, at closing, S would have to turn over to B his right to any insurance benefits on the property.

Under the doctrine of equitable conversion, in the absence of an agreement to the contrary, the buyer does not have the right to occupy and possess the premises before the date set for closing. As a consequence, the seller usually has the right to receive rents and profits as well as the duty to pay applicable expenses such as taxes and utilities during the period of equitable ownership. However, if the buyer lawfully took possession before closing, these rights and duties would be applicable to the buyer.

Breach and Remedies

Where one of the parties does not perform under the terms of a real estate contract and thus commits a breach of contract, the law provides that the nonbreaching party can recover damages for any injuries sustained. The nature and amount of the recovery depend primarily on the type of legal remedy sought and on the event causing the breach. The breach may result, for example, from the seller's refusal to convey title or the buyer's refusal to pay. There are four basic types of remedies: (1) specific performance, (2) benefit of bargain, (3) rescission, and (4) liquidated damages.

Specific Performance

Specific performance is an equitable remedy that compels the breaching party to carry out the specific terms of the contract. The basis of the remedy is that real property is unique and mere money damages cannot adequately compensate the injured party. Thus, it is the buyer who usually pursues a specific performance remedy since the real property the seller contracted to sell cannot be replaced. The courts are less likely to grant specific performance to a seller where the buyer refuses to comply with the terms of the contract, because money damages, in most cases, would provide adequate relief. For example, if the buyer refused to pay for and take ownership interest to certain real property at closing, the seller could always resell the property and recover his/her monetary loss as measured by the difference between the original contract amount and the amount subsequently received from another buyer.

Benefit of Bargain

Benefit of bargain is a remedy at law for money damages as distinguished from a remedy in equity for specific performance. This remedy can be pursued by either party. Where a buyer breaches the contract, the monetary loss to the seller is generally measured by the difference between the contract price and the actual value of the property. If the seller resells the property in good faith within a reasonable period of time, the actual value and resale value become identical, and the loss, assuming the resale value is less than the original contract price, can be readily determined. The same measure of damages is applicable to a seller who commits a willful breach of contract. However, where the seller acts in good faith and discovers that he/she cannot deliver marketable title, even though the seller has technically breached the contract most courts will simply restore the status quo. In other words, the damages recoverable from the seller would be limited to any expenses incurred by the buyer in reliance on the contract.

Rescission

Rescission is a remedy at law that can be pursued by either party. It results in a cancellation or termination of the real estate contract and a restoration of the status quo. For example, if a seller seeks to rescind a contract with a defaulting buyer, the seller would have to return the buyer's deposit. A buyer in possession who defaults must pay the seller a reasonable amount for the period of possession. Sometimes buyers are given a grace period within which time they can by law rescind after signing the real estate contract. For example, under the Federal Truth-in-Lending Act, a buyer has three business days to rescind a transaction where the real property being acquired will secure a loan for its purchase and it is expected to be used as the buyer's principal place of residence.

Liquidated Damages

The parties may agree in their real estate contract to settle or liquidate damages in the event of a breach. The effect of such a liquidated damage clause is eliminated by any of the other available remedies. It is common for a seller to agree to retain the buyer's deposit as liquidated damages in the event the buyer defaults. The courts will usually enforce a liquidated damage clause as long as it is reasonable in amount, regardless of actual damages.

Use of Preprinted Forms

In a transaction involving a real estate broker, the offer to buy is usually put into a standard preprinted form, which serves as the contract pending closing and actual transfer of title. This is particularly true for the sale of residential houses. The preprinted contract has several distinct advantages.

1. It usually represents the best judgment of attorneys and brokers as to the proper language, terms, and conditions that will be upheld in court.

2. It is inclusive in the sense that for the standard transaction, important terms are neither entirely excluded or misstated.

3. It is relatively easy to prepare. Preparation is simply a matter of filling in the appropriate blanks with the correct information.

The use of preprinted forms also has disadvantages.

1. Such forms may not be appropriate for certain real estate transactions—for example, the sale of a going concern where the seller must comply with the state's bulk sales law, installment sales agreements, option contracts, and sales where the seller agrees to finance the transaction. In such cases, the parties usually have an attorney prepare the contract.

2. Preprinted forms tend to favor the seller. The buyer is often reluctant to read the fine print and question terms that he/she may not fully comprehend.

3. In an attempt to make the contract conform to the situation, preprinted terms and conditions may be stricken and others added, which tends to produce confusion and may lead to a result that was not intended by the parties.

In summary, the preprinted form has the distinct advantage of being able to expedite a transaction; however, in using such forms, brokers should consult with attorneys when there are deviations from the standard provisions. In some states the preparation of a contract is considered to be the practicing of law and thus cannot be carried out by a broker who does not have a license to practice law.

QUESTIONS FOR DISCUSSION

1. What is meant by the concept of merchantable title? Give several examples of items or events that would render title to real property not merchantable.

2. What precautionary measures would you advise real estate brokers to take in their relationships with their clients in order to protect themselves from potential liability?

3. What is the difference between legal and equitable title? Why can this difference be important to the seller or buyer?

4. What basic items must contracts for the sale of real property contain to be valid and enforceable? Would preprinted forms be of any help in drafting such a contract?

5. Of what significance are the Statute of Frauds and the parol evidence rule to a contract for the sale of real property?

CASES

Case 1. Plaintiff is a licensed real estate broker. In the course of showing building sites to a representative of Steak House Franchise Company, she showed a specific tract in which the official of the company expressed interest. Plaintiff contacted the owner of the tract, who agreed to pay a commission to Plaintiff if the property was leased due to Plaintiff's efforts. When Plaintiff revealed the identity of the potential lessee of the tract, the owner informed Plaintiff that he and Steak House Franchise Company had had previous dealings and therefore no commission would be paid. The owner and Steak House had had many dealings, but the lease of the specific tract was never discussed between them. Subsequently, the owner and Steak House Franchise Company entered into a long-term lease of the specific tract. Plaintiff has brought suit against the owner for unpaid commissions. What is the likely result of the suit? Why?

Case 2. Plaintiff, who is a licensed real estate broker, learned of Manufacturing Company's interest in purchasing land in the area for construction of a new plant. Plaintiff approached Defendant, who owned a potentially suitable tract for the new plant, and asked Defendant if he was interested in selling. Defendant authorized Plaintiff to attempt the sale. Plaintiff showed the property to the manufacturer's local manager, who did not have authority to purchase the property or negotiate on behalf of Manufacturing Company. The next year, another representative of the same company viewed the land at the suggestion of an official of the city government. After an engineering study by the company's engineers, the company purchased the land from Defendant. Plaintiff brought suit against Defendant for a commission. Is Plaintiff entitled to a commission in this case? Why or why not?

Case 3. Defendant, a real estate broker, represented the buyer of a large tract of land being purchased for developmental purposes. Defendant procured a tract suitable for Buyer's purposes for $200,000 from Plaintiffs, who were the sellers. Before the closing of the transaction, and unknown to the sellers, Buyer's financial condition worsened and it was unable to purchase the property. Before Plaintiffs discovered Buyer's insolvency, Defendant learned of another buyer for the tract for $285,000. Defendant gave $200,000 of her own funds to the original buyer, who completed the transaction and then conveyed the title to Defendant the same day. Defendant then sold the property to the other interested buyer for $285,000. Plaintiffs sued the real estate broker to cancel the original transaction and for damages. Defendant broker defended on grounds that there was no agency relationship between herself and Plaintiffs and she therefore owed no duty to them. What are the likely findings at trial on the merits of Plaintiff's claim?

Case 4. Defendant was owner of a radio station that occupied premises that were destroyed by fire. To retain its operating license, the station was required to find another location on very short notice. The owner approached Plaintiff on Sunday after a brief inspection of the premises and offered to purchase Plaintiff's building in the downtown commercial district. Defendant prepared a written agreement providing that Plaintiff transfer title free and clear of liens and encumbrances, and the agreement was executed by both parties. Some time later it became apparent to Defendant that the building had a party wall shared with the adjoining property owner. The party wall agreement had been recorded thirty years before. The party wall made it quite expensive to remodel the building for radio station purposes, and Defendant refused to consummate the transaction on grounds that the party wall agreement was an encumbrance rendering Plaintiff's title unmerchantable.

Plaintiff instituted a suit in specific performance against Defendant to force the purchase of the property. Could Defendant successfully defend on the grounds that Plaintiff's title was unmerchantable?

Case 5. Plaintiffs entered into a long-term real estate contract for the purchase of a ranch property for $34,000, paying 10 percent down, with the balance payable over ten years. The contract provided that Plaintiffs could prepay the purchase price and receive a deed to the property before final payment. After three years, Plaintiffs entered into another contract to sell the property for $45,000 to Defendants. The contract between Plaintiffs and Defendants provided that the interest in property transferred be free and clear of liens and encumbrances and that the purchase price be paid in cash at settlement. At the time of settlement, Defendants refused to purchase the property, claiming that Plaintiffs were not the owners of the property because title had not passed under the preexisting real estate contract and that therefore Plaintiffs' title was not merchantable. Plaintiffs brought suit to force Defendant-buyers to complete the purchase of the property.

What disposition of the case is the court likely to make in light of the general rules regarding merchantable title? Why?

Case 6. Sellers and Buyers entered into an agreement of purchase and sale of a private residence for $24,000. Prior to the time of the scheduled settlement, Sellers defaulted on a loan in the amount of $750 at a lending institution. Sellers told the institution of the impending sale of the property, and the lending institution began a legal proceeding to execute upon a judgment obtained by reason of the sellers' default. Sellers then refused to consummate the transaction on grounds that the title was not merchantable and refused to pay the money to forestall the execution proceeding. Buyers brought suit against Sellers for specific performance.

What is the most likely result of a trial on the merits of Buyers' claim?

Case 7. Defendant purchased two lots in 1959 by land contract. Two years later he decided to build an office building on the lots. In order to raise the construction money, he assigned his interest in the land contract to a lending institution as collateral for a loan to build the office building. The construction loan was repaid in 1961.

In May 1961, the sellers of the two lots delivered a deed to Defendant and his wife "as tenants by the entirety." In July 1961, the construction loan having been paid, the lending institution delivered a quitclaim deed (a deed where the grantor does not guarantee title) to Defendant and his wife, as "tenants in common" and not as "tenants by the entirety." Plaintiff, independent of the above transactions, obtained a judgment against Defendant in 1970 for approximately $22,000.

Could Plaintiff satisfy his judgment from Defendant's equity in the two lots and office building?

Case 8. Sellers sold Buyers a certain tract of land for $8,500. Included in the written contract was language that specifically related to a parcel of land that was excepted from the sale as follows: "It is also agreed by and between the parties that should the sellers herein fail to build a home on the property excepted herein, the purchasers shall have first option to purchase said land when it is offered for sale, for the sum of $1,000."

Sellers sold the excepted parcel to a third party for $3,500 a number of years later without having first built a home on it for themselves.

Assuming the written contract is a valid option to purchase, what remedy would Buyers pursue for breach of contract against Sellers? What would they recover?

Case 9. Plaintiff and Defendant entered into a written agreement of sale wherein Plaintiff agreed to buy and Defendant agreed to sell certain commercial real property located in Philadelphia, Pennsylvania. Plaintiff maintained that prior to the execution of the Agreement of Sale, he and Defendant had discussed his plans to sell his business and open a new service station on the subject premises. Plaintiff relied in part on these discussions in selling his former business. Defendant breached the contract by not delivering title to the subject commercial property at settlement. Is Plaintiff entitled to consequential damages (damages suffered from loss of business) as a result of being prevented from relocating in the subject property?

Case 10. Purchasers signed a contract wherein they agreed to purchase a 160-acre farm for $80,000. The terms were $12,000 down at the date the contract was signed and the remainder on closing approximately three months later. The contract specifically stated that if Purchasers did not consummate the purchase according to the terms set forth, Sellers could terminate the agreement at their option, "in which case the purchaser shall forfeit all payments made."

In reliance on the contract, Sellers disposed of their farm equipment and prepared to vacate the premises. When Purchasers finally conceded that they could not perform, normal planting dates were past and Sellers could get only a small percentage of the usual yield.

What legal basis would Sellers have in retaining the $12,000 deposit after Buyers could not perform?

Case 11. In 1967, Plaintiff-buyer and Defendant-seller entered into a valid written agreement for the sale of a certain parcel of land. The contract provided that the purchase price would be paid in monthly installments of $100 each at an annual interest rate of 6 percent and that buyer would pay the applicable real estate taxes for 1968 and subsequent years. Several years after the agreement was initiated, the property was sold at a tax sale because Defendant-seller did not pay the 1967 real estate taxes.

What form of legal remedy do you think Plaintiff would seek against Defendant, and in what general amount?

Chapter 6
Title, Title Examination, and Title Protection

CONCEPT OF TITLE

NOTICE

RECORDING STATUTES
  Types of Recording Statutes
  Mechanics of Recording

TITLE SEARCH PROCEDURES
  Principles of Title Examination
  Concept of Chain of Title
  Adverse Conveyances
  Liens and Encumbrances
  Limitations of Title Searches
  Torrens System of Title Registration
    Advantages   Disadvantages   Exceptions   Summary
  Other Methods of Title Registration

TITLE PROTECTION
  Title Insurance
  Certificates of Title
  Abstracts of Title

QUESTIONS FOR DISCUSSION

CASES

As discussed in Chapter 1, the buyer of real property is charged with the dual responsibilities of inspecting the property physically and having the public record searched to determine the quality of the ownership right being transferred. This chapter discusses the real estate law concerning the quality of ownership rights and the ways in which purchasers or encumbrancers can obtain information on land titles so that they can make informed decisions about either the purchase of a real property interest or the acceptance of an interest as security for a debt.

CONCEPT OF TITLE

Title is an ownership interest in real property. It is the right to possession and control over property, including both the power to transfer ownership interests to another and the power to create in others possessory and nonpossessory interests in the property. The title or ownership rights may be vested in one or more individuals such as cotenants or partners, it may be held in trust, or it may be owned by the government.

All land titles originate with a governmental authority. In the United States, title comes from England in a number of eastern states and from Spain in several southwestern states, since the land was originally obtained from England by conquest or from Spain by cession and purchase. Governments obtain original title through discovery, conquest, occupancy, or cession. The government, in turn, transfers the ownership interest in real property to private individuals whose title is then said to be *derivative.* That is, the individual derives authority or title from the state. Individuals transfer title to one another through voluntary methods such as purchase and sale, descent, and devise or involuntarily through actions of third parties.

The foundation of most of the law concerning land titles is the proposition that the mere transfer of land title from one individual to another will not improve the *quality* of that title. For example, if A owns a fee simple determinable estate, A cannot transfer it to B in fee simple absolute. Also, if A conveys his ownership interest first to B, then makes another conveyance of the same property to C, C will obtain no title whatsoever if B records her deed before the conveyance to C.

As real property ownership interests are transferred from one party to another over the years, one owner may create or reserve an easement, grant a mineral deed, bind the property with restrictive covenants, or divest herself or himself of any of the incidents of ownership. Creation of such ownership, possessory, or nonpossessory interests by one owner may affect all successive owners of the real property. For example, an easement appurtenant granted by the owner to a third party continues to bind the property until the easement expires by its terms or is terminated through abandonment or by operation of law. Each successive owner of the servient tenement is bound by that easement, because the transfer of ownership of the property does not affect the nonpossessory right held by the owner of the dominant tenement.

Each transfer of an interest or creation of an encumbrance decreases the quality of the current owner's estate and continues from owner to owner unless the interest or encumbrance is limited in time or scope or an affirmative step is taken to recover or terminate it. Because an interest or encumbrance continues to affect the property through successive owners, subsequent purchasers or encumbrancers should be concerned about the title, not only of their immediate transferor, but of previous owners as well. An interest, easement, or other encumbrance continues even though there is no recitation of the outstanding interest in subsequent deeds.

NOTICE

Interests or encumbrances continue to affect real property after it has been transferred only if a prospective purchaser or encumbrancer such as a mortgagee has a notice of the interest. If a prospective purchaser or encumbrancer physically inspects the property and the public record, neither of which disclose an encumbrance or outstanding interest, then that subsequent purchaser would not be affected if an interest were to be disclosed after he/she has taken title.

For example, A is the owner of a tract of real property that is subject to an unrecorded mortgage in favor of B. A agrees in writing to sell the property to C. C's physical inspection of the premises does not reveal B's mortgage because most mortgagees do not take possession of the mortgaged premises or give other physical evidence of their interest in the mortgaged property. Since B's nonpossessory security interest is not in the public record, unless A, B, or a third party disclosed the encumbrance to C, C would have no knowledge of B's interest and any conveyance to C would be free and clear of B's mortgage. The key issue in this example is whether the transferee has notice of the outstanding interest.

Notice can be either actual or constructive. *Actual notice* is express knowledge. The person who has actual notice has been affirmatively apprised of the existence of a fact or condition. In the preceding example, if A, B, or a third party had told C of the mortgage held by B, then C would have had actual notice of the outstanding nonpossessory security interest in the property. Having had actual knowledge of the existence of the mortgage, C would take the real property interest subject to the rights of B.

Constructive notice is knowledge of a fact or condition that a person is presumed to have because of a duty imposed by law. A buyer or encumbrancer of real property is charged with the duty of physically inspecting the premises for rights of persons in possession or other conditions such as easements that would be revealed by a reasonable inspection. The buyer or encumbrancer is also responsible for completing a search of the public record to discover interests in the property that are not disclosed through a physical inspection. The physical inspection and search of the record are both duties imposed by law. The buyer takes the property interest subject to any interests that would have been disclosed by a diligent completion of the inquiries, whether or not the buyer actually makes them. In the preceding example, if B had recorded his mortgage, but C had failed to make a diligent search of the public record that would have disclosed B's nonpossessory security interest, then C would take title to the property subject to B's mortgage. This is true even though C had no *actual* notice of B's interest in the property, because C is responsible by law for information that a proper search of the record would reveal.

If a prospective purchaser receives notice of a possible outstanding interest or encumbrance on the property being considered for purchase, he/she is under a duty to make further inquiry into the facts. Under such circumstances, the purchaser has constructive notice of all facts that a further inquiry would reveal even though he/she does not actually complete an investigation. A purchaser discharging his/her duties to inspect cannot ignore a suspected fact and benefit from a failure to make further inquiry. For example, if the physical inspection were to reveal that the real property has crops growing on it, and the prospective purchaser knows that the seller-owner is not engaged in the farming business, he/she is under a duty to make an inquiry into the facts concerning the crops. If further inquiry is not made and there is an outstanding farm lease upon the property, the buyer takes ownership subject to the terms and conditions of the farm lease, because the law imposes a duty to make further inquiry into suspected facts.

Just as the purchaser or encumbrancer of real property is under a duty to inspect, the seller is under a duty not to conceal. If the purchaser enquires as to the existence of a fact or condition, the seller must cooperate.   After due inquiry is made, any failure to disclose or misstatement of fact by the seller upon which the buyer justifiably relies to his/her detriment may be considered fraud or misrepresentation. In such cases, the buyer may be entitled to a refund of the purchase price, reimbursement for costs and expenses incident to the purchase, and in some cases, if fraud is proved, punitive damages as well.

RECORDING STATUTES

In ancient England, the rule with respect to priority of conveyances of the same property was "first in time, first in right." Thus, the first person to receive a properly executed deed to the property had better title to the property than subsequent grantees or mortgagees of the same property. Early colonies adopted laws whose purpose was to give owners a central place or registry where their instruments could be deposited and provide an official record of ownership. The first recording statute in the American colonies was adopted in 1640 by the Massachusetts Bay Colony to avoid fraudulent conveyances; it provided that unless a conveyance or mortgage was recorded as prescribed in the statute, it would not be effective against any other person except the grantor and his/her heirs. The Massachusetts concept of a recording statute spread rapidly, and today all states except Louisiana have somewhat similar recording statutes.

Both early and current recording statutes have had certain basic features.

1. They provide that the instrument between the parties is fully operable whether or not the instrument is actually recorded. In other words, the recording of the instrument has no effect upon its validity.

2. In order for the document to be entitled to be recorded, it must have been acknowledged. That is, the execution of the instrument must comply with certain formalities designed to ensure uniformity and reduce the chance of fraud.

3. The major features of the transaction are to be made a part of the public record so that anyone inspecting the record can discover the nature of the instrument, the property transferred or encumbered, the names of the parties, and the date of the transfer or encumbrance, and, in the case of mortgages, find the amount of the mortgage.

4. The recording statute establishes priorities of purchasers and encumbrances according to when their respective interests are placed in the public record.

Only deeds and mortgages were included within the early recording statutes. Today, under most statutes, almost any document affecting title to real property may be recorded. Thus, in addition to deeds and mortgages, records may include assignments, leases, restrictive covenants, powers of attorney, articles of agreement, Uniform Commercial Code security interests, easements, and other similar instruments.

Types of Recording Statutes

The original purpose of recording was to provide security for landowners. This has been supplanted by the modern purpose of providing a comprehensive system of priorities for subsequent purchasers or encumbrancers of the same property. Recording statutes differ from state to state, but their purposes are similar. The major differences are found in the provisions concerning the instruments that are recordable, the time limits within which they must be presented for recording, and the determination of priorities among interests.

There are three major types of statutes with regard to establishment of priorities among subsequent purchasers or encumbrancers.

1. A type of recording statute in use in a minority of jurisdictions is the *race-type statute*. Priority among subsequent purchasers or encumbrancers is given to the first person to place the instrument creating his or her interest in the record. For example, if A were to mortgage the same property to B and then to C, the first mortgage on the property would belong to the winner of the "race to the Courthouse." The race statute is similar to the Old English doctrine of first in time, first in right. The priority of the first to record is not affected by whether that person had actual or constructive notice of a prior interest, provided that fraud was not the reason for the first holder's failure to record.

2. The second group of recording statutes are *notice-type statutes*, under which a subsequent purchaser or encumbrancer of real property is entitled to priority only if, at the time of acquisition, he/she had neither actual nor constructive notice of a prior interest. Notice statutes are an outgrowth of the English common law doctrine that an interest of a subsequent buyer should not be protected if, at the time the buyer took

the conveyance, he/she knew of a prior interest in another. All states except for those with purely race-type recording statutes now require that the subsequent purchaser be without notice of the prior interest in order for his/her interest to be superior to that of a prior purchaser or encumbrancer. With a notice-type statute, if the first purchaser records his/her instrument prior to the second purchaser but at the time of recording has knowledge of the second purchaser's interest, his interest would be subordinate to the second purchaser's. For example, A conveys the property to B who does not record. A then conveys the property to C who also does not record. However, B learns of C's interest and then records. B's interest would be subordinate to C's because C took title without notice of B's interest.

3. *Race-notice* recording statutes combine the features of both race and notice statutes. Under race-notice statutes, a subsequent purchaser or encumbrancer has priority over any prior interest only if he/she is first to record and has no notice of the prior conveyance or encumbrance. For example, A conveys the property to B, who does not record. A then conveys the property to C, who has no notice of B's interest and does not record either. B discovers that C has received a conveyance to the property and records his deed. C then records her deed to the property. C does not receive the protection of the recording statute's priority because she has lost the race to the courthouse and did not record her deed before B, even though she had no notice of B's prior interest.

Under both notice and race-notice statutes, there is either an express or implied requirement that the subsequent grantee must be a *bona fide* purchaser to benefit from the protection offered the recording statute.

Generally, a purchaser is bona fide if he/she has given fair value for the interest conveyed and had neither actual nor constructive notice of grantor's prior interest in the property. In addition, the bona fide purchaser must give "present consideration" for the interest received. The requirement for present consideration is met if there is a bargained-for exchange under which the owner transfers his/her interest to the other in exchange for property, services, or other valuable consideration. The requirement is not met through transfers by gift, devise, assignment for the benefit of previous creditors, or a mortgage where the consideration received by the mortgagor was a preexisting debt.

For example, if A were to transfer his property to B by deed in satisfaction of a prior debt, B would not receive the protection of notice and race-notice recording statutes because he is not a purchaser for value.

The fair value requirement is met if the present consideration given to the transferor reasonably approximates the fair market value of the property. For example, if A were to convey his property to B for the sum of $10,000, and an appraisal of the property reveals that the fair market value of the property is $15,000, the discrepancy would not be such as to raise the inference that "fair value" was not given to the grantor. Most courts would not substitute their judgment for that of the parties to the bargain unless there is evidence of fraud or unless the amount of consideration given by the transferee "shocks the conscience" of the court.

In a minority of jurisdictions, the grantee of a quitclaim deed cannot be a bona fide purchaser even though fair value is given for the interest and the grantee has no notice of a prior interest. The reasoning behind this rule is that the grantee is on notice of a possible defect in the title because of the grantor's tendering of a quitclaim deed rather than a warranty deed. However, this rule has gained disfavor because there may be many valid reasons why a grantor will convey a property interest with a quitclaim deed other than lack of confidence in his/her title to the property. In most states, the receipt of a quitclaim deed does not adversely affect the bona fides of a purchaser.

In almost all jurisdictions, any instrument intended to be recorded must be acknowledged. The absence of an acknowledgment does not affect the validity of the instrument. However, if the document is not acknowledged it cannot be recorded and cannot receive the benefits accorded to recorded documents.

As a general rule, the grantee of an instrument should record the instrument as soon as possible. In states with a race-type statute, prompt recording is essential. In other states, good judgment dictates the prompt recording of instruments so that any subsequent purchaser or encumbrancer has constructive notice of the interest of the grantee. It is possible for two inconsistent instruments to be recorded at the same time, and under either a race or a race-notice statute, the priority would be in doubt. In most recording offices, this will not pose a problem because the same clerk or a limited number of clerks may handle the document and no two are given exactly the same filing time. However, simultaneous filing may post a problem in large metropolitan areas where scores of documents are received hourly and a large number of employees receive documents. Some states provide by statute that the lowest filing number has priority, others provide that the instrument with the lowest document number prevails.

Simultaneous recording is no problem in a state with a notice recording statute. There the problem may arise when two inconsistent instruments are executed and delivered at approximately the same time and neither grantee has any knowledge of the other grantee's interest. In such states, the priority may be accorded to the instrument first presented for recording. In states without specific statutes concerning

TABLE 6   Features of Recording Statutes

Type of Statute	Priority of Subsequent Purchaser	Subsequent Purchaser Required to be Bona Fide Purchaser
Race	Only if first to record	No, unless prior purchaser did not record because of fraud of subsequent purchaser.
Notice	Has priority if had no actual or constructive notice at time acquired interest.	Yes, must pay fair value and have no notice of prior interest.
Race-Notice	Has priority if records before prior purchaser and has no actual or constructive notice of prior interest.	Yes, must pay fair value and have no notice of prior interest.

simultaneous recording, the courts are left to decide the issue should it be raised in litigation.

There always exists the possibility of human error in the recording, transcription, or indexing of documents presented for record. It is a general rule that a person searching the record may rely upon what he/she may reasonably find. In some states, if an instrument is not indexed properly and could not be found other than through a page-by-page search of the entire volume of recorded material, then the subsequent purchaser is not charged with constructive knowledge of the instrument improperly indexed. In others, courts have held that the grantee who records properly, but through error of the recording agents does not receive the protection of the recording statutes, is still protected, and a subsequent purchaser or encumbrancer cannot prevail even though a reasonable search of the indices and records does not reveal the prior interest.

Table 6 summarizes the main distinguishing features of the three types of recording statutes.

Mechanics of Recording

The actual mechanics of recording vary from state to state. Usually, the instrument is presented to the appropriate public official for recording. For most instruments, there is a fee for the service. When the document is accepted, it is assigned a recording number, and a receipt is given evidencing both payment of the fee and acceptance of the document by the official. At that moment, the document is considered to be recorded

FIGURE 8   Recording Receipt

ORIGINAL

OFFICIAL RECEIPT

RECORDER OF DEEDS

Date   September 16,   197 7

Received of   Bruce Brown, et ux

	STATE		COUNTY		TOTAL	
Penna. Transfer Tax						
School Transfer Tax						
Recording Deed		50	8	00	8	50
Mortgage		50	8	00	8	50
Miscellaneous						
Agreements						
Bond & Commission						
Power of Attorney						
Satisfaction of Mortgage						
Release of Mortgage						
Assignments						
Secured Transactions & 287						
Maps						
Acknowledgments						
Photostatic Copies						
TOTAL	1	00	16	00	17	00

Per N.K.

RECORDER   DEPUTY OR CLERK

No. 58385   309844-5

and everyone has constructive notice of the interest conveyed or created.

Figure 8 illustrates a sample recording receipt.

In earlier times most documents were transcribed into the records; today the laborious task of copying by hand has been replaced by photocopy processes. After a transcription or photocopy facsimile of the document is prepared and bound into the record books, the document is classified and indexed according to the method set forth by state statute or local custom and usage. Usually, the instrument is indexed under the names of both the grantors or creators of the interest and the grantees or recipients of the interests, and the index entries indicate the record book and page number where the instrument is bound into the permanent record. The index enables an interested party to more easily find specific instruments evidencing conveyances or the creation of possessory or nonpossessory interests in real property.

There are various types of indexing systems used by recording officials. Most commonly, an instrument is indexed alphabetically by the names of the parties according to the first letter of either the last or first name of each party. Often different types of interests are indexed and bound in separate volumes. It is not uncommon for deeds to have a separate index and a separate set of books with either transcriptions, abstracts, or photocopies of the deeds. In some registries, other documents such as releases, assignments, easements, powers of attorney, and restrictive covenants are separately indexed and bound; in others, such documents are included with the deeds. Most often, instruments creating nonpossessory security interests are indexed and bound separately. Thus, mortgages and Uniform Commercial Code security interests are usually indexed and bound separately. Examples of grantor and grantee indices are shown in Figures 9 and 10, respectively. Note that in the examples the indexing is by alphabetical grouping by first letter of last name of grantors in the grantor index and grantee in the grantee index, but the entries are made chronologically in the order in which they were received by the Recorder. Thus, all grantors or grantees in an alphabetical grouping will be listed together not in alphabetical order among themselves, but in the order in which their documents were presented and accepted by the registry.

In these examples, the deeds, miscellaneous documents such as easements, releases, powers of attorney, and the like are indexed together in one volume. However, the deeds and miscellaneous documents are bound separately in different volumes. The prefix before the book number indicates whether the document is found among the deeds or among the miscellaneous documents.

In addition to the grantor and grantee indices commonly found in

FIGURE 9　Grantor Index

GRANTOR INDEX TO DEEDS and MISCELLANEOUS RECORDS

Month	Day	Year	SURNAME	GIVEN NAMES ABCDEFGH	GIVEN NAMES IJKLMNO	GIVEN NAMES PQRSTUVWXYZ	GRANTEE	KIND OF INSTRUMENT	Book	Page	LOCATION
3	27	74	Smith	Alex		Patricia	Frye, Edward	Deed	D579	223	Newtown
5	7	74	Smithley	James June			Gambol, Jessica	Deed	D580	345	Kneen Township
7	8	74	Smithfield	Albert	Jennifer		Gekki, Joseph	Deed	D581	443	Newtown
9	2	74	Smith			Winand	Jacobson, Henry, Zelda	Deed	D582	001	Royler Township
11	3	74	Smith		John		Wilson, Wanda	Agrmnt.	Misc. 29	334	Knox Township
2	20	75	Smiley			William Mila	Baron, Mary Ann, et al	Release	Misc. 30	007	Alison County
7	25	75	Smithhurst		Lewis		Baker, Mary, William	Deed	D585	867	Newtown
10	4	75	Smith		Johnston	Valerie	Black, Howard	Easement	Misc. 32	555	Newtown
1	5	76	Smith	Howard Ernest			Keene, L. K.	Power of Attorney	Misc. 33	007	Wilson County
4	4	76	Smithley		Jonathan		Whiting, Opal	Deed	D586	111	Flitford Township
7	8	76	Smith	Elsa	Jacob		Holmberg, Anton, Marie	Deed	D587	227	Kneen Township
9	23	76	Smith		Maria Joseph		Beadle, Susan	Deed	D588	019	Newtown
11	3	76	Smiley		Julia		Bentley, Emily	Release	Misc. 35	233	Newtown
3	9	77	Smith			Wilson, et al	Vilman, George, Virginia	Deed	D589	119	Flitford Township
9	16	77	Smith			Samuel	Brown, Bruce, Brenda	Deed	D590	798	Newtown

FIGURE 10   Grantee Index

GRANTEE INDEX TO DEEDS and MISCELLANEOUS RECORDS

Month	Day	Year	SURNAME	GIVEN NAMES ABCDEFGH	GIVEN NAMES IJKLMNO	GIVEN NAMES PQRSTUVWXYZ	GRANTOR	KIND OF INSTRUMENT	Book	Page	LOCATION
3	5	74	Browner			Russell Rose	Jones, Cecelia	Deed	D579	349	Newtown
6	29	74	Brownley		Joseph	Virginia	Adams, Julia Johnson	Deed	D580	956	Hope Township
8	8	74	Browning			Kenneth, et al	Johnson, Terrance, Elaine	Art. of Agrmnt.	Misc. 29	006	Danforth Township
10	7	74	Brown	Harry		Winifred	Alexes, Lawrence, Margaret	Deed	D583	459	Newtown
1	9	75	Brown		Jeffery Louise		Boston, David, et al	Deed	D584	590	Kneen Township
5	8	75	Brownington	Henry		Susan	Dandel, George, et al	Deed	D585	239	Plitford Township
7	25	75	Brownley	Gregg, et al			Ace Development Corporation	Art. of Agrmnt.	Misc. 31	543	Roylen Township
9	6	75	Browning	Helen Henry			Allgood, Jacob, Teresa	Deed	D585	998	Newtown
11	7	75	Brown			Robert Rachel	LaPante, Janet, et al	Easement	Misc. 32	899	Knox Township
2	4	76	Brownington Twp.				Alison County Land Co.	Dedication	Misc. 33	113	Browning-ton Twp.
4	30	76	Brown			Thomas	Brown, Thomas, Sr.	Power of Attorney	Misc. 33	328	Alison County
7	8	76	Browning	Henry Aline			Greater Alison Realty	Deed	D587	230	Kneen Township
9	16	76	Brown	Alfred Gertrude			Sheriff of Alison County	Deed	D587	877	Plitford Township
11	14	76	Browntree		Kevin June		Grately, Brixton Hilda	Deed	D588	378	Newtown
1	6	77	Brown			Theodore, et al	Jenison, Harold, Katherine	Deed	D588	991	Newtown
5	9	77	Brown			William, et al	Apex Oil Company	Release of Lease	Misc. 36	678	Alison County
8	24	77	Brownington Twp.				Alison Land Co.	Dedication	Misc. 36	990	Browning-ton Twp.
9	16	77	Brown	Bruce Brenda			Smith, Samuel Smith	Deed	D590	798	Newtown

recording offices, specific interests in real estate such as mortgages may be indexed separately. A page from a "B" mortgagor index volume is shown in Figure 11. Under this indexing system, there is a separate volume or index for the first letter of the last name of the mortgagor. Within that volume, the names are listed in alphabetical groups according to the first letter of the first name of the mortgagor in the order in which the mortgages were presented for recording.

Alphabetical indexing is still a major method of accessing records, but it is decreasing in both popularity and importance. Technological advances in information processing enable private abstract companies to develop and supplement recording data. Under such systems, rather than indexing according to the names of the parties to instruments, the tracts themselves are numbered and indexed and all relevant documents are keyed to the tracts affected. This method of indexing by parcels of real estate is known as *tract indexing* and has been accepted as a means of indexing public records in a few states. Data are constantly updated to include current information on specific tracts of real property that is easily accessible without resort to the many different public registry indices that use alphabetical indexing.

TITLE SEARCH PROCEDURES

The buyer of real property interests is charged with knowledge of any defect or interest of record that may affect the title to the real property being purchased. Most buyers are not qualified to do a comprehensive search of the public record; therefore, they must rely on others to fulfill the requirement. In some areas within the United States, attorneys perform title searches; in others, professional abstractors and title companies perform this service.

Principles of Title Examination

Title search procedures vary according to the laws of each jurisdiction and local recording statutes and recording procedures. However, there are certain basic principles of construction common to most jurisdictions.

1. As stated previously, the quality of an estate is not improved by a transfer from one party to another. Any lien, encumbrance, or diminution of an estate by one owner affects all subsequent owners of the property unless an affirmative step is taken to correct the defect. Therefore, the person performing the title search or examination must be concerned with the quality of the estate of every person who had an interest in the property.

FIGURE 11 Mortgagor Index

Mortgagor Index

SATISFACTION	MORTGAGORS	MORTGAGEES	BOOK	PAGE	DATE OF MORTGAGE	DATE RECORDED	AMOUNT	LOCATION	REMARKS
	Boversox, Bernice, et bar	First State Bank	300	234	3/3/65	3/5/65	$23,000	Newtown	
	Billiagham, Boston, et ux	Newton Savings & Loan	301	299	3/30/65	3/30/65	$34,000	Flitford Township	
8/7/70	Bass, Barbara	Consumer Finance	314	967	6/25/67	6/25/67	$4,000	Knox Township	
	Bond, Beverly, et bar	First National Bank	325	003	9/16/70	9/16/70	$42,000	Roylen Township	
	Beaty, Bart, et ux	Second Federal Savings	331	667	2/24/71	2/25/71	$10,000	Newtown	Assigned Misc. 33-1
	Bradford, Beulah	First State Bank	333	211	5/4/73	5/4/73	$37,400	Newtown	
	Bilko, Benjamin, et ux	Old Reliance Finance	336	779	6/1/75	6/2/75	$34,600	Flitford Township	
1/3/77	Bernal, Benito, et al	Merchant's Bank	337	233	10/1/76	10/1/76	$78,000	Weaverly Township	
	Brown, Brenda, et bar	First National Bank	339	111	9/16/77	9/16/77	$65,000	Newtown	
	Brown, Bruce, et ux	First National Bank	339	111	9/16/77	9/16/77	$65,000	Newtown	

2. The deed conveys only the property described in the instrument. If there is a variation in the description from one grantor to another, the variation affects the quantity and the title of real property conveyed by all subsequent grantors. Therefore, each description must be verified to be sure that the same land is being transferred.

3. All persons who have an interest in the property must join in the conveyance, or complete title is not passed to the grantee. For example, X and Y are wife and husband, but only Y is owner in fee simple. If Y were to convey the property to a grantee without the joinder of X, a potential title defect may arise because of possible outstanding dower or statutory rights held by X as Y's wife. If a grantor has not joined in a conveyance, that grantor may have retained an interest in the property either intentionally or accidentally. Therefore, the title searcher must be sure that the appropriate grantors have joined in all conveyances.

4. All technical aspects of document preparation and recording must be verified. As a general rule, the recording official will accept any document that has been properly acknowledged. It is not the public official's duty to verify the proper execution of the documents being accepted. If a deed or other instrument is defective in its execution and lacks an element essential to its validity, the act of placing it on the record does not cure the defect. If the instrument is improperly prepared or executed, it cannot be operative. Therefore, the searcher must be certain that the document is properly executed and in fact transfers or creates the intended interest.

There are many other principles affecting title search procedures; however, the foregoing are basic to an understanding of the overall search process.

Concept of Chain of Title

The first step in the title search process is the construction of the chain of title. The *chain of title* is the record of ownership of property as it passes from the government as original grantor to each successive owner of the same tract. Each owner forms a link in the chain of title, and as title is passed to the next owner a new link is formed. The chain of title is constructed through use of recorded documents, and all matters affecting ownership rights in the property become part of the chain of title.

The person performing the search and constructing the chain must necessarily start with the current owner. The name of the current owner is searched in the grantee index because he/she was most recently the grantee of the property. As illustrated in Figure 10, the index entry reveals the name of the current owner's grantor and the book and page number in the record where the deed may be found. After examining the deed to verify the estate, the description, the parties, and the proper execution of the instrument, the first link in the chain of title is complete. Since the grantor of the present owner was once a grantee of the property, his/her name is then searched in the grantee index. The grantee index reveals the name of the previous grantor and the book and page number in the record where that deed may be found. That deed is examined, the grantor of that interest is searched in the grantee index, and in this manner the links of the chain of title are constructed from the present owner back to the original title source.

Sometimes a search of the grantee indices is not necessary because the information is available in the deed itself. For example, the deed may include an explanatory clause that the property conveyed is the same property, or a part of the property, received by the grantor from another. A typical example is the phrase "being the same premises which the grantor herein received by deed of Jeremy Wigglethorpe, dated March 10, 1974, and recorded in Deed Book 350, page 100." These "recital clauses" as they are sometimes referred to, are not essential to the validity of the deed, but they are helpful to anyone searching title to the property.

In the example illustrated in Figure 12, the links are all complete from the present owner back through several past owners to the state. However, not all chains of title are so constructed. Often, there is either a break in the chain or an incomplete link, perhaps because one of the grantors has failed to join in the conveyance or there has been no judicial determination of a deceased owner's heirs. In such cases, there is a defect that adversely affects the merchantability of the present owner's title. Sometimes the defect is corrected by passage of time and the running of the statute of limitations. If the outstanding interest is not remote in time, a quitclaim deed from a prior grantor may be the easiest way to correct a defect.

Some defects may result from incorrect descriptions. Often this type of defect may be corrected through adverse possession, if any of the prior grantors held possession according to the correct description, or it may be possible to procure a corrective deed from a prior grantor.

Technical defects in deeds may be corrected through a quitclaim deed reconveying the property with a properly executed instrument. In some states, the legislature periodically enacts legislation designed to validate or correct some of the technical defects in recorded instruments. However, these statutory validations do not correct substantive defects such as missing grantors or incomplete or erroneous descriptions.

Adverse Conveyances

The running of the chain of title is only the first step in the title search process. The chain of title was constructed link by link through a search

FIGURE 12 Sample Chain of Title

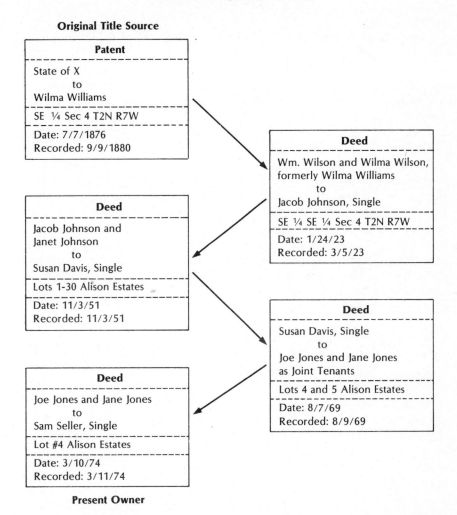

Original Title Source

Patent
State of X to Wilma Williams
SE ¼ Sec 4 T2N R7W
Date: 7/7/1876 Recorded: 9/9/1880

Deed
Wm. Wilson and Wilma Wilson, formerly Wilma Williams to Jacob Johnson, Single
SE ¼ SE ¼ Sec 4 T2N R7W
Date: 1/24/23 Recorded: 3/5/23

Deed
Jacob Johnson and Janet Johnson to Susan Davis, Single
Lots 1-30 Alison Estates
Date: 11/3/51 Recorded: 11/3/51

Deed
Susan Davis, Single to Joe Jones and Jane Jones as Joint Tenants
Lots 4 and 5 Alison Estates
Date: 8/7/69 Recorded: 8/9/69

Deed
Joe Jones and Jane Jones to Sam Seller, Single
Lot #4 Alison Estates
Date: 3/10/74 Recorded: 3/11/74

Present Owner

of the grantee indices of each of the grantors. It is possible that somewhere along the chain of title a grantor conveyed the property to another grantee other than the grantee within the chain being followed. If the property were conveyed twice, another chain would arise that would not be revealed through a running of the original chain whose links are constructed using only the grantee index. In order to discover a conveyance "adverse" to the principal chain of title, it is necessary to check the grantor index for each of the named grantors to be certain that the described property was not conveyed to another. Figure 13 shows an adverse conveyance that would be revealed through a search of the grantor indices.

In the above example, the existence of an adverse chain of title would be revealed when the name of Howard Hall was checked in the grantor index. The record should disclose that Howard Hall made two conveyances of the identically described real property. The priority of ownership between the grantees, Stephen Steele and Richard Randall and Rebecca Randall, would be determined by the recording statute in effect within the jurisdiction. (Note that although the Randall deed has a prior date, it was recorded subsequent to the recording of Steele's deed.)

Obviously, if there were an outstanding adverse interest in the property, the title to the property would be unmerchantable. Often, the duplication of descriptions is an error that may be corrected to conform to the original intention of the grantor who twice conveyed the identically described properties. In other cases, the party in possession of the property may have barred the claim of the other through adverse possession. In any case, the adverse conveyance should be corrected on the record so that future problems are avoided.

Liens and Encumbrances

After the chain of title has been constructed and the absence of adverse conveyances has been verified through a search of the grantor index, each grantor should be checked for liens and encumbrances. As previously discussed, a lien on property continues until it expires by lapse of time or through an affirmative action to remove it. If property is encumbered with a lien, the lien continues no matter who the owner of the property may be so long as the lien was properly entered initially. A recorded lien is notice to the world of the existence of the lienholder's nonpossessory security interest. Therefore, it becomes essential that such liens be discovered through the title search process.

The different types of liens and the rule for their effect upon real property have been discussed in Chapter 4. The searching process will be governed by the applicability of liens to the property interest being transferred or encumbered. There is a wide variation in the applicability of liens and lien search procedures. Suffice to say that any possible lien or encumbrance should be checked in the records to avoid an unanticipated result.

If the chain of title is intact, there are no adverse conveyances of the same property, and there are no liens or encumbrances other than those that may be removed through the proceeds received at settlement between the parties, then the search is completed.

FIGURE 13 Sample Chain of Title With Adverse Chain

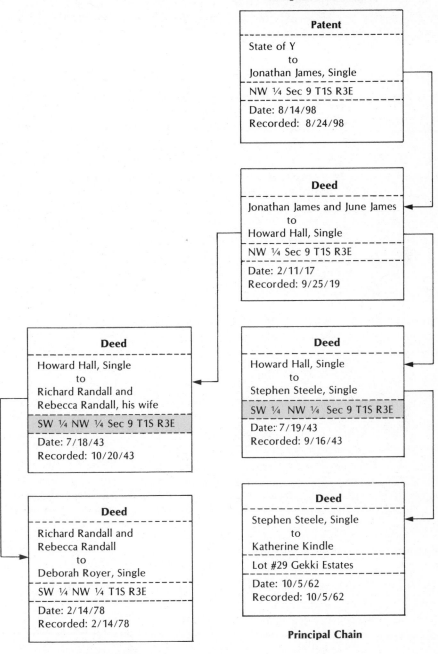

Original Title Source

Patent

State of Y
to
Jonathan James, Single

NW ¼ Sec 9 T1S R3E

Date: 8/14/98
Recorded: 8/24/98

Deed

Jonathan James and June James
to
Howard Hall, Single

NW ¼ Sec 9 T1S R3E

Date: 2/11/17
Recorded: 9/25/19

Deed

Howard Hall, Single
to
Richard Randall and
Rebecca Randall, his wife

SW ¼ NW ¼ Sec 9 T1S R3E

Date: 7/18/43
Recorded: 10/20/43

Deed

Howard Hall, Single
to
Stephen Steele, Single

SW ¼ NW ¼ Sec 9 T1S R3E

Date: 7/19/43
Recorded: 9/16/43

Deed

Richard Randall and
Rebecca Randall
to
Deborah Royer, Single

SW ¼ NW ¼ T1S R3E

Date: 2/14/78
Recorded: 2/14/78

Deed

Stephen Steele, Single
to
Katherine Kindle

Lot #29 Gekki Estates

Date: 10/5/62
Recorded: 10/5/62

Principal Chain

Adverse Chain

Limitations of Title Searches

If the purchaser or encumbrancer has physically inspected the property for rights of parties whose interests are revealed through such an inspection and has had a search of the public record performed, he/she has completed the duties imposed by law. However, the successful completion of a'title search and physical inspection does not eliminate all risk to the purchaser. The public records disclose only that the documents in the record have been duly presented for recording. The authenticity of the documents is not guaranteed because they appear in the record.

Certain "hidden" risks are assumed by a buyer who relies solely on the record and a physical inspection. For example, a forged deed does not foreclose the right of the true owner to reclaim a property interest unless the statute of limitations has run. In titles involving probate or other litigation, a defect in service of process against one who had an interest in the property may render the judicial proceeding ineffective against that individual. Often such defects are not discoverable in the court records. Another potential problem arises when a grantor who has died either testate or intestate has surviving children whose whereabouts or even whose identity are unknown to the survivors. Such missing or unrecognized heirs-at-law may include children born out of wedlock who, under the more modern law, may inherit from either father or mother. In a title involving probate or administration, a title search will not usually disclose the existence of such missing heirs.

To a certain extent, the hidden risks assumed may be minimized through title insurance, which under some contracts insures against such risks. Title insurance is discussed in detail later in this chapter.

Another weakness in relying solely on an inspection of the record is the possible entry of a lien or claim of lien that relates back in priority to a prior date. As discussed in Chapter 4, most mechanic's liens have a provision for the relation back of priority of such claims. In some jurisdictions, purchase money mortgages and other specific liens are accorded such favored treatment and a search of the record cannot protect against the entry of a lien that by statute is given priority over later recorded deeds and mortgages.

Torrens System of Title Registration

The recording systems prevalent in most jurisdictions have major difficulties. First, there may be a defect in the record such as those mentioned in the preceding section. Second, as the years pass and the mobility of the population increases, the volume of recorded instruments increases, making the title search process more cumbersome and thereby increasing the chances of error. Third, with title search procedures, the search must be performed for each transfer. If the search has not previously been performed by the searcher, the search fee will probably reflect either the time needed to complete the search or a price per page for preparation of an abstract. A searcher who subsequently performs the same or a similar search still often charges as if the entire search were performed again when in reality the data obtained during a previous search was simply updated. Thus, the prices charged for title searches do not always reflect the fair value of the work performed in accomplishing the task.

One alternative to recordation systems is the registration of land titles. Robert Richard Torrens, Premier of South Australia in the late 1850s, invented the system of land title registration that commonly bears his name. The Torrens system is prevalent in many countries that use the English legal system and is permitted by statute in several states in this country. Land title registration is somewhat similar to motor vehicle or ship registration. Under land title registration, the appropriate governmental authority issues a certificate to the title holder as evidence of title. Under recording statutes, the *entire record* is an owner's evidence of ownership in the property, not a single document. Under title registration, no liens or encumbrances are effective against any subsequent purchaser until entered on the certificate of title issued by the governmental authority.

Advantages

It is clear that the title registration system avoids the major difficulties inherent in recordation systems. First,

1. All liens and encumbrances will appear on the certificate of the present owner and there is no need to search for such liens.

2. There is no chain of title to be searched, because the purchaser or encumbrancer has the legal right to rely on the registration as evidence of ownership.

3. The fee for searching the title is limited.

Despite these advantages, the system of land title registration has not gained general acceptance.

Disadvantages

In the early part of this century, approximately half the states enacted legislation aimed at implementing title registration. However, many states have since repealed the registration laws, and in those states continuing to permit registration, the use is limited to only a few geographical areas. The major problem with land title registration is the necessity of a lengthy and costly judicial determination of ownership.

Under American Constitutional "due process" requirements, each person having even the remotest possible interest in the property must be joined in the legal proceeding and be served with notice of the pending action. If such a person is not joined or notice is not properly served upon such a party, his/her interest is not foreclosed and any judicial determination is not conclusive against that person. Thus, the legal proceeding involves much preliminary research to select the proper defendants.

In addition, most registration statutes require a survey of the property. At the time and place designated by the court, all parties named in the suit or others having any interest in the property come forward and the court determines ownership and other rights in the property. When the court issues a judgment, it is conclusive as to all parties to the action. Under the typical statute, the court judgment is the basis for the registrar's issuance of a title certificate. Under most statutes, land titles placed into the registration system may not be withdrawn.

In order for a purchaser or encumbrancer to be able to rely on the title registration certificate as evidence of merchantable title in the seller or mortgagor, the certificate must eliminate all reasonable claims of interests to the subject property. If the registration certificate is not conclusive proof that the property is free and clear of all liens and encumbrances except those noted on the certificate, the registration has limited utility. If it is not conclusive, then in order to be assured that the seller has merchantable title, the prospective purchaser or encumbrancer will have to perform a title search, thus eliminating one of the chief advantages of registration over the recordation system.

Exceptions

In some states that permit registration, there are statutory exceptions to the conclusiveness of the title registration certificate. Typical among them are exceptions for short-term leases, current tax liens, public highways, and federal tax liens. Another problem not solved through registration is that it is possible for two adjacent tracts both of which have been registered to have overlapping boundaries. Obviously, the registration certificates cannot both be conclusive proof of complete ownership of their respectively described properties.

Summary

In summary, title registration overcomes several of the major difficulties of the recordation system. However, its initial cost and lack of conclusiveness as to title have limited its attractiveness as an alternative to the recordation systems.

Other Methods of Title Registration

The disadvantages of reliance on recorded information and the complexity and costliness of title registration have been discussed. One alternative method suggested has been the registration of "possessory title." A party in possession of real property under a deed purporting to give him/her fee simple title to property could apply to an established quasi-judicial authority for confirmation of title. Under this system, the owner would only have to present evidence of the boundaries of the property and his/her possession of the property under a deed. The statute permitting this method would establish a ten-year statute of limitations. Such a statute of limitations would be similar to the rule of adverse possession. Before the expiration of the statutory period, any person claiming an interest adverse to "possessory title" of the claimant would be required to institute legal proceedings to eject the party in possession. If no adverse claims were brought during the ten-year period, all claims for adverse parties would be forever barred, and no subsequent purchaser would be required to search the chain of title for proof of the purported owner's fee simple title.

After the ten-year period had run, the party with possessory title or his/her successor in interest could apply to the governmental authority for confirmation of ownership title. Upon proof of his/her continuous possession, title could be confirmed. The costly and complex requirements of a Torrens system of registration would be eliminated, because there would have to be a judicial determination only if a dispute arose between adverse claimants.

Liens, restrictions, easements, and other encumbrances could continue to be entered against property. They would be recorded under a system similar to those in general use, but the indexing would be keyed to tracts rather than alphabetical. The tracts used for indexing purposes would be those presented as "possessory titles" and those titles that were confirmed after the expiration of the ten-year period.

The method of establishment of possessory titles that may ripen into ownership titles overcomes the chief objections to both reliance on recorded data as evidence of ownership and title registration under the Torrens system. However, this general system, which was first suggested by Richard R. Powell, a noted expert in real property, has not found acceptance as an alternative to recordation or registration of titles.

TITLE PROTECTION

Title Insurance

Title insurance is a commonly used device for the protection of a purchaser's or encumbrancer's title or interest in real property. Broadly defined, *title insurance* is an agreement whereby the insurer, for valuable consideration, agrees to indemnify the insured party against a loss sustained because of a defect in the insured's title to or interest in real property. Title insurance was conceived in the mid-nineteenth century in Philadelphia and is in general use throughout the United States. Unlike other forms of insurance such as casualty insurance or life insurance, which insure against future loss, title insurance insures only against events that have happened prior to the execution of the contract. However, like other forms of insurance, it is a contract of indemnity, and the insured will be paid for any loss sustained because of a defect in title to the property existing on the effective date of the policy. The premiums for title insurance coverage are not specifically based on the risks assumed by the insurer, as are other types of insurance, whose premiums are assessed on the likelihood of future loss. Title insurance premiums are set by the amount of coverage obtained by the insured. In most states, title insurance premium rates are either regulated or approved by governmental authority.

The types of title insurance policies available are similar throughout the country. Most title insurance contracts are on standard forms approved by the American Land Title Association and the states within which the insurance company is permitted to do business. Most title policies contain the names of the insurer and insured, the amount of the policy, a description of the real property, and the interest or the estate insured under the contract. The policies contain conditions as to notice of claim, duty to defend, and other procedural matters. The insurance contract will also include a *Schedule B,* which sets forth the specific defects that are not covered by the insurance contract. Schedule B includes all defects or encumbrances, such as easements, unsatisfied liens, restrictive covenants, or leases, that have been revealed through an examination of the title. Usually, Schedule B also includes a broadly worded exception excluding coverage against rights of parties in possession and matters that would be disclosed by physical inspection of the property and an accurate survey of the insured premises. This is sometimes known as the *survey exception.*

There are two common types of title insurance policies: *mortgagee's* or *loan policies,* which insure the interest of the mortgagee against loss, and *owner's policies,* which insure the owner's estate.

Figure 14 shows an example of Schedule A of a title insurance loan policy, and Figure 15 illustrates an owner policy.

Since title insurance insures against past defects in title, the insuring company must have a title search conducted. Often, the insurance company, through a local agent, will search the title, assess the risk, and issue the policy. In other instances, companies may rely on attorneys to

(Continued on page 158)

FIGURE 14   Title Insurance Loan Policy, Schedule A
(Courtesy Commonwealth Land Title Insurance Company)

Issue with Policy No.   SFNM 31074

POLICY OF TITLE INSURANCE
Issued By

COMMONWEALTH/LAND
Title Insurance Company

(a stock company)
PHILADELPHIA, PENNSYLVANIA

POLICY NUMBER
L1378159

SCHEDULE A

Amount of Insurance: $ 65,000.00

File No. Alison County 3511

Premium: $425.00

Date of Policy: Sixteenth   day of   September   , 19 77 , at   3:56   P.M.

1. Name of Insured: First National Bank

2. The estate or interest in the land described in this Schedule and which is encumbered by the insured mortgage is
   Fee Simple   and is at Date of Policy vested in:

   Bruce Brown and Brenda Brown, by deed from Samuel Smith, single, dated September 16, 1977 and recorded in Alison County Deed Book No. 590, page 798.

3. The mortgage, herein referred to as the insured mortgage, and the assignments thereof, if any, are described as follows:

   Mortgage from Bruce Brown and Brenda Brown to the insured dated September 16, 1977 and recorded in Alison County Mortgage Book 339, page 111.

4. The land referred to in this policy is described as set forth in the insured mortgage, is situated in the County of
   Alison   , State of   X   , and is identified
   as follows:

   Lot No. 7, Block 1, Unit II, Tall Timber Estates, as shown upon that plat of survey recorded in Book 19, page 74, records of Alison County.

Countersigned: _____

_____
Authorized Officer or Agent

American Land Title Association Loan Policy - 1970 (Amended 10/17/70)
Form 1006-6 Schedule A

FIGURE 15 Title Insurance Owner Policy
(Courtesy Commonwealth Land Title Insurance Company)

Issue with Policy No. L1378159

POLICY OF TITLE INSURANCE
Issued By

COMMONWEALTH LAND
Title Insurance Company

(a stock company)
PHILADELPHIA, PENNSYLVANIA

POLICY NUMBER
SFNM 31074

SCHEDULE A

Amount of Insurance: $ 83,000.00

File No. Alison County 3511

Premium: $425.00

Date of Policy: Sixteenth   day of September   ,1977 ,at 3:45 P. M.

1. Name of Insured: Brenda Brown and Bruce Brown

2. The estate or interest in the land described herein and which is covered by this policy is Fee Simple
and is at Date of Policy vested in:

The Insured by deed from Samuel Smith, Single, dated September 16, 1977, and recorded September 16, 1977, in Alison County Deed Book No. 590, page 798, records of Alison County.

3. The land referred to in this policy is described in the said instrument is situated in the County of Alison
, State of X , and is identified as
follows: Lot #7, Block 1, Unit II Tall Timber Estates, as shown upon that plot of survey recorded in Book 29, page 74, records of Alison County, State of X.

Countersigned: _____
Authorized Officer or Agent

American Land Title Association Owner Policy – 1970 – Form B (Amended 10-17-70)
Form 1005-6   Schedule A

(Continued)

FIGURE 15—Page 2

COMMONWEALTH LAND TITLE INSURANCE COMPANY

OWNER POLICY OF TITLE INSURANCE

SUBJECT TO THE EXCLUSIONS FROM COVERAGE, THE EXCEPTIONS CONTAINED IN SCHEDULE B AND THE PROVISIONS OF THE CONDITIONS AND STIPULATIONS HEREOF, COMMONWEALTH LAND TITLE INSURANCE COMPANY, a Pennsylvania corporation, herein called the company, insures, as of Date of Policy shown in Schedule A, against loss or damage, not exceeding the amount of insurance stated in Schedule A, and cost, attorneys' fees and expenses which the Company may become obligated to pay hereunder, sustained or incurred by the insured by reason of:

1. Title to the estate or interest described in Schedule A being vested otherwise than as stated therein;
2. Any defect in or lien or encumbrance on such title;
3. Lack of a right of access to and from the land; or
4. Unmarketability of such title.

IN WITNESS WHEREOF, the Commonwealth Land Title Insurance Company has caused its corporate name and seal to be hereunto affixed by its duly authorized officers, the Policy to become valid when Schedule A is countersigned by an authorized officer or agent of the Company.

COMMONWEALTH LAND TITLE INSURANCE COMPANY

Attest: *Edward A Schmidt*
Secretary

By *Fred B Tromhold*
President

EXCLUSIONS FROM COVERAGE

The following matters are expressly excluded from the coverage of this policy:

1. Any law, ordinance or governmental regulation (including but not limited to building and zoning ordinances) restricting or regulating or prohibiting the occupancy, use or enjoyment of the land, or regulating the character, dimensions or location of any improvement now or hereafter erected on the land, or prohibiting a separation in ownership or a reduction in the dimensions or area of the land, or the effect of any violation of any such law, ordinance or governmental regulation.

2. Rights of eminent domain or governmental rights of police power unless notice of the exercise of such rights appears in the public records at Date of Policy.

3. Defects, liens, encumbrances, adverse claims, or other matters (a) created, suffered, assumed or agreed to by the insured claimant; (b) not known to the Company and not shown by the public records but known to the insured claimant either at Date of Policy or at the date such claimant acquired an estate or interest insured by this policy and not disclosed in writing by the insured claimant to the Company prior to the date such insured claimant became an insured hereunder; (c) resulting in no loss or damage to the insured claimant; (d) attaching or created subsequent to Date of Policy; or (e) resulting in loss or damage which would not have been sustained if the insured claimant had paid value for the estate or interest insured by this policy.

American Land Title Association Owner Policy — 1970 — Form B (Amended 10-17-70)
Cover

B 1005 6

(Continued)

FIGURE 15—Page 3

Policy No. SFNM 31074

SCHEDULE B

File No. Alison County 3511

This policy does not insure against loss or damage by reason of the following:

1. Mortgage in the amount of $65,000.00 to First National Bank dated September 16, 1977, and recorded September 16, 1977, in Mortgage Book 339, page 111, records of Alison County.

2. Possible unfiled mechanics' liens and municipal liens.

3. Restrictive covenants upon Tall Timber Estates recorded September 16, 1968, in Misc. Book 22, page 22, records of Alison County.

4. Eight-foot easement for public utilities along the northern boundary of the property.

5. Boundaries, encroachments, deficiencies in quantity of land, unrecorded easements, or any other matter which would be disclosed by a physical inspection and a survey of the premises.

PA 10
American Land Title Association Owner's Policy – 1970 – Form B (Amended 10-17-70)
Form 1005-17 Schedule B

C. L. T. COPY

(Continued)

FIGURE 15—Page 4

CONDITIONS AND STIPULATIONS
(Continued)

7. LIMITATION OF LIABILITY

No claim shall arise or be maintainable under this policy (a) if the Company, after having received notice of an alleged defect, lien or encumbrance insured against hereunder, by litigation or otherwise, removes such defect, lien or encumbrance or establishes the title, as insured, within a reasonable time after receipt of such notice; (b) in the event of litigation until there has been a final determination by a court of competent jurisdiction, and disposition of all appeals therefrom, adverse to the title, as insured, as provided in paragraph 3 hereof; or (c) for liability voluntarily assumed by an insured in settling any claim or suit without prior written consent of the Company.

8. REDUCTION OF LIABILITY

All payments under this policy, except payments made for costs, attorneys' fees and expenses, shall reduce the amount of the insurance pro tanto. No payment shall be made without producing this policy for endorsement of such payment unless the policy be lost or destroyed, in which case proof of such loss or destruction shall be furnished to the satisfaction of the Company.

9. LIABILITY NONCUMULATIVE

It is expressly understood that the amount of insurance under this policy shall be reduced by any amount the Company may pay under any policy insuring either (a) a mortgage shown or referred to in Schedule B hereof which is a lien on the estate or interest covered by this policy, or (b) a mortgage hereafter executed by an insured which is a charge or lien on the estate or interest described or referred to in Schedule A, and the amount so paid shall be deemed a payment under this policy. The Company shall have the option to apply to the payment of any such mortgages any amount that otherwise would be payable hereunder to the insured owner of the estate or interest covered by this policy and the amount so paid shall be deemed a payment under this policy to said insured owner.

10. APPORTIONMENT

If the land described in Schedule A consists of two or more parcels which are not used as a single site, and a loss is established affecting one or more of said parcels but not all, the loss shall be computed and settled on a pro rata basis as if the amount of insurance under this policy was divided pro rata as to the value on Date of Policy of each separate parcel to the whole, exclusive of any improvements made subsequent to Date of Policy, unless a liability or value has otherwise been agreed upon as to each such parcel by the Company and the insured at the time of the issuance of this policy and shown by an express statement herein or by an endorsement attached hereto.

11. SUBROGATION UPON PAYMENT OR SETTLEMENT

Whenever the Company shall have settled a claim under this policy, all right of subrogation shall vest in the Company unaffected by any act of the insured claimant. The Company shall be subrogated to and be entitled to all rights and remedies which such insured claimant would have had against any person or property in respect to such claim had this policy not been issued, and if requested by the Company, such insured claimant shall transfer to the Company all rights and remedies against any person or property necessary in order to perfect such right of subrogation and shall permit the Company to use the name of such insured claimant in any transaction or litigation involving such rights or remedies. If the payment does not cover the loss of such insured claimant, the Company shall be subrogated to such rights and remedies in the proportion which said payment bears to the amount of said loss. If loss should result from any act of such insured claimant, such act shall not void this policy, but the Company, in that event, shall be required to pay only that part of any losses insured against hereunder which shall exceed the amount, if any, lost to the Company by reason of the impairment of the right of subrogation.

12. LIABILITY LIMITED TO THIS POLICY

This instrument together with all endorsements and other instruments, if any, attached hereto by the Company is the entire policy and contract between the insured and the Company.

Any claim of loss or damage, whether or not based on negligence, and which arises out of the status of the title to the estate or interest covered hereby or any action asserting such claim, shall be restricted to the provisions and conditions and stipulations of this policy.

No amendment of or endorsement to this policy can be made except by writing endorsed hereon or attached hereto signed by either the President, a Vice President, the Secretary, an Assistant Secretary, or validating officer or authorized signatory of the Company.

13. NOTICES, WHERE SENT

All notices required to be given the Company and any statement in writing required to be furnished the Company shall be addressed to Commonwealth Land Title Insurance Company, 1510 Walnut Street, Philadelphia, Pennsylvania 19102.

American Land Title Association Owner Policy – 1970 – Form B (Amended 10-17-70)
Cover Page
Form 1005-8

Valid Only If Schedules A and B Are Attached

(Continued from page 152)

conduct the search and report the state of the title to the company for subsequent issuance of a policy. In any case, in order to protect itself, a search of the record must be made by the insuring company or its agent before the policy is issued.

There are four general risks assumed by the insurer, excluding those specifically listed on Schedule B.

1. The company may insure against defects disclosed in the public record. Included in this category are liens and encumbrances such as taxes and restrictions that are either missed or mistakenly excluded from Schedule B.

2. There is the risk of hidden defects not disclosed by the public record. Among the hidden defects covered by the contract of insurance are forgeries of deeds, mortgages, or other instruments in the chain of title; incapacity of grantor or mortgagor; mistaken identity on the record caused by similarity of names; incorrectly filed documents; and misrepresentation of marital status of grantor or mortgagor.

3. The insurance assumes the costs of defending an adverse claim against the insured's title assuming that the attack is not based on a claim specifically excluded in Schedule B. The cost of defending title is borne by the company as part of its contract duty to the insured even if the adverse claim is without merit.

4. The contract of insurance covers mistakes made by the title examiner. The mistake may be the result of failure to properly interpret the information in the record or of negligently overlooking a title defect.

In each of the four risks assumed by the company, the title insurance obtained by a buyer or mortgagee can provide protection that a mere title search cannot.

As part of the insurance contract, the insured has the duty to disclose to the insurance company any defect known to him/her. Failure to disclose such known defects may void the insurance contract.

Under most owner title insurance contracts, coverage continues even after the owner has transferred his ownership interest to another. If a defect for which the insured might have recovered under the policy becomes apparent after the transfer and the insured is sued by the transferee under the warranties of a general warranty deed, the insurance coverage continues. Under these circumstances, the insurance company would defend. Mortgagee or loan policies do not have a life beyond the life of the indebtedness that the mortgage secured. Thus, if the mortgagee is satisfied, the liability of the insurance company terminates. Owner policies are not assignable and benefit only the named insured.

As a general rule, insurance principles of law have been applied by courts for interpretation of title insurance contracts. For example, title insurance contracts are construed most strongly against the insurer, and any ambiguity is resolved in favor of the insured. Under an insurance contract, the limits of loss coverage are established by the policy, and under most circumstances, any excess loss suffered by the insured above the face amount is not recoverable from the insurer. Also, in order for an insured to recover from the insurance company under the indemnity provisions, he/she must actually suffer a monetary loss. For example, if a restrictive covenant is missed by the title examiner and not included in Schedule B, an insured who attempts to build in violation of the covenant cannot recover under the policy unless he/she suffers actual monetary damage.

In many areas, there has been general acceptance of title insurance as an integral part of the real estate transaction. Many lenders require title insurance as part of the mortgage transaction, both as security for their loan and to increase the marketability of mortgages in the secondary mortgage markets. As urban areas develop, the private attorney is no longer in a position to personally conduct or supervise title searches. Instead, attorneys and real estate brokers increasingly rely on title insurance companies to provide title services.

Certificates of Title

In some areas of the United States, title protection is accomplished through a certificate of title issued by an examining attorney or abstract company. A *certificate of title* is not an indemnity contract such as title insurance, but merely a certificate disclosing the state of the title to a certain parcel of real property. (See Figure 16.) Title certificates should not be confused with certificates of title registration issued under the Torrens system.

Before title insurance, the intricacies of land transactions were in the hands of professional conveyancers who prepared documents of transfer and performed title searches. Their opinion as to the merchantability of title was backed by their professional reputation, and persons dealing in real property and even attorneys consulted these conveyancers on land title matters. As times changed, title insurance companies and attorneys gradually supplanted conveyancers in the real property transaction. Today, in many areas where title insurance is not prevalent, the task of examining titles and rendering opinions about the merchantability of such titles is in the hands of attorneys.

In many of these geographical areas, either attorneys or their agents perform title searches and issue written certificates of title based on the records available in the local registry. The title certificate is the personal guarantee of the attorney that the title is merchantable. However, unlike

FIGURE 16   Certificate of Title

Certificate of Title—Published by
The Plankenhorn Co., Williamsport, Pa. 17701

Certificate of Title

To

have examined the title of

in the General Indices to the records in   *County,
Pennsylvania, and in my opinion find the record title good and marketable, and clear of all claims, liens
and encumbrances of record therein, except as hereinafter stated:*

MORTGAGES

Mortgagor.	Mortgagee.	Date.	Recorded.	Amount.

JUDGMENTS

Defendant.	Plaintiff.	Date of Record.	No. and Term.	Amount.

OTHER OBJECTIONS

Require tax receipts be produced for the past four years before making settlement.

*If any new buildings have been constructed or if any renovations, additions or reconstruction on
existing buildings has occurred within the past four months, the Mechanics' Lien Law of 1963 is of concern,
and a release of mechanics' liens must be furnished.*

Inquire as to local ordinances affecting the premises.

*I do not certify to the accuracy of lot lines, nor to the fact that buildings on the property are within
lot lines, nor to the quantity of land.   Purchaser must rely on survey.*

*This certificate is good only to the party addressed, and is issued subject to all rights of persons who
may be in possession of the premises under lease, or title, or claim of title, not of record.*

Taxes and Municipal Claims not filed of record in the Court House are not included.

*Subject of course, to all outstanding equities, easements visible upon the ground and other matters
not appearing of record.*

See reverse side for Remarks.   *Respectfully submitted,*

Dated   19   *By* ....
                                     Attorney-at-Law and Abstractor

title insurance, the title certificate is not a guarantee of indemnity, although an attorney who negligently performs a title search may be liable for damages sustained by the party for whose benefit the certificate was issued and who relied to his/her detriment on the representations made in that certificate. The guarantees of title certificates are limited to matters of record and do not cover "hidden defects" such as those commonly covered by title insurance. Like title insurance, items that would be disclosed by physical inspection of the property and defects that would be revealed through a survey are specifically excluded from coverage.

Most title certificates are specifically limited to matters of record up to the date of the search, and their benefit runs only to the party named in the certificate. Commonly, title certificates are required by lenders who wish to know the state of title of the mortgagor and wish to be assured that their lien will be first on the record to establish priority. When the loan is paid by the mortgagor or when the property is conveyed, the title certificate automatically terminates.

A title certificate is the personal guarantee of the issuing attorney. The certificate is only as good as the attorney's financial responsibility or "errors and omissions" insurance coverage. If the beneficiary of a title certificate should suffer a loss, his/her recourse is against the issuing attorney, and the burden of proving the attorney's negligence is on the certificate holder. In addition, under most certificates of title, the issuing attorney is under no obligation to defend the title of a certificate holder. Therefore, if a spurious claim against the holder's title were made, the issuing attorney would be under no legal obligation to come to the defense of the holder's title. In many areas, title certificates are being replaced by title insurance because of the additional benefits of title insurance.

Abstracts of Title

In some areas of the United States, through general custom and usage, the seller must provide evidence of the merchantability of his/her title. In these areas, the buyer does not bear the expense of having the title search performed. The rule of *caveat emptor* prevails, however, and the buyer must still satisfy him/herself that the title of the seller is merchantable, even though the seller bears the initial burden of providing the evidence. Often, the requirement of providing evidence may be met through a title insurance policy paid for by the seller and issued in the name of the buyer. The seller may also meet the requirement by providing to the buyer an up-to-date abstract of title on the property being transferred.

An *abstract of title* is a complete record of all documents, wills, conveyances, records of judicial proceedings, liens, encumbrances, or any other matters affecting title to real property. It is the product of a title search and includes all matters disclosed by the record. Often, the documents themselves are reproduced in the abstract of title. Sometimes, however, only summaries of the documents are included. Most complete abstracts also include a report of the tax records. Professional abstractor or title agencies who prepare abstracts of title usually issue an accompanying certificate certifying that the abstract of title is complete up to a certain date and time.

The abstract is not a guarantee of title or even an indication that the title is merchantable. It is only a report of the record and a guarantee that the record, as reported, is complete. The seller who orders an abstract of title on the property being sold delivers it to the buyer, who must then interpret the information included in the abstract. Often, the buyer refers the abstract of title to an attorney for an opinion as to the merchantability of the seller's title. The attorney then examines the abstract and issues a formal opinion of title based on the information contained in the abstract. (See Figure 17.) The title opinion is the personal guarantee of the examining attorney, and a buyer who purchases property in reliance on an opinion that is subsequently found to be erroneous has recourse against the attorney.

If the title is merchantable, upon closing of the purchase and sale, the buyer becomes the owner of the abstract of title, which may then be updated or supplemented at the time the property is mortgaged or sold to a subsequent buyer or mortgagee.

The abstract of title system is generally less expensive for the parties after the "base" abstract has been prepared, because the only subsequent expense is in updating the abstract and having a new certificate issued by the abstractor.

Since the abstract of title is only a report of what is disclosed in the public record, it does not cover the "hidden" defects in title or matters that could be discovered by physical inspection of the property. The abstract of title and the opinion issued based on the abstract are only as good as the abstractor and the attorney rendering the opinion, and in the event of loss any guarantee is limited by the financial responsibility of either the attorney or abstractor or their malpractice insurer.

Neither abstractor nor attorney issuing an opinion are obligated to defend title. Buyers generally prefer the guarantees offered by a title insurance policy; however, unless the seller is required by contract to provide a title policy to the buyer, the requirement that the seller furnish evidence of merchantability is met through delivery of an up-to-date abstract of title showing merchantable title in the seller.

The obligations imposed upon a buyer require that the buyer be able

FIGURE 17   Formal Opinion of Title Based on Abstract of Title

Law Offices of

WARING, SMITH & SEAVOR

Alison, State of X

Mr. Joseph P. Gekki
112 Elm Street
Anytown, X

     RE: Formal Title Opinion

Dear Mr. Gekki:

At your direction, I have examined Alison County Abstract Company No. 456839-78 supplemented and certified to and including April 14, 1978, covering the following described real property:

     SE 1/4 Section 2 T2N R73W X Principal Meridian, Alison
     County, State of X

Based upon my examination of the aforementioned abstract of title, it is my opinion that as of April 14, 1978, the owners, Martin S Smith and Matilda S. Smith, joint tenants with rights of survivorship, had merchantable title to the above-described property subject, however, to the following liens and encumbrances:

1. First Deed of Trust in favor of Alison County National Bank dated January 4, 1967 and recorded in Book 269, page 345, Records of Alison County.

2. 25-foot easement along the western boundary in favor of Alison County Ditch and Reservoir Company for maintenance and use of an irrigation ditch dated April 9, 1948, recorded in Misc. Book 294, page 3, Records of Alison County.

3. Easement for public utilities granted to the Alison County Electric Co-op along the northern border of the property, dated November 2, 1957, and recorded in Misc. Book 330, page 789, Records of Alison County.

The deeds within the chain of title make reference to 160 shares in the Alison County Ditch and Reservoir Company, which transfer with the land. The tax certificate appended to the aforementioned abstract of title indicates that all local taxes for the years 1974 through 1977 have been paid in full.

Your attention is specifically directed to the fact that this title opinion is based solely upon the information contained in the aforementioned abstract of title and the examining attorney assumes no liability for errors or omissions committed by the abstrator.

               Sincerely,

               Eleanor H. Seavor

               Eleanor H. Seavor, Esquire

to make an informed decision concerning the merchantability of the seller's title. The satisfactory completion of the buyer's duty requires the assistance of title experts who inspect the public record and interpret the information. Before purchase, each buyer should be well informed as to the condition of title. After purchase, the buyer's title may be protected through title insurance, by a certificate of title issued by an attorney, or through a title opinion based on an abstract of title.

QUESTIONS FOR DISCUSSION

1. Compare the advantages of tract indexing and alphabetical indexing of land title information.

2. If an adverse conveyance search of the chain of title reveals that a grantor conveyed the same property twice, what information must be known before a decision on priority can be made, assuming that the jurisdiction has a race-notice recording statute?

3. The public record cannot provide all the information upon which a prospective purchaser or encumbrancer of real property should rely. What information outside the public record should a purchaser or encumbrancer know before completing the transaction?

4. Recent federal legislation provides for the establishment of model recording and title registration systems. What alternatives are there to the traditional methods of indexing and registering titles that may effectively lower the cost of title examination?

5. Discuss the relative advantages of a purchaser's obtaining title insurance, abstract of title with attorney's title opinion, or title certificate, assuming that their costs are relatively similar.

CASES

Case 1. Owners conveyed unimproved real property to a construction company so that it could obtain a construction loan on the property. By separate contract, the construction company agreed to reconvey the property to the owners. The deed was recorded, but the owners never recorded the contract of reconveyance. The contractor obtained a construction mortgage on the property and defaulted. The mortgagee commenced foreclosure proceedings against the construction company, and the former owners sought to intervene and claim that their interest was superior to that of the mortgagee. What priority is likely to be established by the court, assuming that the jurisdiction had a race-notice recording statute?

Case 2. Under long-term contract, A purchased a tract of land and recorded a memorandum of the contract. During the contract and before final payment, A received knowledge of an unrecorded timber lease and easement on the property when the lessee began timbering the property. The interest of the timber lessee was not visible on the land. Purchaser A brought suit against the seller and the lessee for cancellation of the lease and for damages. The seller and the lessee defended on grounds that the purchase had not been completed and the purchaser's remedy was to cancel the contract and receive back the purchase price. What is the most likely disposition of the purchaser's claim to cancellation of the lease and damages?

Case 3. A purchaser of real property obtained title insurance that listed the standard survey exception in Schedule B of the policy. An adjoining landowner brought suit against the purchaser for an alleged encroachment, and the purchaser called on the title insurance company to defend his title to the property. The title insurance company refused to defend against the claim on grounds that the claim was not insured under the survey exception. The recorded instruments did not reveal the possible conflict. Must the insurer defend against the claim?

Case 4. The owner of a large tract of land was advised by local counsel that some of the tract he thought he owned actually belonged to an adjacent landowner under a double conveyance of the property in the last century. The owner contacted another attorney and requested that he obtain title insurance on the property. The title insurance company did a standard 60-year search, which did not reveal the defect. Subsequently, when the adjacent landowner sought to quiet his title to the property, the owner called on the title insurance company to defend. Must the title insurance company defend title on behalf of the owner-insured? Why or why not?

Chapter 7
Theory of Mortgage Financing

167

Mechanics of Leasehold Mortgage Financing

SUMMARY

QUESTIONS FOR DISCUSSION

CASES

AFTER the buyer and seller have entered into a real estate contract for the purchase and sale of an ownership interest in real property, the buyer's primary obligation is to produce funds at closing to complete the transaction. Sometimes the funds will be available from the buyer's own resources; however, in most cases a major part of the funds will be borrowed. The borrowing of money to complete the purchase creates a new set of legal relationships. Thus, in a typical real estate transaction where the buyer finances the purchase of the property, there are actually two transactions. The first is between the seller and the buyer for the transfer of an ownership right; the second is between the lender and the buyer for the transfer of money.

This chapter and the next deal with the legal relationships created by borrower and lender under various financing arrangements. A complete analysis and explanation of the many forms of financing is more appropriately reserved for a text in real estate finance. In most cases the basic legal relationships are substantially the same no matter what the form of the financing arrangement.

FINANCING THE REAL ESTATE PURCHASE

Among the major sources of real estate loans are savings and loan associations, commercial banks, mortgage companies, insurance companies, pension funds, credit unions, and, in some cases, federal or state governments. Each lender is in the business of placing money with borrowers, making a profit by charging for the use of the money. The charge, usually referred to as *interest*, is generally stated as an annual percentage of the amount of the loan.

169

Factors Considered by Lenders

Since the lending firm is taking a risk in lending money, it will attempt to minimize the chance that the principal will not be repaid and to maximize its potential gain on the investment. Therefore, most lenders will look to one or more of the following factors in deciding whether to lend to a particular borrower:

1. The credit worthiness of the borrower.
2. The value of the property being offered as security or collateral for the loan.
3. The amount of money that the borrower will have invested in the property exclusive of borrowed funds.
4. The priority of the lender's potential security interest in the collateral in relation to other interests in or liens on the property.

Credit Worthiness

The first factor that most lenders consider is the credit worthiness of the borrower. The financial history of the borrower is considered, and great weight is placed upon his/her past record of loan repayment. Net worth and current earning capacity may also be considered indicative of the borrower's financial strength and ability to repay the loan. The data for determining credit worthiness are obtained partly from information supplied by the borrower in the form of a financial statement and partly from other sources such as credit bureaus, independent credit references, and sources provided or suggested by the borrower.

Property Value

The second factor considered is the value of the property offered by the borrower as security or collateral for the repayment of the loan. Under a typical security arrangement, the borrower creates a nonpossessory security interest in the property, naming the lender as the secured party. If the borrower does not repay the loan as it becomes due, the lender has the right to enforce its security interest and have the property sold to satisfy the unpaid balance of the loan. The lender is concerned with the value of the property being placed as collateral because it must look primarily to that value to recover the principal advanced to the borrower under the loan agreement in the event that the borrower defaults. To determine whether the value of the property being placed as security would be sufficient to ensure recovery of the loan plus costs of collection, the lender may hire an appraiser to render an opinion as to the value of the security. The appraisal report is an important element of the loan decision.

Ratio of Loan to Appraised Value

A third factor considered by lenders is the loan-to-appraised-value ratio. This ratio is established by dividing the amount of the loan by the appraised value of the security interest. Since the lender must look to the property placed as security for its remedy in the event of the borrower's default, the greater the value of the security in comparison to the amount loaned, the less the lender's risk. For example, if the property being used as security is appraised at $40,000, it is unlikely that the lender will lend $40,000 to the borrower. If it lends, say, 70 percent of the appraised value of the security, or $28,000, the lender will be more certain that its money will be recovered if it has to resort to a sale of the security.

If the loan is being used to finance the purchase of real property, and the security is to be the property being purchased, the difference between the amount the lender will lend and the total purchase price represents the buyer-borrower's down payment. Thus, if the buyer-borrower is purchasing the property for an amount equal to its appraised value and a lender will lend 80 percent of the appraised value of the property, the down payment will be 20 percent of the purchase price.

Priority of Lender's Interest

The lender generally wants to be assured that title to the property being placed as security by the borrower is merchantable and that the security interest created for its benefit is superior to any other current or potential interest in the property. If the lender is forced to resort to a sale of the property to recover the money advanced to the borrower, the property will have greater value at sale if the title is merchantable.

In addition, the lender's rights to sell the property depend on its having a superior or prior security interest or lien on the property. Unless the lender has a first lien it does not automatically have the right to sell the property to satisfy the borrower's debt. The lender may therefore require a policy of title insurance, an attorney's certificate, or an abstract of title showing that the borrower has merchantable title and that the lender has a first or prior lien upon the property.

Loan Repayment

There are many loan repayment arrangements that may be made between a lender and borrower. During the last forty years, the *direct reduction* or *amortized* loan has become accepted as the basis for most real estate financing. The name describes the method by which the interest charges and the principal are paid to the lender.

Under a direct reduction or amortized loan arrangement, the borrower pays a fixed amount at monthly, quarterly, or annual intervals over a fixed term, which may be as long as thirty years. Interest is charged on the unpaid principal balance, and each payment is allocated between interest charges and repayment of principal. The principal is thus directly reduced or amortized over the entire life of the loan.

In the early part of the repayment term, the bulk of each payment is applied to interest, with a smaller portion being applied to repayment of principal. However, since each reduction in principal proportionately reduces the interest charges for the succeeding payment and each payment is the same amount, a proportionately larger amount of the payment is applied to principal each time.

One common form of financing is through use of a mortgage. A *mortgage* is a commercial transaction that establishes an obligor-obligee relationship and creates a nonpossessory security interest in real property. There are two parties to the mortgage, the *borrower,* who is the *obligor-mortgagor,* and the *lender,* who is the *obligee-mortgagee.* The general rule is that any person or entity with contractual capacity can be either mortgagor or mortgagee.

HISTORY OF MORTGAGE FINANCING

Mortgage financing has its roots deep in English common law. Mortgages were used as early as the twelfth century as a money-lending device. During the term of the loan, the lender was entitled to possession of the real property encumbered by the mortgage and also entitled to the rents and profits from that property. Under the original mortgage concept, the borrower-mortgagor made a conveyance of an ownership interest in the property to the lender-mortgagee. It was the passage of an ownership interest or "title" that gave the mortgagee the right to possession of the security during the term of the mortgage.

The mortgage usually would contain the express or implied condition that upon payment of the underlying debt the title or ownership interest would revert to the borrower-mortgagor, who could then reenter and retake possession of the property. If the debt was not paid when due, the borrower-mortgagor would forfeit the right to reenter and retake ownership and possession from the lender-mortgagee. This form of financing was generally not favored by debtors because they would lose possession of the real property put up as security as well as the opportunity of receiving income that could be produced through use of the property.

Under pressure from debtors, by the middle of the seventeenth century the relationship between mortgagor and mortgagee was adjusted to give the mortgagor the right to possession during the term of the mortgage even though title was held by the lender-mortgagee. However, the repayment terms of the underlying debt or obligation were strictly enforced. Any deviation meant forfeiture of the mortgagor's right of ownership of the property. This rule of strict construction of the terms of the mortgage repayment led to many harsh results and the subsequent development of the mortgagor's *right of redemption.* Under the right of redemption, sometimes called *equity of redemption,* the defaulting mortgagor could get his/her land back upon payment of the entire amount due the mortgagee even after the mortgagee had had the property sold to a third party to satisfy the debt. This worked a hardship on the mortgagee, who had to look to the mortgaged real property for repayment of the original debt. Naturally, real property was difficult to sell to a third party at a foreclosure sale if it was subject to a right of redemption in the original mortgagor, who could come forward at a time subsequent to the sale and redeem the property.

Much of the early theory of mortgage financing has been carried forward to the present day. For example, some states still recognize that there is a shift in the title of the real property used as security from the borrower-mortgagor to the lender-mortgagee. These states are *title theory* states as opposed to *lien theory* states, which do not recognize a transfer of title. In a lien theory state, the interest created in the mortgagee is security for repayment of the loan; the mortgage merely creates a charge on the property that is not released until the underlying obligation is satisfied. However, in modern practice the difference between title theory and lien theory states is more theoretical than real. Under each theory the possession of the property remains in the mortgagor, and the mortgagee has a legally enforceable right to have the property sold at a foreclosure sale if the mortgagor defaults upon his/her obligations.

The equity or right of redemption is still part of the mortgage law in many states. In states where the right of redemption is recognized, a foreclosed mortgagor still has the right to cure a default and regain ownership of property even after a third party has purchased the property at a public sale. The statutory period of redemption may vary from state to state. Also unchanged are the formal requirements for proper execution of a mortgage document.

REQUIREMENTS OF THE MORTGAGE TRANSACTION

The mortgage transaction is basically a commercial transaction. The lender lends money to the borrower in exchange for (1) the borrower's promise to repay the loan as it becomes due and (2) creation in the lender of a nonpossessory security interest that secures performance of the borrower's repayment obligation.

Mortgage financing where the lender looks solely to the credit of the borrower for repayment is called *conventional mortgage financing*. Creation of the legal relationship that will accomplish the transaction requires (1) a promissory note or bond from the mortgagor to the mortgagee and (2) the mortgage document, which creates the nonpossessory interest in favor of the mortgagee. Upon closing the loan, the lender pays the loan proceeds to the buyer-borrower, who then pays those loan proceeds together with the down payment to the seller to complete the purchase. The seller receives the purchase price, the buyer receives the ownership interest in the property, and the mortgage lender receives the bond and mortgage document. (See Figure 18.)

Promissory Note

The *promissory note* is the borrower's promise to pay the lender the money as it becomes due. In some jurisdictions, the promise to pay is called a *bond*. There is no practical difference between a bond and a promissory note.

FIGURE 18   Conveyances Under a Conventional Mortgage

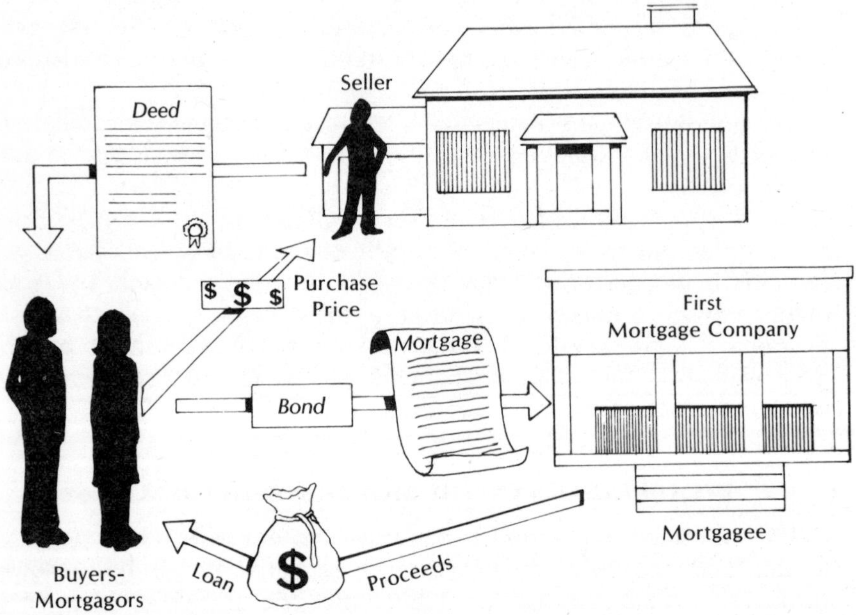

Although not technically required under mortgage law, to be enforceable as a negotiable instrument most notes or bonds must meet the requirements set forth under the Uniform Commercial Code that the instrument (1) be in writing, (2) contain an unconditional promise to pay to a person's order a certain sum in money on demand or at a definite time, and (3) be signed by the maker. In addition to these required elements, most promissory notes and bonds used in real estate mortgage transactions also contain other terms such as provisions for additional charges if a payment is late, default procedures, additional advances, and the mortgagee's right to accelerate the due date in the event of default. The promissory note or bond is signed by the mortgagor and is not signed by the mortgagee.

Mortgage Document

The *mortgage document* is the instrument that creates the nonpossessory security interest in the mortgagee. Like the promissory note, it must be in writing and signed by the mortgagor in order to be enforceable. The mortgage document in a title theory state theoretically transfers title to the property to the mortgagee. However, the "title" transferred does not permit the mortgagee to have possession; it is only for security. The language of conveyance in the mortgage is conditional, so that upon completion of the mortgagor's obligations the conveyance is null and void and title reverts to the mortgagor. In a lien theory state there is no conveyance of title, merely the creation of the nonpossessory security interest. In both title theory and lien theory states, the result is the same.

The mortgage must be in writing to comply with the Statute of Frauds. Most states have a statutory form of mortgage document that sets forth the minimum requirements of a valid mortgage. Such states generally require that the mortgage be properly executed and be delivered to and accepted by the mortgagee. The required contents of the mortgage document will vary among jurisdictions. However, the mortgage should contain the names of the mortgagor and mortgagee, an express intention to create a mortgage relationship between the parties, a description of the property to be encumbered by the mortgage, and the signature of the mortgagor. The mortgagee's signature is not usually required. An example of a mortgage document appears in Figure 19.

Some states require that the underlying obligation for which the mortgage is being given as security be included or summarized in the mortgage instrument so that the obligation being secured can be clearly identified. In addition, the parties may include other covenants and conditions that bind the mortgagor. These additional conditions cannot conflict with applicable law or public policy.

FIGURE 19   A Typical Mortgage Document

<u>REAL ESTATE MORTGAGE</u>

BRENDA BROWN and BRUCE BROWN, for consideration paid, grant to FIRST NATIONAL BANK the hereinafter described real estate in Newtown, Alison County, State of X, being Lot #7, Block 1, Unit II, Tall Timber Estates, as shown on that plot of survey recorded in Book 19, page 74, records of Alison County.

This mortgage secures the performance of the following obligations:

1.   A certain Promissory Note in the face amount of $65,000.00, executed by mortgagors to the mortgagee, dated the 25th day of January, 1978, payable in monthly installments with interest at the rate of 8 1/2% per annum, with collection provision.

This mortgage is upon the statutory mortgage condition for the breach of which is subject to foreclosure as provided by law.   The amount specified for insurance as provided in the statutory mortgage condition is $50,000.00, and the hazard to be insured against is fire with extended coverage, relating to all improvements on the mortgaged property.

In addition to the statutory mortgage condition, it is expressly agreed between the parties as follows:

1.   In the case of foreclosure of this mortgage, the mortgagor shall be obligated to pay all costs and expenses incidental to the foreclosure proceedings, including reasonable attorneys' fees and abstract charges, and all of such costs and expenses shall be deemed to be additional indebtedness secured.

2.   In any action for the foreclosure of this mortgage, the mortgagee shall, upon its request, be entitled as a matter of right, without bond, and without notice to the mortgagor, to have a receiver appointed by the Court with full power and authority to take immediate possession of the mortgaged premises and collect the rents, issues, and profits thereof; and the proceeds thereof, less costs and expenses of receivership, shall be treated as additional security under this mortgage.

3.   The parties agree that the statutory period for redemption after sale of this property shall be reduced to one (1) month.

4.   It is expressly agreed that this mortgage secures the foregoing indebtedness without reference to who may be the actual holder of said indebtedness after it has been initially incurred.

WITNESS our signatures this _____ day of _____, 1978.

_____
Brenda Brown

_____
Bruce Brown

STATE OF X
COUNTY OF ALISON
     The foregoing instrument was acknowledged before me this _____ day of
_____, 1978.

_____
Notary Public

Among the more common mortgage covenants and conditions that bind the mortgagor are the following:

1. Payment of the underlying debt or obligation as it becomes due.
2. Payment of real estate taxes assessed against the property.
3. Maintenance of fire and extended coverage insurance on the property, with mortgagee named as loss payable beneficiary of such insurance.
4. Protection of the real property and improvements from deterioration or impairment of the security.
5. Reduction of the time within which the mortgagor may redeem foreclosed property (statutory redemption period).
6. Compliance with default procedures.
7. Prohibition against transfer or assignment of the mortgage.

One common mortgage condition is the *prepayment privilege*. This is the right of the mortgagor to pay all or any part of the remaining balance of the loan before the end of the term. A morgagor with a loan at a high rate of interest might seek to prepay the balance of the loan if financing could be obtained from another lender at a lower rate of interest. To deter a prepayment by the mortgagor, some mortgagees have required a prepayment penalty that either limits the right of the mortgagor to prepay the loan or assesses a monetary penalty on the mortgagor for such prepayment. In some jurisdictions prepayment is not permitted unless the right is specifically granted in the mortgage document or the consent of the mortgagee is first obtained. The rationale in upholding prepayment penalties is that the mortgagee has bargained for interest over the entire term of the loan and cannot be forced to accept less interest than was originally bargained for. In some jurisdictions, the prepayment privilege is presumed unless restricted in the mortgage. Still other states permit prepayment penalties except in mortgages on owner-occupied residential property.

The rules regulating prepayment of mortgage loans vary from state to state and are often complex. Many problems can be avoided by both mortgagor and mortgagee if the applicable laws are clearly understood at the time the loan is made and the mortgage given.

PRIORITY OF MORTGAGES

A nonpossessory security interest in real property is not usually discoverable through a physical inspection of the property. To give notice to third parties of the existence of the mortgage lien, the mortgagee should have the mortgage document recorded with the appropriate public registry. It is a general rule of law that unless the mortgage document or other evidence of the mortgage is part of the public record, the mortgagee's nonpossessory interest may be subordinate to other interests. Thus, if the mortgage is not in the record and the mortgagor-owner sells his/her interest to another who has no notice of the mortgagee's nonpossessory security interest in the property, the new owner takes title free and clear of the mortgage.

The same property may be subject to more than one nonpossessory security interest. A succession of mortgages may be created intentionally as a specific financing device. If two or more mortgages exist on the same property, the first mortgage to record usually has first priority on the property. That is, if the security is subsequently sold at a foreclosure sale, the proceeds will first be applied toward the satisfaction of the first mortgage obligation. However, there are exceptions. In each jurisdiction the recording statute and lien priority laws will control.

Often an owner's interest in real property will have a greater value than the liens and encumbrances against it. The difference between the value of the real property and the liens and encumbrances against it is the *owner's equity*. Because owner's equity represents value, a mortgagee might accept that equity as security for a loan.

An owner who wishes to obtain a loan but does not wish to satisfy an existing mortgage because it was given at a time of more favorable interest rates on mortgage loans may be able to use his/her owner's equity as security for a second loan, using the same property as collateral. A mortgage created in this way is called a *second mortgage*, because it stands second in priority to the original mortgage.

For example, A owns real property with a fair market value of $100,000. His ownership right is subject to a mortgage in favor of M Mortgage Company in the current amount of $30,000, and thus his equity in the property is $70,000. If A wishes to borrow $20,000, he has two options: (1) to refinance the entire property, giving a new mortgage for a loan of $50,000 and paying off the existing $30,000 mortgage to M Mortgage Company or (2) to borrow $20,000 against a second mortgage with his equity as security.

A loan cannot be obtained at as favorable a rate on a second mortgage as on a new first mortgage because the holder of the second mortgage faces a greater risk in case of default. Assuming that both mortgages are recorded in their proper sequence and there are no intervening liens, the second mortgage is subject to the first. If the mortgagor defaults on both mortgages, the first mortgage has priority in any suit to enforce the lien. The second mortgagee must join the suit of the first mortgagee and will have second priority in the proceeds realized in the event of a foreclosure sale.

Second mortgages are common; however, not all lending institutions are permitted by law or regulation to lend on a second mortgage. There is no legal limit on the number of mortgages that may be placed on an interest in real property, but there is a practical limit. Lenders will usually hesitate to accept a real property interest as security if the loan amount exceeds the borrower's equity in the property.

DEBT COLLECTION AND MORTGAGE FORECLOSURE

If the borrower-mortgagor defaults on payment obligations, the lender-mortgagee has two primary remedies: enforced collection of the mortgagor's promise to pay and foreclosure.

Suit on Promissory Note or Bond

The mortgagee may bring suit to enforce payment of the amount due on the promissory note or bond. Under this remedy, the mortgagee holder is said to be *proceeding upon* the note. The terms and conditions of the note itself will determine the specific rights of the mortgage holder, and the procedural rules of court will determine the remedy or method of collection.

The issues in such a lawsuit will be the amount that is due the holder and any defenses to payment that may be asserted by the mortgagor-maker of the note. The result of the lawsuit will be a court judgment to the effect either that there is an amount due and owing the mortgagee-holder or that the mortgagor-maker of the note has a complete defense to payment. If the judgment is favorable, the mortgagee may proceed to enforce judgment against the mortgagor by executing or levying upon the mortgagor's other property. Specific procedures for suing upon the note vary widely among jurisdictions. Local law must be consulted.

Mortgage Foreclosure

If the mortgagee defaults on payment obligations or fails or refuses to perform any other material covenant or condition in the mortgage document, the mortgagee may proceed with a *mortgage foreclosure*. The mortgage document itself will specify the mortgagee's rights in the event of default, and the procedural rules of the jurisdiction where the property is located will determine how that right may be exercised.

The laws regulating mortgage foreclosure vary widely among jurisdictions. However, each jurisdiction requires a court proceeding in which the mortgagee seeks to have its nonpossessory security interest enforced and the property sold through an order of court to satisfy the balance of principal and interest due and to reimburse the mortgagee for the costs and expenses of collection and foreclosure. The mortgagee proceeds with a foreclosure action, setting forth facts surrounding the mortgagor's default. In each case, it is an adversary proceeding where both parties have certain rights. The mortgagor may impose any viable defenses to the foreclosure action and has all the "due process" guarantees of notice and the opportunity to be heard, to present evidence, and to cross-examine witnesses. After hearing the facts and applying local law, the court will enter a judgment either for or against the mortgagee. In some states, the mortgagor has the right to cure the default up to the time of judgment.

If judgment is entered for the mortgagee, it may follow the appropriate procedures to have the property sold. In some jurisdictions, the sale is conducted by a court-appointed receiver; in others, the sheriff or another public official conducts the sale. The mortgagee's primary right is to have the property sold to satisfy the debt. If the mortgagee wishes to acquire the property itself, it must reserve the right to bid at the public sale. In some jurisdictions, the foreclosed mortgagor has the right of redemption and may come forward within a specified time and redeem the property by paying the successful bidder the purchase price plus all costs and expenses borne by the mortgagee.

If the proceeds of the sale are not sufficient to satisfy the outstanding indebtedness plus costs and expenses of the foreclosure action, the mortgagee may be entitled to a deficiency judgment. A *deficiency judgment* is a personal money judgment against the mortgagor for the balance of the debt, costs, and expenses not received through sale of the security. Some states do not permit a deficiency judgment, and in such jurisdictions the mortgagee must look only to the sale of the security for the satisfaction of the debt of a defaulting mortgagor.

PURCHASE MONEY MORTGAGES

There may be mortgage financing without resort to a third-party mortgage lender, with the seller acting as lender-mortgagee for the transaction. This arrangement is called a *purchase money mortgage*. Under a purchase money mortgage, the seller conveys the ownership interest to the buyer and as part payment of the purchase price takes back from the buyer a promissory note or bond secured by a mortgage on the property. (See Figure 20.) Usually, the seller requires that the buyer make a down payment so that the promissory note or bond secured by the nonpossessory interest is less than the fair value of the property. The greater the down payment, the greater the security for

FIGURE 20   Conveyances Under a Purchase Money Mortgage

Down Payment

Bond

Mortgage

Deed

Seller-
Mortgagee

Buyer-
Mortgagor

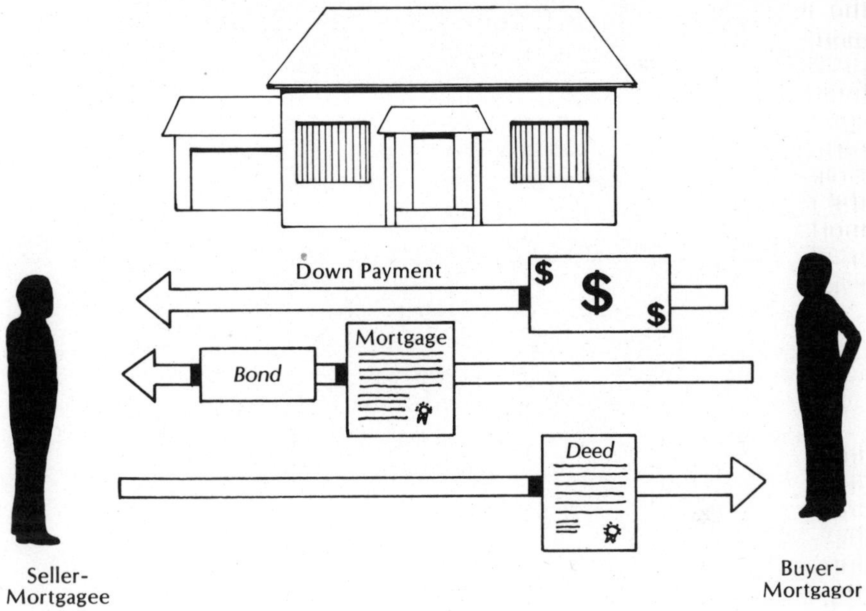

the seller if there is a default and the seller must resort to a foreclosure proceeding to receive the balance of the original purchase price.

The terms and conditions of the bond or note and mortgage document in a purchase money mortgage are a matter of agreement between the parties. Generally, the terms are similar to those used by mortgage lenders.

There is no legal difference between a conventional mortgage and purchase money mortgage, and all procedures for recording, default, and foreclosure are identical. The only difference between the two forms of financing is that with a purchase money mortgage the purchase price is being financed by the seller rather than by a third-party mortgage lender.

Purchase money mortgages are in general use throughout the United States. They may be used when the buyer does not qualify for conventional financing from a mortgage lender or when mortgage funds from such lenders are not available during times of "tight money." They may also be used when the seller does not wish to receive the proceeds of the sale all at one time but wishes to receive the purchase price plus interest over a longer term. Purchase money mortgages are very flexible and may be tailored by the parties to fit their respective interests.

OTHER TYPES OF MORTGAGES

Other mortgage loan arrangements are also in general use throughout the United States. Some introduce a third party into the mortgage transaction, often to guarantee or insure the mortgagor's repayment of the loan. Chief examples of these arrangements are the FHA-insured mortgage loan and the VA-guaranteed loan.

The third party need not always be a guarantor or insurer. Sometimes the third party is another mortgagee; for example, in a *wraparound mortgage* the lender assumes payment of an existing mortgage and provides the mortgagee with a new loan, usually at a higher rate of interest. The new loan is in the amount of the old loan plus an additional amount. The mortgagor makes payments to the new mortgagee, who in turn applies a portion of the payment to the existing loan. The wraparound mortgage is distinguished from a second mortgage because the new mortgagee makes payment to the original mortgagee and the mortgagor pays only the new mortgagee. Wraparound mortgages are used as refinancing devices and are common where the original mortgage cannot be prepaid.

MORTGAGE OF LEASEHOLD INTERESTS

Although most mortgage financing arrangements utilize an ownership interest in real property as security for repayment of the mortgage loan, it is possible to grant a nonpossessory security interest in a possessory interest in real property. Because the possessor of real property usually has the right to receive the rents and profits from its use, a possessory interest or leasehold in real estate may have value. The actual value to the holder of the possessory interest may depend on a number of factors. Among the factors that determine the value of the leasehold are the length of the term of the lease, the use of the leased premises, and the overall real estate market conditions in the geographical area in which the leasehold premises are situated.

If the leasehold is for property in a location where the market forces of supply and demand enhance the desirability of the land for development, then a long-term right to exclusive dominion and control over such land may have considerable value. It is this value that may make a leasehold an appropriate subject for mortgage collateral to finance improvements to the leased real property. Leasehold mortgages are commonly used to finance construction of large office and commercial buildings and on rare occasions to finance residential construction.

Parties to Leasehold Mortgage Financing

The leasehold mortgage usually involves three separate parties: (1) the lessor or owner of the leased premises that are the collateral for the mortgage loan; (2) the lessee or mortgagor, who wishes to construct improvements on the land and places his/her leasehold interest in the leased premises as security for repayment of the mortgage loan; and (3) the mortgagee, who is lending money to the lessee-mortgagor in exchange for the lessee-mortgagor's promise to repay the debt as it becomes due. The mortgagee receives the benefit of the leased premises as collateral to secure the repayment of the mortgage loan.

The advantages to the owner-lessor include the receipt of ground rental on the property over the term of the lease without having to relinquish ownership of the property or perform any affirmative duties to the lessee. At the end of the lease term, the land, together with the improvements made by the lessee, are returned to the owner. Tenants also may have certain advantages in a leasehold mortgage. For example, they may deduct certain costs and expenses, including rental payments, and depreciate the improvements for income tax purposes. They may conserve capital by not being required to purchase the land upon which the improvements are to be made.

Lease Agreement

The lease that is the subject matter of the leasehold mortgage usually is a lease covering unimproved real property. This type of lease, sometimes referred to as a *ground lease,* usually specifies a base rental and payment by the lessee of all charges such as taxes, insurance, and other assessments so that the lessor receives a net rental and does not have to perform any duties for the benefit of the lessee other than give possession of the premises. In order for a lease to be considered as collateral for a mortgage, it must be one that the leasehold mortgagee feels confident will remain in existence throughout the term of the mortgage. In addition, the leasehold mortgagee must be able to "sell" the leasehold to another at a foreclosure sale to recover the unpaid balance of the mortgage should the leasehold mortgagor default. If either of these prerequisites is not met, the lease would probably not be acceptable to a mortgagee as collateral for a loan.

In the event of default, the interest of the mortgagee might be subject to certain rights in the lessor-owner of the fee interest in the property. By statute, many states accord lessors certain rights in the collection of past-due rent from a defaulting lessee, including a priority lien on the property. To avoid a possible conflict with the owner-lessor in the event of default, the mortgagee might request the owner of the underlying fee simple estate to agree in advance to permit the mortgagee to exercise its rights and remedies ahead of any rights that the owner-lessor might have if the mortgagor-lessee defaults in payments of rental. Such an agreement is called *subordination,* whereby the holder of a prior interest agrees in advance to relinquish his/her priority in favor of another. If the holder of the ownership interest subordinates his/her interest to the mortgagee, then the mortgagee has first lien on the property and may have the property foreclosed upon and sold if the mortgagor defaults. The practice of the lessor's subordination is common, and the lessee's right to obtain the lessor's agreement to subordinate is usually a provision of the lease agreement when mortgage financing is anticipated by the lease.

In most cases involving leasehold mortgages, the lease is for a long period of time, with the owner having recourse against the lessee only for nonpayment of rent. In effect, the lessee has a "fee simple" interest in the real property that will terminate only upon nonpayment of rental or upon the expiration of the lease term. The term for such leases varies, but leases for ninety-nine years are not uncommon. Upon termination of the lease, the buildings or improvements on the leased premises revert to the lessor under the law of fixtures.

Mechanics of Leasehold Mortgage Financing

The lender's decision on whether to grant the mortgage loan will usually be based on the credit worthiness of the lessee-mortgagor as well as the value of the leasehold as collateral to secure repayment of the proposed loan. If the mortgagee and mortgagor come to terms on a leasehold mortgage, the actual mechanics of consummating the transaction are similar to those employed in conventional mortgage financing. Instead of pledging an ownership interest as security for repayment, the mortgagor pledges a leasehold interest. Both a bond or promissory note and mortgage document are used to secure the mortgagee's nonpossessory interest in the leasehold. Of course, in a leasehold mortgage there must also be a lease that creates the leasehold interest of the mortgagor. The leasehold mortgage is placed on record to protect the mortgagee's interest against subsequent purchasers or encumbrances, and, as a general rule, leasehold mortgages are foreclosed in the same manner as conventional mortgages.

SUMMARY

Mortgage financing represents a major force in financing the purchase and construction of real property. Through mortgage financing, money is lent by a mortgagee to a mortgagor, who gives a promise to pay in the form of a promissory note or bond and creates a nonpossessory security interest in real property for the benefit of the mortgagee. Each party receives a benefit. The mortgagor has the present right to enjoyment of the real property while he/she is repaying the loan on a regular long-term basis. The mortagee (lender) receives a charge for the money in the form of interest, and its investment is protected from loss through the nonpossessory security interest. Mortgage financing has made the owner-occupant single-family residence an achievable reality for most American families.

QUESTIONS FOR DISCUSSION

1. In some states, statutes prohibit the mortgagee of residential real property from obtaining a deficiency judgment against the mortgagor if the mortgage is foreclosed. What effect, if any, will such statutes have on the factors considered by the mortgagee in deciding whether to make the mortgage loan? What effect do such statutes have on the transferability of real property subject to the mortgage?

2. Is there any such policy basis for the fictional transfer of title from mortgagor to mortgagee in "title theory" states? Why or why not?

3. When might it be desirable for a seller to finance the borrower's purchase of real property through a purchase money mortgage?

4. Why is it essential that the mortgage document contain an accurate legal description of the mortgaged premises?

5. Many mortgages prohibit the assignment of the mortgage to a third party. What is the purpose of such limitations on the assignability of the mortgage? Under what circumstances might it be desirable for a mortgagor to be able to assign the mortgage to a buyer of the real property?

CASES

Case 1. Most mortgages require the mortgagor to carry insurance for the benefit of both the mortgagor and mortgagee "as their interests may appear." Defendant's mortgage provided that he was obligated to insure the premises, which he did. A large portion of the improvements on the premises was destroyed by fire. Defendant continued to make payments on the mortgage and received the total proceeds of the insurance settlement. Plaintiff brought suit against Defendant for a portion of the insurance proceeds. Who should win the lawsuit? Why?

Case 2. In order to protect their security, most mortgagees provide in their mortgages that the mortgagor cannot remove or demolish buildings or other improvements without the prior consent of the mortgagee. Mortgagor's property was subject to extensive damage from vandals. The mortgagor took no affirmative action against the vandals nor did he move to protect the property from the acts of third parties. The mortgagee brought a foreclosure action against the mortgagor under the clause of the mortgage that prohibited the mortgagor from removing or demolishing the improvements without the prior consent of the mortgagee. Should the foreclosure be allowed? Why or why not?

Case 3. Mortgagor entered into a mortgage that was silent as to his right to pay the debt before it was due. The jurisdiction did not have a statute dealing with a mortgagor's right to prepay. When Mortgagee refused to accept the remaining balance of principal and accrued interest, Mortgagor brought suit against the firm to compel it to accept the prepayment. Must the mortgagee be required to accept the prepayment? What arguments can be made on behalf of Mortgagor and Mortgagee?

Case 4. The holder of a first mortgage brought a foreclosure action against a defaulting mortgagor. The foreclosure sale was ordered, and the sale was made. The second mortgagee of the property objected to the sale on the grounds that the mortgagors had not been given proper notice of the pendency of the foreclosure sale, in violation of the Constitutional requirements of due process. In fact, the mortgagors had not received proper notice under the applicable statute but had not raised any objection themselves. Should the sale be set aside? Why, or why not?

Case 5. Defendant Mortgagor failed to pay property taxes on the mortgaged premises, in violation of the mortgage condition that such taxes be paid when due. Under the terms of the mortgage, Mortgagee informed Mortgagor that it was about to institute foreclosure proceedings. While the papers were being prepared by attorneys for the mortgagee, Mortgagor offered to pay the taxes and cure the default. Mortgagee refused, the taxes were not paid, and foreclosure proceedings were begun. The court entered judgment for the mortgagee and ordered the property sold. Defendant-Mortgagor appealed the decision of the trial court, arguing that his offer to pay the taxes should have prevented the sale. On appeal, what is the likely result? Why?

Chapter 8
Other Real Estate Financing Devices

Joint Ventures

Corporations

Real Estate Investment Trusts

Summary

QUESTIONS FOR DISCUSSION

CASES

MORTGAGE financing constitutes a large percentage of all real estate financing transactions, especially in the residential market. However, there are many instances when conventional mortgages are either not available to the parties to a transaction or not appropriate to achieve the desired result. This chapter deals with devices other than mortgages that can be used in financing a real estate transaction.

INSTALLMENT REAL ESTATE CONTRACTS

Theory of Installment Purchase and Sale

An *installment real estate contract* is a promissory agreement between two parties for the purchase and sale of an ownership interest in real estate on an installment or deferred basis. Installment real estate contracts are sometimes referred to as *real estate contracts, articles of agreement,* or *agreements of purchase and sale.* The installment real estate contract should not be confused with the initial agreement or contract between buyer and seller discussed in Chapter 5. The initial agreement sets forth the basic understanding and terms of the contract between the buyer and seller and is generally not used as a financing device. The initial agreement typically requires the buyer to pay the purchase price in cash at closing.

Terms of Installment Real Estate Contracts

The chief characteristic of the installment real estate contract is that the parties' rights are a matter of bargain between them; they may agree on any terms as long as neither law nor public policy is violated. Even though the terms may vary from contract to contract, certain basic terms are usually included.

The essential element of the installment contract is that the seller agrees to sell the ownership interest and the buyer agrees to purchase and pay for that interest over a period of time. Usually, the buyer is required to pay a sum of money at a specific time as a down payment to be applied toward the bargained-for purchase price. The balance of the purchase price plus interest on the unpaid balance is paid from buyer to seller at regular intervals until the purchase price is paid in full. Payments may be made monthly, quarterly, or annually as agreed upon by the buyer and seller.

Upon payment of the down payment, the contract usually provides that the buyer may take possession of the real property and may hold possession during the term of the contract as long as the payments are made and all other material conditions and covenants of the contract are kept by the buyer. The buyer has the right to receive the rents and profits from the real property and, during the term of the contract, enjoys most of the attributes of an owner of the property. Typically, the contract also places certain duties on the buyer incident to possession and control of the property. One such duty commonly imposed is the payment of taxes assessed against the property. Also, if the real property is improved, the seller may require that the buyer insure the improvements for fire under an extended coverage insurance policy, naming the seller as a loss-payable beneficiary of the policy.

Under the contract, the seller also has certain obligations. The seller's chief duty is to convey the property to the buyer by deed upon full payment of the purchase. Usually, the buyer requires that the title conveyed be merchantable title, free and clear of liens and encumbrances. The seller also has the duty to permit the buyer to take possession of the property upon payment of the down payment. Often this latter duty is not expressed in the contract between the parties but is implied at law.

Title to Property under an Installment Contract

Even though the buyer usually has the exclusive right to possession of the real property during the term of the contract, the title or ownership interest remains in the seller until delivery of the instrument of conveyance. Under the typical installment real estate contract, the buyer is not entitled to receive a deed to the real property until final payment is made. Thus, even though the buyer has all of the incidents of ownership such as possession and control and is liable for the duties of ownership such as payment of taxes, he/she is not the legal owner until receipt of the deed.

Protecting the Purchaser's Interest

The fact that the seller has legal title to the property until final payment poses some potential problems for the buyer under an installment real estate contract. First, if the buyer does not take physical possession of the real property, another buyer would not be put on notice of prior interest in the property by physical inspection of the property. In addition, an inspection of the public records would reveal that legal title to the property was still in the original seller. Furthermore, if that second buyer were to purchase the property from the seller and record the deed, the installment buyer's interest would be subordinate to the second buyer's title to the property. This potential problem may be overcome by the installment purchaser placing the contract or a memorandum of contract in the public record.

The presence of the contract in the public record serves as notice to potential third-party purchasers of the buyer's contractual interest in the property. The recording of the contract will also protect the installment purchaser from the seller's being able to mortgage the property during the contract period. Any mortgage or other lien or encumbrance ordinarily would be subordinate to the installment purchaser's rights in the real property. Therefore, a buyer under an installment real estate contract would be well advised to protect his/her interest by taking physical possession of the property or recording a memorandum of the contract in the appropriate public record.

A second potential problem facing the purchaser under an installment real estate contract concerns the transfer of title. The seller is bound by the contract to deliver a deed for the property to the buyer upon full payment of the purchase price. Since the buyer must completely perform his/her obligations before the seller is obligated to deliver a deed, the buyer will not know in advance of making full payment whether the seller will actually deliver the deed transferring title. This places the buyer at a serious disadvantage. If the seller fails or refuses to make the conveyance, the buyer's remedies are to sue for damages for breach of contract, for rescission of the contract and a refund of the purchase price, or for specific performance to force the seller to execute and deliver a deed. The costs and expenses of litigation are borne by the buyer.

Escrow

The failure of the seller to complete performance obligations does not always imply bad faith. The seller may be unable to execute and deliver a deed because he/she is absent from the jurisdiction, physically incapable, acting under some disability, or deceased.

One method the buyer may use to ensure delivery of a deed upon completion of his/her performance is through the establishment of an escrow. Under an *escrow arrangement,* the buyer and seller agree that a third party will take delivery of the executed deed from the seller and hold it during the payment period of the contract. Upon final payment, the escrow agent completes the delivery of the deed to the buyer without regard to the physical or mental condition of the seller. Neither the buyer nor the seller has the right to alter the escrow agreement without the concurrence of the other. Courts have generally upheld the escrow arrangement and consider the resulting conveyance valid if the deed is properly executed and delivered to the escrow agent.

The choice of escrow agent is a matter of agreement between buyer and seller. In many jurisdictions, commercial banks, title companies, and attorneys offer escrow services. Sometimes there is a fee for escrow services depending upon the scope of the escrow agreement. Often, the escrow agent will also collect the payments from the buyer and forward them to the seller or deposit them to the seller's account. The escrow agent provides services to both parties and protects the buyer by ensuring delivery of the deed upon final payment.

Figure 21 illustrates the flow of funds and documents in an installment sale under an escrow arrangement.

Rights upon Default

The exact rights of the parties in the event of default are a matter of contract between the parties. As with other contracts affecting real property, the parties may agree upon any default procedures that do not violate law or public policy. Generally, the seller will want to have procedures that make it possible to easily collect the debt or reenter and retake possession of the real property and cancel the contract. The buyer will bargain for a long grace period within which to cure any default that may occur and to make it more difficult for the seller to retake the property.

Installment real estate contracts provide for specific remedies to be available to the seller if the buyer fails to pay or to perform any other material duty under the contract. Usually the contract provides that upon the default of the buyer, the seller is obligated to give the buyer notice of default setting forth the nature of the default and a time limit within which the buyer must cure it. At the expiration of the pre-arranged time limit for the buyer to cure the default, the seller usually has two options: he/she may declare the total remaining balance on the contract immediately due and payable and may proceed to enforce collection of that amount in a lawsuit for breach of contract, or he/she may reenter and repossess the real property and terminate the contract.

FIGURE 21 Conveyances Under an Installment Real Estate Contract

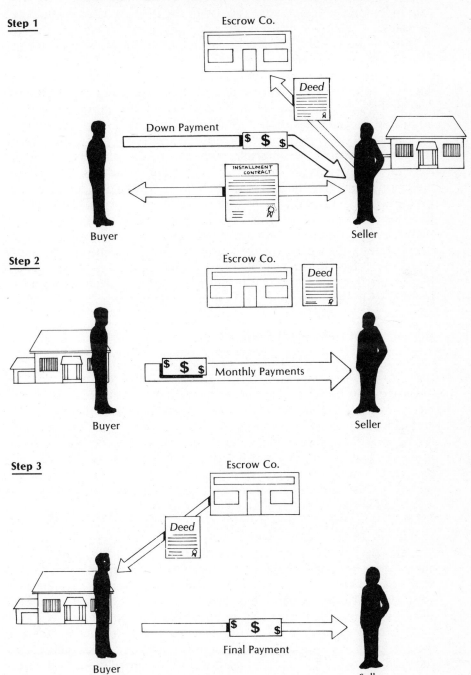

Step 1

Escrow Co.

Deed

Down Payment

INSTALLMENT CONTRACT

Buyer

Seller

Step 2

Escrow Co.

Deed

Monthly Payments

Buyer

Seller

Step 3

Escrow Co.

Deed

Final Payment

Buyer

Seller

In either case, the seller usually reserves the right to retain all monies paid by the buyer as rental for the use of the property and as liquidated damages.

The remedies available to a seller in case of default often work a harsh result. Suppose, for example, that the buyer has paid 75 percent of the purchase price at the time of default. Under a typical contract, the seller would have the right to reenter and retake possession of the property, cancel the contract, and retain 75 percent of the purchase price as liquidated damages and rental. Thus the seller would have the property back plus all but 25 percent of the contract purchase price. Because of the potential of such harsh results, some courts have placed limits on the forfeiture provisions of installment real estate contracts. The exact limitations are indefinite, and most such situations are decided on a case-by-case basis. If the results of a default are unconscionable, or if the forfeiture of a defaulting buyer is such that it "shocks the conscience" of the court, the default provisions of a contract will be denied enforcement in court. However, the limitations imposed by some courts cannot be relied on by a buyer as a safeguard against forfeiture. Buyers should be certain that they can reasonably foresee any default and protect themselves in the installment real estate contract.

Advantages of Installment Contracts

One of the primary advantages of an installment real estate contract is that it may be used when a buyer cannot qualify for a conventional mortgage loan because of either an unfavorable credit rating or a tight money market. Often the installment real estate contract may be used to good advantage as an interim financing device until the buyer can qualify for a conventional loan. Unlike most conventional mortgages, the terms of the installment contract may be tailored to fit the parties' needs. The greater flexibility permits the parties to set terms that are mutually beneficial. An additional advantage is that most of the closing costs associated with conventional financing are avoided.

Sellers favor the installment contract because it provides a great deal of protection to the seller, who usually reserves the right to take the property back without legal process if the buyer defaults. Another key advantage to the seller under an installment sales contract is that receipt of the purchase price can be deferred over several years, providing a tax advantage. Under applicable federal income tax laws, if the seller receives less than 30 percent of the purchase price in the first year, the total amount of seller's gain from the sale need not be included in income for the year of sale. Only that portion of the capital gain actually received is includable for tax purposes. The installment real estate contract provides a method of spreading out the gain over several years and mitigating its impact.

Since the installment real estate sale is between private buyer and seller, the interest rate between the parties is negotiable. The seller may be able to receive a greater return on his/her money through an installment sale than with investments offering comparable safety and security. This is an attractive feature of the installment sales contract for many sellers.

Installment Real Estate Contract and Purchase Money Mortgage Distinguished

The installment real estate contract and the purchase money mortgage are similar in many respects. In both cases the seller is acting as financing agent to the buyer. In both cases, the buyer makes a down payment, with the remaining balance plus interest payable at regular intervals. However, there are also major differences. A comparison of the two financing methods is summarized in Table 7.

Most sellers favor the installment real estate contract as the means of financing a buyer's purchase. The seller is better protected because title to the property is not transferred to the buyer and thus there is a better chance of recovery if the buyer defaults. On the other hand, most buyers prefer the purchase money mortgage when they finance their purchase through the seller. The purchase money mortgagor has legal title to the property. If there is a default, the seller-mortgagee must

TABLE 7   Financing a Real Estate Purchase Through the Seller—A Comparison

	Purchase Money Mortgage	*Installment Real Estate Contract*
Holder of legal title during term of financing	Buyer-mortgagor	Seller
Default procedures	Set by state statute	By contract between the parties
Does default involve legal proceedings?	Yes, mortgage foreclosure action	No
Right of redemption	Permitted in some states by statute	None, unless reserved in contract
Does seller have right to retake property in default?	No, proceeds of foreclosure applied to debt	Yes, if provided in contract
Party with greatest overall protection	Buyer	Seller

bring legal action in foreclosure against the buyer. The legal action affords the buyer the opportunity to defend against the foreclosure and may permit the buyer additional time within which to cure the default. Even if the mortgagee is successful in the foreclosure action and has the property sold, the purchase money mortgagor has the right to receive from the sale any excess above the amount of the debt plus costs. Under an installment contract, the buyer usually has no right to receive any value after a default.

Whether a transaction is financed by the seller under a purchase money mortgage or an installment real estate contract is a matter of bargain between buyer and seller.

DEEDS OF TRUST

In a few states, a deed of trust is employed as security in financing. A *deed of trust,* also known as a *trust deed,* is a written instrument in which the owner of a real property interest conveys legal title to a third-party trustee to secure payment by the owner to the lender. The deed of trust is not another method of financing, but an alternative to the mortgage document as a security device. In a mortgage, the mortgagor creates a nonpossessory security interest in the mortgagee (usually a bank or other financial institution), which continues to hold that security interest in its own name during the term of the mortgage. In using a deed of trust rather than a mortgage, the borrower gives a bond or promissory note to the lender and a deed of trust to a third-party trustee, who then holds legal title for the benefit of the lender during the term of the loan. (See Figure 22.)

The deed of trust, which conveys the property to the trustee, sets forth the terms and conditions by which the trustee holds the title for the benefit of the lender. Under the terms of the deed of trust, the owner of the property continues to hold possession of the property and may exercise all other incidents of ownership; however, any conveyance of the property to another would be subject to the rights of the trustee.

When the borrower has repaid the obligation that gave rise to the deed of trust, the trustee then releases the deed of trust, and the real property interest that was the subject of the trust is freed from the operation of the trust. Under the terms of most deeds of trust, the owner of the property must present proof to the trustee that payment in full has been made to the lender before the trustee can release the deed.

The deed of trust has advantages that make it attractive to a lender. First, since there is no mortgage upon which the lender relies for security, if the borrower defaults a time-consuming and costly mortgage foreclosure proceeding is not required. Second, the holder of the note

FIGURE 22 Conveyances Under a Deed of Trust

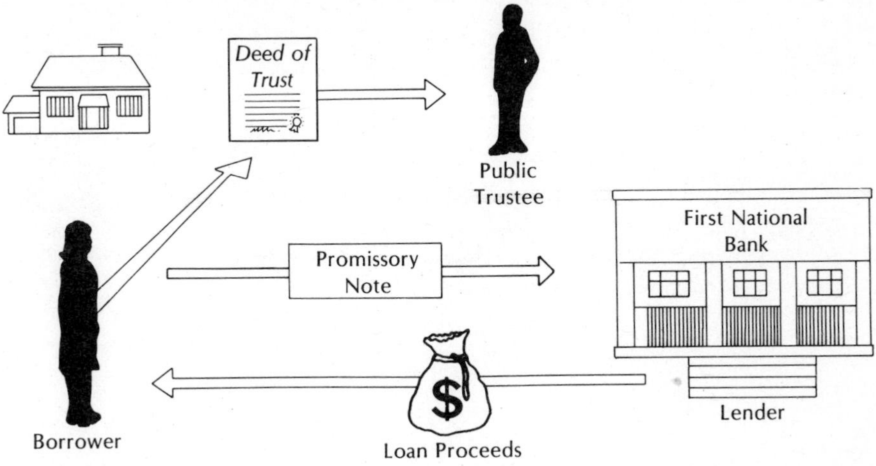

or bond can freely transfer or assign the obligation without executing an assignment as is required with a mortgage. Under a deed of trust, the borrower receives only the protection included in the deed of trust instrument and does not enjoy such mortgage benefits as the statutory right of redemption. In addition, the burden is upon the borrower to prove that the obligations that gave rise to the trust are paid in full. If the notes are not available, the borrower may have difficulty satisfying the trustee that the deed of trust should be released.

The trustee is appointed by the parties to the transaction. In most jurisdictions there are public trustees who perform the services required under a deed of trust arrangement. There is a fiduciary relationship between the trustee and each of the parties, which may subject the trustee to liability if he/she fails to perform his/her duties according to the standard of care required for such relationships.

SALE AND LEASEBACK

A common financing device for commercial and industrial properties is *sale and leaseback,* where the owner of the real property interest conveys an ownership interest to a purchaser and then leases it back from the new owner. In the first step of the transaction, the owner conveys the real property by deed to the buyer, who is usually an investor. In the second step of the transaction, the new owner immediately creates a possessory interest in the property and the former owner becomes the lessee. (See Figure 23.) Often the former owner has

FIGURE 23   Conveyances Under Sale and Leaseback

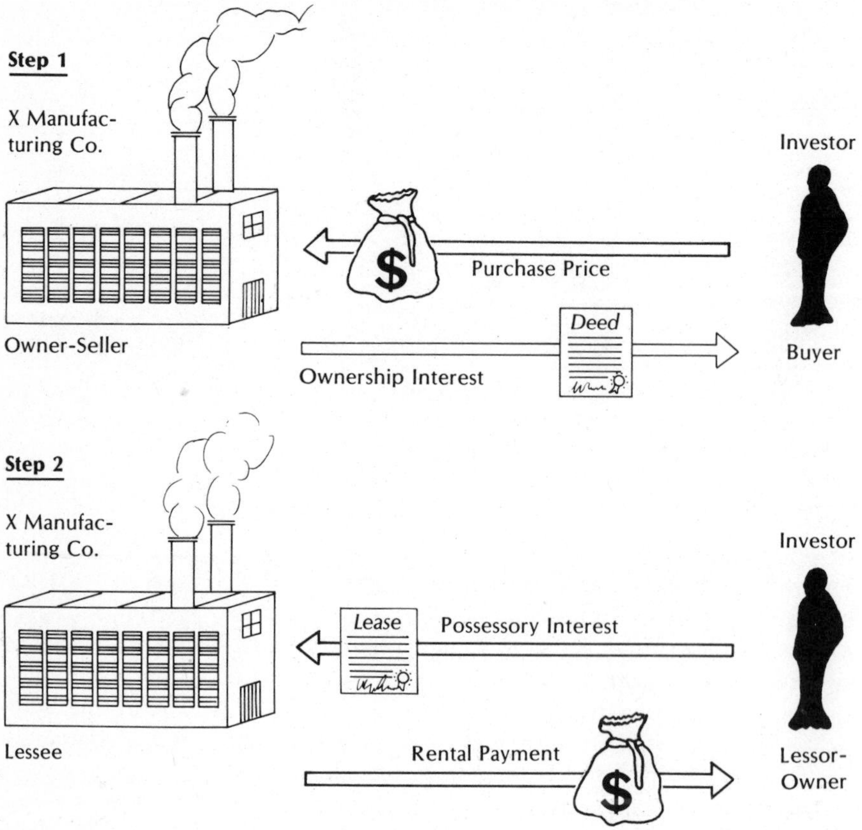

Step 1

X Manufac-
turing Co.

Investor

Owner-Seller

Purchase Price

Ownership Interest

Deed

Buyer

Step 2

X Manufac-
turing Co.

Investor

Lessee

Lease   Possessory Interest

Rental Payment

Lessor-
Owner

the right to repurchase the property at a future time during the term of
the lease. The term of the leasehold interest varies and is a matter of
bargain between the parties, but it is common for the term to be 25 years
or more.

Advantages

Sale and leaseback has several advantages for the seller-lessee. The sale
of the property produces a larger amount of capital than could be
obtained through conventional financing sources, who will lend only an
amount based on a favorable ratio of loan to appraised value. The seller-
lessee frees a large amount of capital that would otherwise be locked into
a fixed asset. In addition, the sale-and-leaseback arrangement avoids an
adverse effect upon the credit of the seller-lessee because the lessee is

freed from long-term debt. The rental payments to the lessor are fully deductible as a business expense for income tax purposes. The terms of the sale and leaseback may be tailored to fit the financial needs of both the seller-lessee and the buyer-lessor.

The advantage to the buyer-lessor is that it receives a built-in tenant and a predetermined return on the investment in commercial property with the security of a long-term lease. The investor will also reap the benefits of any increase in value of the property above the original purchase price. Most sale-and-leaseback arrangements require the lessee to assume payment of all expenses and costs such as taxes, insurance, maintenance, and repair. Thus, the return received by the investor is a "net" return, and little additional expense is incurred in holding the investment. A default does not require a mortgage foreclosure action to free the property from any rights of the lessee. The remedies available to the buyer-lessor are a matter of bargain between the seller-lessee and buyer-lessor. The lessor may also depreciate the improvements on the property for tax purposes.

Disadvantages

There are disadvantages to both parties under a sale and leaseback. The seller-lessee loses the potential increase in value of the asset over time. In addition, the lessee bears all the responsibilities of ownership of the property during the term of the lease but cannot sell or transfer his/her interest in the property to another party without the consent of the buyer-lessor. Often the buyer-lessor acquires a property that may have been used for a special purpose with improvements suited only to a limited number of potential lessees. The lessor runs the risk that the seller-lessee may not be able to complete the term of the lease, leaving the lessor with a vacant property that must be relet to recover the investment.

FINANCING UNDER THE UNIFORM LAND TRANSACTIONS ACT (ULTA)

Basic Terminology and Theory

Often a real estate market will span two or more states, each with its own laws affecting ownership, transfer, and the use of nonpossessory security interests. The variance in laws among the states introduces complexities into multistate transactions and creates problems and uncertainties among buyers, sellers, and mortgage lenders.

The Uniform Land Transactions Act has been drafted by the National Conference of Commissioners on Uniform State Laws to modernize, simplify, and clarify the law of real property. The ultimate goal of the drafters is that the entire act be adopted in substantially the same form by every state. As yet, the act has not gained wide support. However, because it would effectively standardize real estate law, it is an important step toward a unified system for transferring ownership interests and using real property as security for loans.

One of the key changes offered by ULTA in Article 3 is the abolition of the distinctions among mortgages, deeds of trust, and installment real estate contracts. Under ULTA, all such financing arrangements are treated the same. In each transaction in which a nonpossessory security interest is granted, new relationships and rights are created. For example, the real property that is the subject of the nonpossessory security interest is referred to as *collateral;* the document granting a security interest in the property to the *secured party* is a *security agreement;* and the debtor is known as the *protected party.* Article 3 of ULTA clearly sets forth the procedures to be followed by the secured party in the event of default by the protected party. The procedures replace the mortgage foreclosure action and provide for notice to the protected party of its right to cure the default and for a judicial or private sale of the property to satisfy the remaining balance of the debt owed the secured party. Under ULTA, there is no right of redemption after a sale of the collateral. The default provisions of Article 3 of ULTA are a compromise between protection of the protected party from fore-closure of interest without an opportunity to defend and cure the default and protection of the secured party's right to force a sale of the property to recover monies lent.

It has been held by at least one court that the application of different foreclosure provisions such as those in ULTA would not affect existing mortgages, because it would be an abridgment of the right of contract between mortgagor and mortgagee or buyer and seller. Therefore, if ULTA were to become law, its effect would be prospective only, and mortgages and other financing arrangements currently in effect would continue under their original terms unless the parties agreed otherwise. Since some mortgages are for periods in excess of twenty-five years, complete implementation of the proposed law would be more than a generation away.

THE BUSINESS ASSOCIATION AS A MEANS OF FINANCING REAL ESTATE TRANSACTIONS

A *business association* is two or more individuals joined to form an entity to carry on a business purpose. Business associations of several types are in general use in the purchase and development of real property where capital requirements and the need for expertise in various fields necessitate the participation of a number of individuals. Through a business association, individual participants are able to pool resources to accomplish their collective and individual goals. An in-depth study of business associations and their economic and tax consequences is more appropriately reserved for a text in real estate finance. However, a basic understanding of the legal relationship created by such associations is properly included in a study of real estate law.

Partnerships

A *partnership* is two or more individuals engaged in a business for profit, with joint management and control and joint ownership of partnership assets. A partnership is a separate entity; in most states, it can trade under a separate name and hold, transfer, and encumber interests in real property in the name of the partnership. However, the partners are jointly and severally liable to third parties for the debts of the partnership. A creditor of the partnership may sue any or all of the partners separately to collect a debt incurred by the partnership after partnership assets have been exhausted.

The partnership is created by agreement among the partners, and as long as neither law nor public policy is violated the parties may agree upon their respective rights and duties within the partnership. The attribute of flexibility makes the partnership attractive for use in the purchase and development of real property. The agreement among the parties will set out the responsibilities of each partner to use each participant's expertise or other contribution to the greatest advantage. For example, by agreement, one of the partners may manage the project, another may contribute capital, and another contribute design expertise.

General Partnerships

With the *general partnership,* the entity is disregarded for tax purposes and the partners are treated as individuals. Each partner shares the profits or bears the losses of the partnership in proportion to his/her ownership share in the partnership. The partnership form of ownership of income-producing property is favored because it allows tax benefits that accrue to the partnership to "pass through" to the partners. Thus, losses produced by the partnership can be offset against a partner's individual income, and income produced will not be double taxed as it is for corporate owners.

Limited Partnerships

A limited partnership is a partnership business association in which one or more partners are general partners and one or more are *limited partners.* The general partners are jointly and severally liable for the partnership debts and are responsible for management and control of the partnership business. The limited partners are passive investors. They have no liability for partnership debts beyond their equity investment and no right to participate in the management and control of the partnership business.

Like a general partnership, a limited partnership is created by contract among the partners. However, unlike a general partnership, the limited partnership must comply with applicable state registration requirements in order for limited partners to enjoy limited liability. Limited liability is a major attraction to an investor who wishes to be shielded from liability to third parties and has no interest in participating in the management of the partnership. The limited partnership is also attractive to a general partner real estate developer who has the skill to manage an investment and is not concerned about assuming personal liability for partnership debts.

For tax purposes, limited partners are treated the same as general partners. Both income and losses flow directly through to all partners in accordance with their ownership interest in the partnership.

Joint Ventures

A *joint venture* is two or more individuals engaged in a specific business enterprise for profit. The joint venture form of business association resembles a general partnership; however, with a joint venture, the relationship among the partners or joint venturers is limited to a specific project rather than being a continuing business relationship. Joint ventures are created by agreement among the partners in the venture. Since the joint venture business is limited in its scope, the agreement usually sets forth the specific nature of the project undertaken by the joint venturers and their respective rights and duties toward each other.

The joint venture is a separate entity and may own, transfer, and encumber real property interests in its own name. The legal relationship among the joint venturers themselves and third parties dealing with the joint venture is the same as in a general partnership; joint venturers are jointly and severally liable for the duties and debts of the joint venture. However, because the joint venture is limited in the scope of its business operations, the potential liability of a joint venturer is also somewhat limited.

The joint venture form of business association often is used for the acquisition and development of real property, and it is not uncommon for other business entities such as corporations to become joint venturers in a specific real estate development project. The joint venturers may pool their respective resources such as capital, expertise, or equipment, and they share the profits and bear the losses in proportion to their ownership shares. As with other forms of partnership, the entity is disregarded for tax purposes, and the tax consequences of the joint venture business are passed through to the joint venturers individually.

Corporations

A *corporation* is an association of one or more individuals doing business as an entity separate and apart from themselves. A corporation is created under authority of state or federal law; once a charter is granted by the governmental authority the corporation comes into existence as a legal entity. As a separate legal entity, the corporation can own, transfer, and encumber interests in real property in its own name. It may also engage in all activities that are permitted in the corporate charter and by-laws of the state. Ownership interests in the corporation are evidenced by shares of stock, and any or all shareholders may be officers engaged in the management and control of the corporation. However, because the corporation is regarded at law as a separate entity, its shareholders are not individually liable for corporate duties and debts even if they manage the corporate affairs.

As a separate entity, the corporation is taxed on its earnings, and tax benefits that accrue to the corporation are not passed through to the shareholders. Monies distributed in the form of dividends to the shareholders from the after-tax earnings of the corporation are taxed as income to the shareholders. The resulting double taxation on earnings distributed to the shareholders is a chief disadvantage of the corporate form of business association.

Shares in the corporation may be sold to investors as a source of capital for developmental projects. The purchase of such stock is attractive to some investors who do not wish to take part in the management of the corporation but wish to be shielded from liability to third parties for claims against the business entity.

Real Estate Investment Trusts

Another business association used to finance the acquisition and development of real property is the *real estate investment trust* (REIT), which can be used only for real estate and is solely a creation of the tax laws, having been exempted by Congress from corporate taxation. In a real estate investment trust, the beneficial owners purchase and hold certificates of ownership in the trust, which invests the funds in real estate.

The managers of the investments are the trustees, who are responsible directly to the beneficial owners. Any profits realized from the operation of the trust are paid to the owners in proportion to their ownership shares. The trust escapes corporate taxation, but the owners are taxed on the monies distributed to them. Capital gains realized by the corporate trust and distributed to the beneficial owners are treated as capital gains for tax purposes.

To qualify as a real estate investment trust, the entity must have at least 100 owners, it must be a bona fide business trust with centralized control in the trustees, the owners must have limited liability, the investments in real estate must be passive in nature, and there must be free transferability of shares.

The real estate investment trust has certain advantages. For example, it eliminates the double taxation of the corporate form of business association yet provides the owners with limited liability from debts to third parties dealing with the trust. However, depreciation and other losses are not passed through to the owners. In addition, the investments must be passive in nature—for example, the collection of rental or mortgage interest, where the return is limited. Because of the large number of owners and the free transferability of shares, the real estate investment trust usually must comply with applicable laws concerning registration of securities with the Securities and Exchange Commission. This registration process is expensive and subjects the real estate investment trust to certain governmental regulations and controls not applicable to many other forms of business association.

Summary

Each of the business associations has its distinct characteristics, advantages, and disadvantages as summarized in Table 8. As with all such matters, expert counsel should be obtained before an attempt is made to form a business association to achieve a desired legal or tax result.

**TABLE 8   Chief Characteristics of Business Associations Commonly Used
to Finance the Acquisition and Development of Real Property**

Characteristic	Partnership	Limited Partnership	Joint Venture	Corporation
Creation of entity	Contract among partners	Contract among partners	Contract among joint venturers	Under authority of government and pursuant to applicable law
Registration with State required to carry on business	No	Yes, must file certificate with State	No	Yes, articles of incorporation
Ownership	Partners	Partners	Joint venturers	Shareholders
Liability to third parties for entity debts	Yes, joint and several	General partners, joint and several; limited partners, only to extent of equity investment	Yes, joint and several	Shareholder not personally liable
Duration	Terminates on death of partner unless otherwise agreed	Terminates on death of partner unless otherwise agreed	Terminates on death of joint venturer unless otherwise agreed	Indefinite, death of stockholder has no effect
Transferability of ownership share	No	General partners no; limited partners yes	No	Yes
Taxation	Entity disregarded; partners taxed in proportion to ownership	Entity disregarded; partners taxed in proportion to ownership	Entity disregarded; joint venturers taxed in proportion to their ownership shares	Entity taxed; after-tax profits distributed to shareholders; taxed again to shareholders
Passthrough of tax benefits (depreciation) to owners	Yes	Yes	Yes	No
Method used to raise capital	Contribution of partners	Sale of limited partnership shares	Contribution of joint venturers	Sale of stock, bonds

QUESTIONS FOR DISCUSSION

1. In some jurisdictions, statutes require an installment real estate contract to be "foreclosed" in the same manner as a mortgage. What is the public policy behind such laws, and how do they negate one of the major advantages of an installment real estate contract for the seller?

2. Under what circumstances may an installment real estate contract be the most appropriate financing method of purchasing real property?

3. A group of investors are interested in purchasing a warehouse for conversion into a manufacturing plant for a local light industrial corporation that does not wish to purchase the building itself but is willing to enter into a long-term lease. Discuss the advantages and disadvantages of various methods by which the purchase and renovation may be financed, assuming that the investors wish to retain control of the management of the property.

4. What are the advantages to the lender of using a deed of trust rather than a mortgage to finance the buyer-borrower's purchase of real property?

5. What are the chief advantages and disadvantages to the stockholders of using the corporate form of business association for financing the purchase of an improved parcel of real property?

CASES

Case 1. Seller sold a tract of real property to Buyer under an installment real estate contract. Unlike the situation in most real estate contracts, the seller delivered a deed to the property in advance of full payment by the buyer. After Buyer had refused to make any further payments, Seller brought suit against Buyer asking the court to impress a mortgage lien upon the property to secure final payment by Buyer. What is the most likely result of the suit? Why?

Case 2. The deed of trust given by Buyer to Seller provided that upon payment of a certain portion of the purchase price and upon the request of Buyer, Seller would release a portion of the land encumbered by the deed of trust. After paying a substantial portion of the price, Buyer defaulted. Not having asked the Seller to convey the portion paid for, Buyer brought suit to compel Seller to reconvey the portion of the land paid for. Should Buyer be entitled to receive a deed to the portion that was paid for but not released pursuant to a demand? Why or why not?

Case 3. Purchaser was buying a certain tract of mountain land on an installment real estate contract. He made payments for ten years until he found that some of the timber had been removed, in violation of the terms of the contract. Believing that the timber had been removed by Seller, Buyer refused to make any further payments even though the contract required that all payments be made on a timely basis. Seller sought to quiet title to the property against Purchaser for nonpayment. Purchaser offered to pay the remaining balance of the contract price plus accrued interest, but Seller refused. Should the court grant the relief sought by Seller? Why, or why not?

Case 4. Plaintiff and Defendant entered into an installment real estate contract that provided that Defendant-purchasers were to insure the premises for the benefit of Plaintiff-sellers. Plaintiffs later learned that Purchasers had not paid the insurance premiums but that their insurance agent had extended credit to them. Sellers paid the premiums and declared a default. Buyers never did pay the agent or reimburse Sellers for the premiums. In a suit for possession and termination of Buyers' interest brought by Sellers upon the contract, what is the most likely result? Why?

Case 5. A bank purchased land and constructed a bank building facility. Under applicable statutory law within the jurisdiction, the bank could not be the legal owner of the building. Upon discovering this, the bank sold the building to L Company in a sale-and-leaseback transaction. Under the terms of the lease, the bank retained ownership of the land and agreed to lease the building from L Company, paying as rental an amount equal to the mortgage payments to a third-party mortgagee. The bank also had the right to repurchase the building at a price equal to the unpaid balance of the mortgage loan. As a general rule, sale-and-leaseback transactions are recognized for tax purposes only if they are not a sham used to achieve a desired tax result. If the sale-and-leaseback arrangement were to be challenged, what arguments may be made for and against tax recognition of the relationship between the bank and L Company?

Chapter 9
Deeds

211

Exceptions and Reservations

SUMMARY

QUESTIONS FOR DISCUSSION

CASES

A *deed* is a written instrument that provides evidence of the transfer of an ownership interest in real property from an owner, the grantor (or his/her estate if the owner is deceased), to another party, the *grantee*. As was emphasized in Chapter 6, a deed is not the method by which an ownership interest is transferred; no matter which method of transfer is used, some type of deed will act as the document of transfer. For example, the transfer of an ownership interest by gift or by bargain and sale will be accomplished by a deed that is executed and delivered by the grantor donor or seller during his/her lifetime to the grantee donee or buyer. Similarly, the transfer of an ownership interest by devise or bequest will be accomplished by a deed that is executed and delivered by the executor, administrator, or personal representative of the grantor's estate to the grantee beneficiary or devisee. It is important that a deed be accurate in every respect, not only because it is the grantee's primary evidence of ownership, but also because its accuracy may prevent future claims by other parties to the same property.

The parties to a real estate transaction, particularly to a sale and purchase, as well as the brokers and attorneys who may represent them, usually carefully inspect a deed before it is delivered and accepted to make sure that it conforms to a contract of sale, if applicable, or any other understanding that exists between or among the parties. Such an inspection can serve to avoid embarrassment arising from title defects that may become apparent in the future. For example, if the property were improperly described, the grantees who accept and record the deed may, at best, have to request another deed that correctly describes the property or prepare and record a corrective deed. At worst, the grantees might discover that they do not own land they thought was included in the sale.

213

Persons dealing in real property should be familiar with the legal requirements of a deed. This chapter generally describes the requirements of a valid deed, types of deeds, and the property interests that pass by deed.

ELEMENTS OF A VALID DEED

To be valid, a deed must (1) be in writing; (2) contain the names, designations, and description of the parties, a consideration clause, words of conveyance, a description of the real property being conveyed, and the signature of the grantor and his/her witness or acknowledgment; and (3) be delivered and accepted.

Identification of the Parties

The grantor and grantee must be named with sufficient certainty to permit their identification. As long as identification is possible, a mistake in spelling or a difference between the grantor's printed name and his/her actual signature will generally not be sufficient to invalidate a deed. For example, if the name of the grantor were printed in the conveyance clause as Tom Smithe, grantor, and were signed as "Tom Smith" or "T. Smith," the deed would not be invalid if it could be shown that Tom Smith, Tom Smithe, or T. Smith were one and the same person. Such confusion can easily be avoided by careful examination of the deed before acceptance and recordation. If the deed has been recorded, it can and generally should be corrected by filing a correction deed to avoid future confusion.

If the grantor's name does not appear in the body of the deed, the rule in some states is that the deed is valid if it is properly signed and acknowledged by the grantor, whereas other states require that the grantor's name also appear in the body of the deed.

Where there are multiple grantors or grantees, each should be individually named in the deed so that all interests in the property are conveyed and received. For example, if Sunny Acre were owned by A, B, and C as tenants in common, full title to Sunny Acre would not be received by grantees X and Y unless A, B, and C all joined as grantors in a single deed or prepared separate deeds conveying their separate interests to X and Y. Similarly, if X and Y agree to co-own Sunny Acre, both their names must appear on the deed as grantees.

The importance of properly designating and describing the parties to the transaction can best be illustrated by a few examples. If the grantor is single, he should be described as "Tom Smith, single" so that the grantee knows that an intestate interest in the property is not retained by a spouse. Similarly, if the property is in Tom Smith's name alone and he is married, his wife would have to join in the deed as a grantor to convey her intestate interest to the grantee. The grantor would then be designated as "Tom Smith and Mary Smith, his wife" or "Tom Smith et ux." If either of the parties is a corporation, the usual practice is to state "XYZ, Inc., a corporation organized and doing business in the State of . . . " to distinguish it from other concerns having similar names, such as a partnership or an individual doing business using a trade name or a corporation in another state. If the grantor is an estate, the grantor would be designated as "the Estate of A." If either of the parties is a partnership, in some states each partner should be individually named such as "Armstrong, Bradley, and Corso, a partnership, trading and doing business as Arbracor." Under the Uniform Partnership Act, this is not necessary, because a partnership can hold title to property in its own name. Similarly, if a fictitious name is used, the actual name should appear in the deed usually followed by the fictitious name, such as "Armstrong, Bradley, and Corso, a partnership," or "A. Armstrong, an individual," or "Arbracor, Inc., a corporation" trading and doing business under a specified fictitious name.

If grantees want to co-own property as joint tenants, tenants in common, or tenants by the entirety, this too should be clearly specified. For example, a conveyance to "A, B, and C as joint tenants with the right of survivorship" will clearly indicate to subsequent grantees that if A, B, or C is dead, the decedent's signature does not have to appear on the subsequent deed, because of the survivorship characteristic of joint tenancy. But if A, B, and C own property as tenants in common, a decedent's interest would have to be conveyed by his/her estate to fully dispose of all interests in the commonly held property.

A deed will not be valid unless it designates a grantee who is legally capable of taking title. For example, a deed delivered to a corporation that has not come into legal existence or to a grantee who is dead, is invalid. On the other hand, a deed delivered to a minor or incompetent is valid.

Finally, a deed is not valid unless the grantee's name is inserted by the grantor or his/her authorized agent. Thus, a grantee who wishes to convey the property to another or to share ownership with another should not tamper with the deed before it is recorded but record it and then prepare a new deed that provides the desired results. Thus, if Sunny Acre were conveyed to H alone and he accepted and recorded the deed, he would prepare a new deed from H to H and W, his wife, if he wanted his wife to co-own the property, rather than adding his wife's name to the original deed before it was recorded.

Consideration

Consideration in a bargain and sale deed is the price paid for the transfer of title to real property. At common law, a bargain and sale deed had to include a consideration clause to make the deed valid, but the amount of the stated consideration was inconsequential. It became customary, therefore, for deeds to recite either actual or nominal consideration. For example, a typical nominal consideration clause might be: "That in consideration of One Dollar ($1.00) in hand paid, the receipt whereof is hereby acknowledged, ..." The purposes of using nominal consideration of $1.00 instead of the actual amount are privacy and convenience. A grantee might not want the public to know what he/she paid for the property; or, where the price includes both real and personal property, it may be simpler for the grantor to use a nominal amount rather than make an arbitrary allocation of price. Many states have statutes that do not require consideration for title to pass by deed. However, where there are real estate transfer taxes based on some measure of fair market value, actual consideration is usually stated in the deed if it in fact represents fair market value.

If a gift of real property is intended and the grantor includes a statement of consideration, the deed will be valid even though no money actually changes hands. It is therefore common practice to insert a nominal consideration clause in a gift situation, particularly where the state requires consideration for a valid deed.

Words of Conveyance

Every deed should contain words of conveyance. The same type of language is contained in a mortgage in title theory states. For example, in a warranty deed, common conveyancing language would be "the said grantor does hereby grant and convey to the said grantee . . . " or "grant and release unto the party of the second part, his heirs and assigns forever . . . ." In a title theory state, the conveyancing language of a mortgage would be similar except that the words "grantor" and "grantee" would be replaced by "mortgagor" and "mortgagee," respectively. In a lien theory state, since title is not transferred to the mortgagee, words of conveyance would not have to be included in the mortgage.

Description of the Property

Every deed must contain a description of the property being conveyed. The description should be precise enough to permit easy identification of the subject property. For example, a lot described as being located along Route 322, without further identification, would not be adequately described, particularly if the grantor owned many lots along Route 322. To supply the requisite precision, land can be identified in a number of ways—by the technical language of surveyors, that is, by metes and bounds and courses and distances; by lot, block or subdivision number or name; or by the rectangular survey system. The rules applicable to these methods of describing property are given in a separate section later in this chapter. However, a surveyor's technical description is not necessary to convey full legal title if the property can be reasonably identified in other ways. For example, if a grantor describes his property as being "my residence in a certain town and state," and he has only one residence in that town and state, the property can be easily identified. Or when a grantor describes his/her property by a familiar name such as Sunny Acre, it too is an adequate description if it can be easily located.

Even if a description is sufficient for identification of the property conveyed to comply with the minimum requirements of a valid deed, the lack of a precise legal description may adversely affect the merchantability of the title.

Signature and Acknowledgment

A deed must be signed by the grantor to be valid. However, a grantee generally does not have to sign, because he/she is not conveying an estate or any other interest in the land. In most states, the signature must be witnessed or acknowledged either as a requirement to the validity of the deed or as a prerequisite to recording. A *witness* is anyone with legal capacity who subscribes his/her name to a deed for the purpose of attesting to the authenticity of the grantor's signature. On the other hand, an *acknowledgment* is a formal declaration made by a legally authorized person, usually a notary public, to the effect that the grantor was known to him or her and that the grantor's signature was made in his or her presence. Most states require that deeds be acknowledged before being recorded to prevent fraud in the transfer of real property. If the grantor dies prior to signing a deed, the executor or administrator of his/her estate will sign the appropriate deed and deliver it to the grantee.

Delivery and Acceptance

The final step in transferring title to a grantee is delivery of the deed. Delivery depends on the intention of the grantor. Intent can be presumed where, for example, the grantor physically delivers the deed

FIGURE 24   A Typical Deed

DEED

Date

THIS DEED, Made the _____ day of _____ in the year nineteen hundred and _____.

Name and Designation of Parties

BETWEEN _____,
_____, hereinafter called Grantor, and
_____,
_____, hereinafter called Grantees.

Consideration and Words of Conveyance

WITNESSETH, That in consideration of_____
_____, in hand paid, the receipt of which is hereby acknowledged, the said Grantor does hereby grant and convey to the said Grantees, their heirs and assigns ALL that certain lot, piece or parcel of land, with the buildings and improvements thereon erected, situate in the County of Middle, City of Sunnytown, and State of X, bounded and described in accordance with a survey and plan of lots prepared by Joe Surveyor, Civil Engineer, dated June 30, 1978, as follows:

Description

BEGINNING at an iron pin on the South side of Jones Avenue 200 feet West of the Southwest corner of the intersection of Smith Street and Jones Avenue; thence West along the South side of Jones Avenue 100 feet to an iron pin; thence South along the common lot line of Lots 2 and 3, 150 feet to an iron pin; thence East 100 feet to an iron pin; thence North along the common lot line of Lots 1 and 2, 150 feet to the place of beginning.

IN WITNESS WHEREOF, the said Grantor has hereunto set his hand and seal, the day and year first above written.

Signature and Witness

Sealed and delivered in
the presence of:

/s/_____(SEAL)
Sam Smith

/s/_____

_____

STATE OF X
COUNTY OF ALISON   } ss.:

(Continued)

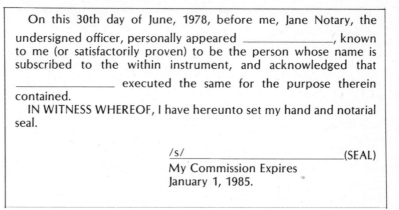

Acknow-
ledgment

On this 30th day of June, 1978, before me, Jane Notary, the undersigned officer, personally appeared _____, known to me (or satisfactorily proven) to be the person whose name is subscribed to the within instrument, and acknowledged that _____ executed the same for the purpose therein contained.

IN WITNESS WHEREOF, I have hereunto set my hand and notarial seal.

/s/_____(SEAL)
My Commission Expires
January 1, 1985.

to the grantee, where the grantee is in possession of the deed, or where the grantor records it him/herself. On the other hand, intent to deliver generally is not presumed when the grantor has the deed witnessed or acknowledged and then retains possession.

A deed can be delivered to a third-party independent custodian, generally known as an *escrow agent,* who will hold it until the occurrence of a specific event. A seller might, for example, give a deed to a bank with instructions to deliver it to the buyer after final payment has been made on the property pursuant to an installment real estate contract. As soon as that event occurs, title passes to the grantee even though the seller may not have received the check. This is because the custodian becomes an agent for the grantee when the specified event occurs. Thus, if an individual custodian absconds with the deed after the occurrence of the event, the grantee's ownership interest will not be impaired.

A deed must not only be delivered; it must also be accepted by the grantee. Acceptance rarely presents a problem, since it is generally presumed if it is beneficial to the grantee and he/she does not actively reject delivery.

A typical deed, with the various parts identified, is illustrated in Figure 24. Deeds commonly contain other clauses in addition to those in Figure 24. Although not necessary to the validity of the deed, these clauses help to further define the rights and duties of the parties. Three examples are as follows:

Warranties   The Grantor will generally warrant and forever defend the property hereby conveyed.

Restrictions   The Grantee, his heirs and assigns, shall erect only a single-family dwelling on said premises with a height not to exceed two stories.

Reservations   The Grantor reserves to himself, his heirs and assigns, the right to
and   use an existing driveway along the West side of said premises.
Easements

Recording

The same rationale that applies to the recording of mortgages is also applicable to deeds. A deed, like a mortgage, can be valid if it is not recorded, but from a practical point of view the purpose is to give notice to the world that the grantee has an ownership interest in the real property, thus establishing grantee's legal priority to such land if he/she records before other innocent grantees of the same property. Recording also has the practical effect of protecting a grantee who loses his/her deed. A certified copy of the original from the office where the deed is recorded is legally just as good as the original deed. Finally, as previously noted, recordation raises a presumption of delivery.

The various state recording acts provide that deeds must be recorded in the county where the land is located. The same rule is applicable to mortgages or any other written instrument that affects the land.

TYPES OF DEEDS

There are different types of deeds for many different specific situations. For example, an *administrator's* or *executor's deed* is used to convey property owned and possessed by an estate, a *sheriff's deed* is used to convey property sold at a sheriff's sale, a *support deed* is used when the grantee agrees to support the grantor for life, and a *corrective deed* is used to correct an error in a prior deed such as the misspelling of an important name or place. Usually, however, these and other deeds fall into one of three groups: quitclaim deeds, warranty deeds, and bargain and sale deeds.

Quitclaim Deed

A *quitclaim deed* conveys only that interest which the grantor may have in the real property at the time of the conveyance. If the grantor did not have any interest, the grantee gets nothing. If the grantor had good title, the grantee takes good title. The legal concept of *caveat emptor* ("let the buyer beware") aptly describes a quitclaim deed. The grantor does not warrant title, which distinguishes a quitclaim deed from a warranty deed.

Quitclaim deeds are used primarily by grantors who are uncertain of the worth of their title. For example, a grantor who purportedly owns 1,000 acres of unsurveyed mountain acreage that he has seen infrequently would probably convey such land by a quitclaim deed, particularly if he knew that the land might be subject to adverse ownership interests and prescriptive rights. Grantees who receive quitclaim deeds should, therefore, understand that they may receive nothing. A quitclaim deed is also appropriate for curing a technical defect in the chain of title and for surrendering or transferring an interest between cotenants of property. For example, pursuant to a divorce settlement, a husband may convey his interest to his wife, or vice versa, in property owned by them as tenants by the entirety. Further, grantees have no legal recourse against grantors based on a quitclaim deed.

A quitclaim deed must contain language specifically stating that the grantor "does remise, release, and quitclaim" a certain parcel of real property to the grantee. Usually, a preprinted quitclaim deed form will identify itself in bold print. If it is not identified as a quitclaim deed or if the term "quitclaim" or similar language is not used in the body of the deed, the grantor may run the risk of warranting the title by implication.

Warranty Deed

A *warranty deed* is a deed containing certain guarantees or assurances that title to the property being conveyed is free and clear of all liens and encumbrances. With some slight variations among the states, there are four basic covenants: (1) the *covenant of seisin,* which means that the grantor is the owner of the possessory interest in the land being conveyed; (2) the *covenant of the right to convey,* which means that the grantor has the legal right and power to effect a conveyance of the land; (3) the *covenant against encumbrances,* which means that the land being conveyed is free of any outstanding interest that might diminish the estate being conveyed; and (4) the *covenant of quiet enjoyment,* which means that the grantor will be responsible for any loss resulting from a disturbance of or interference with the grantee's possession of the property being conveyed.

In some jurisdictions, it is common practice to include these covenants in a warranty deed. In other jurisdictions, they are implied by use of such language as "grantor will warrant and forever defend the property hereby conveyed" or "grantor generally warrants the property conveyed herein." The grantor's obligation with respect to the quality of the title continues after delivery and acceptance of a valid warranty deed. It should be emphasized, however, that a general warranty is personal and hence is only as good as the grantor's credit. The extent of that obligation depends on the type of warranty deed—that is, on whether it is a general warranty deed or a special warranty deed.

General Warranty Deed

Sometimes confusingly referred to simply as a warranty deed, a *general warranty deed* means that the grantor warrants against all defects in title created by him/herself or by any predecessor in the chain of title. If such a defect is found to exist, the grantee can sue the grantor for damages. Thus, where the grantor and a predecessor in title had each obtained a mortgage on property that the grantor conveyed to the grantee, and both mortgages remained unsatisfied after the conveyance, the grantee could sue the grantor for damages to recover an amount necessary to satisfy both mortgages. The grantee's title would then be free and clear of all encumbrances in the chain of title as warranted by the grantor. From the grantee's point of view, therefore, a general warranty deed is the best type of deed to receive. From the grantor's point of view, a quitclaim deed is the best type of deed to deliver, since the grantor does not guarantee the title in any way.

Special Warranty Deed

In a *special warranty deed,* the grantor warrants only against all defects in title created by him/herself during his/her ownership period, but not those created by any predecessor in the chain of title. Thus, under a special warranty deed, the grantor is not responsible for an unsatisfied mortgage of a predecessor in title. A special warranty deed might be appropriately used when a fiduciary such as a trustee or executor transfers property to a grantee, because a fiduciary usually lacks authority to guarantee or warrant title of former owners in the chain. It might also be used when a grantor has not been in possession of the property with the knowledge and consent of the grantee. If a grantee acquires title insurance, the difference between a special and general warranty deed is more academic than real from the grantee's point of view, since title is insured and he/she can recover from the insurance company for any damages sustained.

Bargain and Sale Deed

A bargain and sale deed is substantially similar to a warranty deed in that it transfers title to real property to a grantee; however, it usually does not contain warranties. A bargain and sale deed can also be distinguished from a quitclaim deed, because in a quitclaim the grantor transfers only that interest in the real property that he/she may possess, whereas a bargain and sale deed transfers "substantial title" in and possession of the real property.

Other Deeds

There are many other types of deeds. Usually they incorporate some aspect of a quitclaim, warranty, or bargain and sale deed. For example, an *executor's deed* will identify the source of the power to transfer title. "By virtue of the power and authority given to me by the last will and testament of ..." is typical language. At the same time it may incorporate quitclaim or warranty language. Other types of deeds that accomplish specific purposes are *cemetery deeds,* which convey title to a cemetery plot, *condominium deeds,* which convey title to a condominium unit, *trustee's deeds,* which are executed by a trustee under authority of a declaration of trust, *deeds of trust,* where title is transferred to a trustee, who holds it in trust pending completion of the grantee's performance of certain obligations (usually payment of full purchase price plus interest), and *sheriff's* or *treasurer's deeds,* where property has undergone a forced sale to satisfy outstanding obligations such as unsatisfied judgments or delinquent taxes.

ESTOPPEL BY DEED

The doctrine of estoppel by deed is an outgrowth of warranty law. The doctrine applies to a situation where the grantor conveys an interest or estate in real property that is greater than he/she actually owns or possesses. If the grantor subsequently acquires the full interest or estate, then it will pass by operation of law, that is, by *estoppel,* to the grantee. Therefore, the doctrine of estoppel by deed does not apply to quitclaim deeds or deeds that contain similar language.

Two examples will illustrate the doctrine of estoppel by deed:

1. S conveyed title to a certain tract of real property to B by warranty deed. S did not own the property at the time of conveyance but expected to inherit it after her grandfather's death. If S's expectation becomes a reality, either S's subsequently acquired title would pass to B or B, acting on the warranty given, could sue for damages.

2. If G conveyed to B "whatever interest I presently own" in a certain tract of real property at a time when he did not have an ownership interest, the doctrine of estoppel by deed would not apply, because the conveyancing language merely conveys whatever interest G had at the time, which in this case was none. The language is quitclaim in nature.

PROPERTY PASSING BY DEED

It has been established that one element of a valid deed is a description of the property being conveyed that is precise enough to permit its easy identification. Deeds first generally identify the property by making reference to prior owners or location. For example, "All that certain plot, piece, or parcel of land with buildings and improvements erected thereon, situate, lying, and being in . . . ." makes reference to general location. This type of general identification is followed by a specific legal description.

Importance of Legal Description

The specific legal description should be clear and accurate in order to avoid potential litigation. The description should have a starting point, usually referred to in deeds as the "point of beginning," which is certain and generally accepted. Examples of generally accepted starting points are physical and natural monuments such as government land office monuments, highway station markers, bodies of water, and buildings. The description should completely enclose the property being described, which means that it should end at the same place it began. Without closing, the description is incomplete and is of little value. This is the reason why an insurer of title to real property will carefully plot the land being insured.

Often, where property has been conveyed on numerous occasions, legal descriptions are erroneously transcribed and the error is perpetuated from one deed to another deed. Such description errors can be easily corrected but often cause confusion and delay in closing a real property transaction. In essence, the description must be such as to exclude the possibility that any other parcel of land anywhere in the world will have the same description.

Methods of Describing Real Property

Although there are many ways by which property can be identified, there are generally three legally acceptable methods for specifically describing it: (1) the metes and bounds system, (2) the rectangular survey system, and (3) by reference to a plat of survey.

Metes and Bounds

This method is used by the eastern states as a carryover from the English system. It describes the exterior boundaries of the property by starting at a well-defined point called the *point of beginning,* obtaining a compass reading of the direction the boundary line takes from that point, and then taking linear measurements and compass readings as necessary in following the exterior boundary of the property until the point of beginning is reached. The exterior boundary may also be established by reference to natural or artificial physical monuments such as trees, rocks, streams, roads, buildings, or iron pins fixed in concrete in addition to courses and distances. (In the technical language of the surveyor, compass readings are referred to as *bearings,* linear measurements as *distances,* and the direction a line takes is referred to as a *course.)* Figure 25 shows an example of a metes and bounds description that utilizes this terminology and a plot plan of the property being described.

The general rule is that if descriptions such as courses and distances differ from the physical monuments, the monuments control. This rule does not apply where an obvious error exists or where the monument is difficult to identify and a course and distance or some other form of measurement clearly establishes the boundaries. For example, if the boundary of a certain tract of land were described by courses and distances as going to a large granite rock, and a specific granite rock could not be identified among several that existed in that general area, the course and distance measurement would control.

Where land is described as going to, by, along, etc., a monument, the general rule is that the grantee takes to the center of the monument. If land is described as being bounded by a street or highway, the presumption is that ownership goes to the center of the street or highway. There are a number of exceptions. For example, land described as running along a navigable stream goes to the low water mark, since the water and the land under it are owned by the federal government; in some states, land described as going to a building creates common ownership of the wall on the property line and not ownership of half the building; and in some states, land described as going along an unopened road goes only to the edge of the road. If the description does not fully enclose the property, it is defective, hence, descriptions should not be drafted by laypersons.

Rectangular Survey System

A majority of the states, particularly the western states, use the *rectangular survey system* to describe real property. This method was adopted by Congress after the Revolutionary War to provide a uniform system for describing land throughout the country as settlers moved into new territory. Thus, land in Kansas would be described in the same way as land in California or any other state or territory using the government system.

FIGURE 25   Metes and Bounds Description

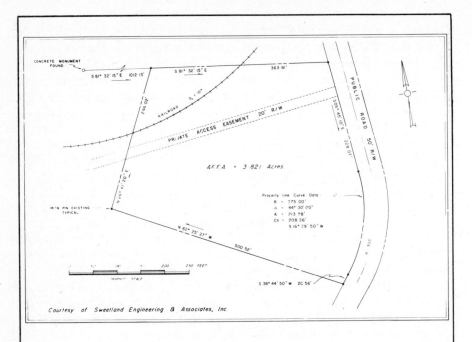

Courtesy of Sweetland Engineering & Associates, Inc.

LEGAL DESCRIPTION

BEGINNING at an iron pin at a northwest corner of the property herein described and being South 81° 32' 15" East 1012.13 feet from a concrete monument; thence South 81° 32' 15" East along lands of J. P. Jones a distance of 363.81 feet to an iron pin at the westerly right-of-way line of Public Road (50 feet wide); thence South 05° 45' 10" East along the aforementioned Public Road a distance of 228.07 feet to an iron pin at a point of curvature; thence along the same by the arc of a curve to the right described as follows:

Radius =	275.00 feet
Central Angle =	44° 30' 00"
Arc length =	213.58 feet
Chord =	208.26 feet South 16° 29' 50" West

to an iron pin at a point of tangency; thence along the same South 38° 44' 50" West a distance of 20.56 feet to an iron pin on the westerly right-of-way line of Public Road and at the northeast corner of lands of James Smith; thence North 62° 25' 27" West along lands of Smith a distance of 500.52 feet to an iron pin; thence North 26° 41' 20" East along the same a distance of 296.02 feet to an iron pin at the place of beginning.

CONTAINING 3.821 acres.

The rectangular survey system is based on a grid formed by east-west lines called *principal base lines* and north-south lines called *principal meridians.* There are a number of principal base lines and 35 principal meridians within the United States. For example, the sixth principal meridian transects the states of Kansas, Nebraska, Wyoming, Colorado, and South Dakota, whereas the third principal meridian passes through Illinois and Indiana. Lines running parallel with the principal base line six miles apart form strips of land called *township tiers.* Lines running parallel with the principal meridian six miles apart form strips of land called *ranges.* Twenty-four miles on either side of each principal base line and each principal meridian, a correction line is run along a true meridian or parallel to correct for the curvature of the earth and maintain fairly constant measures from one range or tier to another.

Six-mile squares called *townships* (the basic unit of measurement within the system) are formed by the intersection of township lines and base lines and thus coincide with the intersection of township tiers and ranges. A township is described and located by counting the number of squares north or south of a principal base line and east or west of a principal meridian and referring to the range or township thus identified. For example, in Figure 26, Graph I shows the location of two arbitrarily selected townships, X and Y. Township X can be described as Township 3 North, Range 4 East of the Sixth Principal Meridian. In practice, this is abbreviated Twp. 3N, Rn. 4E. Township Y can be described as Township 2 South, Range 3 West of the Sixth Principal Meridian, or Twp. 2S, Rn. 3W.

Each township is divided into 36 equal units called *sections.* Each section is one mile square and contains 640 *acres.* The sections are numbered consecutively, beginning in the northeast corner, as illustrated in Graph II of Figure 26. Section 4 in Township X can thus be described as Section 4, Twp. 3N, Rn. 4E.

Each section is divided into *quarter sections,* each of which is described by reference to its location within the section: N.W.¼, S.W.¼, S.E.¼, or N.E.¼. Land within each quarter is further described by reference to its location within the quarter. As shown in Graph III, Sunny Acre is located in the N.W.¼ of the S.W.¼ of Section 4. A complete description of Sunny Acre in terms of the rectangular survey system, which makes reference to all the units discussed, is N.W.¼ of the S.W.¼ of Section 4, Twp. 3N, Rn. 4E of the Sixth Principal Meridian.

A tract can be generally located by using the rectangular survey system and then specifically identified by using metes and bounds. This usually occurs when the land being described does not follow a township, section, or quarter-section line, or when the lot is irregular in shape, or when it is in an urban area and is too small to identify except by use of

FIGURE 26   Identification of Sunny Acre—Rectangular Survey System

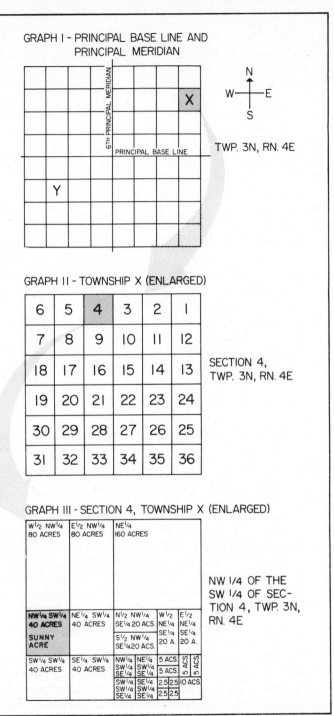

GRAPH I - PRINCIPAL BASE LINE AND
PRINCIPAL MERIDIAN

6TH PRINCIPAL MERIDIAN

PRINCIPAL BASE LINE

X

Y

N
W — E
S

TWP. 3N, RN. 4E

GRAPH II - TOWNSHIP X (ENLARGED)

6	5	4	3	2	1
7	8	9	10	11	12
18	17	16	15	14	13
19	20	21	22	23	24
30	29	28	27	26	25
31	32	33	34	35	36

SECTION 4,
TWP. 3N, RN. 4E

GRAPH III - SECTION 4, TOWNSHIP X (ENLARGED)

W½ NW¼ 80 ACRES	E½ NW¼ 80 ACRES	NE¼ 160 ACRES		
NW¼ SW¼ 40 ACRES **SUNNY ACRE**	NE¼ SW¼ 40 ACRES	N½ NW¼ SE¼ 20 ACS. — S½ NW¼ SE¼ 20 ACS.	W½ NE¼ SE¼ 20 A.	E½ NE¼ SE¼ 20 A.
SW¼ SW¼ 40 ACRES	SE¼ SW¼ 40 ACRES	NW¼ SW¼ SE¼ — SW¼ SW¼ SE¼	NE¼ SW¼ SE¼ — SW¼ SW¼ SE¼	5 ACS. / 5 ACS. / 2.5 2.5 / 2.5 2.5

NW 1/4 OF THE
SW 1/4 OF SEC-
TION 4, TWP. 3N,
RN. 4E

metes and bounds. For example, if an irregular tract of land were conveyed out of the northwest quarter of Sunny Acre as described immediately above, the land would be described as located in "the N.W.¼ of the N.W.¼ of the S.W.¼ of Section 4, Twp. 3N, Rn. 4E of the 6th Principal Meridian bounded and more specifically described as follows . . ." (a metes and bounds description would follow).

Plat of Survey

The third method of describing land is by reference to the plat or a survey. A *plat,* sometimes called a *plot,* is a map of certain land that is usually prepared by a licensed land surveyor or engineer. The platted land is subdivided into basic units called *blocks* and smaller units called

FIGURE 27   Plat of Survey
(Courtesy D. E. Coyne, Developer)

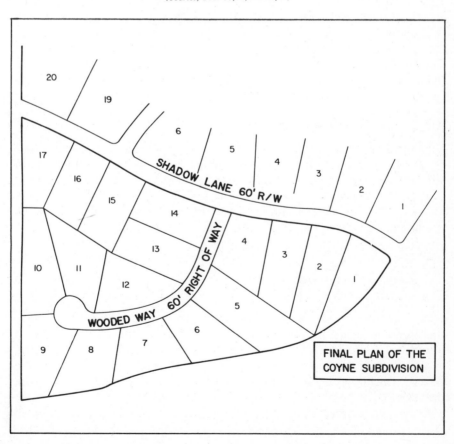

FINAL PLAN OF THE
COYNE SUBDIVISION

lots. A block is made up of a number of lots, and both blocks and lots are numbered and lettered for identification purposes. If a large tract of land is involved, there may be more than one subdivision of the land so that the block and lot would have to be further identified by unit number of the subdivision. Subdivisions are usually given a name, such as a name of the developer or a name with which the land has been identified within the community.

After the plat has been signed and approved by local governmental authorities, it is recorded in the county where the land is located, thus becoming, by reference, another way to describe the land contained therein. An example of a subdivision plat is presented in Figure 27.

Plats may contain other useful data such as the location of easements and rights of way, the names of adjoining landowners and descriptions of their land, engineering data such as the location of flood plains and drainage swales, restrictive covenants, survey data, elevations, and the name and address of the surveyor or engineer who prepared the plat.

This method of describing land is used in all the states. It usually supplements a description under the rectangular survey and metes and bounds systems. As a practical matter, a plat is an extremely useful tool for a buyer or developer, who may want to know not only the general shape of the land, but also how it relates to adjoining tracts, how it could be subdivided if it is a large undivided tract, or how it could be resubdivided if a subdivision previously took place.

Ambiguous Descriptions

Since several methods of describing land can be incorporated into a single deed, ambiguities may arise where one method conflicts with another. When this situation occurs, the general rule is that the intention of the parties controls. In determining such intention, priority is usually given to the description about which the parties are least likely to be mistaken. Hence, the general rules of construction are:

1. Natural or artificial monuments govern over courses and distances.
2. Natural monuments prevail over artificial monuments.
3. Courses govern over distances.
4. A stated acreage or area is the least reliable of any method.

For example, if the distance between a point and a monument were described in a deed as being "north 100 feet to the center of Smith Street, such line forming a 90 degree angle with South Street" and the actual distance between the point and Smith Street was 110 feet, the course (the direction or angle of the line) would prevail and not the distance.

Where necessary, such ambiguities can be clarified by parol (verbal) evidence as long as such evidence is used to explain only the ambiguity and not the written descriptions. They may also be resolved by a course of conduct where the parties rely in fact on an interpretation of a deed description.

Exceptions and Reservations

An *exception* is the exclusion by the grantor of part of the real property conveyed by deed to the grantee. Title to the excepted part of the real property remains in the grantor, but if not excepted in the deed to the grantee, the excepted part would become the grantee's land by virtue of the transfer. For example, if a grantor owned Section 1, he could convey to the grantee "Section 1, excepting the northeast ¼ thereof" and by so doing retain part of the land granted.

A *reservation* creates or reserves a new right out of the land conveyed to the grantee. For example, a grantor conveys Section 1 to the grantee and "reserves to himself, his heirs, and assigns, the right of ingress and egress over an existing road in the southwest corner of such land."

Often the words exception and reservation are taken to mean the same thing because the deed language may say "excepting and reserving . . . ." Technically, however, a reservation creates a new right in the grantor, whereas an exception withholds from the grant part of the property that otherwise would have been conveyed.

SUMMARY

A deed is an instrument of conveyance. A valid deed should include the following elements: the names of the parties, consideration, an adequate description of the property conveyed, the signature of the grantor, and an acknowledgment of the grantor's signature. Grantees who do not regularly deal in real property should have any conveyancing document checked by an expert before accepting it to insure the valid existence of each of these elements.

QUESTIONS FOR DISCUSSION

1. Even though a deed may be valid in the sense that the required elements exist, discuss several reasons why a grantee would be well advised to have it reviewed by a qualified attorney before accepting it for recordation.

2. Discuss the circumstances under which grantors and grantees would be satisfied with the delivery and acceptance of quitclaim, general warranty, and special warranty deeds.

3. Discuss the different methods of describing real property. Does it make any difference which method is selected? Why?

4. What is the difference between a deed and the method of transferring real property?

CASES

Case 1. A certain parcel of land was transferred by deed to Plaintiff, the present owner. The deed specified that the real property consisted of "about four acres of land" and that the northerly boundary of the property was located 20 feet north of the dwelling house on the property. Plaintiff maintained that the northerly boundary was actually located 120 feet beyond the house, and not 20 feet as stated in the deed. In an attempt to reform the deed description, Plaintiff showed that the only way four acres could be obtained was by using the 120-foot measurement. Would a court permit reformation?

Case 2. Plaintiff County had taken title to certain land through tax sales. In 1964, Defendant purchased part of said land and received a quitclaim deed from Plaintiff. The following year, the county issued a correction deed to Defendant that contained the following description: "All unplatted land in this Block and all land west of this Blk. and Pt. lot 1: Pt. lot A. (This deed is given to correct that certain quitclaim deed issued by Summit County July 1964.) The above property was sold for delinquent taxes for the year 1935 inclusive in the name of the Park City

Townsite and an auditor's deed taken by [the] County." Does Plaintiff County's argument that the description in the deed is insufficient based upon the use of certain abbreviations have any merit?

Case 3. Frank, a widower, executed and acknowledged a deed in 1963 conveying his residence to his daughter Wilma. Frank retained possession of the deed until 1970, at which time he gave it to another daughter, Helen. In 1972, Frank died and Helen informed her sister of the deed. Helen thought the deed was valid, gave it to Wilma, and asked her when she was going to move into the decedent's house. Wilma immediately recorded the deed and conveyed the property to her son and daughter. If Frank died without a will, who is entitled to Frank's residence?

Case 4. Plaintiff failed to pay real estate taxes on a certain property. Subsequently, the property was sold to Defendants, who received a treasurer's tax deed that vested title in "L. Michaels or B. Michaels," the defendants herein. Assuming that the property was adequately described, what argument would you make for Plaintiff, who is attempting to void the deed? Do you think the argument is valid?

Case 5. A certain tract of land was described in Grantee's deed as follows: "A certain tract of pocasin land adjoining the lands of the late Henderson Luton and others, lying and being in Chowan County, and State of North Carolina, containing by estimation three hundred nineteen (319) acres, more or less . . . ." There are numerous extensive tracts of pocasin land in Chowan County. Does Grantee have valid title to the land as described in his deed?

Case 6. Plaintiffs own lake front lot 6. A recent title search revealed that a warranty deed conveyed to Plaintiffs' predecessor in title "Lot 6 except . . . and also reserving the East 100 feet [which fronted on the lake] of said lot which is reserved and dedicated to the use of the lot owners of this subdivision." Plaintiffs brought an action to quiet title to the east 100 feet of the property as described in their predecessor's deed. Defendants, being the other lot owners in the subdivision, contest Plaintiffs' quiet title action, claiming that they have a right to use the lake front property in question. What arguments would you make for Plaintiffs and for Defendants?

Chapter 10

Closing the Real Estate Transaction

IN transactions involving the transfer of an ownership interest by bargain and sale, there is usually a date and time when the parties are called upon to complete their agreed-upon performance obligations. Usually the seller presents a deed that transfers title to the property to the buyer, and the buyer pays the seller the agreed-upon purchase price. The process by which the performance obligations are concluded is referred to as the real estate *closing* or *settlement*.

The actual process of settlement is usually carried out according to the prevailing custom of the particular geographical area. The procedures used are generally not controlled by statutory law of the jurisdiction, but certain aspects of settlement may be regulated by laws such as the Real Estate Settlement Procedures Act (discussed in Chapter 14). Settlement may be made through attorneys, banks, real estate brokers, or title insurance companies, or by the individual parties to the transaction. Local custom and usage or agreement by the parties will determine the identity of the agent used to conduct settlement.

THEORY OF SETTLEMENT

The purpose of the settlement is to appoint a time and place for the delivery of the deed and the payment of the purchase price as well as for the adjustment of charges and expenses incident to the transfer of the ownership interest. At settlement, title passes from seller to buyer and all charges and expenses are adjusted between seller and buyer. By establishing a date and place for settlement, the parties can know in advance when and where their performance obligations must be completed. For this reason, most contracts of purchase and sale will specify a

237

date for settlement. Often the settlement date is expressed in terms of "on or before" a certain date, which allows for an earlier closing and establishes a date beyond which the non-performing party is in default.

For purposes of clarity, the closing itself may be divided into two distinct parts. The first part involves the transfer of money and legal documents to complete performance obligations of the parties to the transaction. In addition to the buyer and seller, a third-party lender may be involved in these transfers. The second part of settlement involves adjustment among the parties of expenses for which one or more of the parties is entitled to reimbursement because of the prepayment or accrual of costs. If a third-party lender is involved in the settlement, certain "closing costs" may also be incurred by either buyer or seller or both.

COMPLETION OF PERFORMANCE OBLIGATIONS

The performance obligations of the parties to the transaction will be controlled by the terms and conditions of the contract between them as well as local custom and usage. For example, the contract may specify the type of deed to be delivered by the seller. If the type of deed is not specified in the written contract, the parties may look to local custom and usage to determine what type is to be delivered. A general warranty deed may be the accepted rule when the parties have not spoken to the matter in the contract.

Buyer's Performance Obligations

Most commonly, the buyer's performance obligations include payment of the purchase price and performance of the duties imposed by law. Prior to settlement, the buyer must satisfy him/herself as to the quality of the seller's title and the physical condition of the improvements on the property he/she is buying.

If the buyer is relying on a third party to provide a portion of the funds necessary to complete the purchase of the property, he/she must arrange for appropriate financing in advance of settlement. In this case the buyer usually applies for a loan from either a private or commercial lender. The financing process was discussed in detail in Chapters 7 and 8.

In satisfying the title requirements, the buyer must have the seller's title examined to be certain that the title is free and clear of liens and encumbrances that would render the seller's title unmerchantable. The actual process by which the title requirements are met have been discussed in Chapter 6. In some jurisdictions, by custom and usage, the seller is responsible for providing to the buyer evidence of merchantable title in the form of a title insurance policy or an up-to-date abstract of title. In such jurisdictions, the buyer does not bear the cost of completing the title requirements, although he/she still must satisfy him/herself as to the merchantability of the seller's title.

The buyer may also be responsible for performing other duties imposed by the contract. For example, in some cases, the buyer may be required to make one or more down payments between the time the contract is executed and the date the settlement occurs. In other cases, the contract may have a mortgage contingency clause that requires the buyer to seek financing within a specified time.

Seller's Performance Obligations

Most contracts provide that the seller's performance obligation is to convey merchantable title to the buyer by a "good and sufficient" warranty deed. To accomplish this, the seller must have a deed prepared that transfers title to the property to the buyer, release or arrange to release any liens or encumbrances against the property, and cure any other title defects except those specifically agreed upon by buyer and seller. Often the proceeds of the sale are used to satisfy liens such as mortgages, municipal liens, and judgments. As long as the proceeds of the sale are sufficient to pay off all existing liens, the title is considered merchantable.

If the custom and usage of the area is that the buyer is responsible for checking the seller's title, then it is his/her obligation to report the liens and defects to the settlement agent and the seller. The seller must then make arrangements for payment. If a defect is discovered that cannot be cured by applying a portion of the proceeds toward its satisfaction, then as a general rule the seller must attempt to cure the defect. Often such defects or "clouds upon title" result from an incomplete legal description, the failure of a prior grantor to properly convey the property, or a technical defect in the execution of a prior instrument affecting title to the property. Many times, such defects are easily cured through a survey of the land or by the reconveyance of the property from a prior grantor. In any case, in the absence of an agreement to the contrary, it is the seller who must bear the trouble and expense of providing the quality of title required by the real estate contract as part of his/her performance obligation.

Another performance obligation common to most real estate contracts is the transfer of possession. Usually, the sale of an ownership interest in residential real property involves the transfer of possession. The owner of the property sells to the buyer, who moves into it. However, not all sales involve the transfer of possession. As was discussed in Chapter 4, a sale and leaseback involves a transfer of ownership but no transfer of possession. Sometimes an owner of a rental unit will sell to a tenant who is already in possession of the premises. In these cases, the settlement does not require the seller to vacate the premises in favor of the buyer.

Where the contract is silent as to the transfer of possession, it is the general rule that upon settlement the seller must turn possession over to the buyer. Therefore, in most cases, the inability of the seller to transfer possession upon settlement is a breach of his/her performance obligation. In such cases, the buyer may be entitled to an abatement of the purchase price, to damages, or to rental payments from the seller until possession is transferred. The buyer may also have the option of voiding the contract.

The seller also has performance obligations imposed by law. For example, he/she must permit the buyer reasonable access to inspect the property for the discovery of possible rights of parties in possession. If the property has tenants, the seller must permit the buyer to examine the lease or other documents affecting the property that are not available to the buyer in the public record.

If the property is encumbered by lease contracts, the seller is usually required to assign them to the buyer. If the property has rights such as easements, gas or oil leases, or profits, these must also be assigned or transferred at closing. Usually, the language of the deed includes all appurtenant rights, but in some cases a separate document must be prepared to accomplish the transfer of rights from seller to buyer.

The parties may agree that the seller has additional performance obligations. For example, if the sale of the property also involves the sale of a business, the buyer may require that the seller provide a list of creditors of the business under the bulk sales laws. Or the buyer and seller may agree that the seller must provide an up-to-date survey of the property showing the locations of improvements and easements. Supplementary performance obligations other than those implied at law must be set out in the contract.

Performance Obligations in Mortgage Transactions

In addition to the buyer and seller, there may be other parties to the settlement. In transactions where the buyer is financing a portion of the purchase price, the third-party lender is commonly involved in settlement. Where the buyer has obtained a loan commitment from the lender and a legal relationship has been created between them, the settlement also gives rise to performance obligations.

As discussed in Chapter 7, under a conventional financing arrangement, the lender agrees to supply money to the buyer in exchange for the buyer's promise to repay the loan as it becomes due and a nonpossessory security interest in the buyer's newly acquired property. At settlement, when the funds are provided, the buyer must execute and deliver a bond or promissory note evidencing the debt and setting forth the repayment obligations. He/she must also execute a mortgage document that places a lien on the property to secure the repayment of the loan.

In advance of settlement, the buyer must supply evidence to the lender that after settlement with the seller the buyer will be owner of the property and that the lender's lien will have priority over all other liens and encumbrances against the property. This is usually accomplished through a title insurance binder or a preliminary title opinion, which provide the lender with information about the quality of the title and matters that must be completed before the lender can obtain a first lien on the property. The buyer may also be required to either provide or pay for an appraisal of the property so that the lender may assure itself that the value of the property being placed by the borrower as security for the repayment of the loan exceeds the amount of the loan proceeds.

Prior to settlement, the lender may have performance obligations imposed by law. As discussed in Chapter 14, the lender may be required to provide certain disclosures under Regulation Z or a good faith estimate of the closing costs under the Real Estate Settlement Procedures Act. Failure of the lender to comply may result in a claim for damages by the buyer.

Performance Obligations at Settlement

At settlement, each party must deliver the money or documents to complete the contract. Figure 28 illustrates the transfer of legal documents and money in a typical real estate settlement involving conventional mortgage financing. The buyer's mortgagee provides the loan proceeds to the buyer. The buyer delivers the loan proceeds and the balance of the purchase price to the seller. The seller uses the portion of the purchase price necessary to pay his/her mortgagee the balance of the mortgage loan and retains the balance of the proceeds of the sale. In exchange for the monies received, the buyer's mortgagee receives a bond or promissory note and mortgage; the buyer receives a deed to the property; and the seller receives a release or satisfaction of mortgage and the return of his/her bond or promissory note.

The settlement process requires coordination and the cooperation of all parties. The seller cannot satisfy his/her mortgage until the funds are made available by the buyer. Until the balance due on the seller's mortgage is paid, he/she cannot transfer merchantable title to the buyer. A question frequently raised is whether the buyer can refuse to complete

FIGURE 28   Performance Obligations

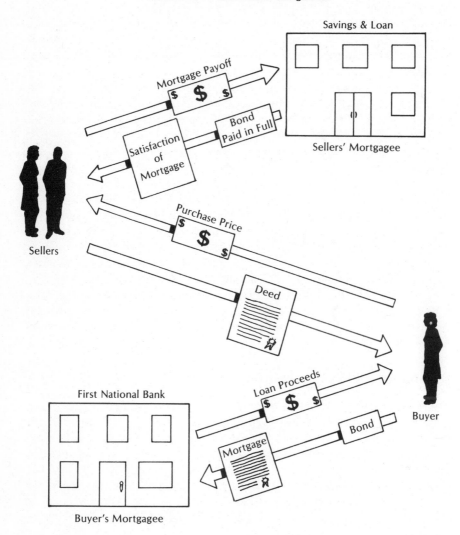

the transaction because at the moment of settlement the seller does not have merchantable title. In most jurisdictions, it is assumed that the purchase price must be delivered if the proceeds of the sale are sufficient to satisfy all liens against the seller's property. In those jurisdictions where no such assumption is made, a clause may be inserted in the contract acknowledging that the purchase price will be used to satisfy any outstanding indebtedness upon the property and that the buyer may not refuse to tender payment as long as that payment can release the liens on the property.

Most settlements are conducted by independent third parties such as title companies, brokers, attorneys, or banks, and the purchase price is tendered to the settlement agent. The settlement agent then makes disbursement to satisfy the outstanding liens. In this manner the buyer is assured that the purchase price is applied to indebtedness before the balance is tendered to the seller.

PAYMENT AND ADJUSTMENT OF COSTS AND EXPENSES

At settlement the parties must pay and adjust among themselves certain costs and expenses incident to the transfer of ownership. The payment of these costs and expenses will be governed by the agreement among the parties and local custom and usage.

Usually the buyer and seller agree that the costs, expenses, and income derived from the property are to be prorated to the date of settlement. This requires the apportionment of income and expenses between the seller and buyer according to the time when each is owner of the property. For example, if the seller pays ad valorem property taxes on a calendar year basis in advance and settlement is to be made on June 30, then the buyer will be responsible for payment of the taxes for the period July 1 through December 31. A seller who has paid the taxes for the entire year would be entitled to reimbursement from the buyer for the portion of the year during which the buyer is the owner. If the taxes have not been paid by the seller, the buyer would be entitled to receive payment from the seller for the period January 1 through June 30, the date of settlement. In the latter case, payment from seller to buyer would usually be made through a reduction in the purchase price in the amount of the unpaid taxes. When expenses have been paid in advance, they are said to be *prepaid*. When payment is made after the expense has been incurred, the expense is said to be *accrued*. Payment or reimbursement will be determined by whether the expense has been prepaid or accrued.

Taxes are not the only item that may be prorated. Often expenses such as insurance, maintenance costs, interest, special assessments, and the like are prorated. When rental property is transferred and tenants have prepaid rents to the seller, a proration of income may be required. For utility costs such as water, electricity, natural gas, and community steam systems, the meter may be read on the day when the prorations are to be made and the amounts to be credited or reimbursed are calculated accordingly. However, not all expenses can be calculated in this manner. In the case of fuel oil or liquefied petroleum gas, where the seller has an inventory of fuel on hand and no way to measure the contents of the tanks, if the capacity of the tank is known it is possible to refill on the settlement date and have the buyer pay the seller the value of a full tank of fuel. In such cases, an adjustment should be made because it may be physically impossible to completely refill the tank.

The rules governing proration of expenses and income are not uniform throughout the United States and are usually governed by local practice and procedure. For example, in some areas, by custom and

TABLE 9   Chart for Calculating Prorations of One Dollar on a Calendar-Year Basis[a]

Days	Jan.	Feb.	Mar.	Apr.	May	June	July	Aug.	Sept.	Oct.	Nov.	Dec.

Days	Jan.	Feb.	Mar.	Apr.	May	June	July	Aug.	Sept.	Oct.	Nov.	Dec.
1	.003	.086	.169	.253	.336	.419	.503	.586	.669	.753	.836	.919
2	.006	.089	.172	.256	.339	.422	.506	.589	.672	.756	.839	.922
3	.008	.092	.175	.258	.342	.425	.508	.592	.675	.758	.842	.925
4	.011	.094	.178	.261	.344	.428	.511	.594	.678	.761	.844	.928
5	.014	.097	.181	.264	.347	.431	.514	.597	.681	.764	.847	.931
6	.017	.100	.183	.267	.350	.433	.517	.600	.683	.767	.850	.933
7	.019	.103	.186	.269	.353	.436	.519	.603	.686	.769	.853	.936
8	.022	.106	.189	.272	.356	.439	.522	.606	.689	.772	.856	.939
9	.025	.108	.192	.275	.358	.442	.525	.608	.692	.775	.858	.942
10	.028	.111	.194	.278	.361	.444	.528	.611	.694	.778	.861	.944
11	.031	.114	.197	.281	.364	.447	.531	.614	.697	.781	.864	.947
12	.033	.117	.200	.283	.367	.450	.533	.617	.700	.783	.867	.950
13	.036	.119	.203	.286	.369	.453	.536	.619	.703	.786	.869	.953
14	.039	.122	.206	.289	.372	.456	.539	.622	.706	.789	.872	.956
15	.042	.125	.208	.292	.375	.458	.542	.625	.708	.792	.875	.958
16	.044	.128	.211	.294	.378	.461	.544	.628	.711	.794	.878	.961
17	.047	.131	.214	.297	.381	.464	.547	.631	.714	.797	.881	.964
18	.050	.133	.217	.300	.383	.467	.550	.633	.717	.800	.883	.967
19	.053	.136	.219	.303	.386	.469	.553	.636	.719	.803	.886	.969
20	.056	.139	.222	.306	.389	.472	.555	.639	.722	.806	.889	.972
21	.058	.142	.225	.308	.392	.475	.558	.642	.725	.808	.892	.975
22	.061	.144	.228	.311	.394	.478	.561	.644	.728	.811	.894	.978
23	.064	.147	.231	.314	.397	.481	.564	.647	.731	.814	.897	.981
24	.067	.150	.233	.317	.400	.483	.567	.650	.733	.817	.900	.983
25	.069	.153	.236	.319	.403	.486	.569	.653	.736	.819	.903	.986
26	.072	.156	.239	.322	.406	.489	.572	.656	.739	.822	.906	.989
27	.075	.158	.242	.325	.408	.492	.575	.658	.742	.825	.908	.992
28	.078	.161	.244	.328	.411	.494	.578	.661	.744	.828	.911	.994
29	.081	.164	.247	.331	.414	.497	.581	.664	.747	.831	.914	.997
30	.083	.167	.250	.333	.417	.500	.583	.667	.750	.833	.917	1.00

Ratios for Apportionment Based on One Dollar

Source: Berks Title Insurance Company

[a] Five hundred dollars prorated as of March 17 is $500 x .214 = $107.00.

usage, prorations are made to the date of settlement and the buyer assumes responsibility as of the settlement date. In other areas, the seller is responsible for the expenses up to and including the closing date. Often prorations are based upon a 30-day month or 360-day year. However, the actual number of days may be calculated and used as the basis of prorating expenses or income. Local custom and usage should control in the absence of an agreement to the contrary. Table 9 is an example of a chart used to calculate prorations on a daily basis using a 360-day year.

In addition to the proration of expenses and income between the buyer and seller, there may be other expenses incident to the transfer of an ownership interest in real property. If the jurisdiction assesses a tax on the transfer of ownership interests, then the applicable tax must be paid in the manner agreed on by the parties. Also, costs such as recording fees are paid at settlement. If the transaction involves conventional mortgage financing, the fees and costs charged in connection with the loan are usually collected at closing. These charges may include credit report fee, appraisal fee, document preparation fee, mortgage recording fee, loan placement fee or discount points, and a charge for conducting the settlement. In most cases involving residential mortgage financing, these charges are set forth in the Real Estate Settlement Procedures Act settlement statement (see Figure 35 in Chapter 14).

If the seller has employed a broker who is entitled to a commission by reason of the sale, then the commission is customarily paid at settlement. If the broker has received an earnest money payment from the buyer that has been held in the broker's trust or escrow account, then at settlement the broker must account to the seller for the funds so received.

If the settlement is conducted by an independent party, an accounting is usually prepared that details the receipts and disbursements involved in the transaction. A settlement statement that explains the disbursements to be made in connection with the transfer of the ownership interest is illustrated in Figure 29.

The settlement statement prepared by the settlement agent should not be confused with the settlement statement required under the Real Estate Settlement Procedures Act. Often, if there is a loan incident to the buyer's purchase of the property, both the HUD Form No.1 required by the Real Estate Settlement Procedures Act and a settlement statement are prepared for closing. However, the HUD form may reflect only those costs and expenses resulting from the loan. The settlement statement usually includes the adjustments between buyer and seller and is commonly used whether or not the buyer has financed the purchase through a mortgage lender.

At settlement, the accounting is made and the legal documents are presented that are necessary to effectuate the transfer of ownership and the release of any liens or encumbrances upon the property. However, in most cases the transaction is not complete.

FIGURE 29   Settlement Sheet

```
                        SETTLEMENT SHEET

Seller:     Samuel Smith

Purchaser:  Bruce and Brenda Brown


Sale Price                                          $83,000.00

Costs of Buyer:
  Preparation of Mortgage              $     25.00
  Realty Transfer Tax (1%)                  830.00
  Recording Deed and Mortgage              17.00
  Real Estate Taxes (prepaid by Seller)
    Borough/Township/County                 86.70
    School                                 394.50
  First Year's Insurance Premium           317.00
  Settlement Charge                         50.00
  Title Insurance                          425.00          2,145.20

Gross Due from Buyer                                $85,145.20

Less:
  Down Payment                         $ 5,000.00
  Due from Mortgage Lender              65,000.00         70,000.00

Net Due from Buyer                                  $15,145.20


Sale Price                                          $83,000.00

Plus Real Estate Taxes (prepaid by Seller)
  Borough/Township/County                   86.70
  School                                   394.50           481.20

Gross Due Seller                                    $83,481.20

Costs of Seller:
  Preparation of Deed                  $     25.00
  Realty Transfer Tax (1%)                  830.00
  Satisfaction fee to Mortgage Lender        2.00
  Agent's Commission (6%)               4,980.00
  Settlement Charge                         50.00
  Mortgage Payoff                      27,570.00         33,457.00
                                                        $50,024.20

Less Down Payment                                         5,000.00

Net Due Seller                                      $45,024.20
```

POST-SETTLEMENT PROCEDURES

Usually, the buyer's title examination is completed sometime in advance of the settlement, and it would be possible for a lien or encumbrance to be entered during the interval between completion of the examination and the settlement. As was discussed in Chapter 6, most recording statutes look to the date and time when a document was recorded to establish priorities among inconsistent instruments. Therefore, if a lien, encumbrance, or conveyance of the property were made and entered on the record after the purchaser's search was completed but before the purchase, the purchaser's interest in the property would be subject to that prior interest, because in most states the purchaser would be considered to have had constructive notice of that prior interest.

To protect against this contingency, after settlement the actual disbursement of the funds is delayed until the buyer or his or her agent has an opportunity to make a final check of the public records to be certain that no additional liens or encumbrances have been entered and that no adverse conveyances of the property have been made. This final check is sometimes referred to as a *bringdown search* because it brings down to the present the title work that was completed earlier. The abstractor, attorney, or title agent will check the indices for mortgages, judgments, and other liens and deeds from the date of the preliminary search up to the actual time of recording.

If there has been no change in the record and the record indicates that the property is free and clear of liens and encumbrances except those accounted for at closing, the deed transferring title from seller to buyer may be presented for recording. If the transaction also involves a form of financing that includes the property's being placed as collateral, then the instrument that creates the nonpossessory security interest in the lender or other secured party is presented for recording as well as the deed. In most cases, the deed is presented first for recording. This transfers title into the buyer-borrower. After the deed is recorded, the mortgage or other document is presented for recording. This establishes the proper sequence of the documents in the chain of title.

After the deed and mortgage or other document are recorded, the settlement agent is notified and the funds are then disbursed to the parties as detailed in the settlement statement. If the transaction involves title insurance, policies are issued to the new owner and the mortgagee. If an abstract of title is used as title guarantee, the abstract is brought up to date to include the buyer's deed and mortgage. If a title certificate is used, the certificate is issued listing the liens and encumbrances after the transaction is completed.

After the recording process of indexing and incorporating the documents in the public record is finished, the original documents are returned by the public recorder. The deed is returned to the new owner or his/her agent, and the mortgage is returned to the mortgagee for inclusion in the loan file. With the return of the documents, the settlement process is completed.

SETTLEMENT PROBLEMS

Most real estate settlements can be carried out without complication in the manner just described. However, occasionally a problem may develop because one or more of the parties is unable to meet his/her performance obligations. For example, the inability to complete performance may result from the failure of a contractor to satisfy all the requirements of a construction contract. If the seller is a building contractor or developer and the house being purchased by the buyer is substantially completed and habitable, the closing may still be made, with a certain portion of the proceeds withheld from distribution to the seller pending completion of the unfinished work. As a general rule, the amount withheld in such cases will exceed the fair value of the unfinished improvements so that if the work is not completed a third party may be hired to finish the project using the funds that were withheld. The amount withheld is a matter of agreement among the parties to the transaction.

If the seller is unable to deliver merchantable title at closing, and the funds produced through the sale are not sufficient to correct the defect, then, as a general rule, the buyer may not be compelled to complete the transaction. For example, if the search of the seller's title reveals that in a prior conveyance of the property one of the property owners did not join in the conveyance, then there would be a cloud upon the seller's title. This type of cloud could not be cleared through the payment of a portion of the proceeds of the sale as could an unpaid money judgment lien. In such cases, the buyer usually has the option of taking title to the property with the cloud upon the title or refusing to complete the transaction because of the seller's inability to convey merchantable title to the property.

The buyer may also be entitled to receive any damages sustained through the seller's breach of contract. These additional damages might include the reasonable and incidental expenses incurred by the buyer incident to the transaction, such as title fees, loan costs, or moving expenses. If the buyer still wishes to complete the transaction and assume the risk of the cloud upon the title, it is possible that the seller and buyer might abate the purchase price to reflect the diminution in value of the property. If a third-party lender is involved in the transaction, the latter alternative may not be acceptable because most loans are made on the basis that the mortgagor will have merchantable title to the mortgaged premises free and clear of all other liens and encumbrances. The cloud upon the title may disqualify the property from being acceptable as security for the repayment of the mortgage loan.

Another problem at settlement can arise through the form in which payment of the purchase price, costs, and expenses is made. If the parties make payment with personal checks rather than cash, any payment so tendered is subject to collection. In some jurisdictions, no actual disbursement of funds is made until all checks have cleared the banks. This potential problem may sometimes be avoided through the use of certified checks that insure the availability of funds for collection. However, certified checks are not generally considered the equivalent of cash. Disbursement can be made if the form of payment at closing may be specified in advance and appropriate arrangements made to insure that payments made at settlement are secured.

Since settlement involves the disbursement of other persons' money, the settlement agent has a fiduciary duty to the participants whose funds are being used to complete the transaction. In most cases, the settlement agent will ask the parties to verify the disbursements made as scheduled on the settlement statement. If the parties agree with the listed disbursements, each is asked to acknowledge his/her concurrence by signing the settlement statement. This verified copy of the settlement statement is usually retained by the settlement agent as evidence of the parties' concurrence.

SUMMARY

The purpose of settlement (closing) is to permit parties to the transaction at a designated time and place to complete their respective performance obligations. The following tabulation summarizes the transfer of legal documents for a typical settlement involving mortgage financing:

Document	From	To
Deed	Seller	Buyer
Mortgage	Buyer	Buyer's mortgagee
Bond or promissory note	Buyer	Buyer's mortgagee
Satisfaction of mortgage	Seller's mortgagee	Seller
Canceled promissory note	Seller's mortgagee	Seller

The flow of monies among the parties to a typical real estate transaction involving mortgage financing is as follows:

Funds	From	To
Mortgage loan proceeds	Buyer's mortgagee	Buyer
Purchase price (down payment and loan proceeds)	Buyer	Seller
Mortgage payoff	Seller	Seller's mortgagee
Proration of prepaid expenses	Buyer	Seller
Proration of accrued expenses	Seller	Buyer
Closing costs	As designated by agreement among the parties	

QUESTIONS FOR DISCUSSION

1. In most cases, the buyer of real property is paying money as consideration for the purchase. If the consideration being paid is other real property rather than money, what effect will this have on the settlement with regard to the transfer of legal documents and the adjustments of costs and expenses between the buyer and seller?

2. Usually at a residential property settlement there is a transfer of possession as well as a transfer of ownership of the property. Sometimes, however, the seller cannot vacate the premises until after settlement, or the buyer moves into the property before settlement. In such cases, what additional matters must be considered in conducting the settlement between the parties?

3. Additional matters must be considered for settlement if the real property being transferred includes a business that is a going concern rather than a residential property. What additional legal documents should be included, and what other charges and expenses usually must be adjusted between buyer and seller?

4. Is it necessary that the buyer and seller be present at settlement if all documents are properly executed in advance? Is there any good policy reason why attendance at closing is desirable?

5. What additional documents must be prepared or matters considered if the transaction is based upon the seller's financing the property through (a) a purchase money mortgage? (b) an installment real estate contract?

6. If either buyer or seller is unable to complete his/her performance obligations at settlement and is in default, the nonbreaching party may be entitled to recover damages caused through the default of the other. What damages would be reasonably foreseeable if the nonbreaching party is the seller? What damages would be reasonably foreseeable if the nonbreaching party is the buyer? What other remedy other than damages may be available to either party?

7. If Seller had a mortgage on the property and Buyer has borrowed a portion of the purchase price in a conventional mortgage transaction, what documents incident to closing should be recorded?

8. The local property taxes assessed against Seller's property for the current year are $375 in school taxes and $278 in county and municipal taxes. Both taxes are assessed on a calendar year basis and are payable in advance. Seller has paid the school taxes but has not paid the county and municipal taxes for the current year. Assuming that the closing is to occur on September 16, by whom is payment or reimbursement to be made, and in what amount? (Use Table 9.)

9. If, after closing, the buyer discovers that a new lien has been entered against the seller since the title search but before recording of the buyer's purchase, what recourse, if any, does the buyer have against the seller?

10. After settlement, all monies having been disbursed and documents of title recorded, it is discovered that the settlement agent did not properly prorate taxes between the seller and the buyer. What recourse does the aggrieved party have against the settlement agent? Against the other party?

Chapter 11
Leases

By Operation of Law

By Occurrence of a Condition Subsequent

By Mutual Agreement

REMEDIES ON DEFAULT OF RENTAL PAYMENT

Distraint

Possession and Mitigation

Anticipatory Breach

SECURITY DEPOSITS

LEASE TERMS AND CONDITIONS

Date

Parties

Lease Premises

Term

Rental

Use Provisions

Renewal

Possession

Rules and Regulations

Maintenance and Repairs

Habitability

Insurance

Destruction

Examples

QUESTIONS FOR DISCUSSION

CASES

IN Chapter 2, a nonfreehold estate was defined as an estate that could be measured in exact intervals of time. It was characterized as being no more than a possessory interest, often referred to as a leasehold interest or estate. Four such leasehold interests—an estate for years, an estate from year to year, a tenancy at will, and a tenancy at sufferance—were broadly defined and discussed. The purpose of this chapter is to examine with more specificity the general nature of a lease, since it creates and defines the landlord–tenant relationship, and the terms and conditions contained in the lease that establish the rights, interests, and remedies of the parties.

LANDLORD AND TENANT DEFINED

The relationship between landlord and tenant is always contractual in nature. The contract is called a *lease*. It can be written or oral, depending on the law of the state where the real property is located, and express or implied, depending on the factual situation. The person who owns or possesses the real property that is the subject of the contract or lease is the *lessor* or *landlord,* whereas the person who enters into possession is the *lessee* or *tenant*. The tenant's interest is often referred to as a *leasehold* interest. Thus, a lease is generally defined as a conveyance of a possessory interest by the landlord to the tenant for a stated consideration called *rent*. Rent usually takes the form of a money payment; however, it can be paid with other property or services.

A lease can be distinguished from a license in that a license is the mere authority to perform an act on another's real property and passes no interest or estate in the land. A license usually cannot be assigned; a lease conveys a possessory interest or estate in the land that can be assigned unless expressly prohibited in the lease agreement. Thus, the prevailing

255

view is that one who occupies land with the consent of the owner in anticipation of entering into a lease agreement is a licensee until a lease is finalized. Someone who occupies an owner's land without consent or without being under the terms of a lease agreement is a mere trespasser.

A tenant can be distinguished from a boarder or lodger by the nature of the possession. A tenant has exclusive legal possession of the premises and consequently is generally responsible for its condition, normal wear and tear excepted. On the other hand, the boarder or lodger has only the right to use the premises. He/she does not have a right to control its use and is not generally responsible for its care and maintenance.

PRELIMINARY NEGOTIATIONS, PRESENT LEASE, AND AGREEMENT FOR LEASE

Particularly in transient or seasonal communities, where there is a high tenant turnover, landlords often attempt to negotiate leases well in advance of occupancy. The question becomes, At what point in time do such preliminary negotiations become binding on the parties? The answer depends on ordinary principles of contract law. If the parties have agreed on all the essential terms, including rental amount, duration of occupancy, and description of the unit, they have formed either a binding present lease or an agreement to make a lease. If a precise understanding has not been reached, neither party is bound.

For example, T had always liked the appearance of a certain residential rental building owned by L, so he wrote to L and stated: "I like your building located at the intersection of A Street and B Avenue. I would be willing to rent a unit if the price is under $300 per month." L replied several days later: "I accept your offer to lease for $300 per month. You can move into Unit #10 any time after the date of this letter." It is clear that T was merely making an inquiry into the possibility of leasing a unit from L. In the law of contracts, T's letter is simply an invitation to negotiate and not an offer capable of being accepted. Here, a landlord–tenant contract has not been formed.

The distinction between a *present executed lease,* which commences now or in the future, and an *agreement to make a lease* in the future is based primarily on the landlord's remedy. Since a present executed lease creates a definite right to possess, it is governed by landlord and tenant law. Thus, it permits the landlord to sue for rent in the event the tenant fails to take possession or pay rent. On the other hand, since an agreement to make a lease in the future does not create a landlord–tenant relationship until such future contract is executed, it is nothing more than an executory contract again governed by ordinary contract principles. Thus, where the tenant breaches the contract by refusing to take possession or pay rent, the landlord's measure of damage would not be the unpaid rent but the difference between the total agreed-upon rental and the fair rental value of the premises for the stated term. Since these two values are likely to be identical, a landlord would certainly prefer a present lease as opposed to an agreement to make a lease.

For example, L owned a certain tract of land upon which he planned to construct an apartment building if his application for rezoning was approved by local government. Before the application was acted on, L agreed in writing that he would rent a certain unit to T for a stated rental amount and term if and when the apartment building was completed. Subsequently, the application for rezoning was granted and the apartment building completed, but T refused to take possession of the unit. Since the written agreement between L and T was to make a lease in the future and not a present lease, L could not sue T for lost rental but only for damages for breach of contract.

REQUIREMENTS OF A VALID LEASE

Since a lease is a form of contract, the requirements of a valid lease are basically identical with those of ordinary contracts.

1. The parties must have legal capacity to enter into the lease agreement. That is, they must have the capacity to reason and understand the significance of the relationship. Minors, insane or incompetent persons, and others with special legal disabilities lack such capacity. In most states, a person becomes a "legal" adult at age eighteen; however, as a general rule of law, minors have to pay the reasonable value of contracts they enter into for necessaries. Essential housing is usually considered to be a necessity. Thus, even though he/she lacks legal capacity, a minor may be bound to a lease agreement if, under the circumstances, it is a necessity.

2. There must be a mutual manifestation of intent, expressed in the form of an offer and an acceptance. This means that the parties mutually agree to and understand the nature of the lease terms, in particular the duration of the lease and the rental amount. If, for example, the landlord offers to rent apartment 1A for $250 per month and the tenants accept, but only on condition that it is unit 2B, there has not been a mutual manifestation of intent.

3. There must be a stated consideration. Rent is the usual consideration given by the tenant for the right to occupy the leasehold premises. Generally, however, any form of consideration will do as long as it results in a benefit to the landlord. For example, performance of a service or the transfer of some other form of personal property by the

tenant could supply consideration since the landlord benefits by its receipt.

4. The purpose of the lease must be within the law. For example, in a state where gambling is illegal, the lease of a building for the purpose of operating a gambling casino would not be valid.

5. In the event the lease must be in writing to comply with the Statute of Frauds, it should be signed by the parties. If the tenant does not sign, his/her substantial reliance on the written agreement as evidenced by his/her taking possession and paying rent will generally serve as an acceptance, thus doing away with the signature requirement.

These requirements are the bare essentials. Most leases will contain many more provisions further defining the rights and duties of the parties. Such rights and duties are more specifically discussed later in the chapter, under the topic "Lease Terms and Conditions."

THE STATUTE OF FRAUDS

Statute of Fraud provisions in most states generally require that certain lease agreements be in writing. In most states, a writing is required when the duration of the lease is more than one year (as many as three years in some states), or when the lease is not to be performed within the space of one year from the making thereof. It is apparent, therefore, that of the various leasehold estates discussed in Chapter 2, the Statute of Frauds could apply only to an estate for years or an estate from year to year if the duration exceeds a year. It is not applicable to a tenancy at will or a tenancy at sufferance. In most states, where the duration of an oral lease exceeds the statutory period, a tenancy at will or some form of periodic tenancy such as tenancy from month to month arises.

The writing requirement does not require a formal lease. The writing can be informal, but at a minimum it should identify the parties and the premises, state the duration of the lease and the rent to be paid, and be signed by the party against whom enforcement is sought. Therefore, a letter written by a landlord to a tenant containing these terms would be sufficient if the landlord was sued on the lease. Some states go further and require that the signed lease be acknowledged and recorded to be valid. But even if a lease does not have to satisfy the requirements of the Statute of Frauds, it is sound practice to reduce the agreement to writing so that future misunderstanding relating to the lease can be avoided.

CLASSIFICATION OF LEASES

Leases can be classified in a number of ways. However, the three most common methods are (1) by duration of the term, (2) by type of use, and (3) by method of rental payment.

By Duration of Term

As discussed in Chapter 2, the estate for years is a leasehold estate that continues for a definite period of time. On the other hand, an estate from year to year, a tenancy at will, and a tenancy at sufferance are leasehold estates of indefinite duration. The difference among leasehold estates of indefinite duration is that the estate from year to year is subject to definite terms, whereas the tenancy at will and the tenancy at sufferance are not. The tenancy at will is with the consent of the landlord only. The tenancy at sufferance results from a tenant holding over from a valid tenancy without the consent of the landlord.

An estate for years can result in what is generally called a *long-term lease,* where the definite duration of the lease is for an extended period of time, usually more than one year. The advantage of a long-term lease to the landlord is that of having an assured tenant and consequently assured rental income for an extended period of time. Sometimes this is a disadvantage, because the landlord may be committed to a low fixed rent that does not keep pace with inflation. This, of course, works to the tenant's advantage. The advantage to the tenant is that of assured possession of the leasehold premises over an extended period of time. *Short-term leases,* by contrast, do not give such assurances to either party, since their definite duration is usually for less than a year. However, a short-term lease tends to be more flexible, since rental rates and tenants may change more quickly to reflect conditions and trends in the economy.

By Type of Use

Generally, the leasehold premises are used for commercial or residential purposes. A *commercial lease* involves tenant use of the leasehold premises for income-producing activities such as a retail clothing store, professional offices, or manufacturing. A *residential lease* does not usually involve income-producing activities. The leasehold premises provide their tenant and his/her family with a place to dwell. Commercial leases are generally for longer terms than residential leases. In addition, rental payments for commercial space tends to be based on net payments, whereas residential space is usually based on gross payments. (See discussion on page 260 for distinction between gross and net leases.)

Since the law applicable to residential leasing varies widely among the states, the Commissioners on Uniform State Laws have drafted a proposed Uniform Residential Landlord and Tenant Act for the stated purpose of simplifying, clarifying, modernizing, and revising residential landlord–tenant law. The act abandons the traditional view that the landlord–tenant relationship is a matter of real property law and in its place substitutes ordinary contract principles. Thus, the traditional concept of rent for possession only is abandoned for that of rent for certain benefits including possession, service, and quality of the unit. In essence, the act attempts to place the landlord and tenant on an equal footing.

Another type of lease based on use is the *ground lease,* which is a lease of land without improvements. Thus, ownership of the land and ownership of the improvements thereon are separate. The leased land may be used for commercial or residential purposes. For example, if the U.S. Forest Service leased mountain land to a private developer for a ski area, a commercial use is intended, but if land were leased to a private individual for a cabin, a residential use is probably intended. Ground leases usually do not run for more than ninety-nine years, since, under the law of some states, a longer term would convert the leasehold to fee simple ownership.

By Method of Rental Payment

There are many different arrangements that a landlord and tenant can make for the payment of rent. Some of the more common classifications of leases by method of rental payment are gross leases, net or net-net leases, percentage leases, and fixed rental plus escalation leases.

In a *gross lease,* fixed rental payments are made by the tenant, and overhead costs such as taxes, utilities, and insurance are paid for by the landlord. A gross lease is often, although certainly not exclusively, used in the short-term or residential situation.

In a *net lease,* the tenant not only pays a fixed rental, but also pays taxes, utilities, maintenance and repairs, and insurance. Where the tenant pays these as well as all other costs incidental to the leasehold premises, it is often called a *net-net lease.* With a net-net lease, the landlord's only responsibility is to collect rent. A net lease is often used for long-term or commercial rentals.

In a *percentage lease,* rental payments are based on some percent of sales made on the premises. The base to which the percentage is applied can be gross sales, net sales, gross sales above a predetermined amount, or some other agreed-upon sales figure. The percentage lease, therefore, is applicable only to income-producing leaseholds such as restaurants, stores, and theaters. Even though it permits a landlord to share the profits produced in part by a favorable location, it is often difficult to accurately determine the sales figures to which the percentage will apply and to enforce it.

In a *fixed rental plus escalation lease,* a fixed rental base is determined at the beginning of the term and adjusted upward periodically to reflect increases in the cost of living. The percentage increase is often tied to a cost of living index published by the United States Department of Labor. Because of the high rate of inflation and associated increases in the cost of living, landlords favor this method of assessing rent. These and other methods of determining rental payments can be tailored to suit the individual situation since leases are a matter of contractual agreement between the parties. Any terms can be used as long as they do not violate the law or public policy.

RIGHTS AND DUTIES OF LANDLORD AND TENANT

The basic right of the landlord is to receive rent. The basic right of the tenant is to exclusively use, enjoy, occupy, and possess the leasehold premises. The landlord's corresponding duty is to furnish the leasehold premises, and the tenant's duty is to pay the rent. Other important legal rights and duties arise from the landlord–tenant relationship, such as the landlord's right to enter the leasehold premises under certain conditions, rights and duties of the parties with respect to maintenance and repair of the premises, and rights and duties of the parties in the event that the leasehold premises are injured or destroyed.

Landlord's Conditional Right to Enter Premises

The general rule is that a tenant is entitled to the exclusive possession of the leasehold premises and that if the landlord enters without an invitation he/she is a trespasser. The rule is subject to two important exceptions: (1) the landlord can come on the premises to collect rent and (2) the landlord can come on the premises to prevent waste or abate a nuisance.

For example, if a landlord had sufficient evidence that a water pipe in a tenant's premises had burst, he could enter the leasehold premises to repair the pipe to prevent possible water damage. The tenant's permission would not be required, because the landlord entered the premises to prevent waste. However, in the absence of a lease provision to the contrary, in many states, the landlord does not have the right to enter tenant's premises without consent for the purpose of repairing or even rebuilding a damaged or destroyed building. Such an entry might be treated by the tenant as an eviction, thus giving the tenant an excuse to terminate the lease or the right to insist that the landlord rebuild the premises. If the landlord wrongfully comes onto tenant's leasehold premises, the tenant can sue at law for money damages in a tort action, in equity for injunctive relief where the trespass is of a continuing nature and the tenant wants to stop it, or in a contract action based on the landlord's express or implied covenant of quiet enjoyment.

Maintenance and Repair of Premises

Historically, a landlord's duty to maintain and repair leased premises was based on the concept of *caveat lessee*, "Let the tenant beware." In essence, the landlord had no duty to maintain or repair the leased premises either before or after its occupancy. The same general principle was applicable to the tenant. The tenant's only responsibility was to preserve what he/she originally received—that is, to prevent deterioration of the leasehold subject to ordinary wear and tear. However, the law has changed, and now the cases and statutes of most states impose an express or implied obligation upon the landlord to maintain and repair the leased premises.

The modern view is expressed in Section 2-104 of the Uniform Residential Landlord and Tenant Act, which provides that a landlord shall comply with all applicable housing and building code requirements affecting health and safety; make whatever repairs are necessary to keep the premises in a fit and habitable conditon; keep the common areas such as halls, stairways, and roadways in a clean and safe condition; maintain all utilities such as electrical, plumbing, and heating systems and appliances that are furnished as part of the premises in good and safe working order; provide and maintain adequate receptacles for the removal of trash; and supply reasonable amounts of hot water.

Section 3-101 of the same act sets forth similar tenant duties. It states that tenants must also comply with applicable housing and building code requirements; keep the leasehold premises in a safe and clean condition; dispose of trash in a safe and clean manner; reasonably use and maintain the plumbing, electrical, and heating systems; not intentionally or negligently devalue the premises or permit another to do so; and conduct themselves in a manner that will not interfere with their neighbors' peaceful use and enjoyment of their premises. A number of states have adopted substantially all or part of these sections of the act.

Although a landlord has the right to enter the tenant's premises to prevent waste, it is a well-established rule that, in the absence of an agreement to the contrary, a landlord does not have the right, during the term of the lease, to enter the premises and make alterations or improvements. Nor does the tenant have the right, without the landlord's consent, to change or alter the leasehold premises even though such improvements might increase their value. For the tenant to do so would constitute waste.

Constructive Eviction

It is a general rule of law that if a landlord unreasonably interferes with a tenant's possessory interest in the leasehold premises, causing the tenant to abandon the premises, a *constructive eviction* has occurred that will suspend rental payments. For example, a tenant may be constructively evicted if the landlord converts all other units in the building into music studios, the sound of which annoys the tenant day and night. Since the tenant has been deprived of the beneficial use and enjoyment of the premises, a constructive eviction has occurred if he/she moves out of the premises. The concept of constructive eviction may apply where the landlord has failed to maintain and repair the leasehold premises. Thus, where the landlord has an express or implied duty to repair plumbing or supply water and heat and the tenant cannot use the plumbing facilities because they are in a state of disrepair and there is no water or heat, a constructive eviction may have been worked where the tenant abandons the premises within a reasonable period of time.

General Condition of Premises

In the past, the landlord owed no special duty to protect tenants from harm that was in some way related to the condition of the premises. This general rule has also been undergoing significant change as landlord and tenant law evolves to meet the needs of modern society. For example, in the past a landowner's liability to a person injured on the premises depended in large part on the status of the injured person. A landlord generally owed no duty to a trespasser but did owe some duty to a licensee or guest to maintain the condition of the premises. The newer rule, which has been adopted by a growing number of states, creates one general standard of care, as opposed to a different standard for each group, whereby a landowner must act as a reasonable person would act under the particular circumstances in maintaining the property in reasonably safe condition.

Also, in the past, the general rule has been that a landlord owes no special duty to protect tenants from criminal acts committed by third parties on the leased premises. Recently, however, a number of courts have stated that a landlord's duty is to take reasonable steps, in view of the surrounding circumstances, to eliminate conditions that might contribute toward criminal activity. Broken burglar alarms or door locks and poorly lighted common hallways or automobile parking areas might be conditions that if improperly maintained would subject the landlord to liability. The trend, therefore, is to subject the landlord to liability for leasehold premises that are not reasonably maintained under the circumstances.

There are three common factual situations where a landlord can subject him/herself to liability based on the condition of the premises.

1. The most obvious situation is where the landlord actively conceals a dangerous condition such as large pieces of loose plaster in a ceiling or

rotted floorboards. Such conduct constitutes fraud. Upon discovery of the fraud, usually the tenant can terminate the lease or sue for damages if any have occurred as a result of the fraud. Where the defect was not known to the parties at the time they entered into the lease agreement, in the absence of negligence, the landlord is generally not responsible for any damages that result from the defective condition.

2. A landlord generally has a duty to maintain common areas such as hallways, stairways, and utility rooms. A landlord who is negligent in the performance of this duty could be responsible for damages that result from his/her negligence.

3. A landlord may subject him/herself to liability for resulting damages by failing to make repairs in accordance with a lease agreement, by negligent performance of repairs, or by not making repairs as required by statute. Usually, a carefully drafted lease will include a repairs provision. If such provision contradicts a statute, the statute will control. The trend, therefore, is toward increased landlord responsibility in the maintenance of the general condition of the leasehold premises.

Destruction of Premises

The general rule is that if a tenant leases an entire building, destruction or injury to the building will not terminate the tenant's obligation to pay rent, since he/she still has possession of the soil underneath the building. Generally, neither the landlord nor the tenant, in the absence of an express provision in the lease to the contrary, is under any duty to rebuild the leasehold premises. Under these circumstances, a tenant can be put in the unhappy position of either having to rebuild at his/her own expense or pay rent for the duration of the lease for space that cannot be used for its intended purpose. This is another reason why the parties to a lease—tenants in particular—should have a lease agreement reviewed by persons fully familiar with such matters. Recently, however, the courts in a few states have excused rental payments where destruction of the entire leased building occurred, on the grounds that such destruction made it impracticable for the tenant to continue to use the building for the intended purpose.

The same rule does not apply where a tenant leases one unit in a multi-unit building. Rental payments cease upon the destruction of the building, since the tenant is not legally considered to have an interest in the land underneath the building.

ASSIGNMENT AND SUBLEASE

In the absence of an express or implied lease provision to the contrary, a tenant has the right to assign or sublet his/her possessory interest in the leasehold premises without the landlord's permission. If a tenant-assignor assigns his/her interest in the leasehold premises to an assignee, the assignee figuratively stands in the shoes of the tenant-assignor. The assignee becomes a third party to the landlord–tenant contract. As a consequence, the landlord and assignee can enforce the original landlord–assignor–tenant contract against each other. The landlord can compel the assignee to pay rent, and the assignee can enforce the various provisions of the lease. If the assignee does not make rental payments when due, the landlord can compel the assignor to make such payments, since, under the law of assignments, the assignor is not freed from his/her original contractual duties. The assignee, however, is never liable for rent for the period before he/she took possession.

On the other hand, if a tenant subleases the leasehold premises, a new contract comes into existence to which the landlord is not privy. Thus, even though the subtenant may take possession subject to the terms of the original lease, the landlord cannot proceed against the sublessee for unpaid rent because the landlord is not a party to the sublease contract. It appears, therefore, that from the landlord's point of view, the assignment situation is the more favorable method of obtaining an alternate tenant, because the landlord can collect from either the assignor or the assignee, whereas in the sublease situation the landlord can look only to the tenant for satisfaction. Because leasehold premises can be assigned or sublet, most written lease agreements contain a specific provision prohibiting transfer of possession or allowing it subject to landlord approval.

Where the tenant lawfully transfers possession of the leasehold premises to a third party, it is sometimes unclear whether the transfer was an assignment or a sublease. If the transfer is for the entire or remaining term of the original lease and is subject to the same terms and conditions, an assignment would be the preferred interpretation. However, where the transfer is for less than the full or remaining term, then a reversionary interest remains in the transferor and, if subject to different terms, a sublease would be the preferred interpretation. The importance of the distinction lies in the landlord's right to sue.

TERMINATION

There are four basic methods by which a lease can be terminated: by expiration of the term, by operation of law, by the occurrence of a condition subsequent, or by mutual agreement.

By Expiration of the Term

Most commonly, leases terminate by expiration at the end of the lease term. Either a lease provision will expressly state a termination date or it will recite the entire term at the end of which the lease terminates. For example, a lease can provide that "the termination date is September 1, 19XX" or "the term is from 1/1/0X to 9/1/XX." In either case it will automatically expire on September 1, 19XX. If the tenant continues in possession at the expiration of the term without the landlord's consent, he/she could be considered a trespasser, but if the tenant remains with the landlord's consent, the tenancy would not terminate. It would be a periodic tenancy, either from month to month or year to year, depending on the circumstances.

By Operation of Law

A lease will terminate by operation of law when the freehold estate is merged with the nonfreehold estate. This can occur when the lease gives the tenant the option to buy the leasehold premises at any time during the term of the lease. If the tenant rightfully exercises the option, the leasehold estate merges into the fee and is thus terminated.

By Occurrence of a Condition Subsequent

There are a number of conditions that can cause termination of a lease after the tenant has entered into possession of the leasehold premises. Two of the most common, in the absence of a lease provision to the contrary, are destruction or condemnation of the leasehold premises. Such events make it impossible for full performance to occur, and consequently the parties are excused. However, unless excused by a specific provision in the lease or by state law, the death of a landlord or tenant, bankruptcy of either party to the lease, or a sale of the leasehold premises will not terminate the lease.

By Mutual Agreement

The parties can mutually agree to terminate the lease any time during the term. Even though such an agreement is usually evidenced by a tenant's surrender of the leasehold premises and the landlord's subsequent possession, it is always advisable for the parties to put their understanding in a formal, written, and signed cancelation agreement to avoid future misunderstandings.

REMEDIES ON DEFAULT OF RENTAL PAYMENT

When a tenant fails to make the rental payments, the landlord has several remedies available, depending in part on the jurisdiction in which the leasehold premises are located. They include distraint, entry into possession for purposes of mitigating damages, and obtaining a judgment for the anticipated breach of contract.

Distraint

The common law right of *distraint* gives the landlord the right to come on the leasehold premises and seize the tenant's personal property as security for any unpaid rental claims. Because of the severity of this remedy, it is not applicable in most states. However, in many agricultural states, a landlord's claim for back rent can be secured by the crops growing on the leased land or chattels brought on the land.

Possession and Mitigation

Often, a tenant will not only fail to pay the required rent but will also abandon the premises. Under these circumstances, a landlord can do one of three things: (1) take possession and excuse the tenant from further payment, (2) let the premises stand empty and sue the tenant for rent as it comes due, or (3) attempt to mitigate the tenant's damages by seeking a new tenant. The courts in a number of states have indicated that a landlord has a duty to mitigate (reduce) damages where a tenant abandons the premises; thus, an option between the second and third alternatives does not exist in states that require mitigation.

Anticipatory Breach

Even where mitigation is required, a landlord can sue for the unpaid rent as it comes due. This may be cumbersome in that it would necessitate a monthly lawsuit; therefore, some states permit a landlord to treat an abandonment as an anticipatory breach of the entire contract whereby the landlord may sue for present as well as future rent. For example, a tenant who abandons leasehold premises in the middle of the year could be sued, under the anticipatory breach theory, for the remaining half year even though that period of time has not passed.

SECURITY DEPOSITS

In many landlord–tenant situations, the landlord will collect a sum of money called a *security deposit* from the tenant prior to the tenant's entering into possession. Even though the deposit may represent one, two, or three months' rent, depending on the laws of the state where the premises are located, it is not treated as prepaid rent. Its purpose is primarily to compensate the landlord for any damage done to the leasehold premises by the tenant during the period of possession. It can also be applied toward unpaid rent by the landlord but generally cannot be used by the tenant to pay the last month's rent.

Under the statutory laws of many states, landlords are required to return the security deposit, less any amount withheld for damages or unpaid rent, to tenants within a fixed period of time after the lease expires. To encourage prompt landlord action, penalties have been provided where the security deposit is not returned within the statutory period. Some states, for example, assess twice the security deposit as a penalty. Further, if the landlord does not specifically set forth in writing and deliver to tenant a statement of damages within a specified period of time—one month after the lease expires in some states—the landlord loses the right to sue the tenant for those damages. This is an important reason why both parties should familiarize themselves with the landlord–tenant law of the state where the leasehold premises are located.

LEASE TERMS AND CONDITIONS

The basic requirements of a valid lease agreement have been identified. The following material briefly discusses those and other common lease terms and conditions as they would appear in an ordinary lease agreement. It is useful to be able to specifically identify such terms and conditions not only to ensure the validity of the landlord–tenant contract, but also to protect one's interest in the leasehold premises by the inclusion of appropriate terms.

Date

Like most other agreements dealing with real property, a lease will begin with the date the agreement was made. Since lease agreements frequently are not acknowledged or witnessed, this date may be important in establishing a tenant's priority to the leasehold premises. For example, if a landlord dated and signed a lease agreement with T1 on 2/15 and with T2 on 2/20 for the same term and the same leasehold premises, and T2 had no actual or constructive knowledge of the previous agreement, T2 would have a superior right to possession of the premises since his lease is dated five days after that of T1. T1's only recourse would be to sue the landlord for damages. However, other than establishing a priority over other lessees of the same premises, a statement of the date is not crucial to the validity of a lease agreement.

Parties

The lease should include the names and addresses of all parties to the lease. The parties should have contractual capacity as previously defined, and all the lessors and lessees should be included. For example, where a married lessor owns the leasehold premises in his or her name alone, most states require the other spouse to join as a party to the lease. A lessee who is not named as a party cannot be held responsible by the lessor to fulfill the provisions of the lease.

Lease Premises

The leasehold premises should be described with sufficient clarity to permit their easy identification. However, the same detail that goes into a deed description is generally not required. Identification by owner, street, or project name, by unit number, or by some other method is usually adequate. A more complete description may be required where unimproved land is being leased or commercial space is involved.

Usually, a description of the leasehold premises is contained in the lease itself. In the alternative, it can be attached to the lease and incorporated by reference.

Term

The *term* is the duration of the lease. It should clearly specify a beginning and ending date and may include a statement of the total duration. For example, a typical term provision would be "for the term of one year, beginning on January 1, 19XX, and ending on December 31, 19XX."

Rental

A tenant's promise to pay rent is consideration for his or her possession of the leased premises. Rental payments to the lessor are usually made on a monthly basis, and the total amount of rental for the entire term is stated in the lease. For example, a typical rental provison would be "The total rent for the term of this lease is $2,400.00, payable in advance in equal monthly installments of $200 per month on or before the first day of each month at the lessor's business office." Additional terms might be included, such as "time is of the essence" or a late payment penalty clause, depending on the nature of the lease.

Use Provisions

Unless the lease restricts the lessee's use of the leasehold premises, the lessee may use the premises for any lawful purpose. A landlord may, for example, restrict the premises to residential use only, to occupancy by no more than a certain number of persons, to the provision or selling of certain services or goods only, or to any other lawful purpose.

Renewal

In the absence of express provision, a tenant does not have the right to renew or extend the term of the lease. Such provisions, however, are commonly included in leases. They usually are negative or positive in nature. A *negative renewal* occurs when a tenant is given the option to renew his/her lease for an additional term or terms and nothing is stated in the lease about giving notice to the landlord to exercise the option. In this case, the option is exercised by the tenant continuing in possession after the original term has expired. For example, a typical negative renewal clause might state, "Either party may terminate this lease at the expiration of the term hereby created, by giving the other two months' notice, but in default of such notice, this lease, with all its conditions, shall continue for an additional term of one year."

On the other hand, a *positive renewal* requires that notice of renewal be given by the tenant before the lease terminates, and in the absence of such notice the lease expires at the end of the term even if the tenant remains in possession. For a positive renewal, the lease language should be such that the tenant would have to provide the landlord with notice of intent to renew. In the absence of such notice, the lease would automatically expire.

The provisions of a renewal should be definite and clear; otherwise it might not be enforceable. Thus, a lease renewal provision that states that "lessee shall have the right to renew the lease under such terms as are favorable to lessor" is too vague and indefinite to be enforceable. At best, it is an agreement to renegotiate the lease at a future date.

Possession

Usually a lease commences when possession or the right to possession is transferred from the lessor to the lessee. If the leased premises are occupied by a holdover tenant or other adverse party, most states require the landlord to take whatever steps are necessary to deliver possession. The possibility exists that a tenant may be damaged by a landlord's inability to transfer possession at the prescribed date; therefore, a landlord can contract away potential liability by inserting a clause in the lease agreement whereby he/she would not be liable for failure to deliver possession at the prescribed date due to events beyond his/her control.

Rules and Regulations

Landlords frequently attach a number of requirements pertaining to lessee's use of the leasehold premises called *rules and regulations* or *covenants*. The rules and regulations are usually incorporated by reference and include such common lease provisions as not to obstruct common passageways, not to keep animals on the premises, not to deface or damage the premises, not to cause loud noises past a certain hour, not to change locks without the landlord's consent, and so forth. The rules and regulations are binding on the lessee, and their breach could terminate the lease.

Maintenance and Repairs

In the absence of an agreement to the contrary, a tenant has a somewhat limited obligation to maintain and repair the leasehold premises. The repairs do not have to be permanent. They need only be of such a nature as to prevent the leasehold premises from further deterioration. Usually, however, a lease contains specific maintenance and repair provisions wherein the lessor is obligated to maintain and repair the entire structure including the interior and exterior. Alterations and improvements are also usually made at the expense of the landlord. A typical maintenance and repair clause would be "The lessee agrees to maintain and keep in good repair the interior of said premises; however, alterations and improvements can be made only with the lessor's consent and on the expiration of the lease become his/her property."

If an express covenant to repair is contained in the lease and the landlord fails to make the necessary repairs, the lessee, after giving notice, can make the repairs him/herself and charge them to the landlord. If the premises become untenable because of the failure to repair, the tenant may leave the premises without paying further rent.

Habitability

As to the habitability of the leasehold premises, the generally accepted rule has been *caveat lessee*. That is, in the absence of a lease provision to the contrary, the lessee assumes the risk of the condition of the premises. For this reason, lessees frequently require a covenant of habitability from the landlord. However, due in part to recent consumer activism, the principle of *caveat lessee* is slowly giving way to an implied warranty of habitability so that even if a lease does not contain a habitability clause, a covenant of habitability exists by implication.

Insurance

A lease should contain provisions pertaining to fire and liability insurance. Usually, the lessor will carry both types of insurance and the lessee will additionally insure his/her own personal property on the premises. If the lease is a net lease where the tenant agrees to pay for the cost of insurance, such payments are usually treated as additional rent. The fact that insurance is paid for by the tenant does not exculpate the tenant from paying rent in the event the leasehold premises are destroyed by fire, nor does it require the landlord to immediately rebuild the premises.

The lease should be clear about fire damage and which party is responsible for it. Otherwise the lessee might find him/herself in the position of not only paying the fire insurance premiums and rent after the premises are destroyed, but also having to rebuild the premises.

Destruction

As previously stated, if a tenant rents an entire building as opposed to a single unit in a multi-unit complex and the premises are destroyed by fire or other casualty, the tenant runs the risk of being responsible for continuation of rental payments. Therefore, the lease should clearly state the obligations of the parties in the event of destruction of the premises.

Examples

The provisions just discussed represent a few of the more common provisions contained in leases. There can be as many different provisions or variations of these provisions as there are different individual situations. The examples of residential and commercial leases presented in Figures 30 and 31 illustrate how the basic requirements of a lease and the many different provisions can be fit together to form a typical lease. Often standard form leases are used; however, even though these forms are adequate under most situations, they often have to be modified or completely redrafted to meet the needs and demands of the individual situation. A well-drafted lease is the key to avoiding potential land-lord–tenant problems.

FIGURE 30 Residential Lease

RESIDENTIAL LEASE

DATE	APARTMENT	TERM BEGINS	MONTHLY RENT	SECURITY DEPOSIT

THIS LEASE, made this _____ day of _____, 19___
BETWEEN _____, the Landlord,

AND

1. _____   3. _____
2. _____   4. _____

WITNESSETH: that Landlord hereby leases to resident and the latter lets from the former, the apartment designated as No. _____ Building _____, located at _____, hereinafter called the "premises," for the term of _____ beginning on the first day of _____ 19 ___, and ending on the last day of _____, 19___ at the rent of _____ Dollars ($_____) per year payable in monthly installments of _____ _____ Dollars ($_____) each on the first day of each month in advance. This letting is upon the following conditions, covenants, and agreements:

1. **Rent.** Resident agrees to pay to Owner or Agent the monthly rent set forth above on the first day of each month, in advance, at the Rental Office of Owner or Agent or such other place as Owner or Agent may from time to time request. Resident further agrees to pay a late payment charge of $1 per day from the first day of the month. If rental is mailed, the postmark date will determine the date of payment. If any check for rent is returned to Owner or Agent for insufficient funds or other reasons, late charges will continue until rent is actually paid by Resident.

2. **Termination by Owner or Agent.** Owner or Agent may terminate this lease without cause by giving sixty (60) days' prior written notice to Resident, but no termination by Owner or Agent without cause may take effect during the initial one-year term of the lease.

3. **Premature Termination by Resident.** Resident may terminate this lease without cause prior to its expiration date only by giving written notice to Owner or Agent, at least two full calendar months in advance of the termination date, and if Resident elects to move prior to the termination date, Resident must pay to Owner or Agent, at the time notice is given, all rent due to the termination date. In any event, rent must be paid to termination date prior to Resident's move. If a termination of the lease by Resident takes effect during the initial one-year term of the lease, Resident shall also pay to Owner or Agent at the time notice of termination is given liquidated damages for premature termination, which shall be $ _____ if the lease terminates during the first nine

(Continued on next page)

FIGURE 30—Page 2

(9) months of the lease term, and which shall be two-thirds (⅔) of that amount if the lease terminates during the tenth or eleventh months of the initial lease term. Should Owner or Agent rent the apartment prior to termination date, Resident shall be entitled to the return of his rental payment in an amount equal to the rent received by Owner or Agent from the new Resident prior to the expiration date, less $_____ toward the cost of re-rental.

   4. **Rent Increases and Renewal.** Owner or Agent may increase the monthly rent or change the terms of this lease on written notice to Resident given at least seventy (70) days in advance of the first day of the month in which the increase in rent or change in lease terms is effective, but Owner or Agent may not make an increase or change in the lease terms which will take effect during the initial one-year term of the lease. The rent increase or change in lease terms shall take effect in the manner specified by Owner or Agent unless Resident shall terminate the lease as provided in paragraph 3 within ten (10) days after notice of a rent increase or change of lease terms is given by Owner or Agent.

   This lease shall continue for a like term of years under the same terms and conditions as stated herein, unless either party shall give notice in writing to the other party at least sixty (60) days prior to the end of this lease of his intention to terminate the lease agreement or continue same under changed terms and conditions.

   5. **Use.** Resident agrees to use the apartment only as the personal residence of Resident and their children, and not to assign this lease or sublet the apartment. Resident agrees not to alter or make additions to the apartment, its painting or its fixtures and appliances without Owner's or Agent's written consent. Resident agrees not to do or to permit any act or practice injurious to the building, which may be unreasonably disturbing to other residents, which may affect the insurance on the building, or which is contrary to any law.

   6. **Utilities.** Resident understands that the equipment for utilities to serve the premises is installed therein and Resident agrees that the cost of the utilities shall be paid as follows:

   Heating for premises to be paid by_____
   Heating of water for premises to be paid by_____
   Electricity for premises to be paid by_____
   Gas for premises to be paid by_____
   Sewer charge to be paid by_____
   Water consumption to be paid by_____
   TV cable service to be paid by_____
   Other_____to be paid by_____
   _____to be paid by_____

   Resident agrees that Owner or Agent shall have the right temporarily to stop the service of electricity, or water, in the event of accident affecting the same or to facilitate repairs or alterations made in the premises or elsewhere in Owner's or Agent's property. Owner or Agent shall have no liability for failure to supply heat, air conditioning, hot water or other services or utilities when such failure shall be beyond Owner's or Agent's control or to enable Owner or Agent to service or repair installations.

   7. **Care of Apartment.** Resident agrees to use due care in the use of the apartment, the appliances therein, and all other parts of Owner's or Agent's property, to give notice to Owner or Agent of the need for repair thereof, and to

(Continued)

FIGURE 30—Page 3

pay for all repairs to the apartment, its contents, and to all other parts of Owner's or Agent's property which are necessitated by any act or lack of care on the part of Resident, members of Resident's family, or his visitors. Owner or Agent will make necessary repairs to the apartment and the appliances therein within a reasonable time after Resident notifies Owner or Agent of the need for repairs.

8. **Owner's or Agent's Liability.** Resident agrees that Owner or Agent shall not be liable for property damage or personal injury occurring in the apartment or elsewhere on Owner's or Agent's property unless the damage or injury results directly from Owner's or Agent's negligence.

9. **Delivery of Possession by Owner or Agent.** If, due to circumstances beyond the Owner's or Agent's control, the premises shall not be ready for occupancy at the beginning of the term, this lease shall nevertheless remain in effect and the rent shall be abated proportionately until the premises are so ready, and Owner or Agent shall not be liable for delay; provided, that if the premises shall not be ready for occupancy sixty days after said beginning, Resident shall have the right to cancel this lease by written notice delivered to Owner or Agent at any time after the expiration of said sixty days, but not after the premises are ready for occupancy. Resident's remedy shall be limited to such right of cancellation, and upon such cancellation, neither party shall have any further right against the other, save that Owner or Agent shall repay any deposits made by Resident. If Resident shall occupy the premises prior to the beginning of the term, such occupancy shall be subject to the terms of this lease, and Resident shall pay prior to occupying the premises rent for the same period from the date of such occupancy to the beginning of said term.

10. **Damage by Fire.** If the apartment is damaged by fire or other casualty, Owner or Agent shall repair it within a reasonable time and rent shall continue unless the casualty renders the apartment untenantable, in which case this lease shall terminate and Resident, upon payment of all rent to the date the apartment is surrendered, shall not be liable for any further rent. If only a portion of the apartment is rendered untenantable, the Resident may, with mutual agreement of Owner or Agent, alternatively choose to continue in possession and shall thereupon be entitled to a pro rata reduction in the amount of rent, provided that election to proceed under this alternative shall not be a waiver of the Resident's right to terminate the lease if repairs are not made within a reasonable time.

11. **Right of Entry.** Owner or Agent, or any person authorized by him, with the prior specific consent of Resident, which consent shall not be unreasonably withheld, shall have the right to enter the apartment at reasonable times to inspect, make repairs or alterations as needed, to enforce this lease, and, after notice of termination is given, to show the apartment to prospective residents; provided, however, that Resident's consent shall not be necessary in case of emergency.

12. **Security Deposit.** Resident agrees to pay the security deposit set forth above prior to occupancy of the apartment. The security deposit shall be held by Owner or Agent as security for the payment of all rent and other amounts due from Resident to Owner or Agent, for the Resident's performance of this lease, and against any damages caused to the apartment or any other part of Owner's or Agent's property by Resident, his family and guests. Resident understands and agrees that the security deposit may not be applied as rent or against any other amount due from Resident to Owner or Agent, without Owner's or Agent's written consent, and that the monthly rent will be paid each month, including the last month of the lease term. Within thirty (30) days following termination of

(Continued)

FIGURE 30—Page 4

this lease, Owner or Agent shall return the security deposit, less any deductions from it on account of amounts owed by Resident to Owner or Agent, to Resident by check payable to all persons signing this lease mailed to a forwarding address which must be furnished by Resident in writing.

13. **Use of Exterior.** This lease confers no rights on Resident to use for any purpose any of the property of Owner or Agent other than the interior of the apartment hereby leased, except the walks and roadways giving access thereto and such other areas, if any, as Owner or Agent may from time to time designate for the use of residents. When the use by Resident of any other portion of Owner's or Agent's property is permitted, it shall be subject to the rules and regulations established by Owner or Agent.

14. **Owner's or Agent's Remedies.** If Resident shall fail to pay rent, or any other sum, to Owner or Agent when due; shall default in any other provisions of this lease; or shall remove or attempt to remove his possessions from the premises before paying to Owner or Agent all rent due to the end of the lease term, Owner or Agent, in addition to all other remedies provided by law, may: (a) discontinue utility service provided by Owner; (b) terminate this lease; (c) bring an action to recover possession of the premises; (d) bring an action to recover the whole balance of the rent and other charges due hereunder, of whatever kind and nature, together with any and all consequential damages caused by Resident's default, including reasonable attorney's fees and court costs.

15. **Regulations.** RESIDENT AGREES THAT HE WILL COMPLY AND PROCURE COMPLIANCE OF MEMBERS OF HIS FAMILY, AND HIS GUESTS WITH THE OCCUPANCY REGULATIONS WHICH ARE PRINTED HEREON AND WHICH ARE ATTACHED.

16. **Subordination.** This lease is subject and subordinate to the lien of all mortgages now or at any time hereinafter placed upon any part of Owner's or Agent's property which includes the apartment, to extensions or renewals thereof, and to all advances now or hereafter made on the security thereof. Resident agrees, upon request, to execute such further instruments evidencing such subordination as Owner or Agent may request, and if Resident fails to do so, Owner or Agent is empowered to do so in the name of Resident.

17. **The Term "Resident".** The term "Resident" used herein shall refer collectively to all persons named above, and signing this lease as Resident, and the liability of each such person shall be joint and several. Notice given by Owner or Agent to any person named as Resident, or by any such person to Owner or Agent, shall bind all persons signing this lease as Resident.

OWNER: _____(SEAL)
                             Resident

BY: _____   _____(SEAL)
                             Resident

                             _____(SEAL)
                             Resident

                             _____(SEAL)
                             Resident

(Continued)

FIGURE 30—Page 5

Guaranty

Intending to be legally bound, and in consideration of the lease with the above Resident, the undersigned, jointly and severally, hereby become surety to Owner or Agent for the performance of the lease by Resident and guarantee payment of all sums becoming owing to Owner or Agent by Resident. This agreement shall remain in effect throughout the term of the lease or any renewal thereof. The liability of the undersigned is absolute, continuing and unconditional and Owner or Agent shall not be required to proceed against Resident or invoke any other remedy before proceeding against the undersigned. Owner or Agent expressly agrees to notify the guarantor in the event of breach or default.

_____(SEAL)

_____(SEAL)

_____
Witness

FIGURE 31   Commercial Lease
(Courtesy PPG Industries, Inc.)

COMMERCIAL LEASE

THIS   AGREEMENT,   made   this   _____   day   of
_____,   19 ___,   by   and   between
_____,   as   Landlord,   and
_____, a corporation of the State of
_____, with its principal office and place of business in
_____, as Tenant:

WITNESSETH: That the said Landlord does hereby demise and lease to Tenant and Tenant does hereby hire from Landlord the following described premises:
_____,
together with all appurtenances thereto and with easements of ingress and egress necessary and adequate for the conduct of Tenant's business as hereinafter described, for the term of _____ years, running from and including the _____ day of _____, 19___, up to and including the _____ day of _____, 19___, for use in Tenant's regular business of _____ or in any other legitimate business, subject to the terms and conditions of this lease.

Amount of Rental

Tenant   covenants   to   pay   to   Landlord   at   Landlord's   office   at
_____
or such other place in _____
as Landlord shall designate in writing as rent for said premises, the sum of $_____ per month, payable in advance commencing
_____.

In addition to the above, Landlord and Tenant mutually covenant and agree as follows:

1. **Tenant's Maintenance and Repair of Premises.** Except as hereinafter provided, Tenant shall maintain and keep the interior of the premises in good repair, free of refuse and rubbish, and shall return the same at the expiration or termination of this lease in as good condition as received by Tenant, ordinary wear and tear, damage or destruction by fire, flood, storm, civil commotion or other unavoidable cause excepted; provided, however, that if alterations, additions and/or installations shall have been made by Tenant as provided for in this lease, Tenant shall not be required to restore the premises to the condition in which they were prior to such alterations, additions and/or installations except as hereinafter provided.

2. **Tenant's Alterations, Additions, Installations, and Removal Thereof.** Tenant may, at its own expense, either at the commencement of or during the term of this lease, make such alterations in and/or additions to the leased premises including, without prejudice to the generality of the foregoing, alterations in the water, gas, and the electric wiring system, as may be necessary to fit the same for its business, upon first obtaining the written approval of Landlord as to the materials to be used and the manner of making such alterations and/or additions.

(Continued)

FIGURE 31—Page 2

Landlord covenants not to unreasonably withhold approval of alterations and/or additions proposed to be made by Tenant. Tenant may also, at its own expense, install such counters, racks, shelving, fixtures, fittings, machinery and equipment upon or within the leased premises as Tenant may consider necessary to the conduct of its business. At any time prior to the expiration or earlier termination of the lease, Tenant may remove any or all such alterations, additions or installations in such a manner as will not substantially injure the leased premises. In the event Tenant shall elect to make any such removal, Tenant shall restore the premises, or the portion or portions affected by such removal, to the same condition as existed prior to the making of such alteration, addition or installation, ordinary wear and tear, damage or destruction by fire, flood, storm, civil commotion or other unavoidable cause excepted.

All alterations, additions or installations not so removed by Tenant shall become the property of Landlord without liability on Landlord's part to pay for the same.

3. **Landlord's Maintenance and Repair of Premises.** Landlord shall, without expense to Tenant, maintain and make all necessary repairs to the foundations, load bearing walls, roof, gutters, downspouts, heating system, air conditioning, elevators, water mains, gas and sewer lines, sidewalks, private roadways, parking areas, railroad spurs or sidings, and loading docks, if any, on or appurtenant to the leased premises.

4. **Utilities.** Tenant shall pay all charges for water, gas and electricity consumed by Tenant upon the leased premises.

5. **Observance of Laws.** Tenant shall duly obey and comply with all public laws, ordinances, rules or regulations relating to the use of the leased premises; provided, however, that any installation of fire prevention apparatus, electric rewiring, plumbing changes or structural changes in the building on the leased premises, required by any such law, ordinance, rule, or regulation shall be made by Landlord without expense to Tenant.

6. **Damage by Fire, etc. Damage Repairable Within One Hundred Twenty (120) Days.** In the event the said premises shall be damaged by fire, flood, storm, civil commotion, or other unavoidable cause, to an extent repairable within one hundred twenty (120) days from the date of such damage, Landlord shall forthwith proceed to repair such damage. If such repair shall not have been completed within one hundred twenty (120) days from the date of such damage, delays occasioned by causes beyond the control of Landlord excepted, this lease may, at the option of Tenant, be terminated. During the period of repair, Tenant's rent shall abate in whole or in part depending upon the extent to which such damage and/or such repair shall deprive Tenant of the use of said premises for the normal purposes of Tenant's business. In the event that Landlord shall fail to promptly commence repair of such damage, or, having commenced the same shall fail to prosecute such repair to completion with due diligence, Tenant may at Tenant's option upon five (5) days' written notice to Landlord, make or complete such repair and deduct the cost thereof from the next ensuing installment or installments of rent payable under this lease.

7. **Damage Not Repairable Within One Hundred Twenty (120) Days.** In the event the said premises shall be damaged by fire, flood, storm, civil commotion, or other unavoidable cause, to an extent not repairable within one hundred twenty (120) days from the date of such damage, this lease shall terminate as of the date of such damage.

8. **Sidewalk Encumbrances.** Tenant shall neither encumber nor obstruct the sidewalk in front of, or any entrance to, the building on the leased premises.

(Continued)

FIGURE 31—Page 3

9. **Signs.** Tenant shall have the right to erect, affix or display on the roof, exterior or interior walls, doors and windows of the building on the leased premises, such sign or signs advertising its business as Tenant may consider necessary or desirable, subject to all applicable municipal ordinances and regulations with respect thereto.

10. **Termination by Reason of Default.** In the event that either of the parties hereto shall fail to perform any covenant required to be performed by such party under the terms and provisions of this lease, including Tenant's covenant to pay rent, and such failure shall continue unremedied or uncorrected for a period of fifteen (15) days after the service of written notice upon such party by the other party hereto, specifying such failure, this lease may be terminated, at the option of the party serving such notice, at the expiration of such period of fifteen (15) days; provided, however, that such termination shall not relieve the party so failing from liability to the other party for such damages as may be suffered by reason of such failure.

11. **Condemnation.** In the event that the leased premises shall be taken for public use by the city, state, federal government, public authority or other corporation having the power of eminent domain, then its lease shall terminate as of the date on which possession thereof shall be taken for such public use, or, at the option of Tenant, as of the date on which the premises shall become unsuitable for Tenant's regular business by reason of such taking; provided, however, that if only a part of the leased premises shall be so taken, such termination shall be at the option of Tenant only. If such a taking of only a part of the leased premises occurs, and Tenant elects not to terminate the lease, there shall be a proportionate reduction of the rent to be paid under this lease from and after the date such possession is taken for public use. Tenant shall have the right to participate, directly or indirectly, in any award for such public taking to the extent that it may have suffered compensable damage as a Tenant on account of such public taking.

12. **Assignment.** Tenant may assign this lease or sublet the premises or any part thereof for any legitimate use, either with or without the consent of Landlord. If any assignment or sublease is made by Tenant without Landlord's consent, Tenant shall remain liable as surety under the terms hereof notwithstanding such assignment or sublease.

13. **Taxes.** Landlord shall pay all taxes, assessments, and charges which shall be assessed and levied upon the leased premises or any part thereof during the said term as they shall become due.

14. **Tenant's Liability Insurance.** During the term of this lease, Tenant at his own expense shall carry public liability insurance in not less than the following limits:

> bodily injury $100,000/$300,000
> property damage $50,000

15. **Landlord's Right to Enter Premises.** Tenant shall permit Landlord and Landlord's agents to enter at all reasonable times to view the state and condition of the premises or to make such alterations or repairs therein as may be necessary for the safety and preservation thereof, or for any other reasonable purposes. Tenant shall also permit Landlord or Landlord's agents, on or after sixty (60) days next preceding the expiration of the term of this lease, to show the premises to prospective tenants at reasonable times, and to place notices on the front of said premises, or on any part thereof, offering the premises for lease or for sale.

(Continued)

FIGURE 31—Page 4

16. **Renewal of Lease.** Tenant shall have the option to take a renewal lease of the demised premises for the further term of _____ (___) years from and after the expiration of the term herein granted at a monthly rent of _____ _____ Dollars ($_____) and under and subject to the same covenants, provisions and agreements as are herein contained. In the event Tenant desires to exercise the option herein provided, Tenant shall notify Landlord of such desire in writing not less than sixty (60) days prior to the expiration of the term hereby granted.

AND IT IS MUTUALLY UNDERSTOOD AND AGREED that the covenants and agreements herein contained shall insure to the benefit of and be equally binding upon the respective executors, administrators, heirs, successors and assigns of the parties hereto.

IN WITNESS WHEREOF, the parties hereto have executed this lease the day and year first above written.

_____(L.S.)

_____(L.S.)

_____(L.S.)

_____(L.S.)

Landlord(s)

_____

_____

ATTEST:

_____

Assistant Secretary

_____

Vice President
(Tenant)

QUESTIONS FOR DISCUSSION

1. Discuss the concept of *caveat lessee* and its applicability to the twentieth-century landlord–tenant marketplace.

2. Is the quality of an owner's possessory interest in a fee simple absolute equal to, greater than, or less than the quality of a tenant's possessory interest in leasehold premises?

3. Assuming that a lease is silent as to which party is responsible for repairing and maintaining the leasehold premises, which party, landlord or tenant, is responsible for repairing and maintaining the leasehold premises, and under what circumstances?

4. Why is it advisable to reduce an oral lease to a writing even though it does not have to comply with the Statute of Frauds?

5. Discuss what steps, if any, a landlord can take to ensure the payment of rent. Also discuss the landlord's remedies in the event the tenant abandons the leasehold premises.

CASES

Case 1. In 1967, Tenants leased the southern portion of the Lewis Building and invested approximately $80,000 in the establishment and operation of a restaurant business. In February, 1972, Landlords acquired the Lewis Building subject to Tenants' lease. A short time thereafter, the owner of the property abutting the Lewis Building on the south demolished its building, exposing the south wall of Landlord's building, which was found to be structurally unsafe and in need of substantial repair. The lease between Landlord and Tenant did not contain an express covenant concerning the responsibility of the parties to maintain the structural components of the building; however, it did require the lessee to make necessary repairs to maintain the leasehold premises. Who, if anyone, is responsible for repair of the Lewis Building's south wall?

Case 2. Plaintiffs and Defendants entered into a written lease agreement wherein Defendants agreed to rent Plaintiffs an apartment for seven months at a rate of $230 per month. Subsequently, a controversy arose as to whether the apartment building complied with the local building code. If Plaintiffs could prove that the apartment building failed to meet local building code requirements, on what legal theory might they sue Defendants?

Case 3. Tenant and her children were required to vacate an apartment she rented from landlord because its condition presented a health hazard to her children. When Tenant moved from the apartment she took some but not all of her possessions. Dishes, silverware, children's clothing, and other items of personal property were left behind. Landlord inspected the apartment, found it "in a mess," and concluded that the remaining items were abandoned junk. Landlord subsequently disposed of all the personal property that he found in Tenant's apartment on the theory that Tenant had abandoned the leasehold premises and her personal property. Do you agree with Landlord's contention? Could Tenant successfully sue Landlord for conversion of her personal property?

Case 4. In 1972, T1 leased part of a lot from L1 to erect a commercial advertising sign. The term of the lease was for "indefinite years, beginning the 1st day of January, 1973, . . . , and continuing year to year thereafter." Consideration for the lease was valid. T1 never constructed a sign or recorded the lease with L1. In 1975, the lot was purchased by L2, who leased it to T2. The term of the L2–T2 lease was to begin on the date a billboard was erected and to run for a period of five years thereafter. Even though T2 did not erect a billboard, they began to make the monthly payments. As between T1 and T2, both of whom have entered into a lease agreement for the same property, which one if either has a valid lease?

Case 5. In November 1975, Tenant leased approximately 26,000 acres of cattle grazing land from Landlord for a term of five years. The lease specifically provided that "the Lessee shall not assign this lease or enter into any sublease without first obtaining the written consent of the Lessor." Subsequently, Tenant entered into an agreement with T, a third party, whereby T agreed to graze his cattle on the leased acreage at a fee of $7 per head. In the same agreement, Tenant agreed to control the range and movement of the cattle, supply salt and hay in emergency situations, repair fences and gates, and generally supervise T's cattle, and T agreed to provide hay if there was an extremely bad winter, haul the cattle in and out, and care for and remove problem cattle. In addition, Tenant would run some of his own cattle. Landlord heard of the agreement between Tenant and T and attempted to terminate his lease with Tenant on the basis that Tenant breached the lease agreement in subleasing or assigning said lease to T. Is Landlord's contention valid?

Case 6. Lessee was a meat packing company subject to rules of the U.S. Department of Agriculture, Meat Inspection Division, which required the entire building in which lessee did business to obtain an MID number. The MID number could be withdrawn if the government found any deficiencies or substandard conditions in the building. After an MID number is withdrawn, business cannot be conducted anywhere in the building. The lessee was notified that the MID number would be withdrawn because of numerous deficiencies found by the government inspectors. Most of the deficiencies were landlord responsibilities as expressly set forth in the landlord–tenant contract. Would the lessee have any legal justification for vacating the premises after he received notification of withdrawal of the MID number?

Case 7. In May, Plaintiff-landlord and Defendant-tenant began negotiations for a lease of the top four floors of Plaintiff's building. The terms of the lease were agreed upon, and Defendant's lawyer drafted a three-year lease in accordance with such terms. A copy of this lease was sent to Plaintiff on May 29. The following day, Plaintiff requested several changes in the lease, and Defendant agreed to make the changes. Plaintiff then stopped by the office of Defendant's lawyer and signed the revised lease on May 31. On June 2, Defendant called Plaintiff and told him he had changed his mind and did not intend to sign the lease. Could Plaintiff enforce the provisions of the lease?

Case 8. Where a tenant brought an action against a landlord for injuries sustained when she fell from a porch after a porch railing collapsed, under what circumstances could she recover from the landlord?

Chapter 12
Cooperatives, Condominiums, and Planned Unit Developments

COOPERATIVES

Characteristics

Organization
Charter   Bylaws   Proprietary Lease

Advantages and Disadvantages

CONDOMINIUMS

Characteristics

Organization
Declaration of Condominium   Bylaws   Deed

Advantages and Disadvantages

PLANNED UNIT DEVELOPMENTS

Characteristics

Comparisions

MANAGEMENT ASPECTS

Condominiums
Condominium Associations   Employment of Professional Management
Functions of Management

Cooperatives
Cooperative Associations   Employment of Professional Management
Functions of Management

Planned Unit Developments
Functions of Management

SUMMARY

QUESTIONS FOR DISCUSSION

CASES

$\mathbf{D}$UE primarily to the increasing need for housing, the escalating cost of construction and maintenance, the dwindling availability of suitable land, and the importance placed on the quality of the living environment, the housing industry has been forced to consider alternative methods of housing development. The traditional approach of total individual ownership of land and house, where each owner was literally a "king" or "queen" within his or her own small domain, for many persons is no longer feasible. Two of the most widely recognized alternatives are cooperatives and condominiums, which address many of the current housing problems by providing for the common ownership of land and even parts of buildings. A more recent housing innovation is the planned unit development (PUD), which also relies heavily for its success on the element of common ownership.

This chapter examines the characteristics and comparative advantages and disadvantages of cooperatives and condominiums. It also describes the characteristics of a planned unit development and, where appropriate, compares the PUD with cooperatives and condominiums. Finally, the basic management aspects of condominiums, cooperatives, and PUDs are briefly mentioned, since professional management is often involved in the operation of such projects.

COOPERATIVES

Characteristics

Cooperative ownership generally refers to ownership of an apartment building by its tenant-occupants as a group. Each tenant in the building has an ownership interest in the entire building. A cooperative can be co-owned by the group as tenants in common or as joint tenants, but most commonly it is owned by a real estate corporation, which owns the land and the building and whose stockholders are the building's tenants.

287

The corporation enters into a written proprietary lease agreement with the tenant-stockholder, whose right of possession is based on the lease and not on his/her status as a stockholder. However, only stockholders can be tenants. The tenant-stockholder can sell his/her interest in the corporation subject to the provisions of the articles of incorporation and the bylaws, which govern this as well as other acts related to the corporation and the tenant's possession of the apartment unit. As usually set forth in their lease, members of the corporate cooperative are periodically assessed, according to their proportionate interests, a fixed amount that goes toward the payment of mortgages, maintenance and repairs, taxes, and other costs of operating the building.

Organization

Since the corporate form of cooperative is the most common, only its method of organization will be discussed. Three basic documents are necessary to the creation and administration of a corporate cooperative: (1) a corporate charter, (2) a set of bylaws, and (3) a proprietary lease agreement between the corporate landlord and the stockholder tenant. All three contribute to establishing the rights and duties of the corporation and its stockholders.

Charter

Before any corporation can legally come into existence, it must file a *corporate charter* in the state where it is organized. The typical charter will contain many provisions, including the name of the association, the place where its principal office will be located, the purpose for which it is being formed, the type and amount of authorized stock, the terms on which persons may become members, meeting dates for members, and term of existence; however, the purpose and capital stock clauses are two of the most important.

For the cooperative corporation, a *purpose clause* will generally state that the corporation is formed for the purpose of providing housing for the stockholders who are entitled to a proprietary lease. The clause should also give the corporation the power to buy, sell, lease, mortgage, and perform any other act necessary to the operation and development of the cooperative. Where local law permits, it is advisable to comply with federal tax laws and state that the corporation is not formed for profit. The purpose clause should be broadly stated so that the corporation does not run the risk of doing something at a later date that is not within the scope of the purpose clause. Otherwise, the act may not be lawful.

In addition, the charter will specify the amount and kind of shares to be allocated to each residential unit. Usually the number of shares of authorized capital stock is the same as the total number of shares allocated to the individual units. However, where expansion is anticipated, the charter can authorize additional shares. Since ownership of a given number of shares entitles the shareholder to lease an individual unit in the cooperative project, shares must always be sold in their original block.

Bylaws

The *corporate bylaws* generally set forth the rights and duties of the stockholders of the association with respect to its internal government, the management of its affairs, and the rights and duties existing between the stockholders themselves. As such, the bylaws constitute a private contract. A typical set of bylaws will state the name and location of the corporation; the purpose of the corporation; terms of membership such as eligibility, certificates, liens, transfer, termination, and sales price; meeting dates, places, and procedures; director election, qualification, compensation, and number; officer election, removal, and compensation; amendment procedure; and fiscal management including fiscal year, books and accounts, audits, inspection of books, and execution of corporate documents.

Proprietary Lease

The *proprietary lease* in a corporate cooperative differs from the normal landlord–tenant lease in that it does not fix a definite rental amount. Each member agrees to pay the corporation a monthly sum, referred to as a *carrying charge,* equal to the member's proportionate share of the expenses of the corporation based on the number of shares held by the member. Thus, in addition to this type of rental provision, the proprietary lease will typically contain provisions relating to a member's option for automatic renewal of the lease; the purpose for which the premises are to be used; the member's right to peaceable possession; the corporation's obligation to manage the project and pay all costs including taxes, insurance, utilities, repairs, and maintenance; the definition and effect of default; the necessity of member compliance with all corporate regulations; and the effect of fire loss on member interests.

Advantages and Disadvantages

The cooperative has the advantage of relative ease in transferability of interest. It requires only that a member's stock interest be transferred from seller to buyer and reflected in the books and records of the corporation. Also, the cooperative may use its entire equity to finance improvements to common areas. Finally, if the corporation has obtained a mortgage, the individual shareholder has no personal liability on the mortgage. It is a corporate obligation. However, this can also be viewed as a disadvantage, since the member cannot arrange individual financing to fit his/her personal needs. A similar disadvantage is that of financial interdependence because all expenses, including debt service, are shared by the members which may result in a tenant paying for more than he/she receives. Another disadvantage to the individual when the cooperative is organized as a corporation is that the corporation and not the individual lessee gets to deduct interest on mortgage payments and tax expenses for individual income tax purposes.

In summary, the advantages of a cooperative are ease in transferability, lack of personal liability, and concentrated use of equity. The disadvantages are lack of individual financing, financial interdependence, and unfavorable tax treatment.

CONDOMINIUMS

Characteristics

The word *condominium* refers to either an entire building that contains a number of separate residential units or the individual unit itself. A condominium is different from a cooperative in that the separate units within the building are individually owned and the common areas are jointly owned by all unit owners in the building. As a consequence of the individual ownership characteristic, each owner receives a deed to his/her unit (not a proprietary lease as in a cooperative), is the mortgagor with respect to any mortgage indebtedness on the unit, and pays taxes on his/her unit independently of the other owners. Since the units are individually owned, the owners are usually free to sell, mortgage, lease, option, or will their units in any manner they desire. However, a grantee takes possession subject to a set of bylaws that govern the operation of the building.

Fees are usually assessed on a monthly basis to each unit owner to cover his/her pro rata share of operating and maintaining the common areas. In that sense, condominiums are similar to cooperatives.

Organization

Every state has statutes authorizing the formation of condominiums. Although they often use different names, the statutes require the filing of a declaration of condominium. The other basic documents necessary to the creation of a condominium are the bylaws and a deed for conveying the individual unit.

Declaration of Condominium

The *declaration of condominium* is the document that subjects the real property to condominium use. It sets forth in detail conditions, covenants, and restrictions that control the rights and duties of condominium owners. Specifically, a declaration of condominium names the project; describes the land, the individual units, and the common areas; and sets forth the voting rights of members and the method for amending the declaration and bylaws. It may set forth the right to assess repair, maintenance, and replacement costs against the individual owner and the right to place a lien against any unit for unpaid assessments. Finally, it may contain restrictions on occupancy and use; options to purchase, rent, or lease; and restrictions on alterations of the individual units.

Bylaws

The declaration usually states that the operation of the condominium property shall be governed by bylaws that are either attached to the declaration or incorporated by reference. Specifically, the bylaws state that each unit owner shall be a member and the requisites for valid meetings of the membership. The powers and duties of the corporation and its officers and directors are usually clearly described and generally include performance of any act that lawfully facilitates the operation of the common areas of the property. For example, the directors are given the power to employ attorneys, accountants, and other professionals as well as workmen, janitors, and gardeners and other nonprofessionals to preserve the equity of the various unit members in the condominium. Like cooperative bylaws, condominium bylaws represent a private contract among the members as to the method of operating the condominium.

Deed

The deed to a condominium is similar to any standard deed that conveys an interest in real property. It must be in writing, sufficiently describe the unit, and be signed by the grantor. Condominium deeds, however, often contain covenants and use restrictions in the body of the deed or incorporate them by reference to the declaration and bylaws.

Advantages and Disadvantages

Perhaps the most significant advantage to condominium ownership is the availability of separate financing. Two examples illustrate the point. First, a new owner with available cash may want to make a substantial down payment as an alternative investment or an estate-planning tool; that is, the buyer may want to be able to transfer at death a debt-free dwelling unit so that proceeds from his/her pension or life insurance can be used for purposes other than paying off a mortgage. Second, the financing arrangement may facilitate the resale of the unit; a second purchaser of the same unit in a cooperative situation will have to come up with a substantially higher down payment, unless the cooperative blanket mortgage is refinanced, than the second purchaser of a condominium.

If a cooperative and condominium unit were each purchased in 1977 for $100,000 with 80 percent financing, and the sales price for each unit in 1985 was $120,000 with 80 percent financing, in 1985 a second purchaser of the condominium could obtain the unit for $24,000 down, but a second purchaser of the cooperative would have to put down $50,000, the difference between the seller's unpaid portion of the original mortgage ($80,000 as originally financed less $10,000 in paid-off principal) and the sales price of $120,000. The increased amount of down payment would severely reduce the number of prospective purchasers.

Another advantage of condominium ownership over cooperative ownership is that of financial flexibility. Not only does the condominium owner obtain his/her own financing, but he/she pays for all other costs related to real property ownership, primarily interest on mortgage and real estate taxes, which are tax deductible on the unit owner's individual income tax return. In the cooperative situation, failure of one cooperator to pay his/her portion of mortgage expenses and real estate taxes becomes a burden to the other cooperators. However, in the condominium arrangement, these expenses are the responsibility of the individual owner only. Common areas continue to be the collective responsibility of all owners.

The advantages of cooperative ownership tend to be the disadvantages of condominium ownership. For example, every time a condominium unit is sold and mortgage financing obtained, the interest rates on the new mortgage will probably be higher than the rate obtained for a cooperative's blanket mortgage. Similarly, the closing costs of transferring an ownership interest in a condominium unit are usually greater than those of a cooperative. Financial independence can result in another comparative disadvantage of condominium ownership in that unit costs for such things as repairs, maintenance, and insurance tend to be higher than for cooperatives. In some cases they are even duplicated.

For example, if condominium unit owners insure their own individual units against fire and theft, the common structural elements such as walls may be insured twice. It probably would be less expensive if the entire building came under one policy as in the cooperative situation.

PLANNED UNIT DEVELOPMENTS

One of the more recent housing concepts that has been used to meet the need for more housing at lower prices and at the same time provide for maximum attainable environmental quality is the *planned unit development,* or PUD. As the name implies, large areas of land are planned as a unit, which may include many different types of residential dwelling units such as individual houses, townhouses, apartments, churches, schools, and even certain commercial uses. The appeal of total development under a unit development plan as defined by the Federal Housing Administration is that such housing development offers (1) lower-priced houses achieved by more efficient use of the land, (2) small, private yards for outdoor living that minimize owner maintenance and free owners' time for recreational activities, (3) large common areas of green open space under the care of experts, and (4) the availability of recreational centers that could not be financed by the average individual homeowner. All these attributes can apply to cooperative and condominium ownership; however, the development of cooperatives and condominiums is usually done on a much smaller scale and tends not to mix different types of housing or commercial or industrial uses in the same development.

Characteristics

In addition to its physical characteristics, a PUD also has unique legal characteristics that differentiate it from a cooperative or condominium. Its most important legal characteristic is the general necessity for the creation of a nonprofit corporation called a *homeowners' association.* The association's basic function is to own and manage common property within the PUD, and each member receives voting rights and is assessed a fee for the management and maintenance of the common areas.

Before a single lot is sold, the land developer is required to incorporate the home association and record a land subdivision plot and restrictive covenants relating to all the land in the PUD. The recorded plat and covenants run with the land and as a result not only establish the rights and duties of the home association and lot owners, but also provide legal continuity for the development.

The *plat* is a map of the total development. It identifies individual residential lots, common land to be transferred by the developer to the home association, land to be transferred to local governments for use as streets or some other public purpose, and land to be used for any other purpose. *Restrictive covenants,* on the other hand, specifically establish the uses that can be made of all the identified land, including parcels designated for private and common use. Generally, the covenants charge the home association with the maintenance and operation of common areas, and in some cases exterior maintenance of private property within the PUD, the enforcement of covenants, and architectural controls for common and private development. In addition, the covenants bind each private landowner within the PUD to pay an assessment fee to the home association to be used by the association in carrying out its duty of maintaining the common area and for other authorized association activity. In return for payment of the assessment, the private owner receives the right to vote and to use whatever common facilities are available to all others in the development.

Comparisons

Because each member of a home association owns his or her own property and is personally responsible for any mortgage against it, a PUD is more closely related to condominiums than to cooperatives. There are several differences between a PUD and a condominium, but they are more physical than legal. A condominium development is usually built on land zoned for multifamily use. Therefore, the land has to be developed in accordance with rigid zoning requirements, and as a result it may end up being used for only one purpose. On the other hand, PUD zoning permits maximum flexibility. A developer who seeks plan approval generally works with local governmental officials in creating a multi-use development that may include residential as well as commercial use. Often, PUDs are specifically provided for in zoning ordinances or are listed as special exceptions.

A legal difference between PUDs and condominiums is that condominium owners do not own the land under their units. It is owned jointly with all other unit owners in the condominium development. Lot owners in a PUD own the land under their houses. Only the common land is jointly owned. Furthermore, in the PUD there is no direct individual legal interest in common areas. They are owned by the homeowners' association in corporate form. Only to the extent that each unit owner in the PUD has a vote in the association does he/she have control over the common area.

MANAGEMENT ASPECTS

Community developments such as condominiums, cooperatives, and planned unit developments may help to solve the problem of providing housing in concentrated urban areas. A unique feature of these community developments in comparison with private houses is that an organized form of management is necessary to preserve the value of the housing units and the rights of the unit owners to use and control the common areas. This part of the chapter describes the organization of management for condominiums, cooperatives, and planned unit developments and some of the functions of management.

Condominiums

Every state in the United States has legislation on condominium ownership, and most of these statutes have specific provisions about the management and organization of the unit owners. In 1962, the Federal Housing Administration (FHA) drafted the FHA Model Act, which established the necessary elements for a condominium statute to be compatible with FHA financing. The act has significantly influenced the legislation in most jurisdictions.

Under the FHA Model Act, and in most cases not coming under the act, the management of a condominium project is under the control of an association of unit owners. However, during the early stages of condominium development, before any units have been sold, the condominium developer often enters into a management agreement to ensure that the project is properly operated until all units have been sold. At one time it was common for a developer to lock a condominium project into a long-term management contract. Currently, however, the average management contract executed by the developer has a life of no more than three years, at the end of which control is turned over to the unit owners' association.

Condominium Associations

The association membership consists of all unit owners acting as a group under rules set by the declaration and bylaws of the condominium. The declaration usually sets forth the percentage of each unit owner's interest in the common areas and facilities for determining voting weights and each owner's proportion of the assessment for the maintenance of common areas. The bylaws lay out the operation of the association and generally make the association responsible for the maintenance and repair of the common elements.

Each unit owner automatically becomes a member of the association upon purchasing a unit in the development and has the right to vote for a board of directors. The board of directors elects the president, secretary, and treasurer from among the board members. The board, the association officers, and often a management agent handle the daily operations of the condominium project. In addition, condominium owners often form committees to distribute the work of the association. The president and board of directors usually determine the method of selection of the committee members and committee chairpersons. Typical committees formed include finance, maintenance, architectural control, rules, and social and recreational committees. These committees assist the board in setting policies and monitoring the operations of the condominium.

The association of condominium owners usually assumes the form of an unincorporated nonprofit association, although it may also be incorporated. In all instances, the management association functions as a distinct and separate entity from the owners themselves. It is imperative that the association set up an active body to provide for the collection of assessments for common expenses, maintain the common areas and facilities, enforce the house rules, and be generally responsible for the day-to-day affairs of the project.

Employment of Professional Management

Ordinarily, the average nonprofessional board will find the maintenance and operational details necessary for the proper administration of the project to be beyond their scope in terms of both their time and their skills. Therefore, these problems are typically turned over to a professional manager who operates under the general supervision of the condominium association. Also, since both conventional mortgages and the Federal Housing Administration normally require that management specialists be employed, the unit owners often have no choice but to engage professional managers.

A management firm or agent does not take away any power from the board of directors. On the contrary, the management agent is employed by the association for the purpose of carrying out the association's directives and making recommendations to the board relative to the operation of the condominium project.

Advantages of a management agent include increased purchasing power, since the professional management agent may deal with several developments and through bulk purchases obtain better prices than could be obtained by purchasing for a single apartment complex. The agent also provides a maintenance-free life style by taking over the day-to-day burden of the association's financial, maintenance, architectural control, and recreational operations, and an objective viewpoint within the association, since friends and neighbors generally do not make good business partners.

Functions of Management

Sound condominium management depends on a management contract that spells out the manager's duties and limits of responsibility. The agreement applies only to the management of common facilities and not to the individual units. The manager's major duties are to insure the property; maintain the common areas; collect reasonable assessments; pay all bills, salaries, or other association obligations; keep proper books and records; and enforce the house rules. Other duties include handling owner requests and complaints, maintaining a separate bank account to meet maintenance costs, handling rental of garage spaces, inspecting the property, and supervising emergency repairs.

Insurance Generally, the manager or board of directors obtains insurance for the property against loss or damage by fire and other hazards. The manager or board of directors acts as trustee to all unit owners, who are insured according to the percentages established in the declaration. Insurance premiums are common expenses. Statutes vary as to whether or not the management of the condominium must insure the entire complex for its full value. As individual unit owners often have insurance on their own unit, legal problems may arise if there is overlapping coverage. The Federal Housing Administration therefore recommends that the association obtain a single policy covering the entire complex rather than many individual policies. Individuals should still obtain insurance on their own unit for items not covered under the main policy.

Maintenance Generally speaking, the management body will be responsible for providing and paying for lawn and exterior maintenance services, utilities, and other services such as pest control, garbage pickup, and the care of indoor and outdoor recreational facilities that benefit the common areas and thus relieve individual owners of maintenance tasks. The agent may be given a limit—for example, $100 to $500—to spend without authorization for maintenance of the condominium's common areas and facilities. Management is also responsible for employing the personnel necessary for operating the building and the common facilities such as parking areas, lighting, and landscaping. Management will also be responsible for paying taxes (which could become a lien on the entire project or common areas if not paid), the salaries of service employees of the common areas, and any other obligations of the association.

Assessment of Common Expenses Common expenses are charged to the unit owner as determined in the declaration or the bylaws or on the basis of his or her interest in the undivided common elements, according to the value of the individual unit as a percentage of the total value of the entire condominium project. In most cases, owners must pay their share of the common expenses regardless of whether or not they use the common elements. The condominium statutes usually determine how collection of assessments will be enforced. Often a provision is included in the declaration of condominium that imposes a lien, with preference over all other liens except tax and mortgage liens, to enforce the collection of common expense assessments.

Books and Records In general and as provided for in the FHA Model Act, the manager or board of directors must keep detailed, accurate records of all receipts and expenditures affecting the common areas and facilities. All common area expenses such as maintenance and repair expenses must be itemized. In addition, the unit owners must be allowed to examine these records and the vouchers authorizing the payments. Such books and records must be kept in accordance with standard accounting procedures and must be audited annually by an independent auditor.

House Rules House rules, which are contained in the bylaws, restrict the owner's use and operation of the property. The bylaws and regulations are administered and interpreted by the board of directors. Activities that might be annoying to the majority of residents may be regulated by the board of directors as long as the restrictions are reasonable and not biased against a particular person. In general, violation of the house rules is grounds for an action by the managing board to recover for damages or injunctive relief.

Right of First Refusal The board of directors of a condominium is usually given the power to refuse admission to a prospective buyer; however, the board must match the offer made by the prospective buyer to whom it refuses admission. The basic reasons for this policy are to promote the project's viability by striving for compatibility among members and to reduce the risk of financial interdependence.

Cooperatives

Cooperative Associations

The management of cooperatives is very similar to that of condominiums. The members of the cooperative, the cooperative association, elect a board of directors who either manage the cooperative directly or select a managing agent. Voting rights of participants in cooperatives usually differ from those of condominium unit owners.

Most cooperatives allow one vote per member, even though the value of the individual cooperators' ownership interests may vary. For condominiums to get federally insured mortgages, however, the FHA requires that the weight of each condominium owner's vote be in the same proportion as the value of the owner's unit to that of the entire condominium project. The basic reason for this distinction in voting rights is the FHA's desire to assure itself of adequate protection for each unit mortgage as compared to just one mortgage for the cooperative.

Employment of Professional Management

As with condominiums, the employment of professional management seems well advised because of inexperience, lack of time, and factional disputes on the part of cooperators. To obtain federally insured mortgages, the managing agent must be approved by and file periodic reports with the FHA, and major policy decisions must be left to the tenant–stockholders or their elected board of directors.

Functions of Management

Generally, the functions of a cooperative's management are the same as those of a condominium. An additional duty of the cooperative's management, arising because cooperators do not own their units as do condominium owners, is that of paying taxes on all of the property owned by the cooperative. In addition, because the members of the cooperative association are tenants and not owners of their housing units, the cooperative association is considered to be a corporate landlord, and many of the principles of landlord–tenant agreements apply. This causes a few differences in the management aspect.

House Rules The house rules of a cooperative are usually contained in the proprietary lease agreement and, as in condominiums, set boundaries on the behavior of the tenants in the use of the property. Ordinarily the project's board of directors has the power to amend the house rules, but sometimes this power is reserved for the stockholders directly. The corporate landlord is considered to be the author of the house rules and regulations, and therefore any ambiguities will be construed against the corporate landlord.

Cooperatives do not offer the same security of interest as condominiums. As long as a condominium owner makes his/her tax payments, mortgage payments, and the association's maintenance assessments, he/she is secure from eviction. In a cooperative, however, a stockholder usually can be evicted not only if he/she fails to pay the maintenance assessment but also if a certain percentage of the cooperative stockholders (usually 75 to 80 percent) determine that he/she is an undesirable lessee because of annoying conduct.

Right of Refusal and Subletting Like condominiums, which set restraints on the unit owner's right to sell or lease to whomever they wish, cooperatives make subletting subject to the approval of the board of directors. Also as with condominiums, the board must either approve the sublessee or match the offer. A difference exists in that cooperatives set a maximum profit allowed from subletting, whereas condominiums do not set such a ceiling on profit. If should also be noted that the right to sublet is a proprietary right and is not a matter of policy or doctrine.

Enforcement Procedures Because the cooperative association is held out as the landlord and the stockholder-members as tenants, enforcement procedures applicable to landlord–tenant relationships are generally applicable to cooperatives. The lease is an important instrument in establishing the rights of the parties. Often the lease provides that annoying conduct on the part of the tenant-stockholder is grounds for cancellation of the lease with an affirmative vote of a certain proportion of the stockholders. If a tenant violates reasonable regulations established by the board of directors, the cooperative association is usually entitled to an injunction. The eviction power of cooperatives is a quicker enforcement procedure than the court proceedings that condominium associations must go through.

Most other areas of cooperative management and administration as established in the bylaws are very similar to those of condominium management. The major difference in management between the two types of organizations is that cooperatives have many established landlord–tenant procedures available for their use, whereas condominiums are more dependent on the statutes and bylaws governing them.

Planned Unit Developments

In a planned unit development, as in condominiums and cooperatives, arrangements must be made for maintaining, operating, and improving the common areas and facilities. These can include the streets, drives, parking areas, open grass areas, and recreation areas. The Urban Land Institute, a nonprofit organization whose purpose is to improve standards of land use and development, found that the most effective management mechanism is a nonprofit incorporated homeowners association with automatic membership for PUD property owners. Each lot owner is given voting rights in the association and is assessed a fee for the operation and maintenance of the common areas. The common areas must be conveyed to the association by the developer. To prevent the homeowners association from selling the open spaces, the developer sometimes deeds an open space easement to the local government. In contrast, condominium statutes make a person's interest in the common areas of a condominium indivisible from his/her unit ownership.

Functions of Management

The PUD homeowners association can hire professional management to handle the day-to-day operational problems. As with condominiums and cooperatives, the manager is only an agent of the association, and the association retains the policy-making power. Duties of PUD management parallel closely those for condominiums and cooperatives. Common areas must be maintained, assessments must be collected, books must be kept of all payments and collections, insurance must be kept up to date, and so on. In the next few paragraphs, several of the differences in the association's operations will be noted.

Assessments The authority of a homeowners association to act or to assess a fee on its members is usually based on previously recorded covenants and restrictions. There are no well-defined statutes to determine questions of authority for the association as there are for condominium associations, and in some states homeowners associations have not been able to enforce the maintenance assessment payments as a personal obligation of the unit owners.

If the assessment charge is set in the restrictive covenants, then an increase in the charge usually must be approved by the original developer and all the homeowners. As this often makes it difficult to meet cost increases, it seems preferable to have the bylaws set the association's assessments. The bylaws allow the charge to be changed by the agreement of a certain percentage of the homeowners.

Because PUDs do not have the statutory restraints that condominiums have, the developer of a PUD has more flexibility in allocating the interests in the common areas, voting rights, and common expenses. These allocations can be tailored to each particular development.

Insurance The covenants of the PUD usually at least require public liability insurance for the common areas. Hazard insurance, usually required by statute for condominiums, is not always required for a homeowners association. The community's appearance, therefore, is usually afforded greater protection under condominium statutes than under homeowners association covenants. In addition, because there is generally a greater separation between the homes and the common elements in PUDs than in condominiums or cooperatives, problems of insurance apportionment caused by overlapping policies can be avoided by having separate policies for each unit and one policy covering just the common elements.

A homeowners association is probably the best method for providing for the maintenance and operation of a PUD's common areas. It is very similar to the associations set up to maintain the common areas of condominiums and cooperatives except that the specific rights and obligations are not as well defined.

SUMMARY

Condominiums, cooperatives, and planned unit developments and their management aspects have had and will continue to have a significant impact upon the real estate industry; therefore, a general understanding of them is indispensable to the person dealing in real property. Of particular importance is an understanding of the comparative legal characteristics of each, because it is these characteristics that are being bought and sold.

QUESTIONS FOR DISCUSSION

1. What is the basic difference between a condominium, a cooperative, and a planned unit development?

2. Why might a condominium, cooperative, or planned unit development appeal more to an older person in retirement than to a younger person?

3. Do you see a need for continued or expanded use of the planned unit development concept? Why?

4. What role does professional management play in the administration of condominiums, cooperatives, and planned unit developments?

5. What are the comparative advantages and disadvantages between condominium and cooperative ownership?

CASES

Case 1. Lessee-stockholders of a cooperative apartment corporation spent $435 to repair rotted "sleepers" and underflooring in the bedroom of their apartment. They had notified the lessor-corporation of this condition, but the lessor failed to make the necessary repairs and refused to reimburse lessees for them. The lessee-stockholders contend that the corporation was bound by a covenant of the proprietary lease executed between the parties that provided: "Lessor shall keep in good repair the foundations, sidewalks, walls, supports, beams." Can the lessee-stockholders recover the $435 from the lessor-corporation?

Case 2. Plaintiff is a nonprofit corporation organized and existing for the express purpose of administering, maintaining, and repairing the common areas of a condominium. Defendants were the builders of the condominium. Due to improper cutting, filling, and compacting of the soil, tension cracks were produced in the ceilings, floors, and foundation of the residences. The occupants began to complain to Plaintiff about the damage, which included part of the common area of the condominium. Plaintiff made the necessary repairs and sought to recover the cost, which exceeded $5,000 for repairing the common areas, from Defendant-Builder. What possible defense might Defendant raise, and with what success?

Case 3. Plaintiffs and Defendants each own a condominium unit in the same building. Each unit in the building has two open balconies of like appearance. Defendants wished to enclose both of their balconies and, with permission of the board of directors of the building, proceeded to do so. Plaintiffs objected and sought to obtain an injunction. If Plaintiffs argued that the approval of the directors was insufficient in that approval of 75 percent of the unit owners was required under the declaration of condominium concerning alteration of common elements, what would Defendants argue?

Case 4. Defendant-shareholder-tenants reside in a cooperative apartment building operated and maintained by Plaintiff-corporation-landlord. Because the defendants played musical instruments, the board of directors of the plaintiff passed regulations to the effect that musical instruments could not be played between the hours of 10:00 a.m. and 8:00 p.m. and in any event no longer than an hour and a half per day by any one person without the special permission of the board of directors. Do you think this regulation is valid?

Case 5. A real estate developer sought approval of a planned residential development pursuant to a township's legislation on the subject. Although the plan as submitted met all requirements of the township legislation, it was denied by the township commissioners because, among other reasons, it was inconsistent with the township's comprehensive plan and was not in compliance with requirements of the township zoning ordinance. Are these valid reasons for denying the request?

Chapter 13
Tax Aspects of Real Estate Ownership and Certain Transactions

OWNERSHIP of and transactions in real property cannot escape the impact of taxation. For example, at the local level, a transfer tax, similar to a sales tax, is commonly assessed against real property when title is transferred to a new owner. In addition, many local governments assess a real estate tax against real property as a means of funding local school systems and other functions of local government. On the state and federal levels, local real estate taxes may, depending on the circumstances, be deducted from the owner's gross income in arriving at taxable income for purposes of calculating income tax liability. In some cases, the cost of real property can be written off, through depreciation deductions, against a taxpayer's gross income. Even interest paid on mortgage loans may be tax deductible. It is apparent, therefore, that the tax implications of real estate transactions and ownership generally play a direct and important role in acquisition and ownership decisions.

This chapter reviews several fundamental tax concepts that relate directly to the ownership of and transactions in real property. First, it discusses tax deductions for depreciation, interest, taxes, and other charges related to the ownership of real property; later sections deal with the tax implications of certain transactions in real property such as selling, exchanging, and trading.

The tax law as it relates to real property, in addition to being complicated, has been traditionally reserved for courses in real estate finance or taxation. However, the purpose here is to acquaint the student with the basic principles of tax law so that those who have not previously dealt with the subject will not overlook a practical future application. The laws discussed will relate primarily to taxation on the federal level. Many states make use of the same provisions.

TAX IMPLICATIONS OF REAL ESTATE OWNERSHIP

For tax purposes, real estate that is held for production of income or used in a trade or business is treated differently from real estate that is held for nonbusiness or personal use, such as a personal residence. The primary difference is that income-producing or business buildings, or other improvements to the land, can be depreciated over a period of time, whereas a private residence that is a taxpayer's home or other nonbusiness property generally cannot be depreciated. In addition, other expenses, such as interest, property taxes, and repairs and mainte-nance, can generally be used as a tax deduction against business property income, but such expenses for nonbusiness property can be deducted from personal income only under certain well-defined circumstances.

Depreciation

When certain real property is used for the production of income or in a trade or business, a presumption exists that over the years the cost of the property is used up by the wear and tear it receives in the business use. For tax purposes, *depreciation* represents an approximation of the amount of annual wear and tear or expense that contributes to the production of business income. The taxpayer is permitted to deduct this expense in a series of deductions extending over the estimated useful life of the asset. In this way, the cost of the building is periodically deducted from income for tax purposes. Since land is not used up in the same sense, it is not subject to depreciation; only buildings and other improve-ments on the land can be depreciated.

Basis and Adjusted Basis

Generally, annual depreciation of an asset is equal to its *depreciable basis* divided by its estimated useful life; therefore, the concept of tax basis should be firmly understood. Basis is usually synonymous with cost or purchase price, but since property can be acquired in other ways, it may not mean cost. For example, where real property is acquired by gift, for tax purposes, with certain minor exceptions, the basis of the property in the hands of the donee is the same as it was in the hands of the donor. Thus, if G purchased a business property in 1950 for $10,000 and gave it to his son S in 1978, the tax basis to S would be $10,000, assuming that G did not take depreciation deductions or adjust his basis in any other way during the period of his ownership.

The tax basis of depreciable real property usually does not remain the same throughout its life. Generally, the cost or other basis can be adjusted upwards for additions made to the property or downwards if the property is depreciated, partially sold, or destroyed. In the example just given, if G built an addition to the business property in 1970 at a cost of $50,000 and had taken $20,000 of depreciation deductions just prior to the gift to S in 1978, the adjusted basis of the business property would be $40,000 (cost of $10,000 + additions of $50,000 – accumulated depreciation of $20,000). Consequently, the tax basis to G on which depreciation would be calculated is $40,000. Not only is the concept of basis and adjusted basis important to the depreciation deduction calculation, but it is also important in determining capital gains on the sale of real property, as will be discussed later in this chapter.

Deductibility

Depreciation is deductible for tax purposes only on real property that has a limited useful life and is either used by the taxpayer in trade or business or held for the production of income. Hence, land (which has an unlimited life) or a personal residence not used by the taxpayer in a trade or business or for the production of income is not depreciable. Similarly, inventories, even though used in a trade or business or for the production of income, are not depreciable, because the valuation of inventory is automatically adjusted for wear and tear.

Methods of Computation

There are two basic methods of computing tax depreciation: the straight-line method and the accelerated method. Straight-line depreciation can be used for all depreciable real property whether new or used. To calculate annual depreciation using the straight-line method, divide adjusted basis minus estimated salvage value by years of estimated useful life remaining. That is,

$$\frac{\text{Adjusted basis} - \text{Estimated salvage value}}{\text{Useful life (years)}} = \text{Annual depreciation}$$

Estimated salvage value refers to the value that the depreciable real property may reasonably be expected to have at the end of its estimated useful life. *Estimated useful life* refers to the period in years over which the depreciable real property is expected to be of use to the taxpayer in a trade or business. Thus, if a taxpayer purchased land and a rental building on it for $120,000, he would first have to allocate the total cost between land and building since land is not depreciable. If a taxpayer estimated that the cost of the building was $110,000 and that it would have a salvage value of $10,000 at the end of a 25-year life, then annual straight-line depreciation would be $4,000:

$$\frac{\$110,000 - \$10,000}{25 \text{ years}} = \$4,000/\text{year}$$

This method is often recommended for its simplicity.

The two most generally recognized accelerated methods of depreciation are declining balance and sum-of-the-years-digits. Both methods provide for greater depreciation than under the straight-line method in the early years of the property's life, with successively less depreciation deductions each year so that the later years produce smaller deductions than under the straight-line method. In addition, for federal tax purposes, the accelerated methods of depreciation have a limited application to real property.

Under the *declining balance method* of depreciation, the straight-line rate is multiplied by the declining balance percentage to arrive at a declining balance rate. The declining balance percentage can never exceed 200 percent for tax purposes. Thus, a property that is assigned a 20-year life depreciates at the rate of 5 percent per year. Under 200 percent, 150 percent, and 125 percent declining balance methods, the declining balance rate would be 10 percent (5% x 200%), 7.5 percent (5% x 150%), and 6.25 percent (5% x 125%), respectively. The declining balance rate is then multiplied by the adjusted basis to arrive at the current year's depreciation. For example, if a taxpayer purchased depreciable real property on January 1, 19X1 for $50,000, assigned a 20-year life to it, and elected to take 200 percent declining balance depreciation, his depreciation deduction for three successive years would be:

	Cost	-	Accumulated Depreciation	=	Adjusted Cost	X	Rate	=	Depreciation
19X1	$50,000	-	$ 0	=	$50,000	X	10%	=	$5,000
19X2	50,000	-	5,000	=	$45,000	X	10%	=	4,500
19X3	50,000	-	9,500	=	$40,500	X	10%	=	4,050

Under the *sum-of-the-years-digits method,* the adjusted tax basis less salvage value is multiplied by a fraction whose numerator is the number of remaining years of the asset's life and whose denominator is the sum of the digits representing the years of the asset's life. For a five-year life, the digits are 1 through 5, and the sum of the years' digits is therefore $1 + 2 + 3 + 4 + 5 = 15$.

For example, Taxpayer purchased depreciable real property on January 1, 19X1 for $100,000 with an estimated salvage value of $10,000 at the end of a five-year life. Her depreciation deductions for three successive years would be:

	Cost Less Salvage	X	Sum-of-Years-Digits Fraction	=	Depreciation
19X1	$90,000	X	$5/15$	=	$30,000
19X2	$90,000	X	$4/15$	=	$24,000
19X3	$90,000	X	$3/15$	=	$18,000

The sum of the years digits can be calculated for longer lives by use of the formula $S = L(L + 1)/2$, where L is the number of years in the life of the asset. This method is not widely used, because of the complicated nature of its calculation and the fact that 200 percent declining balance produces approximately the same result. Nevertheless, the federal tax law specifically recognizes it as well as the straight-line and declining balance methods.

Specific Application to Real Property

Federal tax law provides that the straight-line and accelerated methods of depreciation can be used on depreciable real property acquired before July 24, 1969. However, the fastest methods of depreciation that can be used on residential rental property acquired after July 24, 1969 are 200 percent declining balance on new property and 125 percent declining balance on used property with a remaining useful life of at least 20 years; otherwise the straight-line method must be used. The fastest methods of depreciation that can be used on depreciable real property other than residential rental property acquired after July 24, 1969, are 150 percent declining balance on new property and straight-line on used property no matter what its life. Since depreciation is subtracted from income in arriving at taxable income, the amount of depreciation that a taxpayer can take under the tax laws has a significant bearing upon an investment decision in depreciable real property.

Interest and Taxes

Unlike depreciation, which is deductible only if real property is used in taxpayer's trade or business or is held for the production of income, interest and real estate taxes applicable to real property can be deducted for both business and nonbusiness property for federal income tax purposes. Thus, interest paid on a mortgage that was obtained to purchase an apartment building or to purchase a private residential dwelling is deductible. Real estate taxes paid on the same buildings are also deductible. There is, however, an important difference between the deductibility of interest and taxes for business and nonbusiness real property.

For business real property, applicable interest and taxes can always be deducted, but for nonbusiness real property, under federal tax law, an individual cannot deduct applicable interest and taxes if he/she elects to take a standard deduction. That is, in lieu of the total deductions for taxes, interest, and other deductions (referred to as itemized deductions), a taxpayer can elect to take a standard amount which is a percent of adjusted gross income never less than $1,600 or more than $3,200 depending upon filing status. Thus, if the total of a taxpayer's itemized deductions, including interest and taxes on his home, were less than $1,600, he would elect the standard deduction in lieu of deducting interest and taxes on the home as an itemized deduction. On the other hand, if taxpayer should convert the same home to a rental property, he could deduct applicable interest and real estate taxes in addition to taking the standard deduction.

Other Charges

Interest and real estate taxes are the primary nonbusiness expenses related directly to real estate under federal tax law that can be deducted as itemized deductions on an individual federal income tax return. However, for business or income-producing real estate, most other charges associated with the building can be deducted. Chief among these are salaries and commissions, repairs and maintenance, insurance, utilities, professional fees, and advertising.

An expense may not be fully deductible in the year paid if it is applicable to more than one year. Under such circumstances, it would be capitalized and written off over a period of years. Repair and maintenance expenses are common examples. If, for example, a boiler wears out and is replaced by a new one, the cost of the new boiler, even though it is a repair and maintenance type of expenditure, would be capitalized and depreciated over its estimated useful life.

Some maintenance expenses such as decorative painting may be capitalized and depreciated or deducted in the year incurred, whereas others such as assessments for streets, sidewalks, and sewers must be capitalized. Where real property is in the process of being developed or constructed, the taxpayer can elect to capitalize such costs as loan interest, sales taxes, and other necessary expenditures. But after the election to capitalize is made, it is binding for the period of development and construction. The investor who seeks to maximize his/her tax deductions should investigate carefully the manner in which an expenditure can be written off before deciding on an investment.

TAX IMPLICATIONS OF CERTAIN REAL ESTATE TRANSACTIONS

There are many different types of transactions in real property, all of which, whether business or nonbusiness, have direct federal tax implications. For example, the sale of a personal residence may obligate the seller to pay an income tax on the difference between the adjusted cost basis of the property and its sales price. A gift of the same residence may obligate the donor to pay a gift tax based on the fair market value of the house. Even the condemnation of real property by governmental authority could create a taxable event. It is impossible in a general survey book to set forth in detail the tax implications of every type of real estate transaction. Nevertheless, the tax implications of sales, exchanges, and involuntary conversions of real property are generally discussed so that the student has at least a basic understanding of the tax implications of these common but important types of real estate transactions.

Capital Gains and Losses

Under federal tax law, a capital gain or loss may arise from the sale or exchange of a capital asset, which includes real property, whether a taxpayer's residence or an investment rental property. *Capital gain* or *loss* is measured by the difference between sales price (amount received) and cost or adjusted cost (amount given up). If a capital gain is treated as long-term capital gain, it is taxed at a lower rate than so-called ordinary income, which is generally derived from employment, the operation of a trade or business, the receipt of dividends or interest, or some other activity not associated with the disposition of capital resulting in long-term gain. From the recipient's viewpoint, therefore, long-term capital gain income is preferred over ordinary income.

If the sale or exchange results in a capital loss, the economic effect of such a transaction may be partially offset by the resulting tax benefits to the taxpayer. For example, losses are used to reduce gains and can, to a limited extent, be used to offset ordinary income.

Short-Term and Long-Term Gain or Loss

Capital gain or loss is classified as being either short- or long-term. For federal tax purposes, *long-term gain* or *loss* occurs when a capital asset is held for more than one year and then sold or exchanged. *Short-term gain* or *loss* occurs when a capital asset is held for less than one year and then sold or exchanged. The distinction between long- and short-term gain or loss is crucial, since net long-term gain receives preferential tax treatment, whereas short-term gain is taxed as ordinary income.

For real property that is acquired by purchase, the holding period begins from the date of purchase. But if it is acquired by gift and is disposed of at a gain, the holding period begins on the date it was purchased by the donor and not on the transfer date from donor to donee. For real property acquired from a decedent, the holding period requirement for capital gain treatment will be met even if the property is disposed of within one year after the decedent's death. Investors in real estate, as contrasted with investors in stock, usually plan on holding the asset for longer than one year in order to take advantage of a more gradual appreciation rate plus depreciation deductions. As a consequence, the holding period requirement for capital gain treatment usually does not present a problem to the real estate investor.

Realized and Recognized Capital Gain

When real property is disposed of at a gain, tax on part of the gain may be postponed depending upon the nature of the transaction. The total amount of the gain is called *realized gain*, but the portion that is taxed is called *recognized gain*. For example, under federal tax provisions, if a taxpayer exchanges real property with an adjusted basis of $50,000 for similar real property with a fair market value of $70,000, taxpayer's realized gain of $20,000 ($70,000 – $50,000) is not taxed or recognized. It is postponed until taxpayer disposes of the exchanged property at some later date. It is also possible for realized gain to be partially recognized, as illustrated in the section below dealing with specific transactions.

Computation of Tax

The computation of tax on capital transactions has been significantly changed by the 1978 Revenue Act. Now, under federal tax law for individuals, net long-term capital gains in excess of net short-term capital losses are taxed under the *capital gain deduction method*. This method provides that 60 percent of the excess of net long-term capital gains over net short-term capital loss is deducted from income and the other 40 percent is subject to tax at ordinary rates.

For example, if taxpayer's capital transactions during the tax year produced a $10,000 long-term gain, a $5,000 long-term loss, a $4,000 short-term gain, and a $6,000 short-term loss, the capital gain deduction would be $1,500, computed as follows:

Net long-term gain ($10,000–$5,000)	$ 5,000
Net short-term loss ($4,000–$6,000)	–2,000
Net long-term gain	$ 3,000
60% net long-term gain over net short-term loss	–1,800
Amount included in income	$ 1,200

In the example above, if the net short-term transactions resulted in a gain, the capital gain deduction would have been $3,000 (60% of $5,000) and the remainder taxed as ordinary income. It is apparent that a capital gain deduction will not exist if there is either a net long-term capital loss or a net capital loss.

Corporations under federal law are not entitled to the 60 percent capital gain deduction. Generally, tax on corporate net long-term capital gains over short-term capital losses is calculated by use of the alternative method, where the alternative tax rate is 28 percent.

Effect of Capital Loss

For individuals, if the net effect of the capital transaction was a loss, it may be used as a deduction. Net long-term capital losses can be used to offset ordinary income on a two-for-one basis. That is, it takes two dollars of long-term capital loss to produce one dollar of deductible loss. Net short-term capital losses can be offset on a dollar-for-dollar basis. For example, if a taxpayer's net long-term capital losses were $2,000 and her net short-term capital losses were $1,000 during the tax year, her deductible loss would be $2,000 (50% of $2,000 + $1,000). An individual taxpayer is permitted to deduct only $3,000 of such losses against ordinary income in any single taxable year, but any loss over and above that amount can be carried forward for an unlimited time until it is exhausted.

Corporations under federal law can use capital losses for a taxable year only to offset capital gains for that year and not to offset ordinary income. However, any unused capital losses can be carried back three years and forward five years and applied against any capital gain transactions in those years.

Specific Transactions

Three common types of transactions pertaining directly to real property are sales, exchanges, and involuntary conversions. There are other types of real estate transactions that have significant tax implications under federal law; however, they are beyond the scope of this book. It should also be understood that due to the complicated nature of the tax law, many variations of the examples given can occur, with different tax results. Nevertheless, by understanding the basic concepts of capital gain versus ordinary income and realized versus recognized gain as they apply to simplified examples of sales, exchanges, and involuntary conversions, the person dealing in real estate is better able to cope with investment and other decisions.

Sales

The simplest situation occurs when unimproved land is sold by a taxpayer for cash. For example, a long-term capital gain of $5,000 would arise from the sale of land that cost $15,000, was held by a taxpayer for longer than one year, and was sold for $20,000. The assumption is that adjusted basis equals cost.

A more complicated tax situation arises from the sale of a personal house that is taxpayer's principal residence. Where the taxpayer sells his principal residence and purchases a new residence within 18 months, the realized gain, if any, is recognized only to the extent that the adjusted sales price of the old residence exceeds the cost of the new residence. For example, if T purchased a principal residence in 1950 for $10,000, sold it in 1980 for $50,000, and purchased a new principal residence in 1980 for $50,000, the realized gain of $40,000 would have been fully reinvested and consequently not recognized. But if taxpayer paid only $30,000 for the new principal residence, $20,000 of the realized gain would be recognized and taxed at capital gain rates, since it was not reinvested. In essence, the unrecognized gain of $20,000 is deferred until the new principal residence is sold at a later date.

A taxpayer who is 55 years of age or older is permitted a one-time exclusion of up to $100,000 of profit on the sale of a principal place of residence if he/she has owned and occupied the house for three of the previous five years. For example, if a taxpayer purchased his principal residence in 1960 for $50,000 and sold it in 1979 when he was 60 years old for $150,000, the entire profit of $100,000 would be excluded from taxation.

In each of these examples, the cost basis or purchase price is usually adjusted to reflect events that directly relate to the property. An addition to the property necessitates an upward adjustment to the cost basis. The purchase price is also adjusted upwards to include closing costs such as real estate transfer taxes, title search fees, and attorney's fees. Depreciation, on the other hand, would cause a downward adjustment in the cost basis. Often, the gain realized from the sale of depreciable real property occurs not only because the value of the property has increased over its original cost, but also because of accumulated depreciation. The most extreme case is where depreciation has reduced the cost basis to a point below the property's selling price. For example:

Sales price		$6,000
Less: Cost	$6,000	
Depreciation	($4,000)	
Adjusted basis		2,000
Long-term gain		$4,000

In this example, all the gain is attributable to accumulated depreciation.

It would appear, therefore, that the taxpayer can deduct the value of depreciable real property from ordinary income via the depreciation deduction and later, when the property is sold, have to pay tax on only 40 percent of the gain caused by the depreciation due to the long-term capital gain deduction. In the above example, the taxpayer's ordinary income was reduced by the depreciation taken, or $4,000, but only $2,000 of the long-term gain is treated as ordinary income at the time of sale. In essence, ordinary income has been converted to tax-preferred long-term capital gain income.

It is possible, however, for all or part of the gain attributable to depreciation on real property to be recaptured as ordinary income. Federal tax law provides, in part, for full recapture of all depreciation if the real property is held for less than one year, no matter what depreciation method is used, for no recapture of depreciation for real property held for more than one year and depreciated on the straight-line method, and for full recapture of post-1969 excess depreciation, which is the difference between straight-line and accelerated depreciation.

For example, Taxpayer purchased a newly constructed apartment building in 1970 for $100,000. He deducted $17,000 as depreciation expenses based on the 150 percent declining balance method from 1970 to 1973. Straight-line depreciation for the same period would have been $12,000. Taxpayer sold the apartment building in the last month of 1973 for $120,000. The total long-term capital gain on the sale is $37,000: sales price ($120,000) less adjusted cost ($100,000 – $17,000). According to the rule, the difference between depreciation as calculated under the accelerated method ($17,000) and the straight-line method ($12,000), or $5,000, is recaptured as ordinary income. The remaining $32,000 gain ($37,000 – $5,000) is treated as long-term capital gain and thus is subject to favorable tax treatment.

It should be stressed that the depreciation recapture rules for real property can be more complex than those presented. Nevertheless, it is important to understand the basic concept of depreciation and its possible effect on the sale of depreciable real property so that expert legal or accounting advice can be obtained if necessary.

Exchanges

Often, real estate investors will exchange one property for another. Usually, an exchange results in a realized gain, particularly if the property given up has been held and depreciated for a long period of time. The realized gain would generally be measured by the difference between the adjusted cost basis of the property given up and the fair market value of the property received in the exchange. Federal tax law provides, however, that the taxpayer can elect not to recognize the gain in an exchange situation if it is a "like kind" exchange of property used in a trade or business or held for investment purposes. The "like kind" requirement basically means that the asset given up and the asset received must be real estate. City acreage and farm acreage may be like-kind property, but real estate and personal property such as stocks and bonds clearly are not. Gain in a like-kind exchange is not always deferred. It is recognized to the extent of the cash or other property received, which is called *boot,* and where mortgaged real estate is exchanged, gain is recognized to the extent of mortgage reduction.

For example, a taxpayer could defer the entire realized gain of $25,000 on real property with an adjusted cost basis of $50,000 that was exchanged for like-kind property having a fair market value of $75,000. But, if he received $10,000 in cash or other personal property in addition to the like-kind property, $10,000 of the realized gain of $25,000 would be recognized and taxed as long-term capital gain, assuming the property exchanged was held by the taxpayer for more than one year. Further, if the property given up was encumbered by a $15,000 mortgage that was assumed by the other party to the transaction, and the property received was encumbered by a $10,000 mortgage that the taxpayer assumed, taxpayer's net reduction in mortgage payable of $5,000 would be recognized as long-term capital gain, again assuming the property was held by taxpayer for the required period of time.

As in most transactions where long-term gain is deferred, the tax basis of the property received in a tax-free exchange is adjusted so that the deferred portion of the gain will be taxed when the property received is sold at some later date. The tax basis of real property acquired in any exchange is equal to its fair market value less any unrecognized gain or plus any unrecognized loss.

For example, if taxpayer exchanged real estate with an adjusted basis of $20,000 encumbered by a mortgage of $10,000 for $1,000 in cash plus real estate with a fair market value of $25,000 that was encumbered by a mortgage of $7,000 the realized gain would be the net amount received ($25,000 − $7,000 + $1,000) less the net amount given up ($20,000 − $10,000), or $9,000, of which $4,000 is recognized (boot received of $1,000 cash + mortgage reduction of $3,000). Thus, taxpayer's basis in the newly acquired property is the fair market value of the property acquired in the exchange ($25,000) less the unrecognized gain ($9,000 − $4,000), or $20,000.

From this example and the discussion above, it can be seen that the gain is simply deferred and that a taxpayer can, through a series of simple exchanges, build up sizable equity without the payment of taxes. For example, A acquired certain real property in 1970 for $10,000. In 1974 he traded the property for one with a fair market value of $20,000, and in 1978 he traded that property for one with a fair market value of $35,000. Taxpayer A then had property worth $35,000, having effectively postponed the capital gain tax on each transaction. The original tax basis of $10,000 would, of course, carry over to the 1978 acquisition, so that if he sold the property in 1979 for $40,000, his long-term capital gain would be $30,000 ($40,000 − $10,000).

There may be situations where taxpayer elects not to take advantage of a tax-free exchange. It may be advantageous to pay the tax on the gain and depreciate from a higher basis. This can be determined only after a careful, in-depth analysis of the taxpayer's financial situation. Such an analysis is usually performed by an accountant, an attorney, or a financial advisor familiar with tax matters.

Involuntary Conversions

Involuntary conversion occurs when a taxpayer's property is compulsorily or involuntarily converted into money or other property through destruction, condemnation, or seizure in whole or in part. Two examples of involuntary conversion of real property are the destruction of an apartment building by fire, flood, or hurricane and the condemnation or seizure of land by a local or state government for use as a highway, park, or housing facility. Generally, when the owner receives money as a result of the conversion, such as proceeds from insurance or payment by a local or state government, the transaction is treated as a sale for tax purposes. The gain is measured by the difference between the amount received and the adjusted basis of the real property converted. But since the gain was involuntary, federal tax law allows the taxpayer to defer recognition of the gain in cases where the proceeds from the conversion are fully reinvested in similar replacement property.

Replacement property must be similar property or related in service or use to the property converted. For example, a taxpayer whose apartment building was condemned or destroyed by fire could defer the gain by purchasing or building another apartment building, but not by purchasing a building used as a restaurant. Although the similarity-in-use test is construed narrowly, the broader like-kind test applicable to tax-free exchanges is applied to real property used in taxpayer's trade or business or held for investment. Therefore, in the example above, even though the replacement property does not comply with the similarity-in-use test, it is arguable that it complies with the like-kind test. The replacement period begins either on the actual date of destruction, condemnation, or seizure or the earliest date of threatened condemnation or seizure. The period ends two years (three years for condemned real property) after the close of the first taxable year in which any part of the gain on the conversion is realized, or at a later date if appropriate permission is received from the Internal Revenue Service.

For example, if taxpayer's real property was destroyed by fire on May 1, 1978, when its adjusted basis was $50,000, the replacement period begins on May 1, 1978, and ends on December 31, 1980. If taxpayer received $75,000 insurance proceeds and purchased a replacement property for $75,000 or more before December 31, 1980, the entire realized gain of $25,000 would be deferred. If the cost of the replacement property was $50,000 or less, the entire realized gain would be recognized. If the cost of the replacement property was between the adjusted basis of the destroyed property and the insurance proceeds received therefrom, $60,000 for example, then the reinvested gain of $10,000 would be deferred and the remaining amount of $15,000 recognized.

Casualty Losses

A casualty loss arises when a taxpayer receives less than the adjusted basis of his real property for a loss resulting from fire, storm, shipwreck, or other casualty. Other casualties may include losses due to vandalism, earthslides, quarry blasts, or other events that are sudden, unexpected, or unusual. Such a loss can be deducted in full if it applies to business property. If the loss applies to nonbusiness property, each individual casualty loss is deductible only to the extent that it exceeds $100. Thus, if taxpayer's house was destroyed by fire on March 1 causing a loss, net of insurance reimbursements, of $5,000, and taxpayer's garage was destroyed in a storm several weeks later, causing a net loss of $1,000, taxpayer's deductible loss for the calendar year would be $5,800 ($5,000 − $100 + $1,000 − $100).

Inheritance

One of the most important considerations of a beneficiary relative to real property inherited from a decedent is the tax basis of that property. There have been a number of significant changes in federal tax law that affect the tax basis of real property received by a beneficiary from a decedent. Prior to December 31, 1976, the federal tax law permitted a decedent's beneficiary to take real property at its fair market value on the date of decedent's death or six months thereafter. In other words, the beneficiary received a stepped-up basis. Thus, the capital gain attributable to appreciation on the property during the period it was held by the decedent went untaxed for income tax purposes. Under the Tax Reform Act of 1976, federal tax law generally provided that the adjusted basis of real property at the time of decedent's death will carry over to the beneficiary. Since this law became effective on December 31, 1976, special adjustments called *fresh start adjustments* were made. The effect of this adjustment is to allow real property acquired by a decedent before December 31, 1976, on which substantial appreciation has been realized to be "stepped up" to its approximate fair market value on that date for purposes of establishing a new tax basis in the hands of the beneficiary. Specifically, the Tax Reform Act of 1976 provided that total appreciation be prorated over the decedent's entire holding period and the appreciation applicable to years before December 31, 1976 will be added to decedent's adjusted basis to arrive at the fresh start basis to the beneficiary.

For example, decedent purchased certain real property on 12/31/75 for $50,000 and died on 12/31/77, at which time the property had a fair market value of $70,000. The fresh start basis to the beneficiary would be: number of days property held by decedent prior to 12/31/76 (365) divided by total number of days property held by decedent (730) times total appreciation of $20,000 over entire holding period ($70,000 − $50,000) added to the decedent's adjusted basis of $50,000 equals the fresh start basis of $60,000 in the hands of the beneficiary. To recap, (365/730 x $20,000) + $50,000 = $60,000. The special valuation method operates on the assumption that appreciation occurs uniformly over the entire period of time the property was held by the decedent. This assumption is probably fairly accurate as it pertains to real property.

For estate planning purposes, in order to prevent the unfavorable imposition of a carryover basis that could result in low depreciation deductions, substantial capital gains, and the overall adverse tax implications of appreciation, one suggestion is to enter into a buy-sell agreement, pegging the price at some fair value that is acceptable to the purchaser-beneficiary. In this way, the tax basis of the property would be stepped up to the price established in the agreement, and consequently capital gains could be eliminated or substantially reduced. Such a transaction has both estate and income tax implications for seller and buyer; therefore, it is always advisable that professional tax advice be obtained when considering a buy-sell agreement.

Under the 1978 Revenue Act, the effect of the Tax Reform Act of 1976 on inherited basis has been delayed until January 1, 1980, and the old step-up in basis rules apply. Most tax specialists predict that after the delay period, the old rules will continue to apply.

The tax implications of certain real estate transfers go far beyond those discussed here. Nevertheless, the basic concepts of some of the more important types of transactions have been presented so that the student will be able to apply the rules to relatively simple situations and recognize the tax advantages derived from certain transactions in real property.

QUESTIONS FOR DISCUSSION

1. Why is the tax impact on a real estate transaction an important consideration to investors?

2. What is the basic difference between ordinary income and long-term capital gain income?

3. Define basis and adjusted basis of real property and state what tax effect its computation has on the acquisition of business and nonbusiness real property.

4. Real property is often purchased as a tax shelter. What is meant by that statement?

5. For tax purposes, what difference does it make whether real property is purchased new or used?

PROBLEMS

1. Taxpayer purchased an apartment complex on January 1, 1970, for $100,000, $80,000 of which was attributed to the building and $20,000 to the land. He assigned a 40-year life to the building and depreciated it using the straight-line method. If Taxpayer sold the apartment complex on December 31, 1980, for $80,000, calculate his gain or loss on the sale.

2. Taxpayer purchased a principal residence in 1960 for $50,000 and sold it in 1980 for $100,000. If taxpayer was 58 years old, how much of the realized gain of $50,000 would be recognized? If taxpayer was 50 years old, and within 6 months of the date of sale purchased a new principal residence for $80,000, how much of the gain would be realized and recognized?

3. In a like-kind exchange, Taxpayer exchanged property A, which on the exchange date had an adjusted tax basis of $20,000, for property B, which had a fair market value of $25,000. Taxpayer also received $2,000 in cash. How much, if any, of the realized gain is recognized? How much, if any, of the realized gain would be recognized if, in addition to the above facts, taxpayer assumed a mortgage of $3,000 on property B and the other party to the transaction assumed a mortgage for $4,000 on Property A?

4. Which of the following expenses applicable to real property are deductible for federal income tax purposes? Explain your answer.

(a) Interest expense on mortgage.
(b) Purchase of hot water heater.
(c) Electric repairs.
(d) Real estate taxes.
(e) Insurance.
(f) Destruction by flood.
(g) Loss on sale.
(h) Legal fees.

5. During the taxable year, Taxpayer had the following transactions in capital assets:

Long-term gains	50,000
Long-term losses	40,000
Short-term gains	30,000
Short-term losses	20,000

For federal income tax purposes, how much of the net gain is treated as capital gain deduction and how much is treated as ordinary income?

6. Calculate the first two years' depreciation for depreciable real property having a cost of $10,000, useful life of 20 years, and no salvage value under (a) the straight-line and (b) 200 percent declining balance methods.

Chapter 14
Governmental Regulation of the Real Estate Transaction

THE right of local, state, and federal governments to regulate land use under their police powers has been generally accepted. The specific powers have been discussed in Chapter 2. Traditionally, the transfer of rights and the creation of nonpossessory security interests in real property were matters controlled by state law. Because real estate was purely local, its regulation was considered to have been reserved to the states. In fact, most states have exercised the power to regulate real estate transactions by prescribing the form of documents of title, establishing recording practices and procedures, and granting certain substantive rights to parties to the real estate transaction.

During the last decade, there has been a growing trend toward federal regulation of consumer transactions. There has also been a corresponding general acceptance of the federal government's role in protecting the public from sharp or unfair practices of those who deal in goods and services. The real estate industry has not been free of members who take unfair advantage of unsuspecting or unsophisticated buyers or borrowers. Consumer advocates, members of the real estate profession, and government officals have increasingly expressed concern over such practices. The federal government has responded by implementing three major laws to deal with these problems. The sale of land in interstate commerce is regulated under the Interstate Land Sales Full Disclosure Act; lending practices are controlled by the Truth-in-Lending Act or Regulation Z; and closing costs are regulated by the Real Estate Settlement Procedures Act (RESPA).

INTERSTATE LAND SALES FULL DISCLOSURE ACT

In the early 1960s, the U.S. Senate Special Committee on Aging began inquiries into certain land sale schemes whereby elderly persons were

327

being persuaded to purchase retirement property that was less than desirable and often uninhabitable. As the investigation continued, it was discovered that misleading or fraudulent practices were widespread in the real estate industry. Often investors purchased property in swamps, deserts, and remote areas, having been led to believe that the land had amenities that in fact could not be provided, and their hopes for a retirement home or vacation retreat were lost along with their money. The land was marketed through magazine advertisements, personal solicitation, and sales parties that induced thousands to invest their savings. No regulations existed to protect the individual purchaser or provide a remedy until the investment had been made and the monies lost.

In 1968, Congress passed the Interstate Land Sales Full Disclosure Act (ILSFDA), an act comparable to the Federal Securities Act of 1933, which has been successful in limiting fraudulent stock sales schemes. ILSFDA is administered by the Office of Interstate Land Sales Registration of the Department of Housing and Urban Development (HUD).

The federal government derives its authority to regulate interstate land sales through the Congress's constitutional authority to regulate interstate commerce. The interstate commerce clause of the Constitution has been judicially interpreted to include not only sales to parties in different states, but also sales to parties within a state if the instrumentalities of interstate commerce such as the telephone, mails, or electronic media are used to promote sales. Therefore, almost all land development sales may be interpreted as being subject to Congressional regulation of interstate commerce.

ILSFDA attempts to deal with three separate abuses common in land promotion schemes.

1. Misrepresentation of the nature and general characteristics of the land being sold.

2. The "sight-unseen" method of promoting land sales through high-pressure techniques designed to overcome the unsuspecting buyer's sales resistance and caution.

3. Overcrowding and overdevelopment of available resources such as water. The act prescribes standards of development to help maintain the desirable qualities of the land.

The drafters of the law recognized the desirability of mass marketing of developmental property as long as fraudulent and misleading practices are curtailed.

The act makes it unlawful for any developer or agent, directly or indirectly, to make use of any of the means or instruments of transportation or communication in interstate commerce to dispose of any land in a subdivision in violation of the act. These provisions establish the jurisdictional basis of federal regulation of local land sales. Section 1404(a) of ILSFDA sets forth the requirement that before any sales may be made using the instrumentalities of interstate commerce, the developer must first file a statement of record with the appropriate government official. In compliance with the disclosure act, the developer must furnish a property report to the prospective purchaser before the sale or lease of any subdivision under the jurisdiction of the act. Finally, the act prohibits certain conduct by the developer in marketing the property.

Jurisdiction of the Act

The Interstate Land Sales Full Disclosure Act applies to all subdivisions that are divided into 50 or more lots for the purpose of sale or lease as part of a common promotional plan. It applies not only to subdivisions that contain 50 or more lots, but also to those where future development would bring the total number of lots to 50 or more. By definition, the term *subdivision* does not mean that the lots have to be contiguous to each other. That the lots are part of a "common promotional scheme" is the test employed by the act to determine the number of lots within a subdivision. For example, if two separate noncontiguous subdivisions each containing 25 lots are owned by the same developer or a group of developers acting in concert in the promotion and sale of lots in both subdivisions, then the act would apply even though neither subdivision has the minimum number of lots to bring it within the jurisdiction of the act.

For purposes of the act, a *lot* is defined as any portion, piece, division, unit, or undivided interest in land if such interest includes the exclusive use of a specific portion of the land. Thus, if a purchaser of an interest in property has the exclusive right to the use of a portion of the land, then the interest sold is a "lot." The term "lot" does not require that an ownership interest be given to a purchaser. Thus, a property under long-term lease would qualify as a lot because the lessee has the exclusive use of the property. Also included within the definition of lot are limited partnerships that grant partners exclusive right to a portion of the land. The Department of Housing and Urban Development (HUD) has also taken the position that a condominium unit is a lot, because it grants the exclusive right to possession and use to the condominium owner. Thus, sale of units in a 50-unit condominium may fall within the jurisdiction of the act even though there was only one parcel of real estate involved.

Exemptions

Certain transactions are exempt from compliance with the act. Dispositions of land under court order, transfers of mortgages, real estate

investment trusts, sale or lease of lots by governmental agencies or
authorities, cemetery lots, and transactions involving certain commercial
builders are exempt by statute. The apparent theory behind such
exemptions is that these transactions are already regulated or do not
involve the development of homesites or investment properties. Subdivisions where the minimum lot size is five acres or more per lot are also
exempt by statute. This exemption has been criticized because the
promoter could use fraud in the sale of larger lots such as mini-farms or
"ranchettes." Another exemption under the act is the sale or lease of
lots in a subdivision where the purchaser or spouse personally inspects
the property before purchase or lease and the property is free and clear
of liens and encumbrances except for dedications to the public and local
and state taxes. This so-called "on-site" exemption has also been
criticized because most purchasers are unaware of the information
necessary to make a decision on purchasing a lot, and such matters as tax
rates, distance to schools, hospitals, fire control, governmental maintenance of roads, and the like are not readily discoverable through an on-
site inspection of the property.

The act also exempts lots upon which there is a residential, commercial, or industrial building or the sale or lease of land that requires the
seller to erect such a building on the property within two years.
Apparently, the drafters of the law decided that if a building is involved,
the buyer will be more careful and there is no need to require the
developer to provide the information included in the disclosure requirements of nonexempt transactions.

These statutory exemptions apply only if the developer does not
attempt to structure a transaction or promotional scheme to circumvent
the provisions of the act. Each statutory exemption is conditioned upon
the developer's not using a particular form to evade the protective
provisions of the act. Thus, a developer may not adopt an exempt form
when in substance it is engaging in conduct that would normally come
within the provisions of the act. For example, the developer cannot sell
lots with the requirement that the purchaser erect a building within two
years and then waive the requirement that the improvements be constructed.

In addition to the statutory exemptions, certain regulatory exemptions
have been developed by HUD incident to its power under the act.
Among the regulatory exemptions are lots sold for less than $100, leases
for terms not more than five years, and "intrastate" sales exemptions.
The intrastate exemption is available upon application to HUD where the
subdivision contains less than 300 lots and is located solely within one
state, the offerings of lots are made within the state, the use of
advertising and promotional means is limited to the state within which

the subdivision is located, and no more than 5 percent of the lots are sold to nonresidents within a one-year perid. The intrastate exemption still requires that the developer register with the Office of Interstate Land Sales Registration (OILSR).

Registration Requirements

Section 1404(a)(1) of the ILSFDA states that it is unlawful for a developer to sell or lease a lot in a subdivision unless a statement of record is in effect and a property report has been furnished to the purchaser or lessee in advance of signing a lease or purchase agreement. The filing requirement is designed to provide information to the OILSR about the subdivision, and the property report is required to provide a prospective purchaser information about the subdivision that will enable him or her to make an intelligent decision concerning the land and the developer. The information requirements are established by law and regulation, and current regulations should be checked before any registration is attempted. Following is a brief summary of major items of information included in the statement of record.

Statement of Record

Name of subdivision, developer, agent, owner

Part I.	Administrative Information
Part II.	Developers and Holders of Ownership Interest in Land, Violations, Bankruptcies, and Litigation
Part III.	Identity of Interest in More than One Filing
Part IV.	Topography, Climate, Subdivision Map, Permits and Licenses
Part V.	Condition of Title, Encumbrances, Deed Restrictions and Covenants
Part VI.	General Terms and Conditions of Offer, Proposed Range of Selling Prices or Rents
Part VII.	Access, Nearby Communities, Road System within Subdivision
Part VIII.	Utilities
Part IX.	Recreational and Common Facilities
Part X.	Municipal Services
Part XI.	Taxes and Assessments—Common Facilities
Part XII.	Occupancy Statutes
Part XIII.	Shopping Facilities
Part XIV.	Financial Statement
Part XV.	Affirmation

The information provided in the registration statement must be complete and accurate. The OILSR does not make decisions about the desirability of the subdivisions or the adherence to developmental standards. It merely ascertains that the information supplied is true and complete.

In addition to the registration requirement, the developer must prepare and have approved an illustrative property report, which must be given to each purchaser or lessee prior to the purchase or lease of subdivision property. The property report is substantially similar to the registration statement and is designed to provide basic information about the subdivision to the prospective purchaser. The property report contains a statement that the data contained in the report are for the purpose of informing the potential purchaser about the subdivision and that the Office of Interstate Land Sales Registration does not approve or disapprove of the subdivision. The report further recommends that each prospective purchaser seek professional advice before purchasing. The property report advises the purchaser that unless he or she has received the report 48 hours before signing the contract, each purchaser has the right to revoke the contract until the close of the third business day after signing. This requirement may not be waived by the buyer.

The registration statement is examined by the appropriate governmental authority, and if it is found free of defects and inaccuracies it becomes effective upon the thirtieth day after filing. The act provides that if the accuracy of the information is in doubt or the registration statement is not complete, the developer shall be sent a deficiency notice and shall have the option of either complying or contesting through administrative and judicial processes.

A developer may engage in promotional activities during the period within which its registration statement is being processed by OILSR, but no sales to purchasers may be made until the registration is approved and the property report delivered to prospective purchasers.

Advertising and Sales Practices

One of the major concerns that led to the passage of ILSFDA were the fraudulent sales practices followed by certain developers. The act deals with this through its disclosure requirements and through the prohibition of practices tending to aid those who engage in fraudulent schemes. In addition, the law provides civil remedies for a party who purchases property from a developer who is not in full compliance with the act.

The act prohibits any false statement of record and the distribution of any property report containing any untrue statement of material fact or omitting any material fact required under the act. The purpose of the act is to require full disclosure, not only of those aspects of the development favorable to the developer, but also of those facts that are unfavorable. Under the disclosure requirement of the act, the duty for a developer to disclose to the purchaser is greater than the duty to disclose imposed by common law. As discussed in Chapter 5, under common law the seller must disclose only known latent defects that would not be readily discoverable by the average buyer. The seller may not make a material misrepresentation upon which the buyer justifiably relies to his or her detriment. The seller may not omit a material fact if a special relationship exists between the parties, there is superior access to information engaged by seller, or there is an implied warranty of fair dealing.

The developer is under an absolute duty to disclose all information expressly required by the act. No advertising material and sales techniques employed can discredit the importance of the information contained in the registration statement or property report. The act also prohibits employing sales techniques designed to pressure the prospective purchaser into a hasty decision, and limits the "puffing" that may be engaged in by resourceful salespersons. The standard applied is more strict than the common law standard under *caveat emptor*. Promotional material must not contradict the property report or registration statement.

Remedies Under ILSFDA

The ILSFDA modifies the two chief common law remedies, rescission and damages, for fraud in contract. Under rescission at common law, the plaintiff is required to prove with a preponderance of the evidence that there was a misrepresentation of material fact upon which he/she relied to his/her detriment. The plaintiff in an equity action for rescission also must have "privity of contract" with the defendant. In an action at law for damages, the plaintiff must show an intentional misrepresentation of material fact upon which the plaintiff justifiably relied to his/her detriment. In such a lawsuit, the plaintiff must show fraudulent intent, actual damages, and a causal relationship between the fraud and the damages suffered. In both rescission and an action for damages, the burden of proof is upon the plaintiff. Such remedies are expensive and time consuming.

If the developer has made a material misrepresentation, ILSFDA permits remedies in addition to those at common law. First, it provides that a purchaser has the right of restitution. He/she may also retain the land purchased and sue for statutory damages. The act reduces the elements in a civil suit for damages by eliminating the requirement that the plaintiff show a causal relationship between the alleged fraudulent representation and the damages suffered.

The Interstate Land Sales Full Disclosure Act represents a major attempt by the federal government to establish standards for sale of certain subdivided lands. It attempts to protect unsophisticated and unsuspecting buyers from sharp practices through disclosure requirements. Any persons engaged in the sale of subdivision land should consult legal counsel to determine whether the act is applicable and to ensure full compliance if it is.

TRUTH-IN-LENDING LAWS

The federal Truth-in-Lending Act is part of the omnibus Consumer Credit Protection Act enacted in 1968. Like the Interstate Land Sales Full Disclosure Act, the Truth-in-Lending Act is designed to assist the consumer-purchaser in obtaining meaningful information about the product or service being purchased. The truth-in-lending law does not seek to regulate the charges for credit, such as maximum and minimum interest rates and finance charges, but it does require a complete disclosure to a prospective borrower of the charges incident to the credit transaction. The term *customer* or *borrower* includes each person if joint ownership is involved. Thus, separate disclosures may be required in such cases. The information obtained through the required disclosure is designed to make it possible for a borrower to shop for credit and compare the charges that various lenders assess for the type of credit sought. Armed with this information, the consumer can make better-informed decisions concerning the cost of credit.

Under the law, the Board of Governors of the Federal Reserve System is charged with the responsibility of implementing the law. Pursuant to that authority, the Board issued Regulation Z, which became effective on July 1, 1969. Thus the federal truth-in-lending law is often referred to as Regulation Z. The Federal Trade Commission is the governmental agency charged with administering the regulation.

The major impact of the law is upon those who extend credit to individuals for the installment purchase of large consumer goods such as appliances and automobiles. However, the truth-in-lending law has applicability to certain credit transactions involving real estate purchases and real estate financing.

Applicability

Generally, the disclosure requirements of the law are applicable when the credit is extended to a natural person and is not used for a business purpose other than agriculture. The law does not apply to agricultural purposes where the total credit involved is more than $25,000. In addition, the law is not applicable to credit transactions involving dwellings containing more than four family housing units, because this is deemed to be a business purpose.

As a general rule, most real estate financing transactions are under Regulation Z if they involve the granting of credit to a natural person for household, family, personal, or agricultural purposes and the creditor obtains a nonpossessory security interest in real property. Thus, conventional financing by mortgage lenders or others in the "ordinary course of business" is covered by the law. Most private transactions such as installment real estate contracts or purchase money mortgages are excepted from the operation of the law.

Finance Charges and Annual Percentage Rate

Under Regulation Z, the lender must disclose to the prospective borrower-consumer information concerning the actual cost of credit for the installment purchase of goods, services, or the repayment of a loan. The two most important determinants of the cost of credit are finance charges and the annual percentage rate.

Finance charges are all charges payable directly or indirectly by the customer and imposed directly or indirectly by the creditor incident to or as a condition of the extension of credit. These finance charges must be disclosed to the customer even if the seller or any other person pays them for the benefit of the customer, and whether they are paid to the lender or to a third party. Among the charges that often are included in the finance charge are interest, loan service fee, discount points, premiums for creditor life insurance if made a condition of the loan, commissions, and other fees. Not included in the finance charges are expenses that are incident to the transaction but would be assessed whether or not credit is extended to the customer. Typically, these include sales taxes, transfer taxes, recording fees, legal fees, and title charges. Even though these latter charges are not part of the finance charge, they also must be disclosed so that the customer knows in advance the total cost of the transaction. If the credit transaction creates a first lien on real property, the total amount of the finance charge over the life of the loan need not be disclosed.

The annual percentage rate includes other finance charges in addition to the interest charged upon the loan. Briefly stated, the *annual percentage rate* is the relationship of the total finance charge (as defined in the previous paragraph) to the total amount to be financed. This rate must be computed to the nearest ¼ of one percent. In most conventional mortgage transactions, interest is based on a "simple" annual rate. Thus, the annual percentage rate disclosed to the borrower-

FIGURE 32   Regulation Z Disclosure Notice
(Courtesy State College Federal Savings & Loan Assn.)

NOTICE TO CUSTOMER REQUIRED BY FEDERAL LAW
FEDERAL RESERVE REGULATION Z
(To Be Executed in Duplicate)

REAL PROPERTY TRANSACTION
PURCHASE LOAN SECURED BY   LOAN. NO. _____
FIRST LIEN ON A DWELLING

The FINANCE CHARGE on this transaction will begin to accrue on _____

The AMOUNT OF THE LOAN in this transaction is .... $ _____
less the PREPAID FINANCE CHARGE on this transaction which includes:
1. Service Charge _____ $ _____   5. _____ Interest ____ (Est.) $ _____
2. Sellers Discount _____ $ _____   6. Construction Interest (Est.) ____ $ _____
3. Construction Loan Fee ____ $ _____   7. _____ $ _____
4. Buyers Discount _____ $ _____   8. _____ $ _____
                                                                      TOTAL $ _____

Equals the AMOUNT FINANCED in this transaction .... $ _____

The ANNUAL PERCENTAGE RATE on this transaction is _____ %
Itemized CHARGES EXCLUDABLE from the FINANCE CHARGE in this transaction:
1. Title Fee _____ $ _____   5. _____ $ _____
2. Recording Fee _____ $ _____   6. _____ $ _____
3. Credit Report _____ $ _____   7. _____ $ _____
4. Appraisal _____ $ _____   8. _____ $ _____

Payments for principal and interest on this transaction shall be _____ monthly installments of $ _____
beginning on the last day of _____ , 19 ____ and due on the last day of each month thereafter.

This Institution's security interest in this transaction is a mortgage on property located at _____
_____ also specifically described in the documents furnished for this loan.
The documents executed in connection with this transaction cover all after-acquired property and also stand as security for future
advances, the terms for which are described in the documents.

Describe late payment formula, if any, in accordance with Section 226.8(b)(4) .... Conventional — none, except that unpaid interest
is added to the Principal Balance.   FHA: 2% of each payment more than 15 days late.   VA: 4% of each payment more than
15 days late. _____

Describe prepayment formula, if any, in accordance with Section 226.8(b)(6) .... None. _____

Describe rebate formula, if any, in accordance with Section 226.8(b)(7) .... Not applicable. _____

Miscellaneous disclosures, or explanations, if any .... There is a separate non-interest bearing escrow account for taxes and
insurance. On conventional loans any escrow deficit or unpaid interest may be added to the principal balance of the loan.

INSURANCE

PROPERTY INSURANCE, if written in connection with this loan, may be obtained by borrower through any person of his choice.

CREDIT LIFE AND DISABILITY INSURANCE is not required to obtain this loan. No charge is made for credit insurance and
no credit insurance is provided.

State College Federal Savings & Loan Association   I hereby acknowledge receipt of the disclosures made in this notice.
                  INSTITUTION

_____   _____
            BY   CUSTOMER

_____   _____
           TITLE   CUSTOMER

_____   _____
           DATE   DATE

(RETURN ORIGINAL; RETAIN YELLOW COPY)

mortgagee will usually be at least ¼ of one percent higher than the interest rate actually being paid because the annual percentage rate figure includes other fees and the like which are assessed by the lender at the time the loan is made.

Disclosure Requirements

For real estate transactions, the lender must disclose such information as the total dollar amount of the finance charge; the date upon which the finance charges begin to accrue; the annual percentage rate; the number, amounts, and due dates of payments; delinquency and penalty charges; the "amount financed"; a description of the security interest created for the benefit of the lender; any prepayment penalty; prepaid finance charges; total amount that will be paid (except in first mortgages on dwelling houses); and the method used to refund any prepaid finance charges, including interest. Figure 32 shows an example of the disclosure required by Regulation Z for a first lien upon a dwelling.

Under Regulation Z, the disclosures must be made before the transaction is consummated. The transaction is deemed to be consummated when a contractual relationship exists between the lender and the customer. In mortgage transactions, this may create a problem for the lender because the loan application submitted by the customer is sometimes considered an offer that is accepted by the lender through a loan commitment letter. In such cases, the contractual relationship exists upon acceptance, when many of the charges that are required to be disclosed cannot have been ascertained.

Right of Rescission

Under Regulation Z, the customer has a limited right of rescission by which he/she may cancel the credit transaction with no penalty to him/herself. This right is applicable to consumer goods transactions as well as to certain real estate mortgage transactions. The right instituted under the law is designed to provide a remedy for a customer who has been pressured into signing a financing agreement that places a second mortgage or other lien on the customer's principal dwelling house. The lender is required to furnish to the customer two copies of the form that explains the right of rescission. One copy may be used by the customer to rescind. A typical example is illustrated in Figure 33.

The borrower has the right to cancel or rescind the transaction in writing by midnight of the third business day following the date of the consummation of the transaction or the delivery of the required disclosure and notice of right of rescission, whichever is later. When a complete and accurate disclosure as required by law is not made, the

FIGURE 33   Notice of Right of Rescission

NOTICE OF RIGHT OF RESCISSION

_____ LOAN NO._____
(Identification of Transaction)

Notice To Customer Required By Federal Law:

You have entered into a transaction on_____which may result in a lien,
(Date)
mortgage, or other security interest on your home. You have a legal right under federal law to
cancel this transaction, if you desire to do so, without any penalty or obligation within three
business days from the above date or any later date on which all material disclosures required
under the Truth in Lending Act have been given to you. If you so cancel the transaction, any
lien, mortgage, or other security interest on your home arising from this transaction is
automatically void. You are also entitled to receive a refund of any downpayment or other
consideration if you cancel. If you decide to cancel this transaction, you may do so by notifying
Name of Creditor

at
(Address of Creditor's)
  Place of Business.

by mail or telegram sent not later than midnight of_____. You may also use
(Date)
any other form of written notice identifying the transaction if it is delivered to the above address
not later than that time. This notice may be used for that purpose by dating and signing below.

I hereby cancel this transaction.

_____   _____
(Date)   (Customer's Signature)

EFFECT OF RESCISSION. When a customer exercises his right to rescind under paragraph (a) of this section,
he is not liable for any finance or other charge, and any security interest becomes void upon such a rescission. Within
10 days after receipt of a notice of rescission, the creditor shall return to the customer any money or property
given as earnest money, downpayment, or otherwise, and shall take any action necessary or appropriate to reflect
the termination of any security interest created under the transaction. If the creditor has delivered any property to
the customer, the customer may retain possession of it. Upon the performance of the creditor's obligations under
this section, the customer shall tender the property to the creditor, except that if return of the property in kind
would be impracticable or inequitable, the customer shall tender its reasonable value. Tender shall be made at the
location of the property or at the residence of the customer, at the option of the customer. If the creditor does not
take possession of the property within 10 days after tender by the customer, ownership of the property vests in the
customer without obligation on his part to pay for it.

Received Notice of Right of Rescission in duplicate this date_____

_____   _____
(Signature)   (Signature)

18 — TIL (NR) NOTICE OF RIGHT OF RESCISSION— AS & AS (9/75) (301)

right of rescission continues beyond the three-day limit until three days after full compliance.

In the conventional mortgage financing field, the right of rescission is eliminated if the mortgage is a first mortgage used to finance the purchase or construction of a dwelling house, if the borrower is not a natural person, or if the loan is for business purposes.

The right of rescission is applicable for transactions involving the installment purchase of building lots. Thus, developers who may be exempt from the provisions of the Interstate Land Sales Full Disclosure Act may still be responsible under Regulation Z for providing financial disclosure and the notice of the right of rescission to the purchaser.

The customer may not waive the right of rescission unless a bona fide financial emergency arises, in which case any waiver must be in writing. Preprinted waiver forms for this purpose are illegal.

If the customer does exercise the right to rescind and cancel, he/she must tender to the lender any property or money received by reason of the credit transaction. The tender may be at the location of the property or at the customer's residence. If the lender does not take possession of the money or property within a ten-day period following rescission and tender by the customer, the customer may retain the property or money without further obligation to the lender. The lender must return all property to the borrower, and the customer is not liable for any further charges.

Advertising under Regulation Z

Regulation Z attempts to regulate and require disclosure of certain information concerning credit that may become a part of advertising or promotion of goods, real estate, or loans generally. Under the law's definition, advertising includes media advertising as well as fliers, billboards, and window displays. The law is applicable if the advertisement contains information about down payments, installment payments, finance charge amounts, the number of installments, or length of loan, or even that there is no charge for credit. If any of these items is included, then the advertisement must also disclose the cash price, down payment, number, amount, and due dates of all payments and the annual percentage rate. Advertisements that state an interest rate must also disclose the annual percentage rate applicable to the transaction solicited.

The law is very specific on the language and format of advertising that comes within its purview. Minimum size of letters and boldness of type are prescribed to avoid confusing language and "fine print." The use of certain abbreviations is also proscribed.

In addition, certain types of advertising such as "bait" advertising are forbidden even though such advertisements may be in full compliance with the content and format requirements of the law. For example, advertising that offers real property for "no down payment" when the seller actually requires a down payment in most of its sales violates the law even though all disclosures are present and the format requirements are met.

Before any documents or advertising are prepared for distribution, both their format and content should be carefully examined.

Remedies Under Regulation Z

Regulation Z provides civil remedies to the customer and assesses criminal penalties against the lender who does not comply. Noncompliance is a misdemeanor, and the lender may be liable for a fine of $5,000, one year in prison, or both if convicted of violating the act. A civil penalty for noncompliance may be imposed that amounts to twice the finance charge involved in the transaction. This penalty may be not less than $100 nor more than $1,000 plus attorney's fees and costs. Any damages that can be proved by the customer may also be recovered in addition to the civil penalties. The customer also has the right of rescission provided by Regulation Z.

To a certain extent, noncomplying creditors may avoid the imposition of criminal and civil penalties if there has been a "good faith" compliance with the requirements of Regulation Z. However, such creditors may still be liable for damages incurred by a customer because of the creditor's noncomplicance even though that noncompliance may have been the result of an unintentional mistake.

Summary

The applicablility of the disclosure requirements of the Truth-in-Lending Act or Regulation Z to real estate transactions is limited. However, real estate professionals must be aware of its requirements and when such requirements apply. Special care must be taken to see that advertising requirements are met when promoting the sale of real property on an installment basis.

REAL ESTATE SETTLEMENT PROCEDURES ACT

History

In addition to the Interstate Land Sales Full Disclosure Act and the Truth-in-Lending Act, the Congress of the United States has enacted the Real Estate Settlement Procedures Act of 1974, sometimes referred to as

RESPA. RESPA was passed in response to demands by consumer groups over the rising costs of settlement charges in financing the purchase of single-family dwellings. Like the consumer-oriented laws previously discussed, it was hoped that prior disclosure of all settlement costs would enable buyers and mortgagors to bargain more effectively and shop for the best possible financial arrangement. However, unlike the Interstate Land Sales Full Disclosure Act and Regulation Z, RESPA placed restrictions on certain conduct of lenders, brokers, and others involved in a typical transaction.

RESPA has a great impact upon the real estate profession because compliance with its provisions is required in a large number of standard real estate transactions.

The law was amended in 1975 to modify certain sections that proved to be unworkable. It is directed toward control of three major settlement charge problem areas. The first practice sought to be controlled was the abusive and unreasonable practice of charging home buyers fees for which they received no actual benefit. RESPA seeks to eliminate such charges by prohibiting certain common but undesirable practices such as kickbacks, unreasonable escrow account requirements, and payment of unearned fees. The second problem area was associated with the average home buyer's lack of access to information on costs and procedures. Here, RESPA requires disclosure in advance of the transaction of all charges that will be incident to the settlement. Finally, it was felt that the land title recordation and verification systems unreasonably increased the costs of purchasing homes and satisfying title requirements for mortgage lenders. The act authorized the Secretary of Housing and Urban Development to establish computerized systems of land title recordation on a model basis.

Applicability

RESPA requires compliance with its provisions if the purchase is of a one- to four-family residential dwelling and the financing is "federally related." The following first mortgage financing arrangements are considered by RESPA to be federally related:

1. Loans insured by the Federal Housing Administration or the Veterans Administration.

2. Loans administered by the Department of Housing and Urban Development.

3. Loans intended to be sold by the lender to the Federal National Mortgage Association or similar federal agency.

4. Loans made by commercial banks and savings and loan associations or other lenders whose deposits are insured by federal agencies such as

FIGURE 34   Good Faith Estimate

(Courtesy State Capital Savings)

STATE CAPITAL
SAVINGS
the unbank

108-114 NORTH SECOND STREET
HARRISBURG, PENNSYLVANIA 17101
TELEPHONE (717) 238-8252

Good Faith Estimate of Closing Costs

Mortgage Amount: $
Terms: monthly payments
Interest Rate   %
Monthly Payments $ (prin. & int.)

801	Service Charge .... $
803	Appraisal ....
804	Credit Report ....
805	Inspection Fee ....
806 & 902	Mortgage Insurance
901	Interest ....
1106	Notary Fees ....
1107	Attorney's Fee ....
1108	Title Insurance ....
includes	
1101	Settlement Fee ....
1102	Title Search ....
1103	Title Examination ....
1105	Document Preparation ....
	(to State Capital Savings & Loan)
1201	Recording Fee ....
1202	Realty Transfer Tax ....

Sub-Total .... $
Less Advance Costs ....
Total .... $

This form does not cover all items you will be required
to pay in cash at settlement, for example, your pro-rata
share of real estate taxes and the cost of insurance.
You may wish to inquire as to the amounts of such
other charges you may be required to pay at settlement. These figures are only estimates. Exact figures
can only be known at the time of final settlement.

If this is a construction loan, interest as accrued will be
billed to you monthly until the date of the first amortiza-
tion payment.

Although you will be depositing an amount in your
State Capital Savings Account each month equal to or
exceeding one-twelfth of your annual tax amount, **tax
money is not held in escrow—you are required to pay
all taxes** (Whether with funds from that account or
from other sources) before penalty attaches and you
must supply us with receipted bills from the tax collec-
tor (not cancelled checks) with your next monthly
payment, and all taxes must have been verified as paid
no later than December 1st in any case. All receipts will
be returned to you promptly.

Have your insurance agent list
  State Capital Savings & Loan Assn.
  108 North Second St.
  Harrisburg, Penna. 17101
on your policy as FIRST MORTGAGEE. Please tell him
State Capital does not require a copy of the policy, but
you **must** take your policy to settlement.

The attorney handling your settlement and representing State Capital Savings & Loan Association **only** will
be:

Name _____

Address _____

Telephone Number _____

The charge at line 1107 (with the exception of line 1105
which is paid to the Association) is based on this Attorney's standard fee. There is a business relationship
between this provider and State Capital Savings and
Loan Association.

You and your real estate agent should contact this
attorney to schedule a settlement time.

Make all your checks payable to State Capital Savings
and Loan Association. If you have any further questions or future correspondence please call:

If for any reason this application fails to process to completion satisfactorily to all parties, the savings account money
may be withdrawn, and you are entitled to a refund of the unused money advanced toward closing costs, except the
credit report fee and the appraisal fee amounts are **not** recoverable. **THANK YOU FOR YOUR BUSINESS!**

This form is not a commitment on the part of State Capital Savings & Loan Association to make a loan to you.

I have received a completed copy of this form and have had its contents explained to me.

Date   Borrower

FORM M-52
4M-2-77

LENDER

the Federal Deposit Insurance Corporation or the Federal Home Loan Bank.

It is the fourth definition of federally related mortgage transaction that brings many real estate purchases within the purview of RESPA.

Disclosure Requirements

The disclosure requirements of RESPA are designed to provide advance information to the prospective borrower-purchaser of the residential property. The first requirement is that at the time of loan application the prospective borrower must be given a copy of a booklet that completely details RESPA and the information that must be disclosed to that borrower. The special information booklet is published by the Department of Housing and Urban Development and includes a complete explanation of all forms that are incident to the transaction, as well as an explanation of standard practices and procedures. The booklet also includes suggested questions that the borrower may ask the lender or others involved in the transaction to clarify the practices, services, or prices. Also included in the booklet is a detailed explanation of the remedies available to the borrower if the lender or other party to the transaction is not in full compliance with the terms of the act.

The second required disclosure is a "good faith estimate" of the settlement charges that are likely to be assessed against the borrower incident to obtaining a loan. The disclosure must be actual amounts or ranges of amounts based on the actual experience of the lender for similar transactions. If the lender uses the services of a particular person who receives a fee and there exists a special relationship between the lender and that individual, then the lender must disclose that the special business relationship exists.

For example, if the bank uses only one attorney to conduct settlements, then there must be a disclosure if any business relationship exists between the lender and the attorney. The good faith estimate must be given to the prospective borrower within three business days of application for a loan. An example of a good faith estimate under the requirements of the act is given in Figure 34.

The third required disclosure is the *uniform settlement statement,* which is made on a HUD-prepared form designed to provide complete disclosure of all financial matters involved in the settlement. The uniform settlement statement provides a complete accounting of all charges assessed against the buyer-borrower as well as a list of all disbursements made. The customer has the right to review the settlement statement at least one business day before the scheduled closing. An example of a HUD Settlement Statement is illustrated in Figure 35.

(Continued on page 346)

FIGURE 35   HUD Settlement Statement
(Courtesy State College Federal Savings & Loan Assn.)

HUD-1 Rev. 5/76   Form Approved OMB NO. 63-R-1501

A.	B. TYPE OF LOAN
U. S. DEPARTMENT OF HOUSING AND URBAN DEVELOPMENT SETTLEMENT STATEMENT	1. ☐ FHA 2. ☐ FmHA 3. ☐ CONV. UNINS. 4. ☐ VA 5. ☐ CONV. INS. 6. File Number: 7. Loan Number: 8. Mortgage Insurance Case Number:

C.   NOTE: *This form is furnished to give you a statement of actual settlement costs. Amounts paid to and by the settlement agent are shown. Items marked "(p.o.c.)" were paid outside the closing; they are shown here for informational purposes and are not included in the totals.*

D. NAME OF BORROWER:	E. NAME OF SELLER:	F. NAME OF LENDER:
G. PROPERTY LOCATION:	H. SETTLEMENT AGENT: PLACE OF SETTLEMENT:	I. SETTLEMENT DATE:

J. SUMMARY OF BORROWER'S TRANSACTION		K. SUMMARY OF SELLER'S TRANSACTION	
100. GROSS AMOUNT DUE FROM BORROWER:		**400. GROSS AMOUNT DUE TO SELLER:**	
101. Contract sales price		401. Contract sales price	
102. Personal property		402. Personal property	
103. Settlement charges to borrower (line 1400)		403.	
104.		404.	
105.		405.	
Adjustments for items paid by seller in advance		*Adjustments for items paid by seller in advance*	
106. City / town taxes to		406. City / town taxes to	
107. County taxes to		407. County taxes to	
108. Assessments to		408. Assessments to	
109.		409.	
110.		410.	
111.		411.	
112.		412.	
120. GROSS AMOUNT DUE FROM BORROWER		*420. GROSS AMOUNT DUE TO SELLER*	
200. AMOUNTS PAID BY OR IN BEHALF OF BORROWER:		**500. REDUCTIONS IN AMOUNT DUE TO SELLER:**	
201. Deposit or earnest money		501. Excess deposit (see instructions)	
202. Principal amount of new loan(s)		502. Settlement charges to seller (line 1400)	
203. Existing loan(s) taken subject to		503. Existing loan(s) taken subject to	
204.		504. Payoff of first mortgage loan	
205.		505. Payoff of second mortgage loan	
206.		506.	
207.		507.	
208.		508.	
209.		509.	
Adjustments for items unpaid by seller		*Adjustments for items unpaid by seller*	
210. City / town taxes to		510. City / town taxes to	
211. County taxes to		511. County taxes to	
212. Assessments to		512. Assessments to	
213.		513.	
214.		514.	
215.		515.	
216.		516.	
217.		517.	
218.		518.	
219.		519.	
220. TOTAL PAID BY / FOR BORROWER		*520. TOTAL REDUCTION AMOUNT DUE SELLER*	
300. CASH AT SETTLEMENT FROM / TO BORROWER		**600. CASH AT SETTLEMENT TO / FROM SELLER**	
301. Gross amount due from borrower (line 120)		601. Gross amount due to seller (line 420)	
302. Less amounts paid by / for borrower (line 220)	( )	602. Less reductions in amount due seller (line 520)	( )
303. CASH (☐ FROM) (☐ TO) BORROWER		*603. CASH (☐ TO) (☐ FROM) SELLER*	

RECEIVED COMPLETED COPIES PAGES 1 & 2 BORROWER'S TRANSACTION   RECEIVED COMPLETED COPIES PAGES 1 & 2 SELLER'S TRANSACTION

SIGNATURE   SIGNATURE   DE LAND SERVICE-ALLEGAN MICH RES - 16

L. SETTLEMENT CHARGES	LOAN NUMBER	HUD-1 Rev. 5/76
	PAID FROM BORROWER'S FUNDS AT SETTLEMENT	PAID FROM SELLER'S FUNDS AT SETTLEMENT
700. TOTAL SALES/BROKER'S COMMISSION based on price $ @ %=		
Division of Commission (line 700) as follows:		
701. $ to		
702. $ to		
703. Commission paid at Settlement		
704.		
800. ITEMS PAYABLE IN CONNECTION WITH LOAN		
801. Loan Origination Fee %		
802. Loan Discount %		
803. Appraisal Fee to		
804. Credit Report to		
805. Lender's Inspection fee		
806. Mortgage Insurance Application Fee to		
807. Assumption Fee		
808.		
809.		
810.		
811.		
900. ITEMS REQUIRED BY LENDER TO BE PAID IN ADVANCE		
901. Interest from to @ $ /day		
902. Mortgage Insurance Premium for months to		
903. Hazard Insurance Premium for years to		
904. years to		
905.		
1000. RESERVES DEPOSITED WITH LENDER		
1001. Hazard insurance months @ $ per month		
1002. Mortgage insurance months @ $ per month		
1003. City property taxes months @ $ per month		
1004. County property taxes months @ $ per month		
1005. Annual assessments months @ $ per month		
1006. months @ $ per month		
1007. months @ $ per month		
1008. months @ $ per month		
1100. TITLE CHARGES		
1101. Settlement or closing fee to		
1102. Abstract or title search to		
1103. Title examination to		
1104. Title insurance binder to		
1105. Document preparation to		
1106. Notary fees to		
1107. Attorney's fees to		
(includes above items numbers;		
1108. Title insurance to		
(includes above items numbers;		
1109. Lender's coverage $		
1110. Owner's coverage $		
1111.		
1112.		
1113.		
1200. GOVERNMENT RECORDING AND TRANSFER CHARGES		
1201. Recording fees: Deed $; Mortgage $; Releases $		
1202. City/county tax/stamps: Deed $; Mortgage $		
1203. State tax/stamps: Deed $; Mortgage $		
1204.		
1205.		
1300. ADDITIONAL SETTLEMENT CHARGES		
1301. Survey to		
1302. Pest inspection to		
1303.		
1304.		
1305.		
1400. TOTAL SETTLEMENT CHARGES (enter on lines 103, Section J and 502, Section K)		

RES-26

(Continued from page 343)

Detailed instructions concerning the amounts found on each line are included in a special information booklet, which also includes a sample form for the prospective borrower to use to compare various settlement charges of different lenders. Unlike the good faith estimate, the uniform settlement statement must be accurate and reflect the monies received and disbursed in the transaction. Lenders must retain their copies of the settlement statement for two years following the closing unless the loan is transferred. No separate charge for preparation of the form may be assessed against a borrower by the lender.

Regulation of Practices

In addition to its procedural and disclosure requirements RESPA prohibits those associated with the real estate transaction from engaging in certain practices. Unlike the procedural and disclosure requirements, these prohibitions extend beyond the lender to others who may be involved in providing services to either the borrower or the lender. The abusive practices intended to be controlled include kickbacks and unearned fees, required use of certain title services, and improper escrow accounts.

As a general rule, RESPA requires that the payment and receipt of something of value bear a reasonable relationship to the value of the goods or services provided to the person or company making the payment. To the extent that the payment received exceeds the value of the services provided, then an unearned fee or kickback is presumed. For example, if an attorney prescribed by the lender certifies title to the lender at the expense of the borrower and the attorney's fee exceeds the reasonable value of the service provided, then under RESPA the excess is considered an unearned fee. Under RESPA a "kickback" arises, for example, when an agreement or understanding for the referral of settlement business is given in exchange for something of value and is based on the volume or value of business referred. For example, if a lender were to pay a real estate broker a fee for forwarding to it prospective borrowers, then under RESPA the fee would be considered a kickback and thus specifically prohibited. The kickbacks specifically prohibited include the payment of anything of value including, but not limited to, money, things, discounts, salaries, commissions, fees, or duplicate payment of a charge. However, the act is not intended to prohibit normal promotional activity not directly conditioned on the referral of business. For example, furnishing information and providing items of nominal value such as calendars, pens, and the like are not considered to be illegal.

These "abusive practices" provisions of RESPA are intended to apply to all those involved in providing services incident to the settlement of a loan that comes within the regulation of RESPA. The special targets of such regulation include title insurance companies, attorneys, real estate brokers, builders, developers, and settlement companies.

Under RESPA, the seller of property that will be purchased with a federally related loan is prohibited from requiring either directly or indirectly, as a condition of the sale, that the buyer purchase title insurance from a particular title company.

Often lenders require that borrowers deposit into a special escrow account in advance of settlement certain money to cover the costs of insurance, taxes, and other charges on the mortgaged property. These payments are made in advance of the due date of such charges and are designed to ensure timely payment of taxes, insurance, and other charges. Usually the lender makes disbursement for the charges. In some cases the escrow accounts are not interest bearing. Thus, the lender may have the use of monies for which it pays no interest. RESPA seeks to limit the amount of money that may be required to fund the escrow account. Generally, no more than one-twelfth of the reasonable amount of taxes, insurance, and other charges can be required per month. Lenders may require that an additional amount up to one-sixth of the reasonable charges on an annual basis be deposited into the escrow account as an additional hedge that the account will be funded to pay all charges.

Remedies Under RESPA

RESPA does not specifically provide any remedy at law to the borrower or other person whose rights have been violated with regard to the disclosure requirements of the law or the limitations on the escrow account collection practices. There is no equitable remedy specifically available to the borrower whose rights have been violated under any of the law's provisions including the disclosure requirements. Unlike both Regulation Z and the Interstate Land Sales Full Disclosure Act, there is no right of rescission for noncompliance. However, RESPA does provide treble damages for violations of the "abusive practices" sections concerning kickbacks and unearned fees and the section dealing with a seller's requiring the use of specified title insurance companies. In the former case, the aggrieved party could recover reasonable attorney's fees in addition to treble damages for violation. RESPA also provides a criminal penalty for violation of its requirements.

Under RESPA, it is specifically provided that the law shall not affect the validity or enforceability of any sale or contract for the sale of real property or any loan, loan agreement, mortgage, or lien arising in connection with a federally related mortgage. Therefore, in theory at least, the borrower may contract away his rights to receive full compliance with the requirements of RESPA. In addition, unlike Regulation Z and the Interstate Land Sales Full Disclosure Act, the borrower may waive most rights under RESPA. However, before any waiver is accepted or a borrower is asked to contract away his or her rights under RESPA, current regulations and counsel should be consulted.

RESPA is designed to complement existing state laws and to provide for concurrent jurisdiction of federal and state laws. To the extent that state law provides greater protection to the consumer, it would apply. If federal law provides greater protection to the consumer, it would apply.

FAIR HOUSING PRACTICES LAWS

In addition to consumer-oriented legislation, over the last twenty-five years there has been greater federal involvement in the field of civil rights. Among the areas that have come under greater regulation is that of fair housing practices. The overall purpose of such legislation is to create a free and open real estate market where each person may be dealt with fairly without regard to arbitrary classifications based upon race, color, religion, sex, or national origin.

History

The first attempt at fair housing legislation was the Civil Rights Act of 1866, which provided that all citizens would have the same rights to inherit, purchase, lease, sell, hold, and convey real and personal property. However, in 1883 the United States Supreme Court severely limited the application of these early civil rights laws except where "state action" was involved. Thus, only federal public housing would come within the law. In 1962, President John F. Kennedy issued an executive order that required the elimination of discrimination based on arbitrary distinctions in the sale, rental, and leasing of residential real property if the property was owned or operated by the federal government, provided for through the aid of federal grants or federal loans guaranteed by the federal government, or supported with federal urban renewal funds. A large percentage of residential mortgages were FHA- and VA-insured mortgages and consequently came within the group subject to the order banning discrimination in the housing market. Title VI of the Civil Rights Act of 1964 provided that no person in the United States should be subject to discrimination under any program or activity receiving federal financial assistance. This broadened the scope of the executive order of 1962 and brought federal antidiscrimination regulation into areas wherever the federal government provided any assistance at all.

In 1968 other civil rights legislation was enacted that included the Fair Housing Act of 1968. This act has had the greatest effect on the real estate market because it seeks to regulate the conduct of those engaged in the day-to-day business of real estate brokers as well as individual private sellers or lessors of real estate.

Fair Housing Act of 1968

Under the federal Fair Housing Act of 1968, it is unlawful to discriminate on the basis of race, color, religion, sex, or national origin in the sale or lease of residential property. Under this law the following acts are among those prohibited:

1. Advertising that restricts the sale or lease of property based on an arbitrary classification.

2. Changing the terms or conditions of a sale or lease for individuals based on an arbitrary classification.

3. Altering the conditions of a loan as a means of discrimination.

4. Engaging in the practice of "blockbusting" by inducing owners to sell or lease because of the entry into the neighborhood of persons of a particular race, color, religion, or national origin.

5. Refusing to admit persons into any brokers' organization or multiple listing or other service based on an arbitrary classification.

6. Refusing to sell, rent, or negotiate for the sale or lease with any person, or representing to a person that the sale or lease of a certain property is not available as a means of discrimination.

Certain parties and transactions are exempt from the application of the law. An individual seller or lessor of a single-family home who owns no more than three dwellings may discriminate, provided that he has not employed a broker, salesperson, or agent and that no discriminatory advertising is employed. The exemption applies to only one sale per twenty-four month period. The rental of apartments or rooms by an owner of less than four such units is exempt provided that the owner occupies one of the units. There are also certain exemptions for private clubs and dwellings owned by religious groups.

Even though these exemptions are specifically provided for in the 1968 law, the Civil Rights Act of 1866 has not been repealed and is still in effect. Since the Act of 1866 specifically prohibits *all* discrimination and provides no exemptions, it is possible that all discrimination is prohibited in light of the expanded view of "state action" taken by the Supreme Court in recent years.

The Fair Housing Act of 1968 prohibits the use of threats or acts of violence in connection with real estate sales and leases. The act provides criminal punishment against those who engage in the prohibited activities and civil remedies for those against whom the discrimination is directed. Among the remedies available to an aggrieved party are injunctions, suits for actual and punitive damages, and reimbursement for court costs and attorney's fees. The Department of Housing and Urban Development is the federal agency charged with administration of the law.

State Fair Housing and Antidiscrimination Laws

In recent years a majority of the states have adopted legislation prohibiting discrimination in public and private housing. The development of such laws has paralleled the growth of federal legislation to ensure an open and nondiscriminatory housing market. Most states provide that there can be no discrimination based on race, color, religion, and national origin. More recently, however, with the increased awareness of women's rights, many states have included a prohibition against discrimination based on marital status and sex. Some states also have provision in such laws against discrimination on other grounds such as persons with children, physical handicap, age, political affiliation, or prior criminal record. In each case, the law of the local jurisdiction should be consulted to be certain that no violation of law can occur through the conduct of either the owner or real estate broker or manager.

SUMMARY

All levels of government are increasingly involved in regulation of the real estate transaction and the real estate market generally. The laws regulating transactions are designed to provide the consumer-real estate purchaser with information with which to make intelligent decisions concerning the purchase of subdivided land and the acquisition of mortgage financing. Chief examples of this are the Interstate Land Sales Full Disclosure Act, the Truth-in-Lending Act (implemented through Regulation Z), and the Real Estate Settlement Procedures Act, which require disclosure of information in advance of purchase. The government also regulates the real estate market through fair housing laws designed to ensure free and unbiased access to housing for all persons regardless of race, color, religion, and national origin.

QUESTIONS FOR DISCUSSION

1. The stated purpose behind the Interstate Land Sales Full Disclosure Act and the Real Estate Settlement Procedures Act is to provide the consumer with information upon which to base an intelligent decision concerning the purchase of developmental land. What arguments may be made for and against such consumer protection laws?

2. Over the last several years the government has played an increasing role in the regulation of the real estate industry and real estate development. What argument may be made for and against the greater involvement of the federal government in such matters?

3. Is there a sound policy basis for exempting business or commercial real estate transactions from the operation of laws such as the Real Estate Settlement Procedures Act and the truth-in-lending laws? Explain.

4. The fair housing laws are designed to provide for an open and unbiased real estate market through the imposition of criminal and civil penalties against those who discriminate in the sale or rental of residential property based on arbitrary distinctions. What difficulty, if any, would governmental agencies have in enforcing these regulations? Explain.

5. Attention has been focused in recent years concerning the alleged practice of "redlining" by lending institutions. Under "redlining," lenders refuse to lend money for the purchase of housing in certain geographical areas because the character of the neighborhood gives the investment greater risk. Such practices limit the availability of mortgage funds to certain segments of society. What arguments can be made for or against the practice? Would use of the federal fair housing laws be an effective way to combat this practice?

CASES

Case 1. One of the alleged discriminatory practices among real estate brokers is the practice of "steering." "Steering" is the refusal to show prospective purchasers of real estate property in certain geographical areas in an effort to maintain the racial or religious homogeneity of a particular neighborhood. Prospective purchasers are "steered" away from certain neighborhoods. Plaintiffs brought suit under the federal Fair Housing Act against real estate brokers who were members of a certain multiple listing group, alleging that Defendants had steered them away from certain neighborhoods. Defendants claimed that no suit could be brought against them because it was not they who had refused to "sell, rent, negotiate, or otherwise make available" to Plaintiffs a dwelling because of race. Defendants claimed to be mere intermediaries. If Plaintiffs could prove that the defendants had indeed "steered" them, are they entitled to damages under the Fair Housing Act? Why or why not?

Case 2. Plaintiffs brought suit against the developer's real estate agent under the Interstate Land Sales Full Disclosure Act to recover the purchase price they had paid. Their claim was that the required property report included many recreational facilities that were not built. The defendant agent argued that the act authorized suits only against the developer and not against the agent. What arguments may be made that the act does not apply to the agent? What is the most likely result of a lawsuit where this issue is presented?

Case 3. Plaintiffs brought suit to cancel a real estate contract on grounds that in violation of Regulation Z the defendant had included a liquidated damages and forfeiture provision on the reverse side of the written contract without disclosing the method by which the potential charge was to be calculated. Under the truth-in-lending laws, all charges must be disclosed on the face of the contract. What arguments may be made on behalf of Defendant that the potential default provisions are not "charges" within the meaning of the law? What is the most likely ruling upon this defense if it were asserted?

Case 4. Plaintiffs agreed to purchase a building lot that was subject to the provisions of the Interstate Land Sales Full Disclosure Act. They made a down payment on the lot and executed a promissory note and mortgage for the balance of the purchase price. Within the time prescribed by law, they exercised their right to rescission under the act and received back their down payment. However, before the right of rescission was exercised, the developer had transferred the promissory note to a bank for less than its full value. Under normal circumstances, the transferee of a promissory note takes the note free of any defenses that the maker of the note may have, provided that he does so in good faith. The plaintiffs brought suit against the bank to have their note canceled. They argued that the bank knew that the transaction was subject to the plaintiff-maker's right of rescission under the ILSFDA and that because of such knowledge the bank could not be considered to have taken the note in good faith. What is the most likely result of Plaintiffs' suit to cancel the note? Why?

Glossary*

Abatement A legal remedy for breach of contract resulting in a decrease in price by an amount that usually compensates for the breach.

Abstract of Title A written record of interests in a tract of land summarizing all documents that affect title to the property as taken from the public record.

Accelerated Depreciation Various methods of computing depreciation that provide for the greatest amount of depreciation in the first year and a lesser amount in each successive year. The declining balance and sum-of-the-years-digits methods are the most common.

Accretion The process by which an area of real property is increased by the gradual deposition of soil from the natural action of water.

Acknowledgment Authentication and declaration by an authorized officer that the person executing an instrument is who he/she purports to be and is performing voluntarily the act evidenced by the instrument.

Actual Notice Express or direct knowledge. *Compare* Constructive Notice.

Adjusted Basis The basis of real property adjusted upwards for such things as capital improvements or additions and downwards for such things as depreciation or removal.

Adverse Conveyance A transfer of an ownership interest that is inconsistent with a prior transfer of the same real property interest.

Adverse Possession A method of acquiring an ownership interest in real property by possessing it openly, visibly, notoriously, hostilely, and adversely for a statutory period.

* For more detailed definitions, see Alvin L. Arnold and Jack Kusnet, *The Arnold Encyclopedia of Real Estate* (Boston: Warren, Gorham & Lamont, 1978).

Agency   A relationship wherein one person called a *principal* delegates to another person called an *agent* the right to act on his or her behalf.

Agent   A person authorized by another to act on his or her behalf.

Air Rights   A right or interest in real property above the surface of the land.

Airspace   That space which exists above the surface of an owner's land, limited by its perimeter boundaries extended vertically upward.

Alienation   The transfer of a real property interest from one party to another.

Ameliorating Waste   The results of an unauthorized act on real property by someone in possession other than the fee simple owner that increases the value of the reversionary or remainder interest.

American Land Title Association   The trade association of land title companies that prescribes title insurance contracts for use by member companies.

Amortized Loan   A loan that is repaid gradually through systematic payments of both principal and interest so that at the end of the loan term the balance of principal and accrued interest is zero. Also called a direct reduction loan.

Article of Agreement   A legally enforceable agreement between two or more parties for the purchase and sale of a real property ownership interest. Also called a purchase agreement, contract for deed, agreement for the purchase of real property, or real estate contract.

Assignment   The transfer of possessory or nonpossessory rights in real property.

Attorney at Law   An individual admitted to practice before the highest court of the jurisdiction; person engaged in the practice of law as a profession.

Attorney in Fact   Person acting as agent or representative of another pursuant to a power of attorney. See Power of Attorney.

Attractive Nuisance Doctrine   A tort theory of liability whereby an owner or possessor of real property will be liable for injuries caused to a child trespasser if the owner or possessor knew or should have known that children are likely to trespass and maintained a harmful condition on the property, when children were unaware of the danger and the cost to remedy the dangerous condition was small compared to the harm that could result.

Bargain and Sale Deed A deed that transfers title and possession to a grantee but usually does not guarantee or warrant the interest conveyed.

Base Abstract The original abstract of title of a parcel of real property to which additional information may be attached or supplemented.

Basis A compass reading used to describe real property under the metes and bounds method.

Beneficial Owner Person in whom the incidents of ownership are vested even though legal title may be held by another.

Beneficiary Person entitled to receive the benefits of a trust, will, or insurance contract.

Benefit of Bargain A remedy at law for breach of a contract to purchase and sell real property where the monetary loss is measured by the difference between contract price and the actual value of the real property.

Binder A written memorandum for the purchase and sale of real estate executed by the buyer, seller, or both, intending to bind the parties to the transaction until a formal contract can be prepared and executed.

Block A large unit, usually made up of contiguous lots, into which land is divided on a plat or map.

Bona Fide Purchaser A person who in good faith takes an interest in real property, having paid fair value without actual or constructive notice of any outstanding interest in another.

Bond Promissory note in a real estate mortgage transaction whereby the obligor binds him/herself to pay the principal debt plus accrued interest as set forth in the instrument.

Boot Cash or other property received in addition to like-kind property in a real property exchange.

Breach of Contract A violation of one or more of the terms or conditions of a contract.

Broker A person licensed by a state to be employed as an agent in negotiating the sale, purchase, exchange, or lease of real estate on a commission basis.

Buyer The party to whom title to real property is transferred by contractual agreement.

Bylaws A statement of corporate internal government that sets forth the rights and duties of stockholders with respect to the corporation and among themselves. Bylaws also control the internal government of other forms of ownership such as condominiums and cooperatives.

Capital Asset All property used for the production of income except that which is held by a taxpayer for resale in the ordinary course of business.

Capital Expense A cost incurred to improve and extend the useful life of a capital asset.

Capital Gain Gain arising from the sale or exchange of a capital asset when the value of that which is received is greater than the adjusted basis of that which is given up.

Casualty Loss A loss arising from fire, storm, shipwreck, or other sudden, unexpected, or unusual circumstance.

Caveat Emptor "Let the Buyer Beware." A general rule of law under which a buyer purchases at his or her own risk.

Certificate of Title A written statement issued by an attorney reporting the condition of title to real property.

Chain of Title The recorded history of matters that affect title to real property, beginning with the original conveyance and extending to the present.

Charter A statement that a corporation is required to file in the state where it is organized before it can come into legal existence.

Chattel An item of personal property.

Collateral A real or personal property interest pledged as security for the repayment of a debt or performance of an obligation.

Commission The compensation paid to a real estate broker for services rendered in connection with the sale, purchase, or lease of real property.

Community Property Property acquired by a husband or wife after marriage that is considered by some states to be commonly owned by both.

Concurrent Ownership Ownership held by two or more persons or entities.

Condemnation The legal process by which private land is taken for a public purpose.

Condominium An apartment or other building in which each unit is individually owned and common areas are jointly owned and maintained.

Condominium Association An association of all individual condominium unit owners acting as a group under rules set forth in the declaration of condominium and its bylaws.

Consideration The price paid for the transfer of title to real property.

Constructive Notice Knowledge of a fact affecting title to real property that a person is presumed by law to have; e.g., recorded interests and visible possession.

Contract A legally enforceable agreement between two or more parties.

Conventional Mortgage Financing A mortgage loan with a real property interest placed as security that is not guaranteed or insured by a governmental agency.

Cooperative A building in which each occupant has an ownership interest in the entire building, usually as a stockholder of an owner-corporation.

Corporation A legal entity created under statutory law having a legal existence separate from that of its owner-stockholders.

Correction Deed A deed used to correct an error in a prior conveyance.

Declaration of Condominium A document that subjects certain described land to condomium use and sets forth in detail the conditions, covenants, and restrictions that control the rights and duties of condominium owners.

Declining Balance Method An accelerated method of computing depreciation. *See also* Accelerated Depreciation.

Deed A written instrument, which when signed, delivered, and accepted transfers an ownership interest in real estate from one party to another party.

Deed of Trust A written instrument wherein a borrower conveys title to real property to a trustee who holds title to secure repayment of a debt to a lender.

Deficiency Judgment A personal judgment against a debtor following the sale of security, the proceeds of which were not sufficient to liquidate the entire debt.

Deposit A sum of money or other consideration tendered by a buyer to a seller with an offer to purchase real property. Sometimes called earnest money, hand money, or a binder.

Depreciation A decrease in property value or reduction in worth due primarily to use and the passage of time; for tax purposes, an approximation of the amount of annual wear and tear that contributes to the production of income.

Derivative Title Ownership interest in real property held by a individual under authority of the sovereign.

Descent and Distribution Statutes prescribing the persons who are entitled by law to succeed to property of a person dying without a will.

Distraint The right of the landlord to seize a tenant's personal property as security for the payment of delinquent rent.

Down Payment The cash payment made at the time of purchase of real property.

Due Process Legal safeguards imposed on individuals and governmental authorities designed to protect individual rights in property.

Earnest Money Money paid by the purchaser of real property to the seller at the time of the offer to demonstrate good faith.

Easement A nonpossessory interest in the use and enjoyment of the real property of another.

Easement Appurtenant An easement that one owner of real property may enjoy in the contiguous real property of another.

Easement in Gross An easement that is personal in nature that one party may enjoy in the real property of another.

Eminent Domain A government's power to take private land for public use on the payment of just compensation.

Encumbrancer An individual in whom a nonpossessory security interest in real property has been created either voluntarily by the owner or by operation of law.

Equitable Conversion The fictitious division of an ownership interest in real property that arises after a real estate contract has been executed whereby the seller retains legal title and the buyer acquires equitable title.

Equitable Title The interest that a buyer receives after a real estate contract has been executed; gives the buyer the right to receive full legal title at some future date.

Equity The difference between the value of property and the liens and encumbrances against it.

Equity of Redemption Right of foreclosed mortgagor to cure his/her default and regain ownership to the property.

Erosion The gradual wearing away of land by the forces of nature such as wind and water.

Escheat The reversion to the state of property of a person dying intestate and without heirs.

Estate for Years A nonfreehold estate the duration of which is for a definite period of time.

Estate from Year to Year A nonfreehold estate the duration of which is indefinite in the absence of appropriate termination.

Estate Tax For federal tax purposes, the tax paid on the transfer of property from a decedent's estate to a beneficiary.

Estoppel by Deed The doctrine that when a grantor conveys a greater interest in real property than he/she actually owns, if subsequently acquired, the interest conveyed will automatically pass to the grantee by operation of law.

Exception (Zoning) Permits certain uses in a zoning classification that are not in compliance with the uses generally allowed in that zone.

Exceptions (Title) Matters that are excluded from coverage under a policy of title insurance and listed on Schedule B attached to the insurance contract.

Exchange The trading of an equity interest in one property for an equity interest in another property.

Exclusive Agency Listing A contract for the employment of a real estate broker, under which the employer-seller agrees to employ no other real estate broker but retains the right to sell the property him/herself without being obligated to pay a commission.

Exclusive Right to Sell A contract for the employment of a real estate broker under which the seller is obligated to pay a commission to the broker no matter who sells the property during the term of the contract.

Federal Housing Administration (FHA) A federal governmental agency designed to improve housing standards and conditions and provide financing through the insurance of mortgages.

Fee Simple Absolute The largest freehold estate in real property; the estate to which the greatest number of ownership rights attach.

Fee Simple Determinable A freehold estate that is subject to a condition that, if it occurs, automatically reverts the estate back to the grantor or his/her heirs.

Fee Simple Subject to a Condition Subsequent A freehold estate that is subject to a condition that, if it occurs, causes the estate to revert back to the grantor or his/her heirs if followed by actual reentry or repossession.

Finder's Fee A fee paid to someone who finds a seller willing to sell or a buyer willing to buy.

Fixture An item of personal property that has been attached to real property.

Foreclosure A legal proceeding by which the security interest of the mortgagee is enforced through the sale of the secured property.

Freehold Estate An estate in real property that lasts for at least a life and can be inherited.

Future Interest The right to future enjoyment of real property.

General Lien The right of a creditor against a debtor to have the debtor's property sold to satisfy a judgment.

General Partner Co-owner of a business for profit who is empowered to enter into contracts on behalf of the partnership and is accountable to the limited partners as a fiduciary.

General Warranty Deed A deed wherein the grantor warrants to the grantee against all defects in the entire chain of title.

Gift A gratuitous transfer of an interest in real property from one to another.

Gift Tax Federal tax paid by a donor on the transfer of property by gift.

Governmental Rectangular Survey System A uniform method of describing real property based on its relationship to perpendicular intersecting lines called principal base lines and principal meridians.

Grantee Party receiving an interest in real property.

Grantee Index Public record index that lists individuals who have received ownership interests in real property.

Grantor Party transferring or creating an interest in real estate.

Grantor Index Public record index that lists individuals who have transferred ownership interests in real property.

Hand Money Money paid by the buyer of real estate to the seller to bind a bargain.

Hidden Risks Losses for which an insured under a contract of title insurance may be indemnified even though the matter that results in the loss is not disclosed in the public record (e.g., forgeries, missing heirs).

Homeowners Association As it applies to a planned unit development, an association whose basic function is to own and manage common property.

Homestead Exemption Statutory law under which a portion of the area or value of the real property owned and occupied as a person's residence is exempt from execution by judgment creditors.

Improvement An addition made to real estate.

Inheritance The process of passing property from a decedent to a beneficiary.

Inheritance Tax Tax assumed by the state upon the transfer of property from a decedent to his/her heirs. Also called succession tax.

Installment Real Estate Contract A contract for the purchase of an ownership interest in real property, under the terms of which the buyer makes periodic payments of principal and accrued interest until the total purchase price is paid, at which time title passes to the buyer.

Intangible Personal Property Personal property that has no physical existence, such as a contract right.

Interest The amount of money paid or accrued for the use of money.

Inter Vivos Trust A trust that becomes operative during the lifetime of its creator.

Intestate Without a valid will.

Involuntary Conversion Compulsory or involuntary conversion of property into money or other property through destruction, condemnation, or seizure in whole or in part.

Joint and Several Liability Liability for repayment of a debt or performance of an obligation shared by two or more parties such that a creditor can obtain payment or performance from one or more of the liable parties either individually or collectively.

Joint Tenancy A form of concurrent ownership such that, on the death of any joint owner, his/her interest passes by operation of law to the surviving joint owners.

Joint Venture Two or more persons jointly engaged in a specific business for profit.

Judgment The decision of a court adjudicating the rights or claims of the parties to the adjudication; also, a charge or lien upon property for securing a debt or performance of an obligation.

Judgment Lien A general lien that arises from the entry of a court judgment for money against the debtor and encumbers the real and personal property of the debtor within the jurisdiction.

Jurisdiction The power or authority of a court to hear a case and render a decision that is binding upon the parties to the lawsuit; also, the authority of a governmental unit to regulate rights and legal remedies within its geographical area.

Landlord The person, usually the owner, who rents a real property to another, called the *tenant* or *lessee,* for a stated consideration.

Lateral Support Support of real property from adjoining property.

Lease An agreement between two or more parties for the transfer or creation of a possessory interest in real estate.

Leasehold An estate in real property held under a lease; a possessory right in real estate.

Leasehold Improvements Improvements created by the lessee during a leasehold estate.

Lessee One who holds a leasehold estate.

Lessor One who creates or transfers a leasehold estate in another.

License Permission to use another's real property without holding any estate or interest therein.

Lien Theory State Jurisdiction that treats a mortgage as a specific lien against the mortgaged premises.

Life Estate An ownership estate in real property that is limited in duration to the lifetime of a named individual.

Like-Kind Property Property that is similar in form. For federal tax purposes, an exchange of like-kind property qualifies for favorable tax treatment.

Limited Partner An individual member of a limited partnership whose participation in the association is limited to financial contribution.

Limited Partnership An unincorporated association of two or more individuals in a business for profit, with at least one general partner who assumes control and liability, and at least one limited partner.

Liquidated Damages Damages for breach of contract agreed upon by the contracting parties.

Listing Agreement An employment contract between buyer or seller and a real estate broker.

Loan Policy Title insurance contract with a mortgagee as named insured entitled to indemnification for loss up to the unpaid balance of the mortgage.

Loan to Appraised Value Ratio The amount of the mortgage loan expressed as a percentage of the appraised value of the real property encumbered by the mortgage.

Long-Term Capital Gain Gain received on the sale of an asset held for longer than one year that receives favorable tax treatment.

Lot An individual unit of land in a subdivision that, when combined with other such units, forms blocks of land on a plot or map of such land.

Mechanic's Lien A statutory claim for the purpose of securing the value of work performed or materials furnished in building, altering, or repairing improvements to real property.

Merchantable Title Title to real estate that is free of reasonable claims of third parties.

Metes and Bounds A method of describing real property by its exterior boundaries, with reference to courses, distances, and monuments.

Mineral Rights An interest in the minerals in real estate; may be separate and apart from surface or airspace ownership.

Mitigation A duty imposed by law that requires a plaintiff or party to take appropriate steps to reduce, or not augment, his/her damages.

Monument A natural or artificial marker such as a tree, rock, street, or body of water used in describing the exterior boundary line of real property.

Mortgage Pledge or security of an interest in property for the payment of a debt or performance of an obligation.

Mortgagee   Holder of a nonpossessory security interest in property under a mortgage.

Mortgagor   One who creates a mortgage in another.

Mortgagor Index   An alphabetical index in the public record that lists the names of mortgagors.

Multiple Listing   A cooperative arrangement among real estate brokers for sharing the opportunity to sell listed property.

Navigable Water   A watercourse or lake that can be commercially used.

Nonconforming Use   A use that was in effect at the time a zoning ordinance was passed but does not conform to the current zoning ordinance.

Nonfreehold Estate   An estate in real property that lasts for a term less than a life and is commonly referred to as a leasehold interest.

Nonpossessory Security Interest   An interest in a debtor's real or personal property held by a creditor to secure repayment of a debt or performance of an obligation.

Nuisance   A nontrespassory invasion of the use and enjoyment of the land of another.

Open Listing   Employment agreement between a seller and a real estate broker whereby the seller retains the right to enter into listing agreements with other brokers and to sell the property him/herself without being obligated to compensate the broker.

Ordinary Income   For federal tax purposes, income that is taxed at ordinary rates, i.e., that does not receive preferential tax treatment, as opposed to long-term capital gain income.

Original Title   Ownership interest held by the government; obtained through discovery, occupancy, conquest, or cession.

Owner's Policy   Title insurance contract under which the owner of the property is the named insured.

Ownership   A "bundle of rights" in real property, including the rights of use, enjoyment, possession, and disposition.

Parol Evidence Rule   A rule of evidence that states that oral evidence of events that took place before or at the signing of a contract for the sale of real property cannot be offered into evidence to change the terms of the contract.

Patent An instrument by which the federal or state government transfers its original ownership interest in real property to an individual.

Percolating Water Subterranean water that is not confined to a known or well-defined channel or bed.

Personal Property All property, tangible or intangible, other than real property that may be the subject of ownership.

Planned Unit Development (PUD) A concept in land planning where large parcels of land are totally planned to produce efficient economic and environmental use of the land.

Plat A map of land that usually shows boundary lines and other data relative to ownership.

Police Powers The power of a governmental unit to enact, adopt, and enforce laws that promote the health, welfare, and safety of the public.

Possession The right to occupy and control, but not necessarily own, real property for one's own use and enjoyment.

Power of Attorney An instrument authorizing another to act as one's agent to carry out general or specific duties.

Preliminary Negotiations Written or oral discussion that precedes the formation of a real estate contract wherein the intent and understanding of the parties is crystallized.

Prepayment Privilege Right of a mortgagor or installment real estate purchaser to pay in advance all or any part of the unpaid balance due.

Principal Person employing an agent to act for him or her in dealing with others.

Principal Base Line An imaginary line running east and west that is used as a reference line for locating six-mile square units of land called *townships* under the governmental rectangular survey system.

Principal Meridian An imaginary line running north and south that is used as a reference line for numbering units of land called *ranges* in the governmental rectangular survey system.

Privity Mutual relationship to the same rights of property.

Probate The judicial process of proving a will and administering the estate of a decedent.

Profit a Prendre The nonpossessory right to remove a natural resource from the real property of another.

Promissory Note An unconditional promise in writing signed by the maker to pay to another's order a sum in money on demand or at a definite time.

Proprietary Lease A written lease agreement between landlord-corporation and tenant-stockholder; it differs from the ordinary landlord-tenant lease in that the tenants own the corporation, trust, or partnership that owns the real property.

Protected Party Under ULTA, owner of real property subject to the security interest of another.

Purchase Money Mortgage Bond or promissory note and mortgage are given to seller by buyer as part of the purchase price of the property being acquired.

Quitclaim Deed A deed that conveys only that interest which the grantor may have in the real property at the time of the conveyance; the grantor does not warrant or guarantee the quality of the title.

"Race-Type" Statute Recording statute under which a subsequent purchaser or encumbrancer of real property who records notice of his/her interest first is entitled to priority even though at the time of acquisition of the interest he/she had notice of the prior interest.

Range A unit of land formed by lines running parallel with the principal meridian six miles apart in the governmental rectangular survey system.

Real Estate All things that are fixed and immovable; a portion of the earth extending above and below the surface of the earth and including all things permanently affixed thereto.

Real Estate Investment Trust (REIT) A business association in which investors purchase shares as beneficial owners in income-producing real property.

Real Estate Settlement Procedures Act (RESPA) Federal statutory law that prescribes certain procedures for disclosing settlement costs to prospective purchasers of real property.

Realized Capital Gain The total amount of capital gain on the sale or exchange of an asset.

Recognized Capital Gain The amount of capital gain that will be taxed or recognized in the current tax year.

Recording The process of entering deeds, contracts for the sale of real property, easement agreements, and other documents into the public record for the purpose of alerting interested members of the public to the existence of the documented interests.

Recording Receipt Written evidence issued by the public official that a document has been accepted for recording and that the applicable fee for such recording has been paid.

Recording Statutes Statutes that provide procedures for incorporating documents into the public record and establishing priorities among purchasers and encumbrancers of real property.

Rectangular Survey System *See* Governmental Rectangular Survey System.

Registration Statutes Rules that establish governmental recognition of ownership of real property through compliance with certain procedures.

Remainder Interest The right of someone other than the grantor to the future enjoyment of real property presently in the possession of another.

Rent The consideration paid by a tenant or lessee to a landlord or lessor for the right to possess real property owned by landlord or lessee.

Rescission A legal remedy resulting in cancellation of a contract.

Reservation A provision in a deed or other instrument of conveyance that reserves to the grantor some right or interest in the land conveyed.

Restraint upon Alienation Limitation on the transferability of an interest in real property.

Reversionary Interest The right of a grantor (or his/her heirs) to the future enjoyment of real property presently in the possession of another.

Right-of-Way The right of passage over real property of another.

Riparian Land Land that abuts a watercourse, is under one ownership, and is within the natural watershed.

Riparian Rights Rights incident to ownership of land abutting watercourses.

Sale and Leaseback A financing device whereby the owner of property sells the property to a buyer-investor for full value and then leases the same property back as lessee.

Salvage Value The estimated value of an asset at the end of its useful life.

Schedule B Endorsement to a title insurance contract that lists the matters that are excluded from coverage under the insurance contract.

Section A portion of land one mile square containing 640 acres, as defined under the governmental rectangular survey system.

Secured Party Under ULTA, a person holding a security interest in the real property of another.

Security Agreement Agreement whereby the debtor creates a nonpossessory security interest in favor of the creditor to secure payment of a debt or performance of an obligation.

Security Deposit Money deposited by a tenant or lessee with a landlord or lessor as security for tenant's or lessee's compliance with the terms of the lease.

Seller The party who transfers title to real property by contractual agreement.

Severalty Ownership existing in one person or entity without a joint interest.

Shore The area that borders an ocean between the high and low tide marks.

Short-Term Capital Gain Gain received on the sale of an asset held for less than one year and considered ordinary income for federal tax purposes.

Special Warranty Deed A deed wherein the grantor warrants to the grantee against only those defects created by the grantor during his/her period of ownership.

Specific Lien A nonpossessory security interest in a specific parcel of real estate.

Specific Performance An equitable suit brought upon breach of contract when monetary damages do not fairly compensate the non-breaching party, to compel the breaching party to specifically perform his/her contractual obligations.

Spot Zoning Zoning of a tract of land that does not conform to zoning requirements in the surrounding area.

Statute of Frauds The statutory rule of law that states that no lawsuit may be maintained on certain classes of contracts unless the terms were in writing signed by the party against whom enforcement is sought.

Straight-Line Depreciation A method for computing depreciation that provides for equal amounts of depreciation each year over the asset's useful life. The formula is (Adjusted Basis − Salvage Value) ÷ Estimated Useful Life = Annual Depreciation.

Subjacent Support Support of real property from beneath the surface.

Sublease A lease given by a lessee or tenant to another called a *sublessee* wherein the lessee or tenant retains some reversionary interest.

Subordination An agreement that one who has a superior or prior right or interest shall permit another to assume superiority or priority.

Subsurface That space which exists below the surface of an owner's land, limited by its perimeter boundaries extended vertically downward.

Subterranean Water Water beneath the surface of the earth.

Sum-of-the-Years-Digits Method An accelerated method of computing depreciation, the formula for which is (Adjusted Basis − Salvage Value) multiplied by a fraction, the numerator of which is the number of remaining years of the asset's life and the denominator of which is the sum of the years' digits in the life of the asset.

Surface Water Water that does not flow in a well-defined channel and has not reached a natural watercourse or basin.

Survey Exception A listed exception in a title insurance contract where the insurer excludes coverage for deficiencies in quantity of land, encroachments, boundary disputes, and any matter that would be disclosed by a survey of the insured premises.

Tangible Personal Property Personal property that has a physical existence.

Tenancy at Sufferance A form of nonfreehold estate arising when a tenant continues, without the landlord's permission, to occupy real property after the lease has expired.

Tenancy at Will A nonfreehold estate, the duration of which is indeterminate and can be terminated by either party at any time.

Tenant A person who rents real property from another, called the *landlord* or *lessor,* for a stated consideration.

Tenants by the Entirety A form of concurrent ownership applicable only to a husband and wife, whereby on the death of either spouse his or her interest passes by operation of law to the survivor.

Tenants in Common A form of concurrent ownership whereby each individual owner is treated as if he/she owned an undivided fractional interest in the whole and can dispose of his/her interest by will.

Tenants in Partnership A form of concurrent ownership whereby property in a partnership cannot be disposed of by the individual partners without the consent of the other partners.

Tenement Real property rights that pass from owner to owner as the property is transferred.

Testamentary Trust A trust that becomes operative on the death of its creator.

Testator A person who has made a valid will.

Title Insurance An indemnity contract bertween the insurer and the named insured under which the insurer agrees to pay the insured for losses sustained by reason of title defect in the past and to defend claims against the named insured arising from such defects.

Title Theory State A jurisdiction that treats a mortgage as a conveyance of legal title from the mortgagor to the mortgagee during the term of the mortgage.

Torrens System A system for the registration of land titles used to establish interests in real property without the necessity of searching the public record.

Township A portion of land six miles square within the governmental rectangular survey system; located by reference to a principal meridian and a principal base line.

Tract Indexing A system of indexing recorded documents according to tracts rather than according to names of parties.

Trade Fixtures Items of personal property attached by merchants to the real estate to enable them to store, handle, or display their goods; generally removable upon termination of the lease or sale of the real property.

Transcript of Judgment A document issued by the court upon rendering of a money judgment that is entitled by statute to be entered in the record and become a general lien upon the property of the judgment debtor.

Trespass An intentional intrusion upon another's real property.

Trust The holding of property by one person or entity for the benefit of another.

Truth-in-Lending (Regulation Z) Federal law that requires advance disclosure of the costs of borrowing money or making installment purchases of property.

Undue Influence Exertion of an unreasonable amount of pressure on a person performing an act such that the act does not represent the free will of the party against whom the pressure is exerted.

Uniform Commercial Code Statutory law designed to simplify, modernize, and make uniform among the states laws that apply to commercial transactions.

Uniform Land Transactions Act (ULTA) Proposed statutory law drafted by the National Conference of Commissioners on Uniform State Laws to simplify, clarify, and standardize rights in the transfer, ownership, and financing of real property.

Uniform Residential Landlord and Tenant Act An act designed to simplify, modernize, clarify, and revise residential landlord-tenant law.

Variance Modification of an existing zoning ordinance that has worked a hardship on an owner of real property.

Waste Use or abuse of real property by someone in possession, other than the fee simple owner, that impairs the value of the reversionary or remainder interest.

Witness Anyone with legal capacity who subscribes his/her name to an instrument for the purpose of attesting to the authenticity of the maker's signature.

Wraparound Mortgage A mortgage loan financing device whereby the lender gives a loan to a borrower and assumes payment of an existing mortgage.

Zoning The legislative division of a community into various areas where only certain designated uses of real property are permitted.

Index

Unincorporated associations, 11
Unity of title, 26–27
Unsecured creditors, 89
Use, nonpossessory interests related
     to, 36–43
Use provisions, 269

V

VA-guaranteed loans, 182, 348
Variance, 46–47
Vegetation, 56–58
Visible occupancy, 34
Voluntary transfers, 74–77

W

Warranty deed, 221–222
Waste, 65–66
Water rights, 59–63
Widow's election, 78–79
Wills, 77–82
Witnesses:
   deed, 217
   testamentary transfers, 81
Words of conveyance, 216
Wraparound mortgages, 182

Z

Zoning, 15, 45–46